Asian Economy and Finance

Innovations in Financial Markets and Institutions

Editor:

Mark Flannery
University of Florida

Other books in the series:

Anderson, Seth C. and Born, Jeffery A.:
Closed-End Fund Pricing: Theories and Evidence
Hoshi, Takeo and Patrick, Hugh:
Crisis and Change in the Japanese Financial System
Cummins, J. David and Santomero, Anthony M.:
Changes in the Life Insurance Industry: Efficiency, Technology and Risk Management
Barron, J.M., and Staten, M.E.:
Credit Life Insurance: A Re-Examination of Policy and Practice
Cottrell, A.F., Lawlor, M.S., Wood, J.H.:
The Causes and Costs of Depository Institution Failures
Anderson, S., Beard, T.R., Born, J.:
Initial Public Offerings: Findings and Theories
Anderson, S., and Born, J.:
Closed-End Investment Companies
Kaufman, G.:
Banking Structures in Major Countries
England, C.:
Governing Banking's Future
Hancock, D.:
A Theory of Production for the Financial Firm
Gup, B.:
Bank Mergers: Current Issues and Perspectives

Asian Economy and Finance

A Post-Crisis Perspective

Dilip K. Das

Springer

Dilip K. Das
2869 Battleford Road
Mississauga
Ontario L5N 2S6
Canada

Library of Congress Cataloging-in-Publication Data

A C.I.P. Catalogue record for this book is available
from the Library of Congress.

ISBN 978-1-4419-3619-6 e-ISBN 978-0-387-23383-3 Printed on acid-free paper.

9 8 7 6 5 4 3 2 1

springeronline.com

**To Vasanti,
my true north.**

There is a time for being ahead,
a time for being behind;
a time for being in motion,
a time for being in rest;
a time for being vigorous,
a time for being exhausted;
a time for being safe,
a time for taking risk.
The Master sees things as they are,
without trying to control them.
She lets them go their own way,
and resides at the center of the circle.

— from *Tao Te Ching*

CONTENTS

Preface		xiii
Acknowledgments		xxi
About the Author		xxiii
1.	ASIAN ECONOMY: THE HERITAGE	1
1.1	Past is Prelude to the Future	1
1.2	Alternative Historical Perspective on Asian Economy	2
1.3	Economic Linkages and Interactions in the Second Millennium	4
1.3.1	First Half	4
1.3.2	Second Half	7
1.4	Quantitative Dimensions of Growth	8
1.5	Past Trends in Trade	12
1.5.1	Intra-Regional Trade	13
1.5.2	Global Trade	16
1.6	Industrial Revolution and Its Aftermath	18
1.7	Asian Economic "Miracle" of the Post-War II Era	21
1.8	Summary and Conclusion	23
2.	ECONOMIC DIVERSITY IN ASIA	27
2.1	Heterogeneity	27
2.2	High-Performing Economic Sub-Groups	28
2.3	Regional Economies and Economic Groupings	33
2.4	Japan—the Domineering Regional Economy	36
2.5	Contrasting the Two Populous Giants	43
2.5.1	China	44
2.5.2	India	52
2.5.3	Why India Lagged Behind China?	59
2.6	Newly Industrialized Asian Economies	60
2.7	Southeast Asian Economies	65
2.8	Post-Crisis Performance	68
2.9	Summary and Conclusions	71

3. MARKET-DRIVEN REGIONALIZATION IN ASIA 77
3.1 Introduction 77
3.2 Trends in Intra-Regional Trade and Investment 79
3.2.1 Market-Driven Regionalization 80
3.2.2 Intra-Regional Trade 82
3.2.3 Is Trade Growing More Intra-Regional? 84
3.2.4 Intra-Regional Production Networks 86
3.3 Impact of Other RIAs on the Asia-Pacific Economies 89
3.4 Need for Regional Co-operation in the Aftermath of the Crisis 93
3.5 Impediments to Regionalization 94
3.6 Conclusions and Summary 95

4. CONTEMPORARY INITIATIVES IN INSTITUTIONALIZED REGIONAL INTEGRATION 101
4.1 Regional Integration and the Global Economy 101
4.2 Agglomeration or Clustering Effect 105
4.2.1 Industrial and Sectoral Specialization in an RIA 107
4.2.2 Foreign Direct Investment and RIAs 108
4.2.3 Welfare Implications 110
4.3 Institutionalized Regional Economic Integration 116
4.3.1 Formation of ASEAN 117
4.3.2 Formation of ASEAN Free Trade Area 119
4.3.3 Common Effective Preferential Tariff Framework 121
4.3.4 Impact of Common Effective Preferential Tariff 123
4.3.5 ASEAN's Contribution to Regional Integration 124
4.3.6 ASEAN Economic Community 2020 126
4.4 ASEAN-Plus-Three Grouping 127
4.4.1 Exploring the Future Potential 130
4.5 Asia-Pacific Economic Co-operation Forum 131
4.5.1 Consequences of Trade and Investment Liberalization 134
4.5.2 Economic and Technical Co-operation 136
4.5.3 APEC's Contribution to Regional Integration 137
4.6 Bilateral Trade Agreements 139
4.7 Summary and Conclusion 141

5. TRADE, COMPETITIVENESS AND FOREIGN INVESTMENT AND THE LINKAGES AMONG THEM 147
5.1 Outer-Orientation: The Strategic Stance 147
5.1.1 Adopting Outer-Orientation 148
5.1.2 Global Capital Flows 150
5.1.3 Role Played by TNCs 153
5.1.4 Interaction between Trade and FDI 154

5.2 Trade Performance 155
5.2.1 Trade and Economic Growth Nexus 156
5.2.2 Export Deceleration and the Asian Crisis 158
5.2.3 Emerging Trade Triangle 160
5.3 Growing Cohesion in Trading Pattern 162
5.4 Competitiveness in Global Market Place 165
5.4.1 Quantifying Competitiveness 166
5.4.2 Strengthening Competitiveness 168
5.4.3 Liberalized Policy Stance and Competitiveness 170
5.5 Regional Trends in FDI 172
5.5.1 Medium-Term Prospects 175
5.5.2 Outward FDI Flows 176
5.5.3 Centripetal Forces in China 178
5.5.4 Is China Eating ASEAN's Lunch? 180
5.6 Integrated Production Networks and Refinement of Comparative Advantage 182
5.6.1 Need for Integrated Production Networks 183
5.6.2 Splitting the Value Chain 184
5.6.3 Expanding Opportunities 184
5.7 Outsourcing in ICT and Business-Process Services 186
5.7.1 Igniting Protectionism: Squaring the Circle 188
5.8 China's WTO Accession and its Regional Ramifications 189
5.9 Summary and Conclusion 192

6. FINANCIAL SECTOR DEVELOPMENT: STRUCTURE, INSTITUTIONS AND MARKETS 201
6.1 Financial Sector: Chink in the Asian Armor 201
6.2 The Quality Continuum 203
6.3 Financial Market Structure and Country Classification 205
6.4 Carrying out Financial Market Development 207
6.5 Banking Sector 208
6.5.1 Ascertaining the Dominance 210
6.5.2 Foreign Banks 211
6.5.3 Non-Performing Loans 212
6.6 Intermediate Financial Structure 214
6.7 Bond Markets 215
6.7.1 Bond Market Developments in the Pre-Crisis Period 216
6.7.2 Bond Market Developments in the Post-Crisis Period 218
6.7.3 Market Limitations 220
6.7.4 Market and Institutional Upgrading 221
6.8 Regional Bond Market 223
6.8.1 Facilitating Market Growth 225

6.8.2 Managing Foreign Exchange Reserves to Support Bond Markets 226
6.9 Equity Markets 227
6.9.1 Origin of Equity Markets in China 230
6.10 Risk Management 231
6.10.1 Credit Risk Management 234
6.10.2 Market Risk Management 235
6.10.3 Operational Risk Management 235
6.11 Conclusions and Summary 236

7. POST-CRISIS REGIONAL ECONOMIC CO-OPERATION AND THE EMERGING FINANCIAL ARCHITECTURE 241
7.1 Realistic Dimension of the Asian Crisis 241
7.1.1 Manila Framework Group 244
7.1.2 ASEAN Surveillance Process 245
7.1.3 New Miyazawa Initiative 245
7.1.4 Asian Growth and Recovery Initiative 246
7.1.5 Asian Monetary Fund 247
7.1.6 Other Smaller Proposals and Initiatives 249
7.2 Launching the Chiang Mai Initiative 250
7.2.1 Belated Multilateral Acceptance 252
7.3 Multilateral and Bilateral Swap Arrangements 253
7.4 Future Challenges for the Chiang Mai Initiative 256
7.5 Pros and Cons of Institutionalized Regional Co-operation 259
7.6 Predilection for a Regional Financial and Monetary Institution 261
7.7 Augmenting Foreign Exchange Reserves Holdings 263
7.7.1 Adequacy of Foreign Exchange Reserve Holdings 264
7.8 Monetary and Central Banking Co-operation 266
7.9 Evolution of Exchange Rate Regimes 268
7.9.1 Synchronizing Exchange Rate Regimes 270
7.9.2 Post-Crisis Correction in Exchange Rate Regimes 271
7.10 Lessons from the EU Experience 273
7.11 Monitoring and Surveillance 276
7.12 Summary and Conclusions 280

Bibliography 287
Index 307

PREFACE

"When westerners think of Asia, they mostly think of dollar signs. And with good reason. Call them tigers or dragons, write of thunder in the east or a shining India, whichever imagery you prefer, the Asian economic miracle is exactly that. Across half the world, in a few short decades, hundred of millions of people have been lifted out of abject poverty by a combination of hard work, good policies and benefits of open trade. Yes, there have been problems—remember the Asian financial crisis?—but the truly remarkable thing is how quickly most of the Asian economies have bounced back from them. This year, yet again, it is in Asia that the world's fastest growing economies are to be found."

The Economist. 24 April 2004
"That Other Miracle" p. 10.

Topicality of Asian economy has refused to fade for almost four decades; if anything it has been levitating. The Asian economy has changed markedly since the economic and financial crisis of 1997–98 and is continuing to evolve. As a scholarly subject matter, Asian economy has not stopped attracting academicians, policy mandarins and decision makers in the arena of business. Although Asia includes all the economies in the arch stretching between Afghanistan and North Korea, Asia in this book is defined to include the ten dynamic Asian economies, namely, China, Hong Kong SAR, Indonesia, Japan, Republic of Korea, Malaysia, the Philippines, Singapore, Taiwan and Thailand. Majority of these economies are widely acknowledged to be the high-performers of the post-war era. Although these dynamic Asian economies do not form a formal regional or sub-regional group, all of them except Taiwan are included in the ASEAN-Plus-Three (APT) grouping. The APT concept was born in the latter half of the 1990s.

References and comparisons to other economies like India and those in Indochina have been made wherever necessary and relevant. The reason for excluding the South Asian economies is that over the preceding four decades, they never became a part of the vibrant and high-performing Asian economic scenario. For starters, they attempted a wrong route to economic growth and industrialization, namely import substitution. This group of Asian economies did not seem highly committed to the objective of economic growth and consequently remained mired in low and uninspiring growth and poverty. Although there have been some improvements, their large, inefficient and corrupt government systems kept them at a low-level economic equilibrium.

To be sure, a country-by-country approach for examining the Asian economy has its convenience and advantages, but such disaggregation misses out on the basic unity and integrity of the regional economic entity. Therefore, without decrying or ignoring the former analytical approach, this book takes the regional approach, in both temporal and spatial terms. Asia has been conceptualized as a region, which comprises contiguous countries, which in turn are remarkably interdependent over a range of dimensions. These dimensions have evolved, and would continue to evolve, over time. Indubitably, we discover that the whole is greater than the sum of its parts. This is the principal benefit of following this approach. Pursuing this approach of analysis presents a new perspective on the regional dynamics across time and space.

Unprecedented growth rates in Asia during the post-war era have been the focal point of enormous scholarly analysis. Economists from the academia and professional worlds delved into the hows and whys at length and produced a small library of literature on these and related issues. Asian economies were fondly referred to as the "miracle" economies, which epitomized virtues of the capitalist system, although this capitalism was different from the capitalism of the Western world in several ways. Well-known strengths of the Asian economies were their macroeconomic and political stability, openness to trade and investment, high domestic savings and investment rates, emphasis on human capital development and disciplined work force, and lastly pragmatism, expediency and goal-orientedness in general economic policy structure. Asian economies need to preserve and build on these strengths of the past. This is not to imply that they were free of blemishes and imperfections.

The Asian crisis was a cataclysmic event for the region and brought to the surface several systemic limitations, like those in the financial sector, corporate governance, regulatory oversight, legal framework, and exchange rate management. Managers of Asian economy need to get to the bottom of these acutely problematical systemic issues. Additionally, in keeping with the Latin maxim *tempora mutanture, nos et mutamur in illis,* Asian economies need to change with the demands of time and devise their post-crisis development strategy.

Asia's growth model that served it so well for four decades is overdue for renewal so that it can re-strengthen its bonds with the ever-evolving regional and global economic reality. Well-known total factor productivity (TFP) studies illustrated that economic growth in Asia was driven by input growth or factor accumulation, not by productivity or efficiency growth (Kim and Lau, 1994; Young, 1994, 1995). Asia's growth model was castigated for being factor input-based. No matter how you sliced it, the charge seemed correct, although its consequence in terms of welfare growth was nothing but favorable for the Asian economies. In a short time span, the dynamic Asian economies developed into world's most resilient ones as well as highly successful traders.

The old growth model is likely to be less relevant and effective in the post-crisis future of the Asian economies. It is sure to run into the wall of diminishing returns. As globalization progresses, freer trade, financial and technology flows would make the global economy more competitive than ever. Asia would face numerous regional and global challenges in a globally integrating world economy, which would call for a different growth strategy from the past. At the regional level, the economic performance and relationship of Japan with neighboring Asia, China's economic emergence as a regional economic powerhouse and keen and robust competitor as well as a promising market, brisk growth in the four East Asian economies and a changing and challenging regional economic environment for the Southeast Asian economies are among the important factors that would shape the economic landscape of the immediate future in Asia.

The Asian currency and financial crisis of 1997–98 gave a rude jolt not only to the so-called "miracle" economies but also to the region. These dynamic economies were hit by the crisis and prompted the largest financial bail out in history. However, after experiencing a sharp contraction in GDP growth, the five crisis-affected economies and the region moved on to a recovery trajectory rapidly. The Asian crisis brought to the fore copious shortcomings in the areas of financial structure and markets, corporate governance, regulatory institutions, legal framework, exchange rate management, policies related to financial inflows and exchange rate management and social protection. Palpably, these systemic weaknesses were needed to be overcome without delay. Some progress has been made in this direction, although this work is far from complete.

For the purpose of evolving a new, post-crisis, growth strategy, Asian economies need to make concerted endeavors in the policy areas of financial sector and other institutional reforms, technological innovation, and with it investment in knowledge-intensive sectors and R&D. While rapid growth in the past was based on resource accumulation and input-based, the future growth calls for the creation of an environment of innovation and intensive R&D. That is, the factor-intensity-based growth model needs to be replaced with a technology-based and productivity-driven paradigm of growth. The competitiveness issue needs to be addressed both at macro- and microeconomic levels (Chapter 5). Asian economies need to move up the product value-chain and extend their reach into the services sector. This could not only put Asia back on its high perch as the most dynamic region in the world, but also speed the transition of many Asian economies into the ranks of mature industrial economies. Korea was accepted into the eminent membership of the Organization for

Economic Co-operation and Development (OECD). Several more dynamic Asian economies would be candidates for joining OECD in the foreseeable future. To this end, they need to change their strategic gear, which would not be difficult for the open and competitive Asian economies. They can devise and launch into the new strategy from a position of strength, with adequate supply of resources, and manufacturing skills, albeit in the post-crisis period they have to be aware of their macroeconomic errors, financial missteps and the shortcomings of their educational, financial and research infrastructures and business services.

Various facets of Chinese economy have been provided a special niche in this book. The reasons are, for one, the course that the Chinese economy took after it adopted the "open door policy" in December 1978 is of enormous significance to China, Asia and the global economy. The economy has been on a monotonic ascent since that point in time in the Chinese economic history and has been evolving into a world-class economy. Second, in the late nineteenth century the United States emerged as a major industrial and economic power. A century later, it was China's turn to do the same. This period of China's economic history can be compared to Japan in the 1960s and 1970s, when it emerged as a major economic power and the second largest global economy. Third, China has come to acquire a singular place in the regional economy. Intra-regional trade and investment as well as creation of integrated production networks made China an important economy for the other dynamic Asian economies. Fourth, considered with Hong Kong SAR and Taiwan, the greater China is an economic presence to reckon with. Fifth, although China is not a member of the exalted Group-of-Seven (G-7) or the significant OECD group of economies, in a short span of time it has joined the small number of economies that have global significance. With Japan suffering from recessions and a prolonged deflation, China played the "locomotive" role in Asia. In Chapter 5, I try to establish that vertiginous expansion of Chinese economy should be a boon to the neighboring Asian economies, not a bane. In the newly emerging county grouping like the APT, endeavors like Chiang Mai Initiative or creation of any other similar regional public good, China's role has far-reaching ramifications.

Perpetuating the folklore of Asian economic growth is not the objective of this book. It takes an objective and dispassionate view and delves into the constructive and favorable side as well as adverse and unfavorable side of the Asian economy. The deficiencies and imperfections have not been overlooked. As few analyses of the post-crisis economic scenario in the Asian economy with a forward-looking emphasis are available, this book intends to provide that. Although for covering the post-crisis scenario it does deal with the overture to the crisis and the principal developments leading up to it in the pre-crisis period.

An outstanding feature of this book is that unlike most Asia-related books, it is written in a comprehensive and authoritative manner and covers large areas of Asian macroeconomy and finance. The noteworthy areas of focus include international and intra-regional trade and investment, as well as financial and monetary aspects. In-depth discussions have been provided on regional integration through expanding trade, financial flows, regional production networks and financial and monetary co-operation. I distinctly separate formal regionalism from market-driven regionalization in Asia. This was done because the former was Asia's weakness while the latter is Asia's forte. The overarching focus of the book is how regional integration is unleashing the economic potential of dynamic Asia and providing a basis for the region to reclaim its role as the major force in the global economy in the post-crisis period.

Another outstanding feature of this book is that in taking a contemporary or post-crisis view of the Asian economy, this book offers the newest knowledge related to relevant themes on the Asian economies as well as the latest concepts. In a succinct manner, this book deals with the principal normative and positive strands with which one needs to be properly familiar in this subject area. As it is essential for a book of this kind, parts of the chapters have been written in a "just-the-facts-jack" style. The picture of both static and dynamic aspects of important economic themes related to the Asian economy has been painted with a broad brush. The selection and rejection of the thematic strands for coverage in this book has been done exceedingly carefully.

It is written in a reference book, albeit it can also be used as a textbook style. As noted earlier, students and other readers find the latest knowledge and concepts on several important themes on Asian economy in this book, in a manner in which they can appreciate and absorb them as well as use them as input in their decision-making. Students, particularly those from business schools, who may hold Asian-economy-related jobs after completing their studies, would find this knowledge extremely relevant, usable and helpful.

In a succinct manner, this tightly written volume covers a great deal of ground and imparts knowledge on the Asian-economy-related themes to students, researchers and policymakers alike. It is a worthwhile exercise because a knowledge gap existed among various stakeholders. When the miracle economies of Asia were struck by the 1997–98 crisis, Asian economy specialists, economists, students, policymakers and decision makers in the business community were not only astounded but were also in a state of disbelief. Initially, they did not think it was feasible and did not know what to make of it. In mid-1997, the Asian Development Bank culminated a $1.2 million research project on the future growth potential of Asia and a book entitled *Emerging Asia: Changes and Challenges* was published, forecasting thirty more glorious years of rampant growth. In July 1997, the currency and financial crisis struck Thailand

and the contagion engulfed several "miracles" economies as well as adversely impacted the regional and the global economy. Contrary to the forecast, in 1997 and 1998, GDP in several Asian economies contracted appreciably causing a great deal of economic and social dislocation.

The number of academic institutions offering courses related to Asian economies is already significant and growing. The target readership of the book is master's level students in economics, international political economy, international relations, Asian economy courses as well as MBA students. Ambitious senior-level undergraduates as well as policy mandarins can also benefit from the book. Having a background of initial micro, macro, international trade and monetary economics should be sufficient to comprehend this book because it provides definitions and explanations of terminology and advance concepts used in the text as footnotes.

In addition, it is neither overly technical nor highly model-oriented. Excessive emphasis on technicalities, equations and econometric modeling discourages many potential readers. These characteristics narrow down the market to a small expert readership. The book is easy to access for the target readership because of its descriptive analysis style, which stops short of mathematical formulations and econometric modeling. Many students and other readers who have good analytical minds and sound knowledge of economic principles feel lost in mathematical formulations. This writing style makes it accessible to a much larger number of readers.

As regards the structure, the book is divided into seven chapters. The first one takes an alternative, non-Eurocentric, view of the Asian economic history. It demonstrates that several Asian economies were active participants in and contributors to the global economy of bygone epochs. That Asian economy has a remarkable diversity when considered as individual economies or in country groups is the focus of Chapter 2. A historical characteristic of the Asian economies was their penchant for market-led regionalization. Unlike in the other parts of the global economy (such as Western Europe and Latin America), they preferred it to institution- or government-sponsored regionalism. This proclivity has been examined in Chapter 3. However, somewhat belatedly and in keeping with the global trend, initiatives toward institutionalized regionalism were taken in the recent past, which have been dealt with in Chapter 4. Trade and foreign investment are two vitally important channels through which regional economies have created fundamental linkages with each other. Chapter 5 highlights and analyzes these links and the synergy created by them in the Asian economies. Given the significance of financial sector, Chapter 6 has been dedicated to this subject. Its foci are the pre- and post-Asian crisis financial structure, institutions and market developments. It also examines the options for the immediate future. In the post-Asian crisis period, the Asian economies felt a pressing need for institutionalized co-operation, particularly in the financial and monetary policy areas. The objective of the collaborative regional endeavors was to stall any future crises from precipitating. If they do precipitate in future, their collaborative management may lead to lower cost than that inflicted by the 1997–98 crisis. The developments in these areas are the subject of Chapter 7.

Toronto
July 2004

DILIP K. DAS

ACKNOWLEDGMENTS

A word of gratitude would be in order for Dr F. Charles Adam, Chief Economist, International Monetary Fund, Tokyo; Dr Douglas Brooks, Principal Economist, Asian Development Bank, Manila; and an anonymous referee for reading through the first draft and making critical comments and providing worthwhile suggestions.

I am thankful to Professor Eisuke Sakakibara, Director, Global Security Research Center, Keio University, Tokyo, for formally permitting me to cite from his (with Professor Sharon Yamakawa) Working Papers entitled "Regional Integration in East Asia: Challenges and Opportunities," Part 1 and Part 2. They were published as the World Bank Policy Research Working Papers No. 3078 and No. 3079, respectively, in June 2003. Chapter 1 in particular has benefited from their research. I am also grateful to Ms Deborah Doherty of Kluwer Academic Publishers, Boston, for handling the publication of this book in an exceedingly well-organized and competent manner. I thank my son, Siddharth, for providing prompt and efficient research assistance and my wife, Vasanti, who helped me in preparing the index.

Toronto
July 2004

DILIP K. DAS

ABOUT THE AUTHOR

Professor Dilip K. Das has been associated with several prestigious business schools around the globe, including the European Institute of Business Administration (INSEAD), Fontainebleau, France; the ESSEC, Paris; the Graduate School of Business, University of Sydney; the Australian National University, Canberra and the Webster University, Geneva. He was also EXIM Bank Chair Professor in the International Management Institute, New Delhi. The areas of his expertise include international finance and banking, international trade and World Trade Organization (WTO)-related issues, international business and strategy and Asian economy, including Chinese and Japanese economies. His most recent interest is globalization and global business environment.

Professor Das has worked as a consultant for several international organizations, such as the USAID, the World Bank, and the World Commission on Development and Environment in Geneva. He organized thirteen large international conferences during the last ten years. He is presently a Toronto-based consultant to international organizations.

Dilip K. Das has an immense appetite for research and writing. He has written extensively and published widely. He is the author or editor of twenty books. He edited *The International Finance Reader,* which was published by Routledge, London and New York, in 2003. The last two books he authored were entitled *Financial Globalization and the Emerging Market Economies,* Routledge, London and New York. 2004, and *Regionalism in Global Trade: Turning Kaleidoscope*, Edward Elgar Publishing, Inc., Boston, MA, 2004. He has contributed a significant number of articles to professional journals of international repute and his papers have appeared in many prestigious research paper series. They have also been posted on the well-regarded web sites of many business schools and universities.

He was educated at St. John's College, Agra, India, where is took his BA and MA (Economics) degrees. He went on to study at the Institut Universitaire de Hautes Etudes Internationales, the University of Geneva, Switzerland, where he did his MPhil and PhD in international economics. He is fluent in French.

The author is regarded as a sound scholar in Asian economy. He has lived and worked in Asia and Australia for a long period and has had long-term interest in Asian economy, including Chinese and Japanese economies. He wrote several books on Asian economies, including a successful textbook. He has taught Asian-economy-related courses in several Asian and Australian business schools and did a short-term stint at the economic research division of the Asian Development Bank.

Chapter 1

ASIAN ECONOMY

The Heritage

1.1 PAST IS PRELUDE TO THE FUTURE

T.S. Eliot was not the only one who believed that "time present and time past are both present in time future, and time future in time past".[1] J.M. Keynes concurred with him and counseled his cohorts to "examine the present in the light of the past" so that the future may benefit from it. A creative concern about the future entails an insightful understanding of the past. Notwithstanding the present heterogeneity in the Asian economies, historical links existed between them over a long period, stretching for at least two millenniums. This area of economic history can certainly benefit from more edifying debates and greater scholarly attention than it has received. Yet, there is little doubt that present pace and patterns of changes in the Asian and global economy were influenced by what went on in the past. Strength and significance of relationships between the Asian economies continually vexed and vaned in the past. To comprehend the future of an integrating Asian economy of the contemporary period, it is not only necessary to examine the present relationships between them but also how they evolved over the centuries. Such a historical analysis is the essential objective of this chapter.

Economic historians who examined the longer temporality of Asia came to believe that Asia was a significant region, "having been in the forefront of world development for at least two thousand years, until the sixteenth, seventeenth even early eighteenth century, after which it suffered a relatively brief but deeply felt eclipse." This is the essential hypothesis advanced in this chapter. Most observers of the recent achievements of Asian economies as well as

---

[1] From *Four Quartets* by T.S. Eliot, which were written between 1935 and 1942 and published as a book in 1943. They won him the prestigious Nobel Prize for literature in 1948, and are regarded by many as the greatest philosophical poems of the twentieth century.

the Asian Diaspora concur that "Asia promises to be a great region of the future" (Rozman, 1991). Indeed, the Latin principle of *tempora mutanture, nos et mutamur in illis* would apply to the future growth and development of the region.[2]

The longer temporality enabled the establishment of a link between the present rise of Asian economy and its earlier position in the front line of the global economy. Past researchers put forth the viewpoint that Asia's long-term economic heritage was displaced by colonization, modernization and distressed responses to the rise of the occidental powers; however, deductions of some recent analysts are different. Recent researchers came to an alternative view of the economic heritage. They point out that hybridization and cross-fertilization took place between the Asian economies and the occidental economic and military powers, which became a significant force in the region between the sixteenth and the eighteenth centuries (Arrighi, et al., 2003). In the hybridization and cross-fertilization processes, elements of Asian historical heritage repeatedly reasserted themselves. Together they shaped the economic interactions within the region as well as the global economy. Frank (1998) posited that a global economy existed since the beginning of the thirteenth century, which encompassed the entire Afro-Eurasia. It was joined by North America in the seventeenth century. The coming into existence of this global economy was the result of interaction between the various participating regions.

1.2 ALTERNATIVE HISTORICAL PERSPECTIVE ON ASIAN ECONOMY

Until the recent past, the historical performance of the Asian economies was examined from a completely Euro-centric perspective, according to which they lay at the margins and did not seem to matter materially for the global economy. Their contribution and participation in the global economy was seen as merely peripheral, not worthy of scholarly attention. It was popularly believed that Asia did not have a viable and self-perpetuating economic system of its own and that it was discovered by the Europeans. Its indigenous economic vitality and synergy were seen as virtually non-existent. This perspective was born of both, disinterest and ignorance about the Asian economies and their contribution to the global economic growth over the centuries.[3] Sakakibara and Yamakawa (2003) asserted that "this system may have contributed as much to Europe's economic growth as Europe did to Asia's growth."

---

[2] This Latin proverb means that as the times change, with that we change as well.

[3] Compared to this, the viewpoints put forth by Abu-Lughod (1989), Frank (1998) and Rozman (1991) come as breath of fresh air.

In the background of the recent ascent of the status of Asian economies and rise of the Peoples' Republic of China (hereinafter China) as a manufacturing juggernaut and a large trading economy, more scholarly attention was devoted to Asia's economic history and the old perspective underwent a dramatic transformation. Several recent researchers broke out of the age-old mindset and took a different tack. Their quantitative analyses of economic history provided a clearer, more accurate and balanced perspective of the Asian economic evolution over the centuries, its vitality and its participation in the global economic evolution.[4] This group of researchers inferred that the Asian economies *en masse* were far more economically active, vigorous, productive and participative than what was believed in the past. They found Asia to be an economically open region fully involved in the global economic system, even in the pre-historic era, when Europe was still a vast hinterland having essentially an agricultural economy. Maddison's () estimates for the year 1000 A.D. (Maddison, 2001), put Asia's share of global GDP at 70 percent, vis-à-vis 9 percent for Europe. For certain, three major centers of economic activity prospered in Asia. They covered China, South Asia and the Islamic world of Central Asia. These sub-regions were not only economically active themselves but were also linked among themselves and with Western Europe in a profitable trade relationship.[5]

Abu-Lughod (1989) and Frank (1998) documented international trade between Asian and European economies during the thirteenth and fourteenth centuries. Smooth trade flows were well established and stretched over countries between northwestern Europe and northeastern China. A network of manufacturers, producers and merchants existed, who produced and exchanged an impressive array of goods and commodities. During the first half of the last millennium, there was thriving intra-Asian and Asia–Europe trade in commodities that had high value and low volume, although little trans-border financial flows. Both China and India had emerged as countries with relatively large populations and had significant trade links and trade volumes. China engaged in trade with Southeast Asia, the Islamic world of central Asia and the Middle East and North Africa, the Mediterranean countries and Europe. This trade utilized both the fabled Silk Road and ocean routes. In an identical manner, India traded with the Southeast Asian economies and the Islamic world through the ocean routes and

[4] For a flavor of the new ideas and assessment refer to the recent researches of Abu-Lughod (1989), Akita (1999), Bouchon (1999), Frank (1998), Braudel (1984), Braudel (1992), Clark (1977), Maddison (2001), Sugihara 2003), Bairoch (1981), and Bairoch (1993). Some of these scholars, in particular Abu-Lughod (1989) and Frank (1998) completely broke away from the conventional mould of thinking, and provided a novel and different perspective.

[5] Analysts enumerated in the footnote 4 devoted themselves to quantitative research in economic history and provided a detailed and precise account of production, trade and financial linkages, with appropriate quantification for various periods and sub-periods.

the with Mediterranean and European countries through both land and ocean routes. During this period, the Baltic trade with Eastern and Northern Europe was also substantial (Das, 2004).[6]

During the early part of the second millennium, two of the largest centers of population and economically viable systems were the Islamic world extending between the Atlantic and the Himalayas and the Sung Dynasty of China, covering a large land mass in its own right. These two economic systems had the largest cities of the erstwhile period, considerable manufacturing and commercial activity as well as fairly sophisticated monetary, financial and credit systems that served the commerce of this period fairly well. As noted earlier, during this *mise-en-scene* in Asia, with the exception of the advanced Italian city-states and Flanders, Western Europe was essentially a sprawling agrarian area (Findlay, 1996; Findlay and O'Rourke, 2001).

During the thirteenth century the Mongol Empire had established itself. Thereafter, the Pax Mongolica unified Asia—and also linked it with Europe—leading to the genesis of a global economy (alluded to in the preceding section). China and the Islamic world became both, large traders of commodities from their own respective regions and other parts of the erstwhile global economy. It was a dynamic scenario, and a complex pattern of trade linkages continually evolved. With it not only trade in commodities was promoted through the land routes but also transmission of ideas, techniques and migration of labor took place (Das, 2004; Needham, 1954).

1.3 ECONOMIC LINKAGES AND INTERACTIONS IN THE SECOND MILLENNIUM

Over the first half of the second millennium, Northeast Asia not only had succeeded in creating a vigorous economic system in its own right but also had trade and financial links with the other parts of Asia and Europe. In the second half, three core sub-regions of economic activity emerged. During this period, the so-called "industrious revolution" took place in Asia.

1.3.1 First half

The Mongol emperor, Khubilai Khan[7] lived in the thirteenth century (1214–1294) and founded the Yuan Dynasty in 1279. He succeeded in strengthening and building up the largest trans-continental empire of this period.[8] Khubilai

[6] See Das (2004), particularly Chapter 2.

[7] Mongol emperor Khubilai Khan (1214–1294) was the grandson of Chingis Khan.

[8] The Yuan dynasty, or the Mongol period stretched between 1279 and 1368 AD.

Khan adopted many elements of the Chinese government system and encouraged cross-cultural economic and social exchanges among merchants and traders. In modern parlance, he promoted free trade all through his empire. Dadu was the capital of the Yuan Dynasty, which received foreign visitors from all parts of the vast Mongol empire. Marco Polo (1254–1324) served at the Khubilai Khan's court. A gifted linguist, he was a favorite with the Great Khan and was appointed to high posts in his administration. He was sent on a number of special missions in China, and to Southeast Asia, Burma, and India. That Khubilai Khan sent Marco Polo to different countries as his emissary and tried to establish commercial links was well recorded by Marco Polo[9]. Marco Polo went on great length to describe capital Dadu, ceremonies, hunting and public assistance, and they were all to be found on a much smaller scale in Europe. Marco Polo fell in love with the capital, which later became part of Beijing. Its old name was Cambaluc or Khanbalig, which meant "city of the Khan." The new city, built because astrologers predicted rebellion in the old one, was described as the most magnificent city in the world during that period.[10]

Khubilai Khan's espousal of open-door strategy sustained and promoted trade and commerce, and ushered in an unprecedented era of economic growth and prosperity. During the rise and fall of the Yuan Dynasty, Mongols attempted to unite a vast number of countries and people in Asia and Europe. In his pursuit for greater access to foreign nations, Khubilai Khan planned and implemented a massive transport and communications project. It entailed construction of a roads and canal system for promoting trade and commerce, and was regarded as the most advanced physical infrastructure project of his period.

---

[9] Marco Polo (1254–1324) was the most famous European traveler of the Silk Road. He excelled all the other travelers of this period in his determination, writing, and influence. His journey through Asia lasted 24 years. He reached further than any of his predecessors, beyond Mongolia to China. He became a confidant of Kublai Khan. He traveled the whole of China and returned to tell the tale, which became the greatest travelogue. Interestingly, writing was not his forte. The accounts of his life in the court of Khubilai Khan and those of his voyages were not written by him but by a small time novelist who was imprisoned in Genoa with Marco Polo in the same dungeon, when a war broke out between Genoa and Venice.

[10] Marco Polo was fascinated by the summer palace in particular. He described it as "the greatest palace that ever was." The walls were covered with gold and silver and the main hall was so large that it could easily dine 6,000 people. The palace was made of cane supported by 200 silk cords, which could be taken to pieces and transported easily when the Emperor moved. Even in these palaces Khubilai Khan's kept a stud of 10,000 speckless white horses. The marble Palace, the rooms of which were all gilt and painted with figures of men and beasts, all executed with such exquisite art that you regard them with astonishment." This description later inspired the English poet S.T. Coleridge to write his famous poem "Xanadu" about Khubilai Khan's "stately pleasure-dome."

The vast geographical area covered by the empire benefited from an efficient transport and communication infrastructure. After learning from the Chinese legal system, the Yuan Dynasty also strengthened the legal infrastructure of this period in the Mongol empire.[11] Both of these developments promoted commerce and led to economic growth. Some scholars have argued that accelerated economic and cultural exchanges between Asia and Europe during the thirteenth and fourteenth centuries were the starting point of the subsequent global explorations endeavors by various European nations.[12] It can be argued that the Mongols of the thirteenth and fourteenth centuries were among the pioneers in initiating the concept of economic globalization.

During this period, shipping and nautical systems and the related technology were gradually emerging through a complex interplay of several civilizations and economic systems. Who was the leader and who the follower in this respect inspired endless debates. It was difficult to determine and the last word is not yet in. It was easy to assume that the Europeans led in maritime shipping because they are believed to be the first to develop the necessary nautical technology. However, Abu-Lughod (1989) disproved this Euro-centric assumption by providing comprehensive accounts of the voyages of the Ming Dynasty admiral Cheng Ho (or Zheng He) in the early decades of the fifteenth century.[13] His massive and highly organized fleets sailed in the Indian Ocean between China and Africa, touching and trading with several countries *en route*. This raised the question about technological capability playing second fiddle to economic incentives.

The motivation of the two so-called voyages of discovery was to chart the ocean route to India. It portends to the fact that India had an economically significant place in the global economy during the second millennium. King

---

[11] It was important for Khubilai Khan to ensure economic growth because without economic resources his offensive and defensive military expeditions could not take place. He paid a lot of attention to boosting the Yuan economy, in particular to developing transport and communications infrastructure. He developed a new roads and canal system for transport and a swift mounted courier services. These services were run with the help of 10,000 large post houses, each stabling hundred of horses. Each post house was approximately 40 kilometers from the next. Some of them were so large that they looked like palaces. This new infrastructure project strengthened the existing one and facilitated economic transactions (see Marshall,1993; Mote, 1999). Khubilai Khan also paid a lot of attention to devising and expanding a comprehensive legal and judicial system with the help of legal practitioners. The Yuan Dynasty is credited with the development of a legal code. It was likely that this codified system of law was based on the *yasa* system of the law of the Mongols, which was modified and further developed during the reign of Khubilai Khan (Langois, 1981; Phillips, 1969). Development of a system of legal documentation contributed to the growth of legal professionalism, which in turn helped in an effective administration of justice and property rights. All these developments had definitive economic implications.

[12] See the contributions of Marshall (1993) and Rossabi (1983).

[13] The Ming dynasty covered the 1368–1644 A.D. period.

Manuel I, who commissioned Vasco da Gamma's expedition, knew that India was the source of many spices, which were scarce and costly in Europe.[14] He observed that merchants from the middle and the Islamic and Arab world carried these spices by caravan across the deserts of Arabia to the markets of Mediterranean ports. The king hoped that, by discovering a new sea route to India, he could import spices directly and economically, bypassing the merchants who controlled the caravan routes. Toward the end of the fifteenth century, the much-vaunted and better-chronicled voyages of discovery started transfer of ideas, merchandise, technology, flora and fauna, and diseases on a substantial scale. These voyages *inter alia* provided opportunities "to break the monopoly of the spice trade held by the ruler of Egypt and the Italian city-states, particularly Venice and Genoa" (Findlay and O'Rourke, 2001). This indicated that a good deal of global trade existed in the first half of the second millennium to provide economic incentive to undertake the high-priced voyages of discovery.

1.3.2 Second half

Between the fifteenth and eighteenth centuries these three sub-regions, namely, China in the East, India in the middle and the Islamic and Arab world on the West together formed three "gigantic world economies" served by a maritime force controlling the seas. This nautical force serviced the Pacific Rim and Indian Ocean rim economies. However, Braudel (1984) flashed an amber signal and alerted that the economic interaction between these three sub-regions was far from continuous. In his view, it could be best described as "intermittent." Also, economic activities sometimes benefited the East, while on other occasions benefited the West, affecting functions, division of labor and economic powers in the three sub-regions. During periods when economic interactions ceased completely between the three sub-regions, Asian economy was left splintered into "autonomous fragments" (Braudel, 1984).

---

[14] The two voyages of discovery were first, in the pivotal year 1492 that obscure Genoese, Christopher Columbus, navigated across the Atlantic. He made his landfall in the Bahamas thinking that he was near India. He is credited with accidentally discovering the Americas. The second voyage was made by the Portuguese navigator, Vasco da Gamma, who lived between 1460 and 1524 and discovered the sea route from Portugal to India in 1498. He traveled around the Cape of Good Hope to reach the city of Calicut on the Malabar Coast of India in May 1498. This was a commercial expedition financed by King Manuel I, primarily to promote trade with India. The second objective of King Manuel I was strategic. He believed in the old legends, which described India as a rich Christian kingdom on the eastern rim of the Islamic world. Manuel hoped to contact the Christian King of India, and to negotiate with him an anti-Muslim military alliance. Much to the chagrin of King Manuel I, the Indian king was a devout Hindu, but being liberal, he allowed building of churches in his small kingdom.

Indeed, there were periods when some areas turned to autarky, like China in the mid-fifteenth century and Japan in the seventeenth century. But even during these ostensibly autarkic periods when these economies eschewed trade and closed the outsiders off, evidence is available to show that they were far from completely autarkic. With the help of the economic historic literature cited earlier one can create a realistic scenario of an evolving global economy, trade and financial flows in it, and development of institutional and systemic structures. As regards the technological developments, Asia's strength in shipbuilding, printing, textiles, metallurgy, and transport are well documented by Frank (1998). That Asia had a significant place in the world system throughout this period is clearly brought home by this relatively recent literature.[15]

Founding of Manila in 1571 as a large port and trading center is considered by many as the beginning of truly global or inter-regional trade. The deep-water port and the city around it developed as an active *entrepot*, which facilitated trade between different sub-regions of Asia as much as between different regions of the global economy of that period (Flynn and Giraldez, 1995). Its value as a center for trade in unifying the different sub-regions of Asia remained high until the beginning of the nineteenth century. It contributed significantly to the regional development process, which is not to mean that its value in promoting trade with other regions of the global economy was low.

To be sure, over the centuries spatially Asia has undergone considerable transformations, and many of the cities, territories, and regions have changed beyond recognition, but the contribution of various Asian centers of trade as well as that of Asia as a region to the global economy cannot be denied. Recent researchers have uncovered that during several sub-periods of history the region worked as an integrated economic system and a leading participant in the global economy, making its mark on it. Sakakibara and Yamakawa (2003) inferred that notwithstanding the impermanent and intermittent nature of the flow of economic activity, during the pre-historic period Asia played an "instrumental role in the global division of labor and its conduct in the world economy was open and outreaching."[16]

1.4 QUANTITATIVE DIMENSIONS OF GROWTH

The size of GDP is the first and the best measure of relative and absolute prominence of an economy in the global economy and to a lesser extent is population. Several recent analyses have provided estimates of these and related variables for the 1000–1800 A.D. period.[17] The measures of GDP and other

---

[15] Refer to footnote 5.

[16] See in particular Chapter 1 of Sakakibara and Yamakawa (2003).

[17] See, for instance, Bennett (1954), Clark (1977), Frank (1998) and Maddison (2001).

variables estimated by these studies vary. Notwithstanding the variations, these measures did portend to principal common trends in these measures. Using these estimates Sakakibara and Yamakawa (2003) compared Asia with Europe for the 1000–1800 A.D. period. A generalization that emerged was that the size of population in Europe grew faster than that in Asia during the first half of the second millennium. However, during the following two (that is, the sixteenth and the seventeenth) centuries the growth rate of global population retarded considerably and Asia and Europe were no exceptions. The common and well-known reasons for this slowdown were epidemics, infectious diseases like bubonic plague, wars of varying proportions and urbanization, which is considered to have a declining influence over population growth. As the growth rate retarded more in Europe, the difference between the growth rates of population in Europe and Asia narrowed during the sixteenth and seventeenth centuries. During the eighteenth century Asia's growth rate recorded a sharp spurt—more than 40 percent—leading to a much brisker population growth in Asia than in Europe where the population continued to grow at a sedate pace.

A detailed scrutiny of these historical analyses[18] leads to several significant and appealing conclusions: First, in absolute terms Asia's population was much larger than that of Europe during the entire 1000–1800 A.D. period. In 1000 A.D., Asia's share of global population was four to five times larger than that in Europe. Thus, over this period Asia could support much larger population than Europe. Second, the estimates made by these studies indicated that even in the first half of the second millennium China and India were the two largest concentrations of Asian population, accounting for approximately 70 percent of the Asian population, or 40 percent or higher percent of the world population. Growth rate of population in Asia was strongly influenced by growth rates in these two centers of population, and to a lesser extent by the growth rates in Indonesia and Japan.

Turning to the other measure, the GDP, Angus Maddison found that between 1500 and 1820, Asia's share of world GDP increased significantly. Over the first period (1500–1820), global per capita income increased at a slower pace because the world population was on the rise, with China and India accounting for much of the population rise. The GDP increases in Asia went into a reversal and declined between 1820 and 1945, but began rising rapidly after the War again (Sugihara, 2003). During the first period (1500–1820) world GDP increased only marginally, but during the second period (1820–1945), it recorded dramatic acceleration along with population increases.[19] This shift in gear was caused by a defining period in the economic history of Europe, namely the industrial revolution in Britain. It first spread to Western Europe and subsequently the rest

---

[18] Cited in the footnote above.

[19] See Maddison (1995) and Madisson (1998) for the statistical data supporting these developments in the global economy.

of the world was influenced by it. This was a tectonic period in global economic history.

Statistical analyses by Maddison (2001) and Frank (1998) expounded that in 1500 Japanese economy was depressed because of the disarray caused by the civil war, but in the beginning of the sixteenth century there was a marked improvement in the economic performance. The eighteenth century was marked by stabilization in population growth and rapid increase in production, including agricultural output in Japan. As indicated in the preceding paragraph, between the sixteenth and the eighteenth centuries, Asia enjoyed a period of population growth and rising standard of living, albeit the latter occurred to a modest degree. The factor that supported this development was Asia's response to the natural resources constraints, particularly the scarcity of arable land. To get around this constraint, Asian economies developed a "set of technological and institutional devises for full absorption of family labor" (Sugihara, 2003). The labor-intensive institutions and labor-intensive technology was not developed on the scientific principles of the West. For the most part they were simple rules of thumb and wisdom, rooted in and distilled from the past experiences. One illustration is the Chinese agricultural manuals, which provided information on the method of seed selection for different kinds of soil. Asian countries, particularly China, developed labor-intensive methods of irrigation and water control, double cropping and extensive use of a variety of traditional tools. Commercialization of agriculture in China was far from smooth and steady, but innovations like introduction of the new world crops like silk and sugar, monetization of land tax, played an important role in increasing agricultural output, supporting the rising population from the sixteenth through eighteenth century.

This information was transmitted across different Asian countries in different languages and adapted to the local needs by the adopting economies. Its swift transfer from China to Japan is well documented. Unlike the European peasant society of that period, the farm size was much smaller in Asia, typically one to three hectares. It was the smallest in Japan, less than a hectare. The size continued to remain small until the beginning of the twentieth century (Bray, 1986). As the labor intensity rose, the productivity of land rose in the initial stages, but after a point it did not. The rise in labor productivity at the initial stages was instrumental in facilitating larger number of people per unit of arable land in Asia. Small industrial units, which were often family-based were developed. They tended to absorb the available labor resources. On occasions, these units grew from family-based to village-based, although not all industries could support such growth. This was the "industrious revolution" that occurred in Asia over the sixteenth through eighteenth centuries.[20] It was quite unlike the industrial revolution that occurred in the West during the late eighteenth century. China and Japan were the two countries that were in the forefront of

---

[20] The term "industrious revolution" was devised by Hayami (1992).

this industrious revolution (Hayami, 1992). However, it is believed that the impact of the industrious revolution was smaller on labor productivity than that of the industrial revolution.

For the nineteenth and the twentieth centuries, Maddison also computed and compared the relative economic performance of the West and the East.[21] Drawing on the work of regional specialists, he compared the GDP of six developed Western economies (namely, Austria, France, Germany, Italy, the United Kingdom (UK), and the United States (U.S.) to those of six Asian (namely, China, Japan, Indonesia, Republic of Korea, Taiwan and Thailand) ones for the 1820–1992 period in constant dollars. The result was as follows

Table 1.1. GDP Comparison (in billions of $) of the East and the West in Constant (1990) Dollars

Year	GDP of the West	GDP of the East
1820	128	243
1913	1,138	435
1950	2,422	603
1992	9,781	7,487

Sources: Maddison (1995) and Maddison (1998).

According to this methodology, in 1820, as much as 52 percent of the world GDP originated in Asia, of which China and India accounted for 29 percent. The share of six advanced western countries was 18 percent (see Table 1.1). These statistics represent a general trend.

Acceleration in population growth in the region resulted from two variables, namely, rising fertility rate and declining mortality rate. During the last millennium it was essentially the latter that was the predominant cause of the population increase in Asia. Also, there was a significant improvement in per capita income and life expectancy (Maddison, 2001). It stands to logic that as a rise in per capita income leads to improvement in physical quality of life, increase in life expectancy and accelerating population occurs. Although credible production statistics for large periods during the second millennium are not available for Asia, it is reasonable to assume that rising population and increasing life expectancy can only be supported by a commensurate growth in production. Therefore, assuming that production in Asia grew faster than the population growth rate cannot be unwarranted. Growth in production was essential for sustaining the growing population.

Taking the same line of logic, Frank (1998) and Wallerstein (1989) went further and contended that Asia, along with its sub-regional economies, was "more productive and competitive" than the economies in the Western world and had

[21] Refer to footnote 19.

a far "greater weight and influence" in the global economy until 1800. They argued that predominance of Asia during this era was made feasible partly by growth of technological and economic institutional development. End of the period (1750–1800) GNP estimates by Braudel (1992) buttress this conclusion.[22]

1.5 PAST TRENDS IN TRADE

Some economic historians believe that trade between Asia and Europe is approximately 5000 years old, while others are at variance and contend that it existed only for 2000 years. Recent researches have provided fairly graphic and realistic accounts of the Asian economic scenario during the second millennium. After Christopher Columbus landed in an erroneous part of the globe in 1492,[23] Vasco da Gamma discovered the direct ocean route from Portugal to India around the Cape of Good Hope in May 1498. Charting of trade route to India substantially increased trade between Asia and Europe, both in terms of volume and value. Establishment of a direct maritime route had immense significance for the expansion of trade because, first, it rendered trade between the two destinations more regular; second, it reduced the unit transport cost; and third, it resulted in integration of global economies by joining two important economic regions. After pioneering the direct route from Portugal it dominated Asia–Europe trade throughout the sixteenth century. This dominance did not last for long because in the following two centuries, first the Dutch and then the English shipping services developed at a much faster rate and left the Portuguese traders far behind. Of the two, the Dutch maintained the largest maritime presence. Two historic names stand out in this regard, first the Verenigde Oostindische Compagnie (VOC), a large Dutch shipping and trading company, and second the East India Company, its principal English competitor. The two were involved in large volumes of intra-Asia and Asia–Europe trade. At the end of the eighteenth century, due to domestic reasons, the Portuguese shipping and trading capabilities declined, and were subsequently reduced to almost nil.

For a proper historic perspective, Sakakibara and Yamakawa (2003) divided Asian trade into intra-Asia and extra-Asia trade or trade with the rest of the globe. The former was further sub-divided into trade covering two overlapping regions of Asia. The locus of the first trading region being South Asia, and covering the Middle East, Central Asia, India and Southeast Asia. The hub of the second region was China and encompassed Eastern and Central Asia as well as India. The range of traded goods was wide, stretching from luxury goods to raw and unprocessed goods and commodities. There was large trade in

[22] See also Bairoch (1981), who provides statistical support for this conclusion.
[23] Refer to footnote 14 regarding the two voyages of discovery.

pepper, spices, sugar, silk, textiles, rice, wheat, coffee, opium, precious stones, medicine, weapon and horses. One commodity that was traded in large volumes was precious metals, particularly silver.

1.5.1 Intra-regional trade

Before the Europeans arrived, intra-Asia trade was completely Asian, in all the aspects and functions of trading. Asian traders had their own nautical wherewithal and technology to conduct this trade. A good number of maritime trade routes and ports were well established and busy by the middle of the last millennium, facilitating active intra-regional trade. A network of long and short maritime and land trade routes existed. They connected markets and trading centers in East Asia and Southeast Asia through the Strait of Malacca. There were busy ports on the Eastern and Western coastlines of India, as well as in the Persian Gulf and the Red sea, which were served by maritime shipping. All along these routes trading and financial centers of varying sizes existed, which lubricated the erstwhile trading activities. Since the fifteenth century, European actively participated in intra-Asia trade. Initially the Dutch traders were involved more than traders from the other European countries. VOC was the largest European carrier of intra-Asia trade in terms of volume and value. It dominated the other European shipping companies until the end of eighteenth century, when it ended its operations. The intra-Asia trade of VOC rivaled its Asia–Europe trade. Indonesia was the focal point for the Dutch traders, where they lived, worked, liberally socialized and actively tried to be a part of the Indonesian society. The port city of Batavia, or modern day Jakarta, was the hub of VOC operations.

In the thirteenth century, Japan had significant trade with the neighboring East and Southeast Asian economies. In the following two centuries Japan recorded brisk economic expansion, which supported its trade expansion, turning it into a maritime power of some reckoning in that part of the globe. The strong traditional trade ties with China and Korea became stronger and its exports expanded to other parts of Asia, in particular to the Southeast. The major products exported to China included copper, sulfur, folding-fans, screens, and swords, while imports were raw silk, porcelain products, paintings, medicines, and books. As China withdrew from the world trade for domestic reasons in 1435 (discussed in Section 1.5.2), Japan's trade expanded more vigorously and it picked up the slack in trade caused by the Chinese withdrawal. This was a crucial period in Asian trade. By the mid-sixteenth century, Japan had started producing silver in great abundance, major part of which was intended for export to China. As China had imposed trade prohibition with Japan during this period, it imported Japanese silver through the newly developing *entrepot* port in Manila in exchange for silk. During this period, Japan had established itself as a large exporter of silver, copper, sulfur, and small amounts of gold. European traders were also significant buyers of these products, in particular of silver. Other products of significant export included camphor, iron, swords, lacquer, furniture, sake, tea, and high-quality rice. These Japanese products went as far as India, West Asia and often to Europe. During the seventeenth century, the Tokugawa Shogunate (1603–1868) imposed isolation on Japan.[24] Although the Western countries instantly became pariah, Japan's trade with its Asian neighbors was not affected by this isolation. In fact, trade with China increased during the isolation.[25]

The period between the fifteenth and eighteenth century is acknowledged for the dominance of trade in the Indian Ocean by Asian traders and merchants. Besides, a large number of Asian personnel were active in supporting intra-Asia and Asia–Europe trade conducted by European traders and companies. They provided the necessary services in the areas of shipping, warehousing, inland transport, banking and finance, and in the security forces maintained by the European merchants and traders. To be sure, they energetically competed with each other, and partnerships and collaborations between Asian and European merchants commonly existed. Social links also developed between the European merchants and their Asian counterparts. Pomeranz and Topik (1999) provided accounts inter-marriages. Inter-racial marriages were initiated by the Dutch and the Portuguese.

Portuguese ships were granted lower customs duties by several Asian ports. Asian merchants who owned and ran their own ships flew their own flags as well as under the Portuguese flag, so that they could benefit from the lower customs duties (Braudel, 1984). When the Europeans became actively involved in Asian trade, particularly in the fifteenth and sixteenth centuries, there was a significant exchange of knowledge and technology between Asian and Europeans. There was an influence of Europeans on both the nautical and trading practices in Asia. European also influenced the manufacturing practices. For instance, commercial and profitable ideas of quality consciousness and making products neater, standardized and cheaper were imparted to Asian manufacturers by the European traders (Gaastra, 1999).

Asian trade data for the late nineteenth and early twentieth century (1883–1928 period) were compiled by economic historians.[26] Exports and imports from the West in the region covering South Asia, Southeast Asia, China, and Japan

---

[24] Tokugawa shogunate or *Tokugawa bakufu*—also known as the Edo bakufu—was a feudal military dictatorship of Japan established in 1603 by Tokugawa Ieyasu and ruled by the shoguns of the Tokugawa family until 1868, when Emperor Meiji was reinstated. This period is known as the Edo period and gets its name from the capital city of Edo, now Tokyo.

[25] Refer to Tarling (1992), Sanderson (1995) and Ikeda (1996).

[26] Sakakibara and Yamakawa (2003) compiled these statistics from Sugihara (1985) and Sugihara (1990).

during the period under consideration increased by 4.3 percent and 5.4 percent, respectively. Corresponding increases in intra-Asia exports and imports were 11.2 percent and 13.7 percent, respectively. Consequently, over the 1883–1928 period the share of intra-regional exports in total exports soared from 24 percent to 41 percent and intra-regional imports in total imports climbed from 28 percent to 44 percent. This was a massive increase in less than half-a-century. China and Japan recorded the largest increases in intra-regional exports, while India and Japan recorded the largest increases in intra-regional imports. Likewise, intra-regional exports increased moderately in Southeast Asia, albeit intra-regional imports declined marginally over the period under consideration. During the late nineteenth and early twentieth century, significant development in the cotton textile industry took place in Asia. It was the key sector, leading to industrial growth and promoted large cotton trade. With the passage of time, Asian economies developed a division of labor, with India and Japan concentrating resources on imports of primary products and exports of manufactured products. Conversely, China and Southeast Asia focused on exports of primary products and imports of manufactured products.[27]

The global trading paradigm that emerged toward the end of the nineteenth century and the early decades of the twentieth century was a predictable one, that is, the American and European economies exported manufactured goods to Asia in return for primary and semi-manufactured products. This comprised large part of extra-regional Asian trade. As regards intra-regional trade, Japan's trade with the Asian economies rose substantially during this period, to more than half of the total and remained at this level until 1930, when the Great Depression began. The composition of Japan's trade with Asia went on evolving constantly, and remained in a state of flux. By 1930, Japan's exports to Asia were dominated overwhelmingly by manufactured goods, while its imports were essentially the primary goods.

The reason why Japan's trade with the rest of Asia increased so much was that the Chinese and Indian merchants carried Japanese products to Asia during the early 1900s. This trade was unproblematic because traders from both the countries had established trading networks in Asia, which facilitated trading activity. Secondly, historic association with the Asian economies had made Japan understand the Asian demand—in terms of products and prices—better than that of Western countries. Japan's ability to adopt Western technology and adapt it to Asian circumstances faster than any other Asian economies gave it a head start in the production of manufactured goods for the Asian markets (Akita, 1999). Thirdly, Japan and many large Asian traders, except China, had adopted gold standard by the end of the nineteenth century. It contributed to growth in global trade of Asia. Adoption of gold standard enhanced Asian trade,

---

[27] Ibid.

and especially prepared the ground for importing capital goods from Europe and North America, without which little industrial and transport infrastructure could be developed in Asia and Japan. The intra-regional trade peaked in 1930. Japanese invasion of China in the July 1937 had a destructive impact over the established trade networks. All important cultural and financial cities easily fell of Japan in a short space of time. Beijing was the first to fall, followed by Tientsen, Shanghai, Nanjing, and Hanchow. Over the next decade, important trading economies like China, India, Korea and Southeast Asian economies withdrew from the regional and global trade almost completely because of geopolitical and domestic political problems.

1.5.2 Global trade

Although intra-Asia trade had prime significance, its extension into non-regional or global trade also took place. The Dutch and other European traders and shipping companies that participated in intra-Asia trade also exported Asian products to Europe and sold European goods in the Asian markets. Essentially the European needs were that of silver, which was largely imported from Japan, the secondary source being the Americas. In the past, in the beginning of the nineteenth century, a large part of Asia's maritime trade with European countries was carried on European ships, but Asian ships also carried cargo for the European ports (Feldbaek, 1999). The principal Asian trading economies with Europe during this period were China, India, Japan and the Southeast Asian economies. Of relatively less importance were the economies of the western Asia like Turkey, Armenia, Persia and traders from the Arab and African countries.

Well-researched accounts of China's global trade since the beginning of the twelfth century are available and have been discussed earlier in this chapter.[28] Until the first three decades of the fifteenth century, China was the most dynamic trading economy of Asia. The tradition of building large wooden ships was started by the Sung dynasty emperors, and the Yuan Dynasty founded by Khubilai Khan (discussed in Section 1.3) continued this tradition for expanding maritime commerce. Naval operations of the Ming dynasty emperor Yung Lo (or Yong Le) in the early fifteenth century are also well chronicled. During this period, according to the Chinese world view, the oceans were divided into the "Eastern Oceans" and the "Western Oceans." The former covered the present day East and Southeast Asia, while the latter covered South Asia, the Middle East and Africa. Chinese maritime shipping covered a large part of globe.[29]

---

[28] For instance, see Abu-Lughod (1989), Frank (1998) and Pomeranz and Topik (1999).

[29] During this period China was reputed to be the builder of the largest ships, larger than the European ships.

Chinese ships went as far as the Cape of Good Hope. The large export products included silk and porcelain ceramics. Successes in their export made China earn a great deal of world silver during this era; therefore, it recorded a trade surplus vis-à-vis the rest of the world. Other than trade the objective of naval expeditions was the system of tributary relationships, which represented China's economic and strategic prowess and superiority over other nations. This period culminated with the end of royal patronage for expeditions to the Western Oceans in 1435. The royal court decided that these expeditions did not add to China's security and were too expensive to support, and created fiscal problems. Voyages of Admiral Cheng Ho (or Zheng He) were terminated at this point in time. After this, the large Chinese ships did ply the oceans but they seldom ventured beyond the Eastern Oceans. They focused on short-distance maritime trade, pragmatically utilizing the *entrepots* that existed in these regions.

Between the fifteenth and the early nineteenth centuries, brisk trade was conducted between Asia, Africa and Europe. Indian subcontinent had an active trading economy. India had developed several ports on the long eastern and western coastlines. These ports in turn were not only well connected with inland trade and maritime routes but also served as busy *entrepot* centers. Indian traders filled the void left by the withdrawal of the large Chinese ships, noted in the preceding paragraph. They carried local products and those from Europe and the West Asia to Malacca. Among various merchant communities in India, Gujarati merchant community played the most active role. It is still a thriving merchant community in contemporary India. During this period, Indian exports were much larger than imports and it ran large trade surpluses with Europe and West Asia. It was customary to settle surpluses in silver and occasionally in gold. The trade surplus was essentially created by efficient production and export of cotton textiles and pepper. These exportables had a high demand in Africa, West Asia, and Europe. They were also indirectly exported to the Caribbean and the Americas. The other major products that were exported were rice, pulses, and vegetable oil. They were exported to ports in the East, to the port of Malacca (which was the largest port in the region, developed in 1403) and other Southeast Asian destinations and in the West to ports that existed in the Persian Gulf and the Red Sea. Records are available to show that over this period, India exported silver to China, reflecting a trade deficit with it (Bouchon, 1999; Frank, 1998).

The smaller Southeast Asian economies were also active in trade. They were important *entrepot*. Other than Malacca, these economies had developed several important ports, which remained active for centuries. After 1435, Chinese shipping regarded Malacca as their turnaround point. Manila was another important port that was founded in 1571 (see Section 1.3.2). The *entrepot* trade from the Southeast Asian ports expanded radically after the sixteenth century. Due to its geographical location, this region became the logical meeting point of both regional and global traders. The trade pattern of Southeast Asia reflected all the three patterns in its trade, that is, its local trade, regional trade (China, Japan, and India) and global trade (Europe, the Americas and West Asia). A large number of commodities and products were trades in these *entrepot.* This country group imported textiles from India, silver from Japan and the Americas, and silk and ceramics from China in exchange for its exports of pepper, spices, aromatic woods, resins, lacquer, tortoise shells, pearls, and deerskin. Countries in Indochina, particularly Vietnam, were significant exporters of sugar. Several of the port cities doubled as financial centers. They became multi-service commercial centers where trade financing could also be arranged.[30]

1.6 INDUSTRIAL REVOLUTION AND ITS AFTERMATH

Empirical analyses by Bairoch (1993) provide us with the GDP and GNP computations for the developing economies of the present day and industrial economies, in constant (1960) dollars and prices, for the 1750–1950 period.[31] His country division was between two stylized groups, namely industrial and developing, the latter group contained Asian economies. The results obtained by Bairoch (1993) are revealing and demonstrate that the Industrial Revolution and its aftermath was an extremely significant period for the industrial economies. As it was born in Britain and spread to other industrial economies of the present period, it had a limited and indirect impact on the developing economies. During this period, divergence between the industrial and developing enhanced. The GDP as well as per capita GNP of the former began to rise at a much higher rate vis-à-vis the developing economies. Between the mid-eighteenth and mid-nineteenth centuries, total GDP was found to be much higher—between one-and-a-half to three times—in the developing economies as a group than in the industrial economies. Per capita GNP was a little higher in the developing economies as a group than in the in industrial economies.

This state of affairs began to change around 1900. The causal factor was the long-term cumulative impact of the Industrial Revolution, also called the miracle of compound rate of growth. By this point in time, the Industrial Revolution was in operation for almost a-century-and-a-half. In 1900, the GDP of the industrial economies was more than 45 percent higher than that of the developing economies, while per capita income was 3 times higher. This was reflected in the standard of living in the industrial countries. By 1950, the per capita income of the industrial economies was a multiple of 6 of the average per capital income in the developing economies. These results are also supported

[30] Refer to Frank (1998) and Reid (1993).

[31] See Bairoch (1993), Table 8.2.

by Bairoch's estimate (Bairoch, 1993) of global GDP in 1960 dollars. In 1750, the developing economies accounted for 76 percent of it, while the industrial economies accounted for the balance 24 percent. By 1860, these proportions had changed considerably in favor of the industrial economies and they accounted for 43 percent of the global GDP.

As the population in Asia at this point was much larger than that in Europe, therefore, per capita income in Asia followed a different trend. As stated above, per capita income of the developing economies (including Asia) in 1750 was higher at \$188 compared to the industrial economies (\$182). But this state of affair was transformed by the year 1800, when per capital income in the industrial countries rose to \$198. For the developing economies, it remained stationary at \$188. Bairoch's estimate of per capita income in China for this period was \$210, which exceeded that of both the groups, developing and industrial economies. Both Bairoch (1993) and Braudel (1984) concur that in terms of total GDP, industrial economies overtook the rest of the world toward late nineteenth century. This was the period of a dazzling economic triumph for Europe and industrial countries in other part of the globe. At the end of the colonial period, in 1950, per capital income in the industrial economies (in 1960 dollars and prices) had risen to \$1,180, while that in the developing economies (including Asia) languished at \$214.

As stated in Section 1.4, the measures of GDP and per capital income estimated by these researchers varied from study to study and are not strictly comparable because of differences in definitions, assumptions and regional groupings. Therefore, estimates made by Maddison (2001) and those by Bairoch (1993) and Braudel (1984) are not truly comparable, but the trends indicated by them are strikingly similar. For instance, in his famous 2001 book Maddison[32] estimated these GDPs and reported that total GDP in Asia was higher than that in Europe, until the nineteenth century. According to his estimates, during the 1500 and 1820 period, it was two to four times higher. It was noted in Section 1.2 that for the year 1000, Maddison's estimates (Madison, 2001) put Asia's share of global GDP at 70 percent, vis-à-vis 9 percent for Europe. Asia's share declined to 59 percent by 1820 and 38 percent in 1870. Conversely, Europe's share of global GDP soared at a steady pace, reaching 34 percent by 1870. By 1913, on the eve of the World War I, Europe overtook Asia and maintained its lead.

Similarly the per capita GDP trend estimated by Maddison (2001) was comparable but different from what Bairoch (1993) and Braudel (1984) determined. According to Maddison (2001), while per capita GDP in Asia and Europe were the same in 1000 A.D., by 1500 A.D. Europe surpassed Asia and maintained its lead. Between 1500 and 1770 A.D., Europe's per capita GDP had increased four-fold, while that for Asia had risen by 25 percent, leading to a steady divergence.

[32] It is entitled *The World Economy: A Millennial Perspective.*

During the twentieth century, the gap between the per capita GDP continued increasing between the two regions. Consequently, Europe's per capita GDP reached five times that of Asia by the end of the twentieth century.

Maddison (2001) also estimated China's per capita GDP between the fourth and the fourteenth centuries, and reported it to be higher than that of Europe. The credit for higher GDP was given to China's technological prowess profiled in Section 1.4 and good governance led by a meritocratic bureaucracy. In the fifteenth century and thereafter, the growth rate of per capita GDP slowed in China as well as in the rest of Asia, which continued until the second half of the twentieth century. Although the industrious revolution did contribute to GDP growth, malfunctioning indigenous institutions and incorrect policy stance, followed by Western hegemony and colonial exploitation, which was most intense since the mid-18th century, largely caused the slowdown. In Maddison's view (Maddison, 2001), Western hegemony and colonial exploitation were the principal villains, which reinforced the initial stagnation in China and other parts of Asia.

Although the Japanese economy did not stagnate, its per capita income was lower than that of Asia until the nineteenth century. As noted in Section 1.4. the eighteenth century was marked by stabilization in population growth and rapid increase in production, including agricultural output. In terms of per capita GDP, by 1820 Japan caught up and outpaced China and other part of Asia. As its principal and avowed objective was to catch up with the industrializing West, the Meiji Revolution of 1868 ushered in massive institutional changes and developments, which had a remarkable positive economic impact.

Paul Bairoch and Angus Maddison are in agreement regarding some of the historical findings about the economic prowess of Asia during the last millennium, and in disagreement about others. Needless to say that it is difficult to establish with a high degree of certitude which one of the two scholars is more correct in his estimates, because both of them acknowledged inadequate statistics to base for their estimates. Yet, both of them portend to the fact that Asia did account for the major share of global population and GDP in absolute terms throughout most of the previous millennium. It also seems plausible that Asia had higher per capita income than that in Europe until 1500 A.D.—perhaps even until 1800 A.D. The Industrial Revolution and European colonization and hegemony caused divergence in per capita income between Asia and Europe, with the latter having negative economic consequences for Asia in the nineteenth and the twentieth centuries. The upshot is that Asia's share of world GDP was of substantial and meaningful magnitude for long historic periods and that it cannot be dismissed as a historic lightweight, as was widely considered in the past.[33]

---

[33] Refer to Sakakibara and Yamakawa (2003), Chapter 1, for a detailed presentation.

1.7 ASIAN ECONOMIC "MIRACLE" OF THE POST-WAR II ERA

In the aftermath of the Second World War, the GDP growth rate and per capital income in Japan and subsequently in a group of ten Asian economies began rising substantially faster than that in the mature industrial economies as well as the other developing and non-market economies. As analyzed in greater details in Chapter 2, a pragmatically thought out growth strategy *inter alia* stimulated and sustained growth for a long period. Ten high-performing Asian economies turned Asia into the rapidest growing region in the global economy. They were China, Hong Kong SAR,[34] Indonesia, Japan, Republic of Korea, Malaysia, the Philippines, Singapore, Taiwan, and Thailand. The Japanese economy was the leader in this regard. Its long-term (1955–73) GDP growth rate of 10 percent per annum was unprecedented and a trend-setter, which several other Asian economies consciously tried to emulate. This was termed the Japanese "miracle" and considered a precursor to the Asian "miracle."[35]

Although it is difficult to precisely pinpoint the year when the so-called "miracle" in Asia began, it happened around 1960. As seen in Table 1.1, in the last decade of the last century, the GDP of six Asian economies exceeded that of the six mature industrial economies. Drawing Lorenz curves for 1870, 1950, and 1990 for 199 countries, Maddison (1995) demonstrated that between 1870 and 1950 there was a rise in global inequality. A larger bulge in the curve for 1950 evidenced it. However, after that there was a sustained rise in the GDP in Japan, several Asian economies, and China, strictly in that temporal order. In a short span of time Japan moved up several rungs on the economic growth and industrialization ladder and joined the rank of mature industrial economies. Many Asian economies moved up from the lower rungs to the middle rungs, and some to the higher rungs. Such brisk growth of a small group of economies had global ramifications.

The post-war geopolitical environment favored Japan and the other Asian economies. The United States eagerly supported Japan's rapid economic growth because it was seen as a bulwark to stop the spread of communism in Asia. By

---

[34] On July 1, 1997, Hong Kong was returned to the People's Republic of China and it became a Special Administrative Region (SAR) of China.

[35] The Japanese economic miracle, followed by the Asian one, attracted a great deal of academic attention and spawned voluminous analytical literature delving into causality, linkages and other related aspects. Das (1996) deals with this extensive literature in a succinct manner as well as provides the idiosyncrasies of the economic strategy pursued by Japan and other successful Asian economies. The World Bank dedicated a thorough study of the phenomenon of the Asian miracle, its hows and whys. Its objective was to provide policy lessons for the other slow-growth or stagnating developing economies. Refer to the World Bank (1993).

1950, the policymakers in the United States were convinced that Japan's economic strength would work toward promoting the interests of the "free world" in Asia. This geopolitical environment provided first to Japan and then to the other rapidly growing Asian economies opportunities for importing raw material and exporting manufactured goods to the large U.S. market, and to a lesser extent to the other industrial economies. This geopolitical environment also made it feasible for Japan and the other Asian economies to pursue methodical development of labor-intensive, resource-intensive, and capital-intensive industries, essentially in that order. Low wages and a disciplined labor force *inter alia* successfully supported the rapid growth of these industries.

The other Asian economies, mentioned above, that were perceived as a part of the "free world" in the post-war era and benefited early from this geopolitical environment were Hong Kong, Korea (Republic of), Singapore and Taiwan, which developed at a rapid clip. They were christened the newly industrialized Asian economies (NIAEs) by the International Monetary Fund (IMF). There was a definitive demonstration effect and these economies took a leaf or two from the Japanese experience. Subsequently, Indonesia, Malaysia, the Philippines and Thailand followed suit. The U.S. hegemony in a bipolar world provided these economies an international framework for industrialization. They made a pragmatic use of the U.S. technology and aid, neoclassical economic principles, market-friendly policies of the government and combined it with their disciplined labor force. Their achievements were laudable. Initially China was a part of the communist orthodoxy, and an autarky. As a second thought it adopted the "open door" policy in 1978 (Chapter 2, Section 2.5.1). By the early 1990s, this group of economies had become an energetic part of the rapidly growing and globalizing Asia.

Early in their industrialization process some Asian economies (Korea and Indonesia) took the path of industrialization through heavy and chemical industries, but they soon abandoned it. Industrialization process that would utilize their skilled and disciplined human resources soon found favor. For the most part Asian economies followed outer-oriented,[36] export-led economic strategy. They skillfully located niches in the global market place in the array of products in which they had comparative advantage. A clear division of labor was adopted in that Japan, which was higher on the growth trajectory, focused on the development of capital-intensive industries and the other Asian economies on the labor-intensive sectors. In the 1950s and 1960s, Japan focused on sectors that were neither capital-intensive nor labor-intensive (such as auto and consumer electronics). As China adopted the outer-oriented industrialization strategy, its base of the labor-intensive industrialization process

[36] The term outer-oriented was first used by Anne O. Krueger and it came into currency after that.

broadened. It began its remarkable climb up the economic growth ladder, and with that its reintegration with the global economy (Das, 1996; Hayami, 1997).

1.8 SUMMARY AND CONCLUSION

The old view of Asian economic heritage was that it was a peripheral region of little economic dynamism, which made no contribution to the global economy. In this perspective of things, Asia was bereft of indigenous economic vitality and synergy. However, in the background of the recent ascent of several regional economies, researchers broke out of the age-old mindset and put forth a radically different view of Asia's long-term economic history. The longer temporality enabled establishment of a link between the present rise of Asian economy and its earlier position in the front line of the global economy. Asia has had a dynamic economic past and was in the forefront of world development for at least two thousand years. According to one estimate, Asia's share of global GDP was 70 percent in 1000 A.D. Some researchers put forth the viewpoint that Asia's long-term economic heritage was displaced in the seventeenth and eighteenth centuries by colonization and modernization. Others show that a sufficient degree of hybridization and cross-fertilization had occurred.

Evidence is available to show that a global economy had come into being in the beginning of the thirteenth century. During the thirteenth and fourteenth centuries, trade flows were well established and stretched over countries between northwestern Europe and northeastern China. A network of manufacturers, producers, and merchants existed, who produced and exchanged an impressive array of goods and commodities. During the first half of the last millennium, there was thriving intra-Asian and Asia–Europe trade in commodities that had high value and low volume, although little trans-border financial flows.

Over the first half of the second millennium, Northeast Asia not only had succeeded in creating a vigorous economic system in its own right but also had trade and financial links with the other parts of Asia and Europe. An open-door strategy sustained and promoted trade and commerce, and ushered in an unprecedented era of economic growth and prosperity. In the second half, three sub-regions of economic activity emerged, which were served by a maritime force controlling the seas. An important conclusion is that during several sub-periods of history the region worked as an integrated economic system and a leading participant in the global economy. Conversely, there were periods when economic interactions ceased completely between the sub-regions, and Asian economy was left splintered into "autonomous fragments." Indeed, there were also periods when some areas turned to autarky, like China in the mid-fifteenth century and Japan in the seventeenth century. A highly significant development took place during the sixteenth through eighteenth centuries. It is known as the "industrious revolution."

Some economic historians believe that trade between Asia and Europe is approximately 5000 years old, while others are at variance and contend that it existed only for 2000 years. In the previous millennium Portugal pioneered the direct route to India, and it dominated Asia–Europe trade throughout the sixteenth century. In the following two centuries, first the Dutch and then the English shipping services developed at a much faster rate and left the Portuguese traders far behind. Of the two, the Dutch maintained the largest maritime presence during this period. Two historic names stand out in this regard, first the Verenigde Oostindische Compagnie (VOC), a large Dutch shipping and trading company, and second the East India Company, its principal English competitor. The two were involved in large volumes of Asia–Europe trade. By the end of the eighteenth century, due to domestic reasons, the Portuguese shipping and trading capabilities declined, and were subsequently reduced to almost nil.

Before the Europeans arrived, intra-Asia trade was completely Asian, in all the aspects and function of trading. Asian traders had their own nautical wherewithal and technology to conduct this trade. A good number of maritime trade routes and ports were well established and busy by the middle of the last millennium, facilitating active intra-Asia trade. In the thirteenth century, Japan had significant trade with the neighboring East and Southeast Asian economies. In the following two centuries Japan recorded brisk economic expansion, which supported its trade expansion turning it into a major maritime power of that part of the globe. The strong traditional trade ties with China and Korea became stronger and its exports expanded to Southeast Asia. The major products exported to China included copper, sulfur, folding-fans, screens, and swords, while imports were raw silk, porcelain products, paintings, medicines, and books. China withdrew from the world trade in 1435.

Trade of Asian economies with the other non-regional economies was an extension of their intra-Asia trade. For instance, the Dutch and other European traders and shipping companies that participated in intra-Asia trade also exported Asian products to Europe and sold European goods in the Asian markets.

In the aftermath of the Second World War, the GDP growth rate and per capital income in Japan and subsequently in a group of ten Asian economies began rising substantially faster than the mature industrial economies as well as the other developing economies and non-market socialist economies. They were China, Hong Kong SAR, Indonesia, Japan, Republic of Korea, Malaysia, the Philippines, Singapore, Taiwan, and Thailand. Pragmatically thought out growth strategy *inter alia* stimulated sustained growth for a long period.

Together these 10 Asian high-performing economies turned Asia into the rapidest growing region in the global economy.

REFERENCES

Abu-Lughod, J. 1989. *Before European Hegemony: The World system A.D. 1250–1350.* New York: Oxford University Press.

Akita, S. 1999. "British informal empire in East Asia, 1880–1939: A Japanese perspective," in R.E. Dumett (ed) *Gentlemanly Capitalism and British Imperialism: The New Debate on the Empire.* New York: Addison Wesley Longman. pp. 141–159.

Arrighi, G., T. Hamashita and M. Selden. 2003. "The rise of East Asia in regional and world historical perspective," in G. Arrighi, T. Hamashita, and M. Selden (eds) *The Resurgence of East Asia.* London and New York: Routledge. pp. 1–16.

Bairoch, P. 1981. "The main trends in national economic disparities since the Industrial Revolution," in P. Bairoch and M. Levy-Leboyer (eds) *Disparities in Economic Development Since the Industrial Revolution.* London: The Macmillan Press. pp. 3–17.

Bairoch, P. 1993. *Economics and World History: Myths and Paradoxes.* Chicago: University of Chicago Press.

Bennett, M.K. 1954. *The World Food: A Study of the Inter-relations of World Populations, National Diets, and Food Potentials.* New York: Harper.

Bouchon, G. 1999. "Trade in the Indian Ocean at the dawn of the sixteenth century," in S. Chaudhury and M. Morineau (eds) *Merchants, Companies and Trade: Europe and Asia in the Early Modern Era.* Cambridge: Cambridge University Press.

Braudel, F. 1984. *Civilization and Capitalism; 15th to 18th Century. Vol. III: The Perspectives of the World.* London: Collins.

Braudel, F. 1992. *Civilization and Capitalism; 15th to 18th Century. Vol III: The Perspectives of the World.* Berkeley: University of California Press.

Bray, F. 1986. *Rice Economics: Technology and Development in Asian Societies.* Oxford: Basil Blackwell.

Clark, C. 1977. *Population Growth and Land Use.* London: The Macmillan Press.

Das, Dilip K. 2004. *The Economic Dimensions of Globalization.* Houndmills, Hampshire, UK: Palgrave Macmillan.

Das, Dilip K. 1996. *The Asia–Pacific Economy.* London: The Macmillan Press; New York: St. Martin's Press.

Feldbaek, O. 1999. "Country trade under Danish colours: A study of economics and politics around 1800," in K.R. Haellquist (ed) *Asian Trade Routes: Continental and Maritime.* London: Curzon Press. pp. 96–133.

Findlay, R. 1996. *The Emergence of World Economy: Towards a Historical Perspective.* New York: Columbia University. Economic Discussion Paper No. 9596. April.

Findlay, R. and K.H. O'Rourke. 2001. "Commodity market integration 1500–2000," paper presented at the NBER Conference on *Globalization in Historic Perspective,* Santa Barbara, California, May 11–12, 2002.

Flynn, D.O. and A. Giraldez. 1995. "Born with silver spoon: The origin of world trade in 1571," *Journal of world History.* Vol. 6. No. 2. pp. 201–221.

Frank, A.G. 1998. *ReOrient: Global Economy in the Asian Age.* Berkeley: University of California Press.

Gaastra, F.S. 1999. "Competition or collaboration? Relationship between the Dutch East India Company and Indian merchants around 1680," in S. Chaudhury and M. Morineau (eds)

Merchants, Companies and Trade: Europe and Asia in the Early Modern Era, Cambridge: Cambridge University Press.

Hayami, A. 1992. "The industrious revolution," *Look Japan.* Vol. 38. pp. 8–10.

Hayami, Y. 1997. *Development Economics: From the Poverty to the Wealth of Nations.* Oxford: Oxford University Press.

Ikeda, S. 1996. "The history of the capitalist world system vs. the history of East–Southeast Asia," *Review.* Vol. 19. No. 1. Winter. pp. 49–78.

Langois, J.D. 1981. *China Under Mongol Rule.* Princeton, NJ: Princeton University Press.

Maddison, A. 1995. *Monitoring the World Economy.* Paris: Development Center, OECD.

Maddison, A. 1998. *Chinese Economic Performance in the Long Run.* Paris: Development Center, OECD.

Maddison, A. 2001. *The World Economy: A Millennial Perspective.* Paris: Development Center, The Organization for Economic Co-operation and Development (OECD).

Marshall, R. 1993. *Storm From the East: From Genghis Khan to Kublai Khan.* Los Angeles: University of California Press.

Mote, F.W. 1999. *Imperial China: 900–1800.* Boston, MA: Harvard University Press.

Needham, J. 1954. *Science and Civilization in China,* Vol. I. Cambridge: Cambridge University Press.

Phillips, E.D. 1969. *The Mongols.* New York: Frederick A. Praeger Publishers.

Pomeranz, K. and S. Topik. 1999. *The World that Trade Created: Society, Culture, and the World Economy.* New York: M.E. Sharpe.

Reid, A. 1993. *Southeast Asia and te Age of Commerce 1450–1680*, Vol. 2. New Haven, CT: Yale University Press.

Rossabi, M. 1983. *Khubilai Khan: His Life and Times.* Los Angeles: University of California Press.

Rozman, G. 1991. *The East Asian Region: Confucian Heritage and its Modern Adaptation.* Princeton, NJ: Princeton University Press.

Sakakibara, E. and S. Yamakawa. 2003. *Regional Integration in East Asia: Challenges and Opportunities*, Part I and Part II. Washington, DC: Policy Research Working Paper Nos. 3078 and 3079.

Sanderson, S.K. 1995. *Social Transformation: A General Theory of Historical Development.* Oxford: Blackwell.

Sugihara, K. 1985. "Ajiakan-Boeki no Keisei to Kozo 1880–1913" [Patterns and Development of intra-Asia Trade], *Shakai Keizai Shigaku* [The Socio-Economic History], Vol. 51. No. 1. pp. 123–146.

Sugihara, K. 1990. "Japan as an engine of the Asian international economy, 1980–1936," *Japan Forum.* Vol. 2. No. 1. April. pp. 127–145.

Sugihara, K. 2003. The East Asian path of economic development: A long-term perspective," in G. Arrighi, T. Hamashita, and M. Selden (eds) *The Resurgence of East Asia.* Routledge: London and New York. pp. 78–123.

Tarling, N. 1992. *The Cambridge History of Southeast Asia,* Vol. I. Cambridge: Cambridge University Press.

Wallerstein, I. 1989. *The Modern World System,* Vol. 3. New York: Academic Press.

The World Bank. 1993. *The East Asian Miracle: Economic Growth and Public Policy.* New York Oxford University Press.

Chapter 2

ECONOMIC DIVERSITY IN ASIA

2.1 HETEROGENEITY

Geographically, Asia stretches between Afghanistan in the west to the Korean peninsula in the east. This crescent-shaped region comprises several discernible, distinct, and dissimilar sub-regions and countries, which are at different stages of economic growth, and have widely differing economic characteristic attributes. While diversity is a universal feature, Asia represents an extreme form of it. Asia comprises some high-performing sub-groups of economies and those that have performed relatively poorly during the post-war era. Each economy has its idiosyncratic set of assets and liabilities.

Diversity exists not only in economic aspects of Asian life, but also in social, political, religious, cultural, ethnicity, linguistics, geographical features and systems of governments. Some eleven languages and eighty-seven dialects are spoken in the Philippines. Eight of these are native tongues for about 90 percent of the population. All eight belong to the Malay–Polynesian language family and are related to Indonesian and Malay, but no two languages are mutually comprehensible. Indonesia, the most ethnically diverse country in the world has three hundred ethnic groups that follow four major religions, namely, Buddhism, Christianity, Hinduism and Islam. The Indonesian government takes pride in its pluralistic society and describes it as "unity in diversity." The diversity on various fronts was, and continues to be, far greater than that in European Union (EU) of 15[37] and in North American Free Trade Area (NAFTA). Compared to them, Asia has much greater diversity in terms of levels of economic development, sizes of GDP, economic and industrial structures, depth and sophistication in financial markets, and broad economic and financial institutional frameworks.

[37] In May 2004, the membership of the EU increased from 15 to 25.

A statistical comparison of economic indicators of the Asian economies clearly brings home their inter-country diversity. Added to that is the intra-country diversity, which is also enormous. Many countries contain differing ethnic groups of different races, who follow different religions and social norms and practices. For instance, the Han people are the China's largest ethnic group, but 56 ethic groups inhabit this vast country; 18 of them have population of one million or more. The largest of these minority ethnic groups is Zhuang, with a population of 16 million. Various ethnic minority groups live with the majority Han population, while some minorities prefer to live in separate compact groups. This diversity exists all over Asia. A small country like Myanmar has 135 different ethnic groups of eight races. Large Chinese, Indian and Malay populations are found in many East and Southeast Asian countries. In many countries they are minorities, and in some they are either large minorities or even majorities. These populations groups have maintained many of their native characteristics, yet have assimilated well in their societies of domicile. Families that are part of the Chinese Diaspora have earned a reputation for being astute business people and their business acumen is admired all over Asia. For instance, while the Chinese constitute less than three percent of the total population in Indonesia, they control as much as seventy percent of all private sector economic activity. The phenomenon has been attributed to a natural affinity the Chinese possess for business endeavors. This acumen is believed to be rooted in the Confucian work-ethic, the hierarchal structure of the family, which lent itself to effective creation of large businesses, even conglomerates.

Social indicators like literacy and life expectancy data for these countries also display extreme diversity in Asia. This heterogeneity reflects the economic diversity of the Asian economies. For instance, Korea was the most literate country having 1 percent illiteracy among male population and 4 percent among female. Cambodia was at the opposite extreme, with the corresponding proportions being at 41 percent and 79 percent, respectively. Likewise, life expectancy varies widely. In Hong Kong SAR and Japan it is more than 80 years, while in countries in Indochina (Cambodia, Lao PDR and Vietnam) it is merely 54 years.

2.2 HIGH-PERFORMING ECONOMIC SUB-GROUPS

The dynamic Asian economies began to be recognized as a distinct group of high performers in the latter half of the 1980s. If long-term GDP growth rate is taken as a yardstick, Thailand and countries east of it performed stupendously better than the seven south Asian economies. The reason for excluding the South Asian economies from this book is that over the preceding four decades, they never became a part of the vibrant and high-performing Asian economic scenario. Economic growth did not seem to be the priority of South Asian economies. Their success in eliminating absolute poverty between 1981 and 2001 was also small. The World Bank reference line of poverty of $1.08-a-day remained virtually stationary. In 1981, there were 474 million people living below the poverty line in the seven South Asian economies. In 2001, this number did not decline appreciably and was 431 million—of these, 83.1 percent lived in India. The higher World Bank reference line for poverty was $2.15-a-day. The number of poor people living below this poverty line increased from 821 million to 1,064 million during the period under consideration—of these, 77.7 percent lived in India (Chen and Ravallion, 2004).[38]

When we say that the economies east of Thailand performed remarkable better, to be sure, the three former non-market economies in Indochina are unmistakably an exception. The successful sub-groups among Asian economies and their performance can be divided in the following manner. The dynamic Asian economies comprise a mélange of countries that can be justly called matured industrialized economy (like Japan), emerging market economies (EMEs)[39] and developing economies at varying strata of economic development. Following Japan, the four newly industrialized Asian economies (NIAEs) were the first and the most successful country group in adopting export-led or trade-induced growth, followed by the ASEAN-4 and subsequently the Peoples Republic of China (hereinafter China).[40]

As regards the individual countries, it was stated in Chapter 1 (Section 1.7) that the successful economies of Asia in this book are defined to include the ten dynamic Asian economies, namely, China, Hong Kong SAR, Indonesia, Japan,

---

[38] See Chen and Ravallion (2004), Table 3. The other tables also buttress the same point.

[39] What are the emerging market economies? Other than the rapid endogenous growth endeavors, respect of property rights and respect of human rights are some of the basic prerequisites of becoming an emerging market economy. The national government should offer protection to property and human rights of both, the citizens of the country and the non-residents alike. An indispensable condition for an emerging market economy is its sustained ability to attract global capital inflows. Only an assurance of protection of property rights will attract global investors to a potential emerging market economy. Thus, protection of property rights is a fundamental, non-negotiable, condition, which an economy needs to meet before embarking on its road to becoming an emerging market economy. So far there is little agreement on the country count. In the industrial economies the emerging market economies were thought of as the newly industrialized economies (NIEs) and some middle-income developing countries. The latter group included those countries in which governments and firms are creditworthy enough from the perspective of global investors to successfully borrow from the global capital markets and/or attract institutional portfolio investment. Different international institutions include slightly different sets of countries in this category (Das, 2004b).

[40] Hong Kong SAR, Korea, Singapore and Taiwan are called the newly industrialized Asian economies (NIAEs), while Indonesia, Malaysia, the Philippines and Thailand are called the ASEAN-4 group of countries.

Korea, Malaysia, the Philippines, Singapore, Taiwan, and Thailand. Majority of these economies are widely acknowledged to be the high-performers. The Philippines in thisgroup is a marginal case. Eight of them (excluding China and the Philippines) were called the "high-performing Asian economies (HPAEs)" by the well-regarded 1993 World Bank study, which tried to identify the ingredients that go into a recipe for rapid economic growth, with improvement in income distribution. The HPAEs were characterized by fundamentally sound development policies, outer-orientation, plus tailored government interventions. With high rates of GDP growth, the HPAEs recorded steady improvement in the Gini coefficient.[41] The market-oriented aspects of the experience of HPAEs were recommended to the policymakers in the developing world as well as transition economies with few reservations. However, whether government intervention should be attempted everywhere was another matter.

Japan, the second largest economy in the world after the United States (U.S.), the third largest exporter ($471.9 billion) accounting for 6.3 percent of world exports in 2003, and the sixth largest importer ($383.0 billion) accounting for 4.9 percent of world imports, is a denizen of Asia. Besides, China's importance in the global economy as well as world trade went on rising monotonically. By 2000, China had become the largest developing-country exporter, accounting for 3.5 percent of global merchandise exports. Global GDP growth rate decelerated from 4.7 percent in 2000 to 2.3 percent in 2001 and then recovered slightly in 2002, to 3.0 percent.[42] However China remained unaffected and continued to emerge rapidly as a highly successful trading economy, and accounted for 5.9 percent ($438.4 billion) of the global merchandise exports in 2003. It was the fourth largest exporter in the world after Germany, the United States and Japan, in that order. It also accounted for 5.3 percent ($412.8 billion) of merchandise imports in 2003, making it the third largest importer in the world after the United States and Germany, in that order (World Trade Organization [WTO], 2004).[43] As opposed to these, there are many regional economies, particularly in South Asia, which did not succeed in carving out a niche for themselves in the arena of international trade. Their export volume and value are so small that they do not appear on the WTO league table of traders.

The three small economies of Indochina suffered under the yoke of non-market economic system and remained impoverished. Myanmar's self-imposed autarky partially explains its abject poverty. Long-term GDP growth rate of the South Asian economies was not only low but they were also the last to adopt economic and financial liberalization measures and the slowest to

---

[41] See *The East Asian Miracle: Economic Growth and Public Policy*, New York: Oxford University Press, 1993.

[42] The source of GDP growth statistics is IMF (2003), Table 1.1.

[43] Refer to WTO (2004), Appendix Table 1.

embark on export-led or trade-induced growth path. Their affinity for the import-substituting industrialization (ISI) regime was so strong that it could not be rooted out completely from their growth strategy. Setting up large and inefficient public sector enterprises is the characteristic feature of this set of economies. They did not consider a liberalized and diversified multilateral trade regime useful for their economies. This sub-group failed to develop and hone its supply-side synergy so badly needed for rapid economic growth. Little wonder they lagged behind the successful sub-groups of Asian economies, which were located east of them in the same region.

An admixture of bilateral trade ties, neo-mercantilist policy stance, and liberalized and diversified multilateral trade regimes were the driving forces behind the emerging trade patterns in the rapidly growing Asian economies. Market forces played a notable role in the developments of these trends. As the economies grew and the supply-side synergy gained momentum, Asia's intra-trade not only expanded rapidly, but also advanced ahead of regional institutional arrangements like the ASEAN[44] Free Trade Area (AFTA) and the Asia Pacific Economic Co-operation (APEC) forum. In October 2003, the members of ASEAN proposed to form an EU-like ASEAN Economic Community by 2020 (Chapter 4, Section 4.3.7). There was a steady growth of the internal Asian markets and, therefore, in intra-regional trade. Expanding intra-regional and global trade turned the high-performing Asian economies into traders of global significance. The WTO league tables of leading global exporters for 2003 included nine Asian economies. Other than Japan (3rd) and China (4th) noted above, it included Hong Kong SAR (11th), Korea (12th), Taiwan (15th), Singapore (16th), Malaysia (19th), Thailand (24th), and Indonesia (29th).[45]

Substantial intra-regional trade had existed in Asia since the beginning of the twentieth century. It had markedly increased among the successful economies of Asia. When the crisis broke out in mid-1997, most successful Asian economies were carrying on as much as 50 percent of their total trade with the other regional economies.[46] The only exception in this regard was Indonesia. Apart from this,

---

[44] ASEAN stands for the Association for Southeast Asian Nations. It was established on 8 August 1967 in Bangkok by the five original Member Countries, namely, Indonesia, Malaysia, Philippines, Singapore, and Thailand. The ten present ASEAN members are Brunei Darussalam, Cambodia, Indonesia, Lao PDR, Malaysia, Myanmar, the Philippines, Singapore, Thailand, and Vietnam.

[45] Refer to WTO (2004), Appendix, Table 1.

[46] The Asian crisis began on July 2, 1997 in the financial sector of Thailand, but the contagion engulfed Indonesia, Korea, Malaysia, and the Philippines in no time. Other Asian economies were indirectly affected by it, including the relatively strong economies of China and Japan. Ultimately the crisis dampened the global economic growth. The immediate trigger was the devaluation of currencies in the region, which eroded the value of Asian currencies, making it much more difficult for Asian businesses and banks to pay back debts that they incurred in

only China saw the proportion of its intra-regional trade share decline during the decade of 1990s, essentially because of brisk expansion of its trade share with the United States. Over the recent period, most of the successful exporters in Asia held or reduced their share of trade with Japan, the dominant regional trader. Although Japan's significance as a regional trade partner has declined over the years, in absolute terms it has expanded its exports to the region. During the last decade and a half, the most rapid growth in trade opportunities came instead from the four NIAEs, as well as the ASEAN-4.

Essentially driven by market forces, a hierarchical trade and investment structure developed in the dynamic sub-groups of economies over the last three decades in Asia, which expanded both intra-regional trade and investment, in turn integrating the region. Lee and Roland-Holst (1998) show that the market expansion that took place in Asia was both vertical and horizontal. First, the NIAEs and then the other EMEs of Asia fit into the lower tiers of complex trade hierarchies. The NIAEs were the initial recipient of foreign direct investment (FDI) from Japan and the United States. Second, as labor costs in NIAEs rose, Japan and the United States became investors in the economies further below on the economic development ladder. This tendency was conspicuous in association with the large flows of FDI into the ASEAN-4 economies[47] and China, in that order.

Over the preceding quarter century, Japan, Taiwan and Korea provided massive amounts of FDI to the ASEAN-4 economies and subsequently to China, in the process increasing their commitments in these markets. Firms in the investing countries built subsidiaries or partnerships in these economies, which in turn exported intermediate goods to the investor firms in the home countries. These intermediate goods could also be exported to the subsidiaries of

---

foreign denominations. A wave of loan defaults resulted and much of Asia's financial sector loomed toward bankruptcy. Unable to raise enough financial capital to fix their ailing economies, several Asian governments were forced to ask for international help. The help arrived in the form of loans from the International Monetary Fund (IMF) and several Asian countries pledged to provide around $100 billion in loans to help shore up Southeast Asia's struggling financial systems. China and Japan took lead in this respect. In return for the liquidity support, recipient countries were expected to implement a series of austerity measures designed to contain the crisis and improve their free-market economic policies. The Asian crisis and the IMF bailout kindled a wide-ranging debate on the merits of Asia's economic model. That model—called government-led development—is characterized by a strong alliance between government and business that gives political leaders a substantial role in shaping the private sector's course of development. Some analysts believed that the cozy, sometimes corrupt ties between government bureaucrats, bankers and the family-owned businesses that dominate Asian markets created an inept financial system that was doomed to failure. They generally back the IMF's demand that Asian countries sharply limit the government's intrusion into business and that corporate governance needs to be significantly improved.

[47] ASEAN-4 economies are Malaysia, Indonesia, Indonesia and Thailand.

the investing firms in other parts of the world. This kind of trade expansion was usually supported by complex commercial alliances in which both the partners enjoyed many growth externalities (Lee and Roland-Holst, 1998). Trade between China, Hong Kong SAR and Taiwan[48]—together referred to as greater China—is large and increasingly closely linked. Initially a great deal of China's exports went to the world through Hong Kong, but its trade dependence on Hong Kong SAR progressively declined in 1990, because its capability to trade directly had increased. Presently China trades much more directly both intra-regionally and globally. This interplay of trade and investment has been dealt with at length in Chapter 3, Section 3.2.

2.3 REGIONAL ECONOMIES AND ECONOMIC GROUPINGS

The Treaty of Amity and Co-operation (TAC) in Southeast Asia was signed at the First Association for Southeast Asian Nations (ASEAN) summit on 1967. It was intended to a political treaty of friendship and non-interference. The five founding members of ASEAN (namely Indonesia, Malaysia, the Philippines, Singapore and Thailand) were a fairly homogeneous group. As this group was enlarged to include Brunei Darussalam, Cambodia, Lao PDR, Myanmar and Vietnam, its diversity increased dramatically. Presently the ASEAN has ten members, ranging from tiny island republic of Singapore to Indonesian archipelago, which comprises over 17,000 islands. The areas they cover vary from 1,000 square kilometer for Singapore on one extreme to 2 million square kilometer for Indonesia on the other. Likewise, population size for this small country group varies between 300,000 for Brunei Darussalam to 207 million for Indonesia. Gross national income (GNI) per capita also has wide differences in this small country group, with Brunei Darussalam and Singapore having more than $24,000 and the three new members (Cambodia, Lao PDR and Vietnam) having per capital GNI in the neighborhood of $300 (see Chapter 4, Section 4.3.1).

Since 1997, ASEAN was endeavoring enlargement to include China, Japan and Korea, and become the ASEAN-Plus-Three (APT), which naturally would have much greater economic and social heterogeneity than the ASEAN of 10 members (or ASEAN-10). The members of ASEAN have held meetings with Japan, China and South Korea for seven years in a row, between 1997 and 2003. In 2002, ASEAN began work on a trade agreement with China, and in October 2003 ASEAN signed accords with Japan and India. In October 2003,

[48] Although Macao should be added to this definition of Greater China, it is conventionally not. Hong Kong is the special administrative region of China and is referred to as Hong Kong SAR.

the members of ASEAN proposed to form an ASEAN common market by 2020. China's population of 1.3 billion dwarfs the individual populations of the remaining 12 countries in the APT grouping. Likewise, Japan which is the second largest global economy, dwarfs the GDP of all the APT economies. Its current per capital GNI is the highest for the APT groupings, substantially higher than that of Brunei Darussalam and Singapore.

As set out in Section 2.1, in comparison to the European Union of 15 (EU-15) members, heterogeneity in Asia is much larger.[49] To be sure, there are variations in population size ranging from Luxembourg (400,000) to Germany 82 million, which is a far cry from the Chinese population of 1.3 billion. Asia and the EU-15 comprise different countries from the perspective of level of economic development. As indicated earlier, Asia comprises developing economies, EMEs and one matured market economy industrial economy. As opposed to this, the EU-15 consists of all industrial economies, although Greece, Portugal and Spain are at a much lower level of industrial development than the other members of the EU-15. These three economies also have the lowest per capita GNP in the EU-15. With the signing of treaties of accession with 10 more countries in April 2003, the membership of the EU extended to 25 in May 2004.[50] The EU of 25 members would come close to Asia in terms of diversity.

As the county group size is reduced, the smaller countries begin to matter more and become significant. In the APT grouping, the share of ten ASEAN countries is 8.6 percent. Japan is the largest economy in this group accounting for 69 percent of the ATP GDP, while the other two members, namely, China and Korea account for 15 percent and 6 percent of the ATP GDP. When the country group is enlarged to include all the 21 economies of the APEC forum, which includes both Asian and Pacific economies, the United States is the domineering economy accounting for 51 percent of the total APEC GDP. The ten ASEAN economies add up to only 3 percent of the total APEC GDP.

If the Asian regional groupings are compared to those of Europe or North America, differences in economic growth and the group sizes become obvious. With a GDP of $18 trillion APEC is the largest regional trading group (RTA),

---

[49] On December 1, 1991, agreement was reached in Maastricht on the Treaty on European Union, with a timetable for the Economic and Monetary Union (EMU). The European Single Market was completed on January 1, 1993. On November 1, 1993, the Maastricht Treaty came into force after Danes voted yes at the second try, and the EEC became the European Union (EU).

[50] The Treaty of Accession between the European Union (EU) and ten countries, namely, the Czech Republic, Estonia, Cyprus, Latvia, Lithuania, Hungary, Malta, Poland, Slovenia, and Slovakia was signed in Athens, Greece on April 16, 2003. These 10 countries are to acquire formal membership status of the EU in May 2004. Save for Cyprus and Malta, these are all Central and East European Countries (CEEC) countries. Until the collapse of the Soviet Union in 1990–91, these eight economies were the satellite economies of the Soviet Union. Bulgaria, Rumania and Turkey, three candidates for future membership, are waiting on the sidelines.

accounting for 58 percent of the global GDP. The United States, the largest global economy, with $9 trillion GDP is part of the APEC forum. The 20 percent GDP share of the APT is not much less than the GDP share of the European Union (EU-15) and 33 percent of NAFTA[51]. The share of ASEAN-10 is very small in the global GDP—1.75 percent of the total—in comparison to these large RTAs.

Another comparison can be made with the Free Trade Area of the Americas (FFTA), which is a mega free trade area (FTA), comprising almost the entire Western Hemisphere.[52] The 34 countries of the FTAA account for 38 percent of the global GDP, which is larger than that for the ATP (20 percent), NAFTA (33 percent) and the EU (27 percent), although significantly less than that of APEC (58 percent). In case of the FTAA, the U.S. economy dominates the group again, without which the FTAA would account for merely 8.5 percent of the global GDP. For the APEC this proportion is considerably higher at 29 percent (excluding the United States) of the global GDP.[53]

The heterogeneity among Asian economies is also visible in the structures of GDP and economic development. When the value-added as a percent of total GDP is analyzed for the agricultural, industrial and services sectors, it is easy to see that the economies of the newer members of ASEAN (Cambodia, LAO PDR, and Myanmar) are highly reliant on agriculture. Conversely, in Singapore, the Philippines, Thailand and Vietnam, it is the services sector that provides the largest contribution to the GDP. Indonesia and Malaysia fall between these two extremes, the largest share of GDP originates in the industrial sector.

---

[51] NAFTA came into effect on January 1, 1994, and created the largest free trade area (FTA) in the world of that period. At the time of creation it covered some 360 million people and nearly $500 billion in yearly trade and investment. NAFTA maintained the tariff elimination schedule established by the Canada—U.S. free trade area (CUSFTA) for the bilateral trade between Canada and the United States. Both countries negotiated separate bilateral schedules with Mexico for the elimination of tariffs. However, the three member countries agreed to abolish tariffs and non-tariff barriers completely by 2009. NAFTA had an enormous demonstration effect in Latin America. In fact, it is said to have had a "domino effect."

[52] The Free-trade area of the Americas (FTAA) has 34 members. As a hemisphere-wide FTAA was proposed in 1994 during the Miami Summit of the countries in the Americas. Since then the negotiations have managed to make a good deal of progress. The countries participating in the negotiations of the FTAA held their Seventh Ministerial Meeting in Quito, Ecuador, on November 1, 2002, with the intent to review progress in the FTAA negotiations so as to establish guidelines for the next phase of the negotiations. They are scheduled to conclude on January 2005 in accordance with the terms agreed by the Heads of State and Government at the Third Summit of the Americas, held in Quebec City in April 2001. The negotiations worked towards FTAA's entry into force as soon as possible after January 2005, but in any case no later than December 2005.

[53] The source of statistical data used in this paragraph is *World Development Indicators 2001*, the World Bank.

When an aggregated view is taken, largest (47 percent) contribution to GDP in the ASEAN economies is made by the services sector, industry is close at the heels of the services sector (39 percent), with a large part of the contribution being made in the manufacturing sector. In comparison, in the European Monetary Union (EMU), the services sector dominates the GDP, accounting 71 percent of the GDP.[54] Industry and agriculture account for 27 percent and 2 percent of the GDP in the EMU. This is a reflection of wide differences in the overall development levels of Asia and Europe. While individual economies like Singapore and Thailand can be compared to the EMU in terms of the structure of the GDP, the region as an aggregate cannot be compared to EMU in a similar manner.

Investment rates, measured by the ratio of gross capital formation to gross domestic product (DCF/GDP), are more consistent in the ASEAN economies than the rate of savings. The two exceptions in this case are Cambodia and Myanmar. Investment rate for the other eight ASEAN economies ranges between 20 and 30 percent. If the APT group is considered, China comes out at the top with 37 percent rate of investment. It can finance its recent rate of investment from its domestic savings, but it does not have a saving surplus like some of the ASEAN economies. Indonesia, Malaysia, Singapore and Thailand have consistently shown a saving surplus. For the low-income ASEAN economies even high rates of saving provide little investable capital, and these economies have little alternative but to rely on multilateral and bilateral development assistance.

The savings and investment rates in the Asian economies are higher than those in the other regions. In the ASEAN region, at 35 percent, the savings rate is almost double that of NAFTA and one-and-a-half times that of the EMU. Western economies are well known for a low long-term savings rate. For instance, the ratio gross domestic savings to gross domestic product (GDS/GDP) was 16 per cent in the UK and 18 percent in the United States in 1999. As for the investment rate, ASEAN was comparable to NAFTA and the EMU. However, when investment rate in APT is compared to that of NAFA and EMU, it becomes much higher because of the inclusion of China.[55]

2.4 JAPAN—THE DOMINEERING REGIONAL ECONOMY

Japan is the leading geese in the flying-geese paradigm of Asian economies (Akamatsu, 1961). In 1952, when the Allied occupation ended, Japan was called

---

[54] All the 15 members of the European Union (EU) are the members of the European Monetary Union (EMU). They are Austria, Belgium, Denmark, Finland, France, Germany, Greece, Ireland, Italy, Luxembourg, The Netherlands, Portugal, Spain, Sweden, and United Kingdom; only 12 participate in the Euro Zone (EZ). Greece became the 12th member of the EZ in January 2001.

[55] Discussion in this section is styled after Sakakibara and Yamakawa (2003).

a "less developed country." Building on the remnants of the war-ravaged infrastructure, Japan rapidly reconstructed and rejuvenated its economic strength. Since the early-1950s, it recorded high real GDP growth rates, sustained it for almost two decades, and began to catch up first with Western Europe and subsequently with the U.S. economy. At the end of this period, Japan moved several rungs up the industrialization ladder to acquire the "developed" or industrialized economy status. In 1968 the Japanese economy became the second largest in the world, after the United States.

Japan's brisk post-war economic recovery, followed by acquisition of economic and industrial strength, had enormous demonstration effect in Asia. The salient characteristics of this high-growth era were high rates of savings and investment, an industrious labor-force with strong work ethics, supply of cheap oil, adapting and adopting new technologies in the manufacturing sector followed by technological innovation and effective intervention by the government, particularly by the Ministry of International Trade and Industry (MITI). The strategy of "picking the winners" was a Japanese innovation. The government and bureaucracy led growth efforts in a neo-mercantilist fashion. Rapid export-induced growth led to immense changes in industrial structure. It shifted from agriculture and light industry to heavy and high-technology industries and services. Dominating the industrial sector were iron and steel, shipbuilding, machine tools, motor vehicles and subsequently, electronics.

Japan was a major beneficiary of the swift growth attained by the global economy during the period after the War, under the principles of free trade advanced by the multilateral organizations, particularly the International Monetary Fund (IMF) and the General Agreement on Tariffs and Trade (GATT). The macroeconomic policies followed in Japan were largely based on neo-classical economic principles and outer-orientation of the economy, which implies openness to trade and foreign investment. Openness has been clearly and positively linked to economic performance by numerous empirical studies and regression analyses (Bhagwati and Srinivasan, 1999).[56] The well-thought-out economic strategy was meticulously implemented. Exchange rate was not allowed to be overvalued. In the early stages, Japan had a "repressive" financial system (Chapter 6, Section 6.2). The high-growth period in Japan is also known for steadily rising competitive strength of the industrial sector. It is widely acknowledged that exports were the major contributor to GDP growth during the high-growth period. In the 1960s, they grew by an average rate of 18.4 percent annually. The size of the external sector (exports plus imports) as a proportion of GDP went on increasing by the year. Beginning the mid-1960s, current account balances began recording surpluses, although the post oil shock (1973) years were an exception.

---

[56] A large volume of empirical and theoretical literature exists on the openness-growth nexus. In a recent survey of this literature Bhagwati and Srinivasan (1999) re-established this positive link.

The economy was buffeted by several external and domestic shocks in the 1970s. These included the two oil shocks, double-digit inflation and recession. The rate of domestic investment declined and real GDP growth rate for the 1974–79 dipped to an apathetic 3.6 percent. Economizing on energy consumption became an important objective after the first oil shock (1973), which affected the industrial structure. Notwithstanding the shock, major export sectors retained their competitiveness in the global markets by cutting costs and increasing general efficiency. Particularly, the automobile industry improved its over all competitiveness in the global market place. Energy demand was slashed down. The second oil shock (1979) created another shift in Japan's industrial structure. This time the emphasis shifted from heavy industry to development of higher technology products like the computer, semiconductor, along with other technology and information-intensive industries. This started a second period of rapid growth in Japan in 1980. Current account balances continued to remain positive and in 1985 Japan moved ahead of Britain, with net external assets of $130 billion. By the late 1980s, Japanese per capita income, at market exchange rates, exceeded that of the United States.

The yen remained undervalued until the Plaza Accord of September 1985 between the Group-of-Five (G-5) economies.[57] The Accord was the most significant economic event of the 1980s. It planned for a methodical, coordinated and steep appreciation of the yen, which in turn had an enormous and far-reaching impact over the Japanese, Asian and global economies (Das, 1992). During the latter half of the 1980s, a "bubble economy" was created. It was called the bubble economy because growth was not supported by economic fundamentals.[58] An appreciated currency affected the competitiveness of exports adversely, albeit fiscal and monetary measures increased domestic demand, which started contributing more than the export to GDP growth. In 1988 and 1989, corporate investment rose sharply. New equity issues rose in value and banks sought to fund real estate developments. Corporations used their real estate holdings as collateral for stock market speculation. Consequently, land prices doubled and Nikkei index rose by 180 percent. The bubble economy later became the legacy of large non-performing loan (NPL) overhang of the banks.

---

[57] Ministers of Finance and Central Bank Governors of France, the Federal Republic of Germany, Japan, the United Kingdom, and the United States, or the G-5 economies, met on September 22, 1985, at the Plaza Hotel in New York. They *inter alia* agreed to a coordinated market intervention by their central banks with the express objective of engineering an appreciation of the yen and the deutschmark and a depreciation of the dollar, which was considered highly overvalued at that time.

[58] Investors were buying up stocks at inflated prices not because they expected a solid dividend return but because they expected further gains in the market value. Real estate prices were so out of line that at one time the land beneath the Emperor's Palace in Tokyo was considered more valuable than all of California.

In May 1989, monetary authorities reacted by tightening policies to contain rise in asset values. Next year, the Nikkei index fell by 38 percent, wiping out over $2 trillion worth in stock market value. Land prices collapsed burdening financial institutions with massive bad debts. Banks became overly cautious and a severe credit crunch followed. The economic bubble of the late 1980s burst on the last day of 1989, which signaled the end of the second era of rapid growth and more than two decades of rapid overseas business expansion. The economy went into a deflationary phase and suffered four recessions during the 1990s. The economy became a classical example of a Keynesian "liquidity trap."[59] The deterioration in the economic performance was serious, with little endogenous mechanism for reforms. Until the late 1980s, Japan was the fastest growing economy in the Organization for Economic Co-operation and Development (OECD). During the 1990s it made a somersault and became the slowest one, with an annual average GDP growth rate of 1.1 percent over the 1992–2002 period. In one generation, Japan turned from having global economic driving force to a nation faltering on the brink of economic despair. Lavish fiscal spending packages and extensive monetary easing failed to show any consequences. The deflation persisted. This was the first time after the 1930s that an industrial economy had experienced this monetary phenomenon. Japan essentially went from an economy that was enjoying above peak level growth in the latter half of the 1980s, with soaring real estate and stock prices and major overseas expansion of industrial and banking operations, "to a 60 percent decline of asset prices within a period of two years. It was a decline that rivaled the Great Depression" (Hutchison, 1997).[60]

Several structural limitations came to the fore. For instance, in comparison to the other matured industrial economies, wage structure in Japan had become exceedingly high. Business services were high-priced and so were the prices of intermediate inputs, particularly those supplied by non-manufacturers. Although deregulation has been taking place, several sectors were completely left out of the process. Consequently they remained fettered by stringent licensing requirements and sector-specific regulations. These regulations and

[59] The asset-price bubble burst in 1990 in Japan. To ward off a recessionary tendency, monetary authorities followed highly expansionary policy bringing interest rates down to zero. Although several reasons have been put forward to explain the sustained weakness of the Japanese economy, none is more intriguing from the viewpoint of a central bank than the possibility that monetary policy had been largely ineffective because the Japanese economy entered a Keynesian "liquidity trap." J.M. Keynes posited that the monetary authority would be unable to reduce interest rates below a non-zero positive interest rate floor if market participants believed that interest rates had reached bottom. Any subsequent monetary expansion, then, would lead investors to increase their holdings of idle cash balances and to become net sellers of government bonds.

[60] Hutchison (1997) provided a detailed analytical account of how the Japanese economy, after performing so well, fell into such a torrid quagmire of successive recessions and a deflation in 1990.

customs in the economy continued to impede the functioning of market mechanism. A recent study (NRI, 2002) inferred that the more highly regulated a sector was, the lower was its productivity growth and the more likely it was to pass on wage increases as direct price increases. Under the umbrella of regulations, inefficient wage structures tended to persist, in turn exacerbating the price gap and whittling away the competitiveness.

Another persistent structural problem was weak innovative activity, low productivity and relatively high prices in numerous key sectors of the economy. In many instances, the price line in Japan was as much as 50 percent higher than the OECD average (Cotis, 2003). In many important sectors Japanese prices were as much as 30 percent higher than those in the United States. Poor corporate governance was the other serious structural problem. In addition, as cost structure in the economy became high, total factor productivity (TFP) suffered. It rationally encouraged "hollowing out" of the industrial sector. Besides, the economic and financial environment of the 1990s strengthened the hollowing out and relocating trend of industries to China and other Asian economies. Competitively priced imports from China and the other Asian economies raised the specter of continuing deflationary trend in prices. In an increasing number of product lines these economies became highly competitive and Japanese manufacturers were not able to compete with them. These economies increasingly began to compete with Japan in the global market place.

Owing to high wages and prices, manufacturers in Japan face a serious challenge from China, where wages are lower by a factor of 20 to 30. Similar firms in the OECD economies also pose a serious challenge to the Japanese manufacturers for the same reason. There was a steady migration of production of low-cost mass-produced manufacturing products to Korea, ASEAN-4 economies, China, and other lower-wage Asian economies. Such products have also been seeping out of many other mature industrial economies.

Japan has the large electronics sector. Digitalization has changed the nature of production and competition in this sector. Besides, several digital products have rapidly become mass-produced items. This category includes DVD players, mobile phones, and digital cameras. Digitalization has proved to be beneficial to economies like China and other Asian economies that were playing catch-up in electronics technology. Now these economies can leapfrog the technologically difficult analogue production stages and manufacture newer and easier digital products.

Japanese firms could not compete with other Asian economies in low-cost manufactured items—and very seldom from the domestic base. A recent, albeit rare, example is that of Suzuki Motors, which became highly competitive in a stripped-down budget scooter that costs one-third as much as a regular scooter. The response of the Japanese manufacturers to this situation is to keep the core technologies and its output at home and move low-value-added production activity and assembly operations abroad. Japanese firms become more secretive about the core technologies. Toshiba, the biggest chip maker in Japan and the inventor of DRAM[61] chip, has been busy developing high-end chips. It had developed DRAM in collaboration with a Korean firm, which soon became a commodity and rival Asian firms overtook Toshiba in a short time span. Learning a lesson from its past, Toshiba is determined not to let any other firm in on its high-end chips technology secrets. This new attitude would allow Japanese firms to hold on to high-technology end of manufacturing for a longer period in the future. Besides, notwithstanding the structural limitations, Japanese firms have certain inherent strengths. They excel at producing products whose manufacturing entails designing of many components in great detail, and close co-operation among teams in the firm and its suppliers. Therefore, the twenty-first century manufacturing strategy of the Japanese firms should be to focus on manufacturing products that allow them to cash in on this strength.

The bursting of the bubble marked the beginning of a crisis in the banking industry. A massive (8 percent of the total bank credit) overhang of NPLs persisted on the balance sheets of banks throughout the 1990s and beyond (NRI, 2002). Cost of NPLs in terms of undermined profitability and eroded capital base of the banks is high. Heavy infusion of capital did not resolve the Naples conundrum. They went on rising. A deflationary environment, marked by falling asset markets and recession, is not a solution for resolving the NPLs. If anything, deflation exacerbates the NPL problem. As all these daunting factors crowded in during the 1990s, they were christened the "lost decade" of Japan (see Chapter 6, Section 6.4.3).

After the bubble burst, growth efforts in Japan began to rely heavily on capital accumulation (Cotis, 2003). Although there was a declining trend in the 1980s, the rate of business investment continued to outpace the rate of GDP growth. Over-investment led to constantly rising capital-output ratio in the economy which, in turn, depressed return on investment (ROI), causing financial fragility. To return to growth, Japanese economy needs to reduce its reliance on the factors of production and increase depending more upon productivity growth. Because of demographic idiosyncrasy of expansion in the proportion of retired people, possibility of positive contribution of an expanding labor force is remote. The trend of declining investment in the background of "capital overhang," would indeed help in reducing the capital–output ratio.

Hindsight reveals that the strategic response of lavish fiscal spending and extensive monetary easing to combat deflation was barely enough. For a financial recovery, several concerted and bold measures were called for. Insolvent

[61] DRAM is the abbreviation for dynamic random access memory chip.

institutions had to be allowed to fail, weak institutions had to be merged into stronger ones, and good assets had to be separated from bad. The short route to resolve the problem of outsized NPL was writing them off swiftly and simultaneously, easing the pain with loose monetary policy. The United States and Scandinavia provide examples of countries that had swiftly dealt with bad debt problems and gone on to revitalize economic activities. Japan did not take this route and this major failing continued to fester in the banking system, casting its shadow over the entire economy for a fairly long period.

The decade of 1990s was a highly disappointing period for Japan. Its per capital income fell relatively to the other OECD economies. As set out above, slowdown in Japan had structural roots. One of the crucial causal factors behind the deceleration of GDP growth rate was deceleration in the TFP. Bold and well-conceived measures were needed for making TFP the principal source of growth. Long-standing structural problems of high prices, weak innovative activity and low productivity need to be tackled head on. Promoting competition in the industrial and services sector would have gone a long way in resolving these problems. For sure, it would have brought down the prices. This implies that the potential for gains from intensification of competition in the Japanese economies was high. Aggressively promoting competition should, therefore, be a high priority of the policymaking community.

Although Bank of Japan (BoJ) reduced interest rate to zero and has been following the strategy of quantitative easing, but the monetary measures did not show any result on the real economy because of the numerous structural bottlenecks in the economy, particularly in the banking and corporate sectors. Persistence of deflation for a long time posed the danger of deflation turning into a self-reinforcing spiral of falling prices, output, employment and profits. For bringing the deflationary trend under control, the BoJ needed to continue its aggressive policy of supplying liquidity.

The corporate debt level peaked in 1996, at 125 percent of GDP. By early 2004, Japanese companies had repaid some loans and brought the debt level down to 90 percent of the GDP. The pre-bubble era average was 80 percent.[62] Having addressed the NPLs, Japan would need to earnestly turn to broader financial reforms and restructuring of the financial sector if it is to recapture its former economic vibrancy and dynamism. Financial sector needs to be more transparent and governed by the rules of self-governance. The Ministry of Finance (MoF) and the Bank of Japan (BoJ) still have a large presence in the financial system. Banks and other financial firms march in synchronized manner on orders from the MoF and the BoJ. Market forces and competition take the backseat in the financial markets. Artificial barriers need to be brought down

---

[62] Based on calculations of Merrill Lynch in Tokyo and cited by *The Economist*, "Japanese Debt: End in Sight," 14 February 2004. pp. 67–68.

and market forces and competition needs to be given full play in the financial markets as well. This is a large order of business awaiting the policymaking community in Japan.[63]

Driven by large fiscal spending and export demand, two fleeting cyclical upturns occurred in 1996 and 2000, but the pressure of myriad structural problems of the economy subdued them. In mid-2002 there was another discernible indication of a macroeconomic upturn and the economy gave a signal of being on the mend. Real GDP showed positive, albeit seasonally adjusted, growth for several subsequent quarters after that. The GDP growth rate in 2003 was a commendable 2.7 percent (IMF, 2004). This revival was supported by other indicators. According to the survey of business confidence, *Tankan,* business sentiments and business outlook had begun improving.[64] This applied more emphatically to large Japanese firms and the transnational corporations (TNCs). Both investors' and consumers' confidence were on the rise. Other indicators that underpinned this revival were inventory, capacity utilization, and corporate profits. Improvement in the macroeconomic situation was reflected in the upsurge in the stock prices (Hilpert, 2003). This broad indication of a moderate recovery spread to a large majority of industrial sectors. In March 2004, Moody upgraded Japan's debt rating to AA+—only one notch below the AAA maximum—and furtherupgraded to AAA in the second quarter. In 2004, deflation was moderating, GDP grew by an annualized 6.1 percent in the first quarter and IMF upgraded the GDP growth estimates for 2004 to 3.4 percent (IMF, 2004). Strong external demand—particularly from China—and laterally a pick up in domestic consumption and investment led to upward growth revision in estimated GDP growth. Unlike the previous two fleeting upsurges that had fizzled out, this one seems to be turning into an upswing of business cycle, albeit the structural snags in the economy are yet to be addressed.

2.5 CONTRASTING THE TWO POPULOUS GIANTS

It has been conventional wisdom to make comparison between China and India, two geographically large countries having long common border, entrepreneurial trading heritage, and enormous internal diversity. Until the end of 1980, the two countries were "impoverished" but comparable. India's population was 687 million, 300 million fewer than China's. Living standards as measured by purchasing power per capita, were roughly the same. As China adopted economic liberalization and modernization in 1978, it left India behind.

[63] See *The Economist*, "Japanese Debt: End in Sight," 14 February 2004. pp. 67–68.

[64] *Tankan* is regularly conducted quarterly by the Bank of Japan.

India outperformed its neighbor in nothing but population growth rate. By 2001, China's national income per capita was $890, nearly double India's $450. Adjusted for purchasing power, the Chinese were 70 percent wealthier than Indians. Between 1992 and 2002, Indian per capita income grew at 4.3 percent per year, compared to China's twice as fast. In 2002, some 5 percent Chinese lived below the national poverty line, compared with 29 percent of Indian population (*The Economist,* 2003a). China's ability to attract FDI has far outpaced that of India. In 2002, $52.7 billion of FDI made its way to China, compared to $2.3 billion in India. China has emerged as a low-cost manufacturing juggernaut invading global markets in a large array of products, with total merchandise exports of $438.4 billion in 2003. The comparable figures for India are $49.3 billion. India fell behind in every indicator of economic and social well being.

2.5.1 China

Until 1980, China was grouped with the poorest economies of the world. Adoption of market-oriented reforms and economic liberalization was done under the doctrine of "open-door policy," conceived by Deng Xiaoping in 1978.[65] Their earnest implementation was responsible for transforming China from a small, low-income, centrally planned economy to a large "socialist market economy" as well as for its vertiginous economic growth of the last two-and-a-half decades. China has established new standards of sustained growth and dynamic resource allocation by any economy.

Open-economy reforms were essentially carried out in the areas of trade, exchange rate and foreign investment. The consequences of wide ranging liberalization and reforms were reflected in the real GDP growth rate. China recorded the average annual growth rate of 9.7 percent for the 1979–2000 period. Its GDP sextupled in real terms over this period, while its per capita GDP quintupled.

---

[65] At the Third Plenary Session of the 11th Central Committee of the Chinese Communist Party (CCP) in December 1978, the People's Republic of China adopted its "open door policy". This became famous as the Deng doctrine because Deng Xiaoping was the intellectual father of this liberal economic strategy. This marked a turning point in Chinese economic performance as well as economic history. It grew with a healthy clip through the 1980s and 1990s. Gross domestic product (GDP) increased by 10 percent per annum in real terms over the 1980–2000 period. In a short span of two decades China economically transformed itself. Between 1978 and 2000, the GDP grew almost fivefold, per capital income quadrupled, and 270 million Chinese were lifted out of absolute poverty (*The Economist*, 2001). In 1990, China's GDP was $378.8 billion and per capital GDP was $341.60. A decade later, in 2000 GDP reached $1,080 billion, while per capital GDP rose to $853.40. Between 1981 and 2001, China succeeded in bringing down the population living below the World Bank poverty line of $1.08-a-day from 634 million to 211 million, a reduction by 66.7 percent. If the poverty line is moved up to $2.15-a-day, the population below the poverty line declined from 875.8 million to 593.6 million, a decline by 32.2 percent (Chen and Ravailion, 2004).

In 2003, with a GDP of $1.4 trillion, it was the sixth largest global economy, and had earned global kudos for its buoyant economy and well-documented emergence as a global export powerhouse. In 2003 China's imports expanded by a remarkable 40 per cent in nominal dollar terms (i.e. not adjusted for price changes) while its exports expanded by 35 percent—unprecedented levels of expansion for a country with such substantial trade volume.[66] The United States is China's largest market, accounting for one-fifth of China's exports. China's large and growing trade surplus with the United States reached $103 billion in 2002 and $124 billion in 2003 fueled trade friction.[67] In purchasing power parity (PPP) terms China was the second largest economy after the United States. It should be noted that while the PPP measure overstates China's GDP, the conventional measure underestimates it (Wong and Ding, 2003). Rapid growth ensured political stability, the Communist party survived the 1989 Tiananmen Square clampdown. Its present political leadership is widely considered well-educated, capable and pragmatic.

The Deng doctrine succeeded in integrating China with the regional and global economies. China's exports increased with an impressive annual pace of 17.4 percent during the 1979–2000 period. China gradually became the most successful EME in terms of attracting FDI. Between 1988 and 2000, the average rate of growth in FDI flows, as against approval, was 23 percent per annum. The cumulative total of FDI was $340 billion in 2000 (Wong and Ding, 2003). Only the United States receives more FDI than China. In the first quarter of 2004, it was the second largest holder of foreign exchange reserves ($403 billion) in the world after Japan ($730 billion). Chinese economy globalized at a brisk pace and dictated global prices of many products from cement and steel to microchips. While the four tiger economies (see the next section) were badly mauled by the Asian currency and financial crisis of 1997–98, China remained unaffected and offered to assist the crisis-affected neighboring economies. For all appearances, China's economic momentum would continue into the next quarter century. It is a highly diverse and continent-size economy; its internal dynamics can sustain growth for much longer than small economies.

The reforms were launched without a plan, sequence or a timeframe in China, rendering them a degree of tentativeness. The absence of a plan was officially referred to as the "process of crossing the river by feeling the stones" and was characterized by gradualism. They were essentially evolutionary in nature. Hindsight reveals that this reform strategy worked reasonably well. When the reform process was launched, domestic economy was far from integrated—it still is not. It continues to be an agglomeration of regional economies with

---

[66] World Trade Organization (WTO). 2004. *World Trade 2003, Prospects For 2004*. Press Release. No. Press/373. 5 April.

[67] This is based on the statistics published by the U.S. Census Bureau.

widely differing resource endowments and comparative advantages. Various regions are known to resist trade and factor flows. This was one reason why China adopted a "dual track" liberalization and growth strategy.[68] The two tracks were the market track and the central planning track. Initially they coexisted, but with the passage of time the market track was to become more important of the two tracks and take over from the plan track. Establishing special economic zones (SEZs) was part of the first track of this strategy. This approach was an innovative solution to the political constraints on the direction and speed of reforms.

An important achievement of the dual track reform process was that China successfully avoided the so-called "supply failure" that badgered other transition economies of Eastern Europe and the former Soviet Union. The rapid transition strategy followed by these countries, referred to as the "big bang," apparently had its blemishes that became obvious in implementation. Economic analysis of the dual track approach showed that it was Pareto-improving (Laffont and Quin, 1999).[69] In fact, this approach to liberalization is by design Pareto-improving. It has minimal additional informational and institutional requirements and minimizes political opposition to reforms (Lau et al., 2000). One of the objectives of this reforms strategy was not to create losers. The dual track strategy not only succeeded in accomplishing this but also worked successfully in product- and labor-market liberalization. This strategy was all-pervasive, and all the facets of economy and policymaking reflected it. Sectoral and policy reforms were no exceptions to this generalization. Several well-regarded and comprehensive studies of China's reform process are now available.[70] Of all the areas of economic reform, those in the area of trade, exchange rate, and FDI were the most significant (Das, 2001b).

Setting up of SEZs was the mainstay of open-economy reform process. By establishing them, China endeavored to attract FDI, modern technology and managerial skills. Initially this was done in a cautious, experimental manner.[71] The SEZs were provided substantial decision-making autonomy. Each one of them decided on its own strategy for attracting FDI, particularly the tax incentives. Foreign firms based in SEZs were not only offered preferential tax and administrative treatment but were also given a more or less free hand in running their operations.

---

[68] This was the polar opposite of the so-called "single track" or "big bang strategy" followed by Russia.

[69] Pareto-improving economic effects imply improvements in welfare without any systemic losses.

[70] Although this list is long, reader can refer to one, Zhang (2000).

[71] The first four and the best known SEZs were Shenzhen close to Hong Kong SAR, Zhuhai, close to Macao, Shantou, in Guangdong facing Taiwan and Xiamen, close to Taiwan across the Taiwan Straits.

When it was observed that the SEZ strategy is fructifying, it was expanded (in 1988) and called the coastal development strategy. The expansion was pragmatically planned and aimed at capitalizing on the transformations in global industrial structure. As many mature industrialized economies were abandoning their labor-intensive and low-end manufacturing industries and moving toward information-technology-intensive and knowledge-intensive sectors, China planned to attract their labor-intensive and low-end manufacturing industries to its coastal areas. The strategy essentially entailed importing industrial raw materials to the coastal areas in these carefully identified sectors, manufacture the goods and then export the finished products to the industrial countries. Given China's abundant labor resources, this was a sagacious and well-conceived re-positioning of industrial activity. This strategy successfully relieved the large pressure of surplus agriculture labor as well as relative scarcity of industrial raw materials. Exports generated the much-needed hard currency, which in turn contributed to the development of industry and services sectors. The coastal development strategy turned out to be a stellar success and was an important factor in China becoming an export-oriented economy (Das, 2001b).

Liberalization of trade policy regime led to substantial export growth in goods and services in China. The average annual increase was 12.9 percent for the decade of the 1980s and 15.2 percent for the 1990s. Import growth rates were comparable to those of exports for these two decades; consequently by 1980 China's trade to GDP ratio was 18.9 percent, by 1990 it reached 34.0 percent and by 2000 it soared to 49.3 percent. China's presence is being felt in Asian and global economies. In a short time span, it gained export competitiveness in a large array or products, from labor-intensive ones to high-technology products. Competing economies apprehend that China's rapid industrialization could allow it to become an industrial economy in a shorter time period than that taken by the mature industrial economies.

In 1982, China's constitution legitimized private sector economic activity or the "individual economy." A rapid increase in domestic entrepreneurial activity followed. Since then its fledgling private sector showed impressive growth. Several measures of output and investment in the state-owned enterprise (SOE) sector indicated toward its decline. Its shares in the fixed-asset investment as well as gross industrial output fell from 80 percent in the 1980s to 40 percent in case of investment and to 47 percent—when all the different kinds of SOEs are taken into consideration—in case of output in 2002. As opposed to this, industrial value-added data show that the SOE output declined from 54 percent in 1994 to 48 percent in 2002, which is not a dramatic decline by any stretch of imagination. The output of the private sector was 12 percent of the gross industrial output in 2002, up from 5 percent in 1999 (Lo, 2004). According to another estimate, made by the World Bank, private sector contributed approximately 30 percent to the GDP in 2003.[72] This cannot be taken to mean that the private sector has become large and robust. Despite rapid growth it has remained small, fragile, fragmented and constrained, as China is toiling through its bumpy economic transition. Private sector cannot offer an effective counterweight to the SOEs. Private sector enterprises feel discriminated against, particularly in their lack of access to capital. This shows that China's structural changes have moved much slower than perceived. A significant recent development in this regard is the decision of the National People's Congress (NPC) in March 2004 to include private property rights in the constitution, which was a significant reform step forward. It means private property has now the same legal status as state-owned property.

High profile reforms were launched in banking but progress was much slower than necessary. After two failed recapitalization programs, in 1998 and 1999, financial authorities started another bailout of the Big Four state banks in 2004. They controlled over 60 percent of all banking assets. The bailout maneuver dealt with the banks individually and uses some $45 billion of China's large foreign exchange reserves to strengthen the capital base of these NPL ridden banks. Although the banks needed $300 billion for sustaining and rejuvenating them, the small capital infusion was made earlier than necessary. The banks should have first proven their commercial viability before they were granted liquidity. The former two recapitalization programs failed to transform the manner in which the state banks do their business. They are not driven by commercial consideration but by political criteria.

Bank credit expansion accelerated in 2001, as the monetary authorities tried to boost growth in the face of a global slowdown. Subsequently, the monetary authorities tried to clamp down on lending in late 2003, especially on property loans, because they apprehended overheating. It was customary for monetary authorities to direct boom-bust lending cycles. The Chinese banks are still taking orders instead of lending to viable investment projects on the basis of creditworthiness. In such a policy milieu banking reforms are likely to remain a mere myth. Authorities publicly promised to improve bank management, corporate governance and risk controls by bringing in foreign investors as both managers and strategic investors. The People's Bank of China (PBC) also took steps, albeit very slowly, to liberalize interest rates and some overtures have been made in this direction. Since January 2004, Chinese banks are allowed to charge up to 70 percent over the PBC's benchmark lending rate—instead of 30 percent previously—according to the borrowers' credit risks. However, such plans and proposed changes would certainly be slow to filter through the system (Lo, 2004). The Marxist mindset continues to be a serious drag on banking reforms.

---

[72] This is according to "the Country Assistance Strategy Report" of the World Bank for 2003, which was cited by Ahmed (2004).

As alluded to above, there is a growing perception that China may join the ranks of industrialized countries by truncating the usually long industrial development process. As China has been effectively competing with Japan in many markets in high-technology and information technology (IT) products, many Japanese analysts are convinced about this leapfrogging hypothesis and tend to think of China as a future threat. Because of the growing strength of IT exports from China it is believed by some that the export structure of China is nearly on par with that of Japan. Evidence of these assumptions is generally drawn from isolated cases, rather than systematic analysis and comparison. One reason for this flawed perception is that while there are indicators to evaluate the international competitiveness of individual products and industries, an index to evaluate the competitiveness of the export structure of an economy does not exist. Kwan (2002) developed a methodology to measure the level of advancement of each economy's export structure, based on the weighted average of the level of sophistication or value-added of products that comprise the export structure. This study concluded that while manufactured goods and IT products have become a substantive part of China's fast expanding exports, its competitiveness still lies in low-value-added exportables. Even in the fast growing IT sector, China's competitiveness lags behind Japan's. Although there are overlapping areas, a clear division of labor was found between Japan and China, by Kwan (2002). The former having competitive advantage in high-value-added products, while the latter in the low-value-added products. This trend is in keeping with the Kaname Akamatsu (1961) age old "flying geese paradigm," and until the early 2000s China's industrial structure had not leapfrogged over Japan's.

Notwithstanding the outbreak of SARS (Severe Acute Respiratory Syndrome), the GDP and industrial growth of China was having a great deal of impact over the regional and global economies in the early 2000s.[73] Its accession to the WTO in November 2001 and the increasing contribution to domestic growth made by its own voracious consumers, made it feasible for the economy to depend far less on the problematic SOE sector for domestic growth. As a result, it is also exerting an unprecedented degree of influence over the regional and world trade. Several industrial sectors, including steel, are considered competitive in the global market place. Its imports of iron ore surpassed those of Japan in 2003, making it the largest consumer of iron ore and steel in 2003. Because of heavy construction activity, China became the largest importer of cement in 2004. According to the WTO trade statistics, China accounted for 5.9 percent ($438.4 billion) of the global merchandise exports in 2003, up from

[73] Real GDP growth forecast by the Economic Intelligence Unit (EIU), London, for the 2003 to 2007 period is of 8 percent growth, comparable to the rate recorded in the previous five years (EIU, 2004).

2.7 percent in 1995 (WTO, 2004). Rising level of intra-regional and global trade put severe pressure on China's fast-growing ports. In mid-2003, the southern Chinese city of Shenzhen overtook Kaohsiung in Taiwan to become the world's fifth-largest container port (*The Economist,* 2003b).[74] The TNCs regard China as a special economy in their strategic plans. That China is being regarded as an important market is indicated by the fact that General Motors announced (June 2004) plans to double its capacity and introduce 20 new models into China over the next 3 years. Given that every important car manufacturer on the planet was making similar plans, it appears that the industry could be driving toward excess capacity as early as 2007. Nonetheless, General Motors remained convinced that it can continue to succeed in China, largely at the expense of less-experienced local players. General Motors has been highly successful in China, increasing its market shares from 4.5 percent in 2001 to 10 percent in 2004 (EIU, 2004).

Notwithstanding the commendable achievements, Chinese economy is still in transition from one system to another. Additionally, several structural, institutional and sector-specific quandaries persist. Despite rapid and meaningful progress, reforms are incomplete. The financial sector as well as institutions continued to remain problem ridden, which have not been addressed so far. Infirmities in the semi-reformed fiscal system encouraged rent-seeking behavior at the provincial level and cause frequent budgetary problems. Performance of the SOE sector reached nadir in 1996, when it incurred huge losses. Since then some improvement has been observed due to large layoffs, corporatization, and external factors, but reforms that enhance internal efficiency in firms have not been launched so far. Of the 520 large SOEs, only 10 generated 77 percent of total profits in 2002. All these 10 enjoyed monopoly or semi-monopoly positions in telecommunications, power, oil, and tobacco industries (McNally, 2002). SOE reforms are in a poor state. Closure of loss-incurring SOEs rendered large number of workers redundant. Inaction in this area would have high economic and social costs. China still does not have a truly competitive global firm, which is regarded a failure of its industrial development strategy.

In addition, the ownership structure in the economy still distorts resource allocation, in the process creating large systemic inefficiencies and losses. Interprovincial and inter-regional disparities are large and have not declined, in the process threatening social stability. Of the 1.3 billion Chinese, 900 million live

---

[74] The rapidly growing export value and volume in China is reflected in its fast expanding ports. The Chinese city of Shanghai, which overtook Kaohsiung as the world's fourth-largest port (after Hong Kong SAR, Singapore and South Korea's Pusan), in 2002 saw traffic rise by almost 40 percent during 2002–03. Thanks to a surge in exports from southern China, throughput at Hong Kong SAR's container terminals is soaring. Traffic at the Kwai Chung terminal, for instance, was up by 25 percent in the first half of 2003 compared with the same period in 2002, according to the Port and Maritime Board of Hong Kong SAR (*The Economist,* 2003b).

in the rural areas and work on farms. This neglected constituency is rapidly becoming aware of the growing economic chasm between them and the rising urban middle class, as China rushed on to modern age. With the WTO accession, competition has intensified in the domestic economy and the structural snags became more challenging and problematical. Majority of the SOEs either run at break-even or worse, and their working capital is tied up in "uncollectible bills or unsaleable inventory." SOEs are more concerned with maintaining patronage and employment than operating in a commercially profitably manner (Ahmed, 2004). In general, they cannot be expected to be competitive commercial enterprises.

It was set out above that in their quest for rapid GDP growth, state-owned banks went on providing easy credit and have managed to create massive over-investments and large NPLs. The sclerosis in China's financial sector has been worsened by the mountain of NPLs. Stock markets have remained moribund, incapable of efficaciously allocating capital and creating long-term wealth. The corporate bond market is tiny and venture capital industry is insignificant. The silver lining behind this dark cloud is that the Chinese policymakers have begun to take financial market reform seriously (Ahmed, 2004). Foreign enterprises operating in China feel that the most pressing need is of protection of property rights and strengthening of financial laws. This has been a bane of the business and economic life of the foreign companies operating in China.[75] Where such laws exist, enforcement is woefully feeble.

In the early 2000s, Chinese policymakers worried about overheating because price bubbles were being generated in several sectors, conspicuously in property, steel, and automobile. Several industrial sectors were identified as having overinvestment. Consequently, a large number of goods were in over-supply. Still investment in fixed assets grew by 30 percent in 2003, and contributed 47 percent of GDP. According to the IMF estimates, three-quarters of China's growth comes from capital accumulation, yet TFP on an average rose by 2 percent per year between 1995 and 1999.[76] The real GDP growth rate was 9.1 percent in 2003. In the first quarter of 2004, the economy grew by an annualized 9.8 percent, and growth in fixed investment soared at an annualized 50 percent. In some sectors it grew by 170 percent. New lending by some banks was rising at 40 percent. Inflation rose to a seven-year high in the first half of 2004 and overinvestment problem worsened. The PBC called for restraint in credit disbursement. In April 2004 PBC upped banks' reserve requirements for the second time in eight months, and took the novel step of telling a clutch of

---

[75] Ahmed (2004) provided graphic accounts of several instances of American and European companies falling victims of fraud and loosing their valuable assets because of their naiveté and limitations in the legal system.

[76] Cited in Ahmed (2004).

big banks to stop lending in the near future. These drastic measures raised fears of a credit crunch leading to a "hard landing."

The spillover effects of China's slowdown would be both regional and global. Given that "China accounted for about a third of the growth in the world economy over the past three years (in purchasing power terms), a credit crunch in the Middle Kingdom could also spell trouble" for the regional and global economy (The Economist, 2004a). The Australian dollar and Korean stock market plunged at the news. China's insatiable demand for energy (6 million barrel of oil per day in June 2004), raw materials and inputs for manufactures—both to meet domestic demand and to feed its massive export machinery—has made it an increasingly important export market for other countries.[77] In 2003, it was the largest consumer of steel, tin, copper, zinc, platinum, and the second largest consumer of aluminum, lead, oil and the third largest consumer of nickel. To modify an old metaphor, it is increasingly becoming the case that when China sneezes, the world catches cold (EIU, 2004). If consumers in the United States ignited the recent global economic upturn, Chinese producers played an equally important role on the supply side (Roach, 2004).

2.5.2 India

All-round weaknesses in infrastructure continued to be a perennial feature of the economy, but many non-economic characteristics of the society contributed much more to the underperformance of the Indian economy. Lackadaisical long-term economic performance is often blamed on *inter alia* rambunctious democracy and multiplicity of political parties, leading to chaos, compromises, inordinate delays, acceptance of erroneous economic policies and a massive network of subsidies. In a democratic environment, governments at federal and state levels remain short-term oriented, with their time horizon limited to the next election. They are tempted to give in to populist policies as against adopting sound, positive, pragmatic and well thought out macroeconomic strategies that spawn real GDP growth. In addition, for decades India has creaked and groaned under dull, unimaginative and low-quality political leadership and highly corrupt, inapt, intrusive, albeit powerful, bureaucracy, that seems to belong to another time period, India's feudal past. Besides, India did not adopt serious economic reforms and liberalization process until quite late, and progress in its implementation was tentative, grudging and tardy. The bureaucratic behemoth has not been dismantled. Systemic efficiency is not part of Indian culture.

---

[77] China accounted for 35 percent of global rise in oil demand in 2003, which gave the oil industry a demand shock. When benchmark price for West Texas crude reached a record of $42 in mid-2004, 50 percent higher than the average crude price for 2002–03, Chinese oil consumption was being regarded as part of the reason.

Indian politicians and bureaucrats have stubbornly remained reluctant to unleash the market forces. Creating an efficacious economic system was never a part of their priorities. Indian economy remained highly distortion-ridden for decades.

Since its independence (1947), Indian government was run by the Congress Party, which did not cast aside its Fabian socialistic ideas about the economy until the mid-1990s. These erroneous ideas *inter alia* included public sector dominance of the economy, meticulously drawn out five-year plan exercises, a large and active (meaning excessively intrusive) government superstructure, and the age-old Gandhian maxim of *swadeshi* or economic self-reliance.[78] Private sector economic activity was considered unnecessary and was kept under harsh control with Byzantine requirements of licenses. Neo-classical economic principles like capitalizing on comparative advantage were rejected out of hands and inward-looking import-substituting industrialization (ISI) policies were vigorously, even devotedly, followed until 1991. Labor and bankruptcy laws were inflexible and archaic. A strong anti-market and anti-private sector environment had existed for decades. Market forces were either quashed or allowed to work only on the periphery. Hindsight reveals that these were all wrong-headed, inimical and pernicious policies. The GDP growth rate barely kept pace with population growth rate. The latter remained high and population crosses the one billion mark. This policy environment kept India mired in poverty for decades. It was accepted as a way of life by the docile Indian society. While the dynamic Asian economies continued to grow rapidly, India hopelessly, if somewhat smugly, stagnated. The economy languished and lost ground vis-à-vis the dynamic regional economies by the year.

---

[78] On the one hand, neither Mahatma Gandhi nor Jawaharlal Nehru was an economist. Both were trained lawyers and had some naïve, unidimensional notions that they thought were sound economics. On the other hand, the two national leaders enjoyed enormous popularity and mass adulation in India. Their economic legacies, that is, Fabian socialism in case of Nehru and *swadeshi* in case of Gandhi, were adopted by the Indian society and the government, without the least bit of analysis and questioning. Trained economists did point to the inappropriateness of the former concept and absurdity of latter, but they were treated by the society and the government with contempt for being nerds, who did not know what they were talking. In contrast to these two Indian leaders, Lee Kwan Yew, also a trained lawyer, and Chung Hee Park, an army general, honestly believed that while they were successful individuals in their own right as well as well-intentioned, they were not economists. This realization made them seek high-quality economic advice in running Singapore and Korea, respectively. What they succeeded in achieving for their countries in a short span of time is history. Deng Xioping was also not an economist, but he learned from the failure of the centrally planned economic system in China. Also, he was a clear-headed, dispassionate, result-oriented and pragmatic political leader, not an ideologue. His oft-repeated dictum was, "How does it matter whether the cat is white or black, as long as it kills the rats?" The moral of the story is that the quality of political leadership makes enormous difference in determining a country's economic future.

Although methodical reforms and liberalization was not adopted, something meaningful and durable happened to the supply-side of the economy in the 1980s, and significantly affected the labor productivity. It grew at an average rate of 0.9 percent per year in the decade of 1970s. The average for the 1980s was 3.7 percent. This growth was triggered by an attitudinal shift on the part of the national government toward a pro-business—as opposed to pro-liberalization—approach. When the Congress government returned to power in 1980 after an electoral defeat, it stopped breathing populist fire and sought to court the business constituency. It intended to signal to the market that India is a safe place for business and investment (Rodrik and Subramanian, 2004).

Economic liberalization and reforms were not taken up until it was quite late. Some minor reform measures were taken in the mid-1980s, albeit there was little change in the mindset of the bureaucracy and politicians. Even these half-hearted liberalization measures had a small favorable effect over the GDP growth rate. Between 1987 and 1990, economic growth rate spurted to an average annual rate of 7.6 percent, much higher than the annual average (4.8 percent) for 1980–86. Small relaxation in distortions leading to a significant response in growth rate need not be surprising because it is explained by the theory of distortion. The larger the degree of initial distortion, the greater is the benefit from the marginal reforms and liberalization. When Manmohan Singh, the maverick Finance Minister, launched a relatively comprehensive economic reform program in July 1991, in his budget speech he called it the continuation of the old efforts.

The 1991 stabilization and reform program was launched in the hope that India would be able to emulate the dynamic economies of the east.[79] It was a move away from the ISI strategy that India followed for over four decades, to the outer-oriented growth strategy. It cannot be ignored that the immediate motivation for launching into the liberalization and reform program was a major fiscal-cum-balance-of-payment (BoP) crisis, which brought foreign exchange reserves down to a $1.2 billion, sufficient for three weeks of imports. The Reserve Bank of India (the central bank) had to send its gold reserves to the Bank of England to borrow hard currency from it. The International Monetary Fund (IMF) had to be approached for assistance.

Many economists believed that the deep fiscal-cum-BoP crisis was caused by incorrect and contradictory macroeconomic policies followed during the

[79] Indian bureaucracy and politicians, two of the most powerful groups in the society, are of firm belief that there is little wrong with Indian economy and that it is doing as well as, if not better, the dynamic Asian economies. They have made make-belief an art form. Logic is not their long suite when they compare Indian economic performance to that of the dynamic Asian economies. Although they are perturbed about the global accolade earned by the Chinese economic performance, they are convinced that it is spurious and based on incorrect statistics. Ostrichism knows no bounds.

1980s and earlier. Other believed that the BoP crisis, and growing inefficiencies and non-competitiveness of Indian products in the global markets were caused by subversion of market forces for decades through an array of controls and regulations, quantitative restriction and the public-sector dominance of the economy. Inefficiencies in the public sector had multiplied over time, were of gargantuan proportion, and had existed since its inception. As you will sow so shall you reap. Thus, the economic system created under the guidance of the socialist-minded Prime Minister, Jawaharlal Nehru, had problems galore and served India poorly. A major reform program was long overdue. The stabilization and reform program adopted in 1991 entailed broad measures for macroeconomic policy improvements, measures to improve the efficiency levels in the economy, opening up of the economy to foreign trade and investment, and dismantling the stifling industrial licensing system. It had an unmistakable imprint of the Washington consensus over it.[80]

Reforms program was not only launched belatedly but also implemented in a hesitant, halting and inept manner; therefore, progress in implementation has been slow and tardy. Privatization moved only in fits and starts and foreign ownership of Indian firms was liberalized piecemeal, with a glacial pace. When the government changed in 1998, privatization program regressed.[81] Quantitative restrictions (QRs) on imports and tariff barriers have been reduced in the 1990s, but in terms of the IMF's restrictiveness index for 2001, India (along with Bangladesh) was the most closed Asian economy. India's average tariffs were three time the Asian average. This IMF ranking also applies to non-tariff barriers (NTBs) in India (IMF, 2002). There are well-known static and dynamic gains from free trade, which include domestic efficiency gains through market discipline and integration with the global economy and markets. By devising a rigid system of high tariffs, NTBs and QRs India deprived itself of the benefits of a liberal free-trade regime.

Bardhan (2002) noted that there were flagrant disjunctures in the Indian reform process, particularly "between the policy of economic reforms and the political and economic processes." Therefore, one should not be surprised to see

---

[80] The term "Washington Consensus" is considered synonymous with "neo-liberalism" and "globalization." John Williamson propounded the concept as a set of neo-liberal policies, which in turn referred to the lowest common denominator of policy advice that was being given by the Washington-based Bretton Woods twins to Latin American countries in 1989. This policy advice essentially entailed: fiscal discipline, a redirection of public expenditure priorities toward fields offering both high economic returns and the potential to improve income distribution (such as primary health care, primary education, and infrastructure), tax reforms (to lower marginal rates and broaden the tax base), interest rate liberalization, a competitive exchange rate, trade liberalization, liberalization of inflows of foreign direct investment, privatization, deregulation (to abolish barriers to entry and exit), and secured property rights.

[81] The Congress Party lost election in March 1998, and a new Bharatiya Janata Party (BJP) led coalition government took over.

a lack of direction and indifferent results of the post-1991 liberalization measures. The reforms still lack a political constituency. To succeed, reform process needs to have a long-term framework to which governments can credibly commit and in reference to which progress, or lack of it, may be calibrated. This framework did not exist. In the process of day-to-day political wheeling-dealing, the weak political commitment to reform process constantly eroded. There was little reason to feel assured that even the weak government commitment to the reform process and implementation. It was observed that a government that proposed certain reform measures began to oppose them when it was no longer in power. In addition, the powerful Indian bureaucracy was more than merely apathetic to the liberalization and reform program. If anything, it remained committed to perpetuating the status quo of the pre-reform period. Red tape continued to thwart all economic and financial activities. Bureaucratic antagonism toward implementation was easy to comprehend. This group saw reforms as measures that would loosen its stranglehold over the economy and in turn reduce their rent-seeking opportunities.

Even slow and tardy implementation was reflected in improvement in GDP growth rate and some progress in poverty alleviation. Annual growth rate of per capita GDP in real terms accelerated from 1 percent in the 1960s and 1970s to 3 percent during the 1990s. In nominal terms, GDP growth rate during the 1990s was 6 percent. This implied about one-third increase in per capita consumption over the decade of the 1990s and 5 percent to 10 percent increase in the rate of poverty alleviation, depending upon the methodology and data used (Ferro et al., 2002).[82] Given that one-third of world's poor live in India, this can rationally be considered a valuable contribution of the liberalization and reform program. If implementation of reforms becomes earnest and efficient in future, the power of the market forces would be unleashed and long-term growth trend would surely improve.

The current macroeconomic scenario of the Indian economy presents a mixed picture. Its growth performance for the decade of 1990s was exceeded by only 19 out of 139 countries. However, troublesome levels of fiscal deficits persist. Unlike the dynamic Asian economies, Indian economy was always plagued with fiscal profligacy, a long-lasting weakness. In 2000, 74 countries with population over 10 million were arranged in order of descending fiscal deficits for the decade of the 1990s. Only seven countries, including India, had government fiscal deficits of 7 percent or above. Besides, only Turkey and Zimbabwe had recorded higher fiscal deficits than India (Srinivasan, 2001). In

[82] Change in survey methodology of National Sample Survey in 2000 (the 55th round) made comparison of results with the previous rounds of survey impossible. Empirical studies attempted to correct for the changes in survey methodology. Most new estimates indicated that there was a 5 to 10 percent improvement in the incidence of poverty.

2000, India's fiscal and debt indicators were comparable to Argentina, Brazil and Turkey, all three fell to major macroeconomic crises over the 1998–2003 period. In spite of macroeconomic weaknesses, India was not considered immediately vulnerable to a crisis because of its high foreign exchange reserves (discussed later), restrictions on both inward and outward capital flows, flexible exchange rate, and substantially large public sector ownership of the banking sector. This situation contrasted with the circumstances in 1991, when India suffered a major fiscal-cum-BoP crisis with fiscal deficits of comparable size and lower debt levels (Pinto and Zahir, 2004). Notwithstanding the lower probability of a 1991-like crisis, the macroeconomic health of the economy is far from robust and there is a pressing need to tame the precariously, if not perilously, high levels of government deficits, which currently runs at 10 percent of the GDP and absorbs far too much of the budget.

Unlike China, India follows an old and established system of common law, inherited from the British colonial rule. Property rights are generally well protected and financial and corporate laws are far superior to those in China. However, the legal system is over burdened and, therefore, moves with glacial pace. Every now and then, plans of reforms are made but they remain merely on paper.

Globalization—or to be more precise expanding global trade in services—created new opportunities for India in a small segment of its economy. By virtue of having a large educated, English-speaking young population available to work at low salaries compared to the industrial economies norms, India first found comparative advantage in software and computer programming. Second, it found a profitable niche in back-office outsourcing of business services and call centers. India became world's largest recipient of the U.S. outsourcing in the IT sector, Canada took the second place (Scoffield, 2004). One direct outcome of this success was rising level of foreign exchange reserves. They doubled in 2002 and again in 2003, reaching $103 billion in early 2004, creating pressure on the rupee to appreciate beyond what the fundamentals could justify. The Reserve Bank of India had to purchase huge quantities of dollars to keep the rupee from appreciating.

The business-process outsourcing (BPO) firms have been expanding the range of work that can be performed remotely. Its applications are virtually endless. There were some 3000 BPO firms and a large number of outsourcing jobs. Revenue from BPO alone grew by 50 percent in 2003 to $3.6 billion. Four kinds of firms were scrambling for performing these white-collar jobs. First, the large Indian software firms like Infosys and Wipro, which aspired to be full-service providers to their clients. Second, the specialist third-party outsourcing firms like Evalueserver, Cognizant and Daksh, which provided narrowly specialized services to their clients. Of these IT firms, Daksh was set up in 1999; its turnover doubled every year since its establishment. Third, large captive units created by TNCs, particularly by financial services TNCs, like GE Capital, American Express, HSBC, Citigroup and Standard Chartered. Fourth, the establishments created by the gigantic global professional-services consultancies, like IBM, Ernst & Young and Accenture (*The Economist,* 2004b). India's thriving BPO industry faced two major uncertainties, namely, growing protectionism in its important markets, particularly the United States, and the usual meddling of an incompetent and parasitic government. Besides, competition from the other countries (such as Barbados, Brazil, Bulgaria, China, Malaysia, Mexico, the Philippines, Rumania, Russian Federation, South Africa, and Vietnam) is likely to start making inroads and challenge the Indian IT-enabled services and BPO industry (see Chapter 5, Section 5.4 for greater details).

India's GDP growth rate was 6.8 percent in 2002 and 7.4 percent in 2003, which is far superior to the past achievements. Trade balance recorded a surplus in 2003. However, India has not been attracting global financial resources commensurate with its size and potential. Its engagement in the world trade is also not comparable to those of the dynamic Asian economies. Despite considerable improvement in policies and performance, all the usual economic indicators confirm that India's integration with the global economy has been moderate, at best. Indicators like trade to GDP ratio, FDI to GDP ratio, and country credit rating place Indian economy in the slots far removed from the dynamic Asian economies. Future growth prospects are at best tepid because of slow and inadequate macroeconomic and structural reforms, high levels of fiscal deficits, which crowds out investment in export-related industrial sectors and slow privatization. Global investors are generally unimpressed with the large deficits. As noted above, the level of protection is still very high, both in absolute and relative terms. Inefficiencies and weaknesses of an overstretched infrastructure continue to badger the economy. Power outages impose sizable costs on firms. Labor force has serious quality problems, which is compounded by inflexible and archaic labor laws. Under this set of circumstances, the large domestic market that should have furthered prospects of integration with the global economy, discourages Indian firms to pay attention to the external sector. The Congress-Party-led coalition came back in power in May 2004. In their budget (July 2004), again nothing was done to advance the reforms. Status quo continued even on pressing issues like privatization, labyrinthine subsidies, and labor laws. If the new government does not adhere to the philosophy of rapid liberalization and deregulation, and removing itself from all the things it does not do well in the area of business and economy, and focuses its energies on areas where markets alone do not provide the answer, Indian economy is certain to continue to underperform. Decades of flawed macroeconomic policies *inter alia* provide little reason to be optimistic about the future of Indian economy.

2.5.3 Why India lagged behind China?

It is evident from the above exposition that adoption of wrong economic philosophies (Fabian socialism, *swadeshi* or economic self-reliance) and strategies like ISI, a shackled private sector tied down with Byzantine requirements of licenses and controls, smothering of market forces, rejection of neo-classical economic principles like capitalizing on comparative advantage had high and perpetual costs for the Indian economy. Gigantic public sector enterprises and intrusive governments soon became albatrosses around the neck of the economy. The Chinese economy also suffered when it was a centrally planned economy, but with the adoption of the Deng doctrine these unproductive ideological notions were rejected in China and the economy made a complete volte-face. Despite being a communist country, China adopted capitalist economic philosophy and moved pragmatically toward an open market economic system. No such turnaround in economic philosophy and strategy ever took place in India. Design and successful implementation of the SEZs and coastal development strategies enabled China to prepare a firm and sizeable base for modern manufacturing industries and put China ahead in terms of manufacturing output and exports. India not only did not have any strategy parallel to this but also its industrialization process progressed lethargically.

Systemic rigidities in India have not declined and cause much more constriction in India than in China, leading to high costs to the economy. For instance, in the Global Competitiveness Report for 2000, in terms of restrictions on hiring and firing of workers, India ranked 73rd out of 75 countries, while China ranked 23rd. Bankruptcy laws in India are still archaic and it is an impossibility for large enterprises. Over 60 percent of the bankruptcy cases take more than 10 years in Indian courts. At the other end of the spectrum, starting a new small business takes much longer in India than in China. It takes 90 days and 10 permits in India, while 30 days and 6 permits in China (Wolf and Luce, 2003).

To add to the woes, non-economic malaise like low-quality political leadership, unimaginative governments, large, inefficient and corrupt bureaucracy, exceedingly delayed adoption of economic reforms followed by poor implementation kept India way behind China. Conversely, not having a democratic system helped China at crucial points in its recent economic history. Deng Xiaoping could never have launched his 1978-reform program—which immediately caused a spike in the unemployment rate—if he had to muster a parliamentary majority and hope to be reelected.

It has been debated why the response of liberalization measure was weaker in India than in China. Other than the reasons put forth above, there is a structural explanation for it. Over the 1980–2000 period, substantial structural transformation took place, essentially due to declining significance of the agricultural sector in the two economies. In India, the entire decline in the agricultural sector was added to the services sector. Its industrial sector did not rise as a proportion of the GDP. China experienced similar transformation in its economic structure but in China, initially the size of the industrial sector as a proportion of GDP was twice that of India. Over the next two decades, it rose further. Therefore, in 2000 the share of services sector in China was 33.2 percent of the GDP, while in India it was as high as 48.2 percent. The industrial sector was 50.9 percent of the GDP in China, as opposed to 26.9 percent in India.

This change in the economic structure matters a great deal. When a developing economy takes to liberalization, its prospects of exporting goods, particularly labor-intensive products, from its industrial sector improve. If it has a large industrial sector, its export industries can try and find niches in the global market place for initially low-technology exportables and then move up the product value chain. As China's industrial and manufacturing sectors were much larger than that of India, it benefited more and succeeded in globalizing at a far brisker pace than did India. The same logic applies to FDI. Compared to China, India received modest amounts of global FDI and there are little prospects of a sharp pickup. Investment in industry has remained sluggish. This includes both domestic and foreign investment. Global investors feel hesitant for the same reason as do the domestic ones. The formal services sector can absorb FDI in India, but its capacity to do so is limited. Owing to these structural factors India has lagged further behind China over the preceding quarter century (Panagaria, 2004).

2.6 NEWLY INDUSTRIALIZED ASIAN ECONOMIES

The four newly industrialized Asian economies (NIAEs), namely, Hong Kong SAR, Korea, Singapore and Taiwan earned the fond sobriquet of the "tiger" economies and the "little dragons." These economies are known for their rapid and sustained GDP growth, between the early 1960s and the mid-1990s, and are of interest to the developing economies in that they were able to graduate from developing country status to industrial economy status in a short span of three decades and were able to progress past other developing economies in Africa, South Asia and Latin America. They provided large investment opportunities and attracted attention of the global investment and financial community (see Chapter 1, Section 1.7). Their growth was characterized by even income distribution, that is, they recorded consistent improvements in the Gini coefficient along the growth trajectory. The rapid growth in this sub-group of economies in a short span of time is exemplified by the Korean economy, which is known to have doubled its per capita income every 5 years between 1961 and

1996.[83] It not only became a NIAE, but also a member of the prestigious club of industrialized economies, namley the OECD in 1996.[84] In early 2000s, Korea led the world in broadband Internet access; nearly 60 percent of the population could access the web at ultra-high speed.

In the early 1960s, the four NIAEs were characterized by their low-income and excess labor supply. Though the exact timing of the beginning of rapid growth varies from economy to economy, their growth performance for the following decades was noteworthy—the Asian crisis of 1997–98 was an aberration. Their economic policies contain both similarities and differences. They were largely based on pragmatic and result-oriented neo-classical economic principles. They learned lessons from the impressive economic growth of Japan and espoused the model of outer-oriented, export-induced growth, with relatively closed domestic markets and rejected the ISI at an early stage in their economic growth process. Like Japan, their financial system was "repressive" in the initial stages. Tailored government intervention was a hallmark of their growth strategy, although Hong Kong was an exception in this regard. As they followed outer-orientation, they were open to FDI, which helped them in achieving rapid GDP growth, with technological catch up. In the initial stages of their growth, Japanese TNCs and large firms invested massively in these economies and became a source of industrial learning and technology transfer (Das, 1996).

The four NIAEs together accounted for less than 2.5 percent of world merchandise exports in 1971. Compared to that, in 2003 their exports added up to 9.5 percent of the world's total merchandise exports, which is only a trifle less than that of the Germany (10.0 percent). As a proportion of world's merchandise exports, these four economies were almost equal to the United States (9.7 percent), the second largest exporter in the WTO league table of exporters after Germany, and substantially higher than Japan (6.3 percent), the third largest exporting economy.[85] These statistics make it clear that brisk

[83] In 1960, Korean economy was agrarian and poor, with scarcity of arable land and a large part of labor force underemployed or unemployed. Conversely, today's Korea is an industrial-urban society, with almost 80 percent of the population in urban areas having exceedingly low unemployment rate. In 1960, Korea was nearly an autarky, with heavy dependence on the U.S. aid, which accounted for 10 percent of its GNP. Today's Korea is the 12th largest trading nation in the world, and has turned from a recipient economy to a donor economy, providing official development assistance to other developing economies.

[84] On October 25, 1996, Korea became the 29th member nation of the OECD, the second country in Asia—the first was Japan—to accomplish this feat. This membership was expected to raise Korea's level of credit and push the country toward a full status as an advanced economy and a progressive society. It was also expected to help the country to deregulate and to fully open its economy to the world.

[85] See WTO (2004), *Leading Exporters and Importers in World Merchandise Trade, 2003.* Appendix Table 1.

growth in trade has been an important element in the development of these dynamic economies. Large trade and investment flows closely integrated the NIAEs with Japan. As the industrialization process progressed, the composition of exports evolved toward higher capital-labor ratio products. They started to export more sophisticated manufactured products, such as machinery and equipment. Subsequently, they became important exporters of computers and IT products. This shift in the composition of exports reflected a major shift in the industrial landscape of these economies. Services sector recorded rapid growth, particularly in Hong SAR and Singapore.

Structural transformation of this nature required large investment and until 1970 these economies only had rudimentary financial systems. Government mandates and schemes encouraged savings and they played an active role in mobilized savings for financing export-oriented industrialization—Hong Kong was an exception again. In Singapore, government encouraged high private savings through mandatory provident fund contributions by both employers and employees. A member of a provident fund could use savings for housing, education, medical care, or retirement. Though less formal and limited in scope, the governments of Korea and Taiwan also operated various specialized saving instruments. These savings were utilized to establish government-owned development banks in all the three economies. In addition, in keeping with the strategy of "picking the winners," which was learned from Japan, special funds were created for financing the targeted sectors of industries (Section 2.4). Commercial banks also played a noteworthy role in mobilizing domestic savings. In Korea and Taiwan, the governments required commercial banks to extend credit to industries targeted in the government development plans. Interest rates on these loans were regulated and kept below the market rate.

Economic development in the four NIAEs, in particular in Korea, followed the Japanese model of government-bureaucracy-led growth within a mercantilist framework (Das, 1991). Korea carried the Japanese model so much further that it was often referred to as the Korean model of growth. Korean government and political system was much more intrusive in the economic affairs than was the Japanese government (Krause, 1997). Often the chosen instrument of government intervention was control over financial resources. In all the four NIAEs, resource allocation process treated export industries and sectors as well as large infrastructure projects as priority sectors. In the early stages of growth, exchange rate policies were carefully crafted, currency overvaluation was meticulously eschewed and the real effective exchange rate (REER) was never allowed to get out of line.

In the early stages of growth, more than half of bank credit went to the manufacturing sector. Contribution of manufacturing sector to GDP remained substantial and policy emphasis on this sector persisted, although in the early 1980s the Korean government discontinued an ambitious policy to create large heavy and chemical industries and had to address banking sector problems with a massive credit infusion (Das, 1991). In Taiwan, the pattern was similar, that is, more than half of the bank credit was allocated to the manufacturing sector in the early stages, and manufacturing output contributed even more than Korea to the GDP. In the 1990s proportion of bank credit going to manufacturing sector declined significantly in both Korea and Taiwan.

Although government channeling of credit from state-owned institutions to the targeted industrial sector was done in Singapore also, commercial banks were not involved in the process. Proportion of bank credit going to the manufacturing sector was smaller in Singapore than in Korea and Taiwan. Taking advantage of its geographic location, Singapore developed itself as *entrepot* and regional financial center. Therefore, controls on interest rates, foreign capital, and entry barriers in banking were abolished in the 1970s. In comparison, removal of these restrictions was carried out piecemeal in Korea and Taiwan in the mid-1990s. Although Singapore still strictly limits offshore transactions on its currency, it allowed liberal international financing operations for both domestic and foreign financial institutions. It was necessary for guaranteeing transparent and unencumbered operations of commercial banks for fostering a vibrant financial sector.

Hong Kong's case clearly differs from the other three NIAEs because the government did not support the financing of the industrial sector and took a *laissez faire* stance. The financial and industrial sectors developed their own relationship without any external interference. Government kept its role limited to maintaining the rule of law and did not intervene in most facets of economic activity. Despite such disparate arrangements between the industrial and financial sectors, the four NIAEs collectively achieved remarkable growth, raising the oft-asked question of whether the structure of the financial sector really matters much for growth.

In addition, there was a strong government commitment in all of the four economies to improving education, particularly elementary education, and to egalitarianism, in the form of adoption of land reforms. The strategic priorities of these societies were clear. Unlike the South Asian economies, they assigned economic growth high priority, while other social objectives were relegated to secondary positions. They subordinated the objective of social goals to economic growth. Civil liberties were deemed unimportant at the early stages of growth. All the three NIAEs, except for Hong Kong, initially maintained somewhat non-democratic, and rather stern and authoritarian governments, which contributed to disciplined economic growth.

TFP growth in the ANIEs was slow but steady. The causal factors were low growth in labor productivity, rising capital intensity, and changing pattern of reallocation of resources. Much debated TFP studies showed that economic growth in Asia was essentially driven by input growth not by productivity or efficiency growth (Kim and Lau, 1994; Young, 1994, 1995).[86] The growth model of these economies was castigated for being factor input-based. No matter how you slice it, the accusation seemed correct. Among the industrial economies, TFP growth is considered to be the key to GDP growth. During rapid post-war growth period in Japan, the TFP increases contributed about half to GDP growth. The average annual GDP growth rate of Japan between 1953 and 1971 was 8.8 percent, of which 4.9 percent was attributed to technological progress (Denison and Chung, 1976). Various calculations of GDP growth in the United States attribute half of it to TFP.

Until the mid-1970s it was not clear whether the four NIAEs comprised a particular group known for rapid growth and whether their development model produced superior results to either non-market or ISI models. Gunnar Myrdal's Nobel Prize winning *Asian Drama* (1968) made no mention of the ANIEs.[87] Myrdal vaxed eloquent about the planned developmental efforts of India and its neatly drawn out five-year plan exercises. However, soon thereafter ANIEs' success began to draw a lot of global attention. During this period, Taiwan had recorded brisker GDP growth than China, and was frequently presented as an example of the triumph of market-economies over the non-market systems. The spectacular ascent of the NIAEs to economic prominence attracted much scholarly interest and led to numerous theoretical analyses and explanations. Many economists, and notably at the World Bank, depicted NIAEs' economic ascent as a vindication of free-market system or neo-classical economic principles. This interpretation of their success formed a large part of the Washington consensus. It was expected that the other developing economies would take a leaf from the development paradigm of the NIAEs and move on to a higher growth trajectory.

The Asian crisis (1997–98) mauled the Korean economy severely. Export growth in the NIAEs decelerated in 1998, although there was a huge depreciations of the Korean won (33.3 percent), which had resulted from the financial crisis. This was counter-intuitive because currency depreciation normally leads to spurt in export performance. At least Korean exports did not recover following the steep won depreciation. There were three reasons for the drop in exports in the NIAEs. For one, the build-up of capacity in the electronics industry, which had led to large inventory build-up as well as a collapse in world

[86] In a dissenting empirical study Drysdale and Huang (1997) concluded that both TFP growth and factor accumulation were equally responsible for output growth in Hong Kong SAR, Indonesia, Japan, Korea, and Thailand, while this did not apply to output growth in Malaysia and Singapore. In another dissenting paper, Liang (2002) reached the inference that TFP was the major source of economic growth in Taiwan over the 1960–93 period.

[87] Gunnar Myrdal shared Nobel prize in 1974 with his ideological rival Friedrich von Hayek. He received it for his classic work entitled the *Asian Drama: An Inquiry into the Poverty of Nations,* published in 1968.

prices for semiconductor and electronic goods, forced a slowdown in economic growth in the NIAEs. Second, intraregional trade accounted for around 50 percent of the total. Therefore, when the crisis-affected economies reduced their imports—which included their regional imports—exports of the other regional economies declined, which propelled the spread of contagion. Third, the credit crunch that emerged in the regional economies because of the collapse of financial markets and institutions, additionally hamstrung NIAEs' exports. Many firms found themselves hard pressed for working capital, and they could not import their raw materials and parts and components.

There was a clear disparity in how badly the Asian crisis, and the contagion generated by it, affected the NIAEs (Chapter 7, Section 7.1). Among the ANIEs, Korean economy had suffered the maximum, while Taiwan the minimum. The recovery was rapid, although the same observation of diversity applied to the recovery. Korea was the first to show signs of an upturn, in the fourth quarter of 1998. Rapidity in the recovery was supported by three major developments. First, exports of semiconductor and the other IT-related product lines demonstrated a strong pick-up. Second, the much-needed inventory adjustment was completed during the crisis period. Production suffered during the crisis due to difficulties in importing components and intermediate materials, which led to a fall in inventories. Relaxation in domestic fiscal and monetary policies also helped in bringing down the level of inventories. The NIAEs had successfully completed inventory adjustment by the second quarter of 1999. The third contributing factor was revival in domestic consumption. As opposed this, unemployment remained higher than the pre-crisis level even in 2000. However, it did not rise because of rejuvenation of the production machinary.

2.7 SOUTHEAST ASIAN ECONOMIES

This diverse sub-region comprises Brunei Darussalam, a petro-rich economy, four relatively better-off ASEAN-4 economies (namely, Indonesia, Malaysia, the Philippines, and Thailand), which are included in the EMEs group by some definitions, and three low-income, small economies of Indochina (namely, Cambodia, Lao PDR and Vietnam), which are in a state of transition from centrally planned to market economies. Brunei Darussalam is the richest economy of the sub-region, with its enormous oil wealth. Although Singapore is geographically located in this neighborhood, in terms of GDP, growth rate, economic structure and level of industrialization and development it resembles the other NIAEs and is justly included with them. Three of world's mega-cities, population exceeding 10 million, are located in this sub-region. They are Bangkok, Jakarta, and Metro Manila. The sub-region has enormous economic, social and cultural diversity.

The resource-based economy of Brunei Darussalam is small and rich, and encompasses a mixture of foreign and domestic entrepreneurship. The source of its riches is sizeable oil and gas reserves. The energy sector accounts for around 90 percent of exports and the same proportion of government revenue. Brunei's GDP per capita of about $18,600 is among the highest in the sub-region. The government provides a wide range of free or heavily subsidized public services, and it employs over half of the labor force. Under a currency board arrangement, the exchange rate of the Brunei dollar is maintained at par with the Singapore dollar.

Some of the noteworthy features of the individual sub-regional economies are as follows: From 1966 to 1999, Indonesia was under the New Order regime of President Suharto. It benefited from the oil boom of 1973–85. As a member of the Organization of Petroleum Exporting Countries (OPEC) its production quota is 5.2 percent of the total OPEC production.[88] In Malaysia, ethnicity impinged upon both pattern of development and government policies. The New Economic Policy (1971–93) was designed to restructure Malaysian society and economy to assure the long-term dominance of ethnic Malays, or the *bhumiputra*, over more recent immigrant communities of Chinese and Indian origin. The Philippines has been regarded as an exception among the market economies of Southeast Asia in the sense that its economic growth has been far less stable or rapid than that of the neighbors. Since independence it has been plagued by a series of crises, both in the economic and political spheres. Unlike the other sub-regional economies, Thailand never became a colony of a foreign metropolitan power. It is difficult to comprehend whether it made any substantive difference to its post-World War II pattern of development. The country was ruled by a series of military dictatorships, until the early 1990s.

At the time of independence, the agricultural sector in these economies dominated the economic structure. Since the 1960s, several sub-regional economies benefited from the Green Revolution, a term coined by William Gaud, director, USAID, in 1968. It was a movement to increase agricultural yields by using new crop cultivars, irrigation, fertilizers, pesticides and mechanization. To be sure, agricultural output improved, but its impact on income distribution, distribution of land holdings, employment in the rural sector and more generally on national economic and social development has been controversial. In this regard, Vietnam was a special, if somewhat complex, case. Frequent and major changes buffeted the agricultural sector in Vietnam. It carried out a radical land reform in the 1950s and then, as the socialist model was implemented after 1959, agriculture was collectivized. After the re-unification of the country in 1975, the socialist model of collectivization was imposed on the South as well.

---

[88] The largest OPEC production quotas are held by Saudi Arabia (32.5 percent), Iran (14.7 percent) and Venezuela (11.5 percent).

However, increasing difficulties in the agricultural sector led to a gradual process of de-collectivization and the re-establishment of family-based farming in the 1980s. In 1988, the agriculture sector began to be run in normal market-economy fashion.

As regards the policy structure for industrialization, Indonesia, Malaysia, the Philippines, and Thailand began with adopting the inward-looking ISI strategy, but by mid-1970s they had observed the favorable results of the outer-orientation in Japan and the NIAEs. They pragmatically switched to the export-induced industrialization strategy. Although ISI was never completely abandoned, as a strategy for this group of economies it had a marginal influence. Outer-oriented industrialization led to high rates of industrial growth as well as rapid changes in socio-economic structure. As these economies were learning strategic lessons from Japan and Korea, governments in these economies played a decisive role in the growth and industrialization process. The consequences of intervention were favorable in some cases and unfavorable in others. Birth and abuse of "cronyism" is a notorious illustration of the latter.

Indonesia, Malaysia, and Thailand turned in stellar performances, albeit individual economic differences remained. The contributing factors essentially included adoption of outer-orientation in growth strategy, sound macroeconomic policies, high savings and investment rates, substantial investment in human resource development, favorable demographic shifts, flexible labor market policies, low price distortions in the economy, eagerness to absorb advanced technology, and absence of bias against agriculture. Consequently, this country group was able to achieve real GDP growth rates well above the norm for the developing economies. Little wonder, the 1993 World Bank report classified Indonesia, Malaysia and Thailand as "miracle" economies. Between 1985 and 1995, there were signs of a turn around in the Philippines as well, which was an underachiever in comparison to the other three economies.

Asian crisis, which began in Thailand and the contagion spread to the other economies of this sub-group, was a veritable economic trauma. Before the outbreak of the Asian crisis, these economies were posting rapid GDP growth rates, ranging between 6 percent and 10 percent per annum. Between December 1996 and October 1997, stock market indices plummeted sharply. In Indonesia they fell by 21 percent, in Malaysia 41 percent, in the Philippines 39 percent and in Thailand by 39 percent. During the crisis-induced downturn, GDP contracted in these economies. It was most severe in Indonesia and Thailand (see Section 2.8). Many banks and other financial institutions collapsed under the weight of NPLs, and had to be taken over by the respective governments. Consequently, in Indonesia three fourths of the banking sector had to be nationalized, while in Thailand this proportion was one-third (see Chapter 7, Section 7.1).

With over 6 percent GDP growth rate in 1999, a V-shaped economic recovery set in Southeast Asia. The recovery broadened and deepened in 2000 (ADB,

2003). The driving forces behind the recovery included robust external demand for the sub-region's products and a slender increase in the domestic demand. The export growth in the sub-region was supported by strong U.S. growth in 2000 as well as recovery in the Asian economies. Also, expansionary fiscal and monetary policies underpinned domestic demand in the sub-region. Since the recovery began, public sector consumption and investment picked up in the sub-region. Conversely, private sector consumption and investment remained somewhat subdued in spite of tax breaks. The overall GDP growth trends for the sub-region masked a good deal of diversity in economic performance. For instance, while Malaysia recorded GDP growth of 5.8 percent in 2000, the Philippines posted a weak performance of 3.9 percent (ADB, 2003).

Transition to market economy proved to be a difficult proposition for Cambodia, Lao PDR and Vietnam. When the transition exercise began, the production structure collapsed and severe supply problems arose; consequently these economies grew poorer than they were before adopting the transition measures. However, by 2000 these economies had managed to reduce the levels of absolute poverty. Vietnam is regarded as the most successful in this respect. It is considered a special case in this sub-group of economies and has performed markedly better than its two neighbors.

To be sure, the transition process was difficult and complex for Vietnam. The war had a disastrous impact over economic development endeavors. Although by 1989 central planning had been abandoned entirely, many political and institutional features of the old system continued to influence Vietnamese economic development, especially the preponderance of state-owned firms and a system of highly interventionist government regulations. During the decade of 1990s, agriculture-led growth helped in cutting down the level of absolute poverty from half the population to one quarter. Its growth endeavors were supported by increasing liberalization of the economy, growing exports and adoption of far-reaching economic reforms. The present political leadership seems committed to this economic strategy.

2.8 POST-CRISIS PERFORMANCE

Although five Asian economies (Korea, Indonesia, Malaysia, the Philippines and Thailand) were categorized as crisis-stricken, Asian crisis affected virtually all the regional economies, some more others less. Seven Asian economies recorded negative GDP growth rates—that is, it contracted in 1998. Maximum contraction was recorded by Indonesia (−13.1 percent) and Thailand (−10.5 percent). The crisis was deep, not wide. In 1999, the five crisis-affected as well as the other Asian economies made a V-shaped recovery and the average regional growth rate improved from 1.7 percent in 1998 to 6.4 percent in 1999. The East Asian economies recovered more than the Southeast Asian ones. During 2000, regional GDP growth rate was 7.1 percent, although next year it dipped to 4.1 percent. The following two years were also moderate GDP growth years, with a GDP growth rate of 5.7 percent in 2002 and 6.3 percent in 2003 (ADB, 2003).

To be sure, much was accomplished after 1998. One sign of how far Asia has come is that all the five crisis-affected Asian economies completed their IMF-supported reform and restructuring programs. Indonesia was the last to do so at the end of 2003. Most economies shifted to sounder macroeconomic and financial policy frameworks than before the crisis. Monetary policy became more focused. Fiscal policy reforms were under way in several countries, albeit not completed. Between 1999 and 2003, Asia excluding Japan, was the most rapidly growing region of the global economy, although GDP growth rates did not reach their pre-crisis levels. Even Indonesia, laid low by the crisis, got back on its feet (Krueger, 2004). In March 2004, it succeeded in issuing the first bond in the global financial markets in eight years. Emerging market spreads dropped dramatically from 760 basis points to 420 basis points between January 2003 and April 2004. That being said, much remains to be done, especially in the area of macroeconomic, financial, structural and institutional reforms. Even in 2004, Asian economies were not in the pink of health. Indubitably the recovery from the crisis was rapid, the crisis left some lasting blemishes over the region before retreating.

One post-crisis commonality in sub-regions and economies in Asia was that real GDP growth rate declined markedly after the crisis. A comparison of average annual real GDP growth rates for the pre- (1990–98) and post-crisis (1998–2002) periods demonstrated that it declined for China from 10 percent in the former period to 7.6 percent in the latter, for Hong Kong SAR from 4 percent to 2.3 percent, and for Southeast Asian economies the decline was sharper. For instance, in Indonesia it declined from 5.3 percent to −0.1 percent over the two periods. Likewise, in the South Asian economies, which were affected only indirectly by the crisis, there was a small decline. The imperative of arresting and reversing the declining GDP growth rates applied to all the Asian economies.

Macroeconomic policy framework adopted during the post-crisis period was in general thoughtfully devised and well calibrated, but for the fiscal deficits where a lot more was needed to be achieved. This macroeconomic limitation was acute in South Asian economies as well as in the Southeast Asian ones, particularly in Malaysia and the Philippines. It was also growing serious in Hong Kong SAR (ADB, 2003). Measured as percentage of GDP, South Asian economies had the highest levels of fiscal deficits in the post-crisis period. Expanding fiscal deficits started raising the cost of capital, in turn, affecting volume of investment in several Asian economies. Real cost of capital was

6 percent in South Asian economies in 2002, which was double of the other Asian economies including China (Wolf and Luce, 2003). High cost of capital is a major disincentive to augmenting the rate of investment in an economy. As the fiscal deficits are financed by public borrowings, they tend to increase the level of public debt and interest payment burden as well as crowd out private investment. Share of public investment in many Asian economies declined appreciably; in India and Thailand it fell steeply to almost half the pre-crisis levels.

Inadequacies in regulatory framework and supervision further raised the cost of capital, particularly in economies where the banking sector has substantial public sector ownership. The large amounts of NPLs, spawned by the crisis in several Asian economies, also led to higher interest rates and a credit crunch. NPLs tend to shrink bank profits by cutting down interest income and raising loan loss provisions. For meeting the capital adequacy ratios Asian banks had to raise capital in the equity markets, which was not easy during periods of financial distress. Thus, NPLs put banks under severe financial strain, resulting in interest rate hikes and stringent assessment of loan quality for the new loan applicants. Therefore, credit growth has slowed down significantly in many Asian economies (ADB, 2003). The principal attributes of the post-crisis macroeconomic environment were growing budget deficits, rising public debt, high cost of capital, and deceleration in the growth rate of bank credit. Consequently, governments were unable to provide essential social services, infrastructure weaknesses could not be removed, and high costs of capital raised production costs. In this *mise-en-scene,* at the enterprise level, TFP has suffered in many Asian economies.

The post-crisis restructuring and reform endeavors were far from uniform. There was a variety in their intensity and scope. It was increasingly felt that other than fiscal stability noted above there was a pressing need for further strengthening of the financial sector. On this count, NPL overhang and corporate governance were among the most important issues to be addressed. Until 2004, banks and corporations were still struggling with weak balance sheets in several crisis-affected economies. To be sure, this weakness undermined growth opportunities. It was no coincidence that those economies that were more aggressive in the area of financial sector reform after the crisis were enjoying better growth performance. Second, in many economies there was a need to put effective bankruptcy laws in place, and improve prudential oversight and supervision in the capital markets. Until this is accomplished, Asian economies would be far from having open and competitive environments, which can best foster the sustainable, rapid growth. Third, more efforts were needed to deepen financial markets, with an express objective to extend the number and variety of instruments available. Asian economies need to rapidly shift toward equity and bond financing, because it would reduce the heavy reliance on the banking sector—a long-term characteristic of the Asian financial sector. It would improve the assessment and management of credit risk as well as help in the creation of a thriving financial market (Krueger, 2004). Chapter 2.7 addresses these issues in sufficient details.

The Asian crisis forced the affected economies off their de facto exchange rate pegs. Past experience demonstrated that for the post-crisis period, Asian economies either need to adopt floating exchange rate or its polar opposite fixed exchange rate. This imperative has been necessitated by a financially integrating global economy. Hernandez and Montiel (2001) raised doubts about the post-crisis exchange rate policies of the crisis economies. They contended that these economies seem to be returning to the same set of policies that served them so poorly during the pre-crisis era. That is, the currency values have been stabilized at new levels without adopting any commitment mechanism. As the "soft" currency pegs have little prospects of surviving in the present global financial milieu, resumption of such practices in the crisis makes these economies as vulnerable as they were before the crisis (see Chapter 7, Section 7.9.1).

As officially declared and found in the IMF classification, crisis caused Indonesia, Korea and Thailand to move in the direction of greater flexibility in their exchange rate regimes. Malaysia moved in the opposite direction and adopted a fixed exchange rate. While the Philippines did not make any changes and retained its pre-crisis independent floating exchange rate regime (Chapter 7, Section 7.9). Knowledgeable observers believe that these official positions are not correct and that little has changed during the post-crisis period. With the exception of Thailand, currencies in crisis-affected and non-crisis economies returned to formal or informal dollar pegging, and they fluctuated in much the same way as they did before the crisis, meaning thereby, they are not fluctuating at all (Calvo and Reinhart, 2000; McKinnon, 2000). To be sure, the post-crisis floaters have allowed their currencies much more flexibility than they did during the pre-crisis era, but they are far from the so-called "clean" floats practiced in the mature economies.

2.9 SUMMARY AND CONCLUSIONS

The dynamic group of Asian economies represents enormous diversity in economic as well as in social, political, religious, cultural, ethnicity, linguistics, geographical features and systems of governments. The heterogeneity among Asian economies is also visible in the structures of GDP and economic development. This group can be divided into sub-regions and countries that are at different stages of economic development, and have widely differing economic characteristic attributes.

The Association for Southeast Asian Nations (ASEAN) is the oldest regional grouping and has ten members, ranging from tiny island republics like Singapore to Indonesia, which comprises over 17,000 islands. ASEAN has enlarged to include China, Japan and Korea. The new group is ASEAN-Plus-Three (APT), which has more heterogeneity than the ASEAN of 10 members.

Japan is the leading geese in the flying-geese paradigm of Asian economies. Its brisk post-war economic recovery had enormous demonstration effect in Asia. The salient characteristics of this high-growth era were high rates of savings and investment, an industrious labor force with strong work ethics, supply of cheap oil, adapting and adopting new technologies in the manufacturing sector followed by technological innovation and effective intervention by the government. The government and bureaucracy led growth efforts in a neo-mercantilist fashion. Rapid export-induced growth led to immense changes in industrial structure. It shifted from agriculture and light industry to heavy and high-technology industries and services. Dominating the industrial sector were iron and steel, shipbuilding, machine tools, motor vehicles and subsequently electronics. In 1989, monetary authorities reacted by tightening policies to contain rise in asset values. Next year, the Nikkei index fell by 38 percent, wiping out over $2 trillion worth in stock market value. Land prices collapsed, burdening financial institutions with massive bad debts. Banks became overly cautious and a severe credit crunch followed. The economic bubble of the late 1980s burst on the last day of 1989, which signaled the end of the second era of rapid growth and more than two decades of rapid overseas business expansion.

China adopted market-oriented reforms in 1978 and economy was liberalized under the doctrine of "open-door policy," which transformed China from a small, low-income, centrally planned economy to a large "socialist market economy," noted for its vertiginous economic growth of the last two-and-a-half decades. China has established new standards of sustained growth and dynamic resource allocation by a large economy. Open-economy reforms essentially cover the areas of trade, exchange rate and foreign investment. China recorded real GDP growth rate of 9.7 percent for the 1979–2000 period. China's GDP sextupleted in real terms over this period, while its per capita GDP quintupled. In 2003, with a GDP of $1.4 trillion, it was the sixth largest global economy. In PPP terms China was the second largest economy after the United States. It should be noted that while the PPP measure overstates China's GDP, the conventional measure underestimates it. The flip side of the coin is that Chinese economy is still in transition from one system to another and several structural, institutional and sector-specific quandaries persist.

Lower real growth rate and slow progress in the Indian economy is sometimes blamed on *inter alia* rambunctious democracy and multiplicity of political parties, leading to chaos, compromises, inordinate delays, acceptance of erroneous economic policies, and all round weaknesses in infrastructure. In a democratic environment, governments at federal and state levels remain short-sighted, with their time horizon limited to the next election. They are tempted to give in to populist policies as against adopting sound, positive, pragmatic and well-thought macroeconomic measures. Reforms program was not only launched belatedly in 1991, but also implemented in a hesitant, halting and inept manner; therefore, progress in implementation has been slow and tardy. The favorable recent developments include India first finding comparative advantage in software and computer programming, and second finding a profitable niche in back-office outsourcing of business services and call centers. Also, the BPO firms have been expanding the range of work that can be performed remotely.

The four NIAEs are known for their rapid and sustained GDP growth, between the early 1960s and the mid-1990s, and are of interest to the developing economies in that they were able to graduate from developing country status to industrial economy status in a short span of four decades. Their economic policies contain both similarities and differences. They were largely based on pragmatic and result-oriented neo-classical ecomnomic principles. They learned lessons from the impressive economic growth of Japan and espoused the model of outer-oriented, export-induced growth, with relatively closed domestic markets and rejected import-substitution at an early stage in their economic growth process. Like Japan, their financial system was "repressive" in the initial stages. Tailored government intervention was a hallmark of their growth strategy, although Hong Kong was an exception in this regard.

In the diverse sub-region of Southeast Asian economies, Indonesia, Malaysia, and Thailand turned in stellar performances, albeit individual economic differences remained. The causal factors essentially included adoption of outer-orientation in growth strategy, sound macroeconomic policies, high savings and investment rates, substantial investment in human resource development, favorable demographic shifts, flexible labor market policies, low price distortions in the economy, eagerness to absorb advanced technology, and absence of bias against agriculture. Consequently, this country group was able to achieve GDP growth rates well above the norm for the developing economies. The Philippines became a marginal member of this sub-group of economies. In 1997–98, Korea, Indonesia, Malaysia, the Philippines and Thailand were roiled by a serious currency and financial crisis.

REFERENCES

Ahmed, S. 2004. "Behind the mask: Survey of business in China," *The Economist.* 20 March. After p. 60.

Akamatsu, K. 1961. "A theory of unbalanced growth in the world economy," *Weltwirtschaftliches Archiv.* Vol. 86. No. 1. pp. 56–68.

Asian Development Bank. (ADB). 2001. *Asian Development Outlook 2003.* Hong Kong: Oxford University Press.

Asian Development Bank (ADB). 2003. *Asian Development Outlook 2003.* Hong Kong: Oxford University Press.

Bardhan, P. 2002. "Disjuncture in the Indian reform process: Some reflections," paper presented at *The Indian Economy Conference,* Cornell University, Ithaca, New York, April 19–20.

Bhagwati, J.N. and T.N. Srinivasan. 1999. *Outward Orientation and Economic Development: Are Revisionists Right?* Available at: http://www.columbia.edu/~jb38/Krueger.pdf. Accessed September 17.

Calvo, G. and C. Reinhart. 2000. *Fear of Floating.* Cambridge, MA: National Bureau of Economic Research. NBER Working Paper No. 7993. November.

Chen, S. and M. Ravallion. 2004. *How Have the World's Poorest Fared since the Early 1980s?* Washington, DC; The World Bank. Available at: http://www.worldbank.org/research/povmonitor/MartinPapers/How_have_the_poorest_fared_since_the_early_1980s.pdf. Accessed April 20.

Cotis, J.P. 2003. "Towards sustainable economic growth in Japan: The new mix of monetary and fiscal policies," presentation made at the Policy Research Institute, Ministry of Finance, Tokyo, June 23.

Das, Dilip K. 1991. *Korean Economic Dynamism.* London: The Macmillan Press.

Das, Dilip K. 1992. *The Yen Appreciation and the International Economy.* London: The Macmillan Press; New York: New York University Press.

Das, Dilip K. 1996. *The Asia–Pacific Economy.* London: The Macmillan Press; New York: St. Martin's Press.

Das, Dilip K. 2001b. "Liberalization efforts in China and accession to the World Trade Organization," *The Journal of World Investment.* Vol. 2. No. 4. pp. 761–789.

Das, Dilip K. 2004a. *The Economic Dimensions of Globalization.* Houndmills, Hampshire, UK: Palgrave Macmillan.

Das, Dilip K. 2004b. *Financial Globalization and the* Emerging *Market Economies.* London and New York: Routledge. Drysdale, P. and Y. Huang. 1997. "Technological catch-up and economic growth in east Asia and the Pacific," *Economic Records.* Vol. 73. No. 2. pp. 201–211.

Denison, C. and P. Chung. 1976. "Economic growth and its sources," in H. Patrick and H. Rosovsky (eds) *Asia's New Giant.* Washington, DC: The Brookings Institution. pp. 94–122.

The Economist. 2001. "Enter the dragon." 10 March. pp. 21–24.

The Economist. 2003a. "Two systems, one grand rivalry." 21 June. pp. 21–23.

The Economist. 2003b. "On a roll". Available at: http://www.economist.com/agenda/displaystory.cfm?story_id=1872018. Accessed June 27, 2003.

The Economis., 2004a. "Cheap money, pricey oil." Available at: http://www.economist.com/agenda/displaystory.cfm?story_id=2682614. Accessed May 15, 2004.

The Economist, 2004b. "Japanese Debt: End in Sight", 14 February. pp. 67–68.

The Economist Intelligence Unit ViewsWire. (EIU) 2004. *"China: Economic Analysis*". London. Available at: http://www.viewswire.com/index.asp?layout=display_print&doc_id=374521. Accessed May 8. Ferro, M., D. Rosenblatt and N. Stern. 2002. "Policies for pro-poor growth in India," paper presented at *The Indian Economy Conference,* Cornell University, Ithaca, New York, April 20, 2004.

Hernandez, L. and P. Montiel. 2001. *Post Crisis Exchange Rate Policy in Five Asian Economies: Filling the Hollow Middle?* Washington, DC: International Monetary Fund. IMF Working Paper No. WP/01/170.

Hilpert, H.G. 2003. "Japan: Is the crisis over?" *CESifo Forum.* Vol. 4. No. 4. pp. 49–61.

Hutchison, M. 1997. *The Political Economy of Japanese Economic Policy.* Cambridge, MA: The MIT Press.

International Monetary Fund (IMF). 2002. *India: Selected Issues and Statistical Appendix.* Washington, DC: IMF Country Report No. 02/193.

International Monetary Fund (IMF). 2003, April. *World Economic Outlook.* Washington, DC: IMF.

International Monetary Fund (IMF). 2004, April. *World Economic Outlook.* Washington, DC: IMF.

Kim, J. I. and L. Lau. 1994. "The sources of economic growth of the East Asian newly industrialized economies," *Journal of Japanese and International Economics.* Vol. 8. No. 3. pp. 235–271.

Krause, L.B. 1997. *Korea's Economic Role in East Asia.* Stanford: Stanford University. Asia-Pacific Research Center.

Krueger, A.O. 2004. *Lessons From the Asian Crisis.* Keynote address at the SEACEN Meeting held in Colombo, Sri Lanka, February 12.

Kwan, C.H. 2002, August. *The Rise of China and Asia's Flying Geese Pattern of Economic Development.* Tokyo: Nomura Research Institute. NRI Papers No. 52.

Laffont, J.J. and Y. Quin. 1999. "The dynamics of reform and development in China: A political economy perspective," *European Economic Review.* Vol. 24. No. 4. pp. 1105–1114.

Lau, L.J., Y. Qian and G. Ronald. 2000. "Reforms without losers: An interpretation of China's dual-track approach," *Journal of Political Economy.* Vol. 108. No. 1. pp. 120–143.

Lee H. and D. Roland-Holst. 1998. "Prelude to the Pacific century: Overview of the region," in H. Lee and D. Roland-Holst. (eds) *Economic Development and Co-operation in the Pacific Basin.* Cambridge: Cambridge University Press. pp. 3–36.

Liang, C.Y. 2002. *The Total Factor Productivity Growth in Taiwan 1960–1993.* Taipei, Taiwan: The Institute of Economics. Academia Sinica. Discussion Paper 2002–04.

Lo, C. 2004. *China's Economic Reform Myth.* Hong Kong SAR. (unpublished manuscript)

McKinnon, R.I. 2000. *After the Crisis, the East Asian Dollar Standard Reconstructed.* Stanford: Stanford University. Available at: http://www-econ.stanford.edu/faculty/workp/swp00013.html. Accessed May 15, 2004.

McNally, C.A. 2002. "China's State-Owned Enterprises: Thriving or Crumbling?" *Asia-Pacific Issues.* Hawai'i. East West Center. No. 59.

Nomura Research Institute (NRI). 2002, December 3. *Medium Term Outlook for the Japanese Economy.* Tokyo: NRI. Research Paper No. 2002–27.

Panagaria, A. 2004, March. *India in the 1980s and the 1990s: A Triumph of the Reforms.* Washington, DC. IMF. IMF Working Paper No. Wp/04/43.

Pinto, B. and F. Zahir. 2004, March. *India: Why Fiscal Adjustment Now?* Washington, DC: The World Bank. Policy Research Working Paper 3230.

Roach, S. 2004. *Global Economy: When China Sneezes.* New York: Morgan Stanley Global Economic Forum. Available at: http://www.morganstanley.com/GEFdata/digests/20040503-mon.html#anchor0. Accessed May 3, 2004.

Rodrik, D. and A. Subramanian. 2004. *From Hindu Growth to Productivity Surge.* Cambridge, MA: National Bureau of Economic Research. NBER Working Paper No. w10376.

Sakakibara, E. and S. Yamakawa. 2003. "Regional Integration in East Asia: Challenges and Opportunities", June. Part I and Part II. Washington DC. Policy Research Working Paper Nos. 3078 and 3079.

Scoffield, H. 2004. "Outsourcing a major boon to Canada," *Globe and Mail, Report on Business.* April 2. p. B4.

Srinivasan, T.N. 2001. *India's Fiscal Deficits: Is There a Crisis Ahead?* Palo Alto, CA: Stanford University. Center for Research on Economic Development and Policy Reform. Working Paper No. 92.

Wolf, M. and E. Luce. 2003. "India's slowing growth: Why A hobbled economy cannot meet the country's needs?" *The Financial Times.* April 4. p. 11.

Wong, J. and L. Ding. 2003. *China's Economy Into The New Century: Structural Issues And Problems*. Singapore: East Asian Institute. National University of Singapore.

World Trade Organization (WTO). 2004, April 5. *World Trade 2003, Prospects For 2004*. Press Release. No. Press/373.

Young, A. 1994. "Lessons from the East Asian NICs: A contrarian view," *European Economic Review.* Vol. 38. No. 5. pp. 946–973.

Young, A. 1995. "The tyranny of numbers: Confronting the statistical relationship of the East Asian growth experience," *Quarterly Journal of Economics.* Vol. 110. No. 3. pp. 641–680.

Zhang, W.W. 2000. *Transforming China: Economic Reforms and Its Political Implications.* Basingstoke, Hampshire, UK: Macmillan Press.

Chapter 3

MARKET-DRIVEN REGIONALIZATION IN ASIA

3.1 INTRODUCTION

Although approximately half of world trade is at present intra-regional, institutionalized regionalism was slow to lay down its roots in Asia. Formal regionalism and market-led regionalization are two different, albeit parallel, concepts. The latter implies market-driven increase in economic interdependence that occurs through expansion of trade, investment, technology and migration flows, without any formal government-led framework of co-operation. Relative to other regions, Asia-Pacific region was slow to catch on the concept and phenomenon of regionalism, and espoused formal and institutionalized regionalism relatively late. Policy mandarins in Asia for a long time ignored the concept in its institutional form. A market-driven regionalization spontaneously and logically took its place. This chapter considers whys and wherefores of this situation.[89]

As discussed in the preceding chapter, economic growth in Asia had a certain distinctive pattern to it. Following a brief flirtation with the import-substituting industrialization (ISI) strategy, over the preceding four decades, the ten high-performing Asian economies adopted outer-oriented strategies, promoting openness to trade and foreign investment. A brisk market-led expansion in intra-regional trade and investment followed. Asia-Pacific regionalization was essentially uninstitutionalized. Development of regional production networks was the consequence of market-led economic dynamics of the region. Large corporations, including transnational corporations (TNCs), contributed to the growth of a pan-Asian industrialization and integrated production networks (refer to Chapter 6 for greater details).

---

[89] Refer to Chapter 4 for distinction between regionalization and regionalism.

A large body of research is available proving that trade and outward economic orientation were the principal forces behind rapid economic growth in Asia. This literature is too well-known to be referred to here. Several empirical studies have concluded that with rapid growth, the economic structure of Japan, the newly industrialized Asian economies[90] (NIAEs), the ASEAN-4 economies[91], and the People's Republic of China (hereinafter China) underwent substantial structural transformation, which had a direct bearing on factor endowments in individual economies. Growth, structural transformation and changing factor endowments naturally ushered in transformation in the manufacturing sector, followed by that in the services sector. The Heckscher–Ohlin theory supports and provides an explanation for the resulting transformation in the comparative advantage of different Asian economies and/or country groups (Das, 1998). However, Asian economies did not record high (or low) trade in relative and absolute terms only in certain product lines or sectors. Similarly, trade in these economies was not concentrated in only a few select sectors (Das, 2000a). Another noteworthy observation in this regard is that there was no characteristic Asian export path or Asian export route and few generalizations could be made in this regard for the region.

There were several reasons why the Asian economies did not adopt formalized regional co-operation in an extensive, enthusiastic and functional manner for promoting regional trade and investment. The heterogeneity of the region discouraged launching of such institutionalized regional integration initiatives. Second, several neighboring economies did not have amicable historical and political relationship, while there were others that were hostile to each other. Third, emphasis on nationalism in economic policies was another reason. Many economies were more focused on promoting their narrow national interests and specific industries than on underpinning the regional economic strengths. Fourth, because of their outward economic orientation the dynamic Asian economies established liberalized trade and foreign direct investment (FDI) policy regime early on in their growth endeavors, which ran counter to the doctrine of formal regionalism. Lastly, several Asian economies developed strong trade and investment bonds with the industrial economies, particularly the United States (U.S.), during the post-World War II era, which in turn delayed the formation of formal regional groupings. Until the early 1990s, the United States had a strong commitment to multilateralism.[92]

---

[90] Hong Kong SAR, Korea (Republic of), Singapore and Taiwan.

[91] Namely, Indonesia, Malaysia, the Philippines, and Thailand.

[92] With the formation of North American Free Trade Area (NAFTA) on January 1, 1994, this commitment to multilateralism dissipated.

3.2 TRENDS IN INTRA-REGIONAL TRADE AND INVESTMENT

Asia has a long history of intra-regional trade (Chapter 1). It was well developed in the early decades of the twentieth century. Share of intra-trade in total trade in Asia was 45.5 percent in 1928 (WTO, 1995). After 1931, the Japanese colonial pattern of economic relations—which was nothing more than exchanging raw materials for manufactured goods—gave way to building independent industrial capacity outside Japan, essentially in China, Korea and Taiwan. This manner of economic relations between Japan and Asian economies led to significant intra-regional investment as well as development of regional transportation and communications infrastructure networks. In the late 1930s, during the Japanese imperial domination of East Asian economies, intra-regional trade in Asia was high. Development of production networks by Japan supported mutually reinforcing trade and investment patterns in Asia.[93] Both Beasley (1987) and Sakakibara and Yamakawa (2003) have provided a graphic account of how a sophisticated set of economic linkages between Japan and other Asian economies grew during the pre-war period. Economic complementaries within the region underpinned a rapid expansion of intra-regional trade and a decline of trade between Asia and the rest of the world.

The World War II radically changed the pre-war trading patterns of the Asian economies. After the War ended, the directionality of trade and investment patterns in Asia, particularly in East Asia, were re-directed from Japan to the United States. Economic linkages and intra-trade ties between Japan, Korea, China, and Taiwan were weakened considerably in the aftermath of the War. Besides, the civil war in China had a devastating impact over the trade and it had virtually collapsed. Japan experienced an abrupt redirection in its trade ties at the end of the War. Its trade with Asia, both East and Southeast, fell from 73 percent of total trade in 1940 to 31 percent in 1951 (Petri, 1994). Thus viewed, the War broke down the old trading pattern between Japan and Asia and the new pattern that emerged was of diversified trade. Japan's trade concentration on East Asia declined markedly. This was the nadir in intra-regional trade and investment.

American economic policy in Asia after the World War II worked counter to this trend and sought to re-establish and re-strengthen Japanese trade ties with the regional economies so that the regional synergy of the yorecould be recreated to stimulate the impoverished Asian economies. The expectation was that

[93] Refer to Chapter 4 of "Regional Integration in East Asia: Challenges and Opportunities" by E. Sakakibara, and S. Yamakawa, Part II. Keio University. Tokyo. June. (2003). p. 5.

a steady expansion of trade and investment would not only strengthen regional economic ties but also contribute to political stability in the region. The legacies of pre-War economic relationships in Asia and the post-War endeavors ensured that in the period immediately after the War—notwithstanding the ravages of the War—intra-regional trade was not completely discontinued. Although a sharp fall was to be expected, on an average intra-regional trade stabilized around 41 percent of all Asian trade between 1951 and 1958. It is noteworthy that this intra-trade was driven by market forces, without any institutional support.[94]

3.2.1 Market-driven regionalization

As alluded to above, traditionally East and Southeast Asian economies used to export industrial raw materials to Japan and import intermediate and capital goods. The contemporary period has seen complete reversal in this trend due to remarkable supply-side developments in the Asian economies. By the early 1990s, more than 60 percent of their exports to Japan were manufactured goods. The NIAEs exports to their ASEAN-4 neighbors also expanded. Exports among the NIAEs jumped to $22.4 billion or 10 percent of their total exports in 1988, from $5.9 billion or 5 percent of their total exports in 1986.

NIAEs exports to the ASEAN countries rose from $6.4 billion in 1986 to $14.5 billion in 1998, or from 5 percent of the total to 7 percent (Das, 1993). Likewise, ASEAN exports to NIAEs also rose from $8.2 billion or 21 percent of the total to $15.5 billion or 24 percent over the 1986–88 period. Intra-ASEAN exports also rose in terms of value, from $1.5 billion to $2.3 billion during this period. The share of internal market for the ASEAN economies remained constant and low at 4 percent of the total (Das, 1993).

As envisioned in the Deng doctrine and the "open-door policy," China had gone on liberalizing its economy for FDI inflows and had established itself as the largest emerging market recipient of FDI (Chapter 2, Section 2.5.1). Toward the end of the 1990s, when China was making concerted endeavors to join the World Trade Organization (WTO), previously closed sectors for FDI had to be liberalized under the WTO requirements. This led to a surge in FDI in high-technology industries like semiconductor and electronics from the other Asian economies that had strong high-technology bases. During the latter half of 2000, prices of semiconductor chips were on a downward trajectory. Severe competitive pressure was pushing Asian chipmakers to relocate to cheaper production bases and areas where some domestic marketing potential existed.

[94] For greater details regarding the achievement of stability in trade and investment in the immediate aftermath of the War, please refer to Das (2004); Ikenberry (2000), WTO (1995) and WTO (1999).

China met both the conditions. Thus the pan-Asian wave of industrialization in the high-technology areas has not abated. Until 2000, the electronics industry in China met 86 percent of its semiconductor needs by imports from Malaysia, the Philippines, Singapore and Thailand. In the latter half of 2000, China was attracting Taiwanese investment in new semiconductor capacity and building up its electronic production facilities. Taiwanese venture capitalists launched several initiatives involving billions of dollars in building high-end wafer plants in China, which in turn helped China in upgrading its industrial mix. In 2000, it was projected that by 2003, China would not only meet its semiconductor requirements from domestic production but also have capacity to export semiconductor. This would put pressure on all current Asian semiconductor exporters to move up the value chain and be more competitive (Credit Swiss First Boston [CSFB], 2000).

Other than expansion of mutual trade and investment, Asian economies were also endeavoring to create a mechanism for mutual support in central banking and exchange rate stability. Market-driven regionalism could not take place without co-operation in these vital regional financial spheres. In 1966, the SEACEN (South East Asian Central Banks) was created with a mandate of providing training and organizing seminars for the regional central bankers. Co-operation and collaboration among the regional central banking authority was also considered an imperative by the APEC forum. In 1991, eleven central banks of the Asia-Pacific region established Executives' Meeting of East-Asia-Pacific Central Banks (EMEAP), which began organizing high-level meetings and hosted working groups on financial markets, central bank operations, and prudential supervision.[95] This group of eleven also included Australia and New Zealand. In 1995, the Hong Kong Monetary Authority (HKMA) and the central banks of Indonesia, Malaysia, and Thailand announced re-purchase (or repo) agreements designed to provide mutual exchange rate support. Singapore, the Philippines and Japan joined this network subsequently. At the April 2000 meeting of the Asian Development Bank, in Chiang Mai, Thailand, the ASEAN-Plus-Three (APT)[96] countries agreed to establish a pan-Asian liquidity backstop—a so-called Asian Regional Financial Arrangement (ARFA)—to prevent future speculative crises in the region. Under the AFRA, the old $200 million network of re-purchase agreements, where reserves were provided only against valuable collaterals, were replaced by a new network of swap agreements

[95] Eleven central banks and monetary authorities participate in EMEAP. They are those from Australia, China, Hong Kong SAR, Indonesia, Japan, Korea, Malaysia, New Zealand, the Philippines, Singapore, and Thailand.

[96] The abbreviation ASEAN stands for the Association for Southeast Asian Nations. The ASEAN-Plus-Three (APT) grouping comprises the ten members of ASEAN, and the three Northeast Asian economies, namely, China, Japan and Korea.

where central banks were simply going to swap currencies. Under the ARFA, the Asian economies have freer access to one another's support. This theme has been taken up in Chapter 7 (see Section 7.8) for an intensive treatment.

3.2.2 Intra-regional trade

Intra-regional trade increased to 47.0 percent in 1963, but again declined to around 41 percent all through the 1970s (WTO, 1995). The reason behind this decline was the brisk real GDP growth in the NIAEs, and subsequently in the ASEAN-4 economies and *pari passu* rapid growth in their export volumes, which justified the establishment of trade linkages outside the region. More importantly, all these economies had adopted similar economic development paradigms and sought to achieve growth through the movement toward higher value-added manufacturing production geared toward export expansion. This made it crucial for them to look for markets outside the region. For many of these economies it increasingly meant the large U.S. market.

During the 1970s, a synergetic triangular production relationship developed between Japan, the NIAEs and the United States, bringing the former two sets of economies closer together. Japan supplied the necessary technology and capital goods and components to the NIAEs, which in turn produced and competitively marketed industrial products to the U.S. market. After the Plaza Accord[97] in September 1985, the currency value configuration changed significantly. The dollar had reached a high against the yen in early 1985, which intensified imports from East and Southeast Asia into the U.S. market, and Japan was able to maintain its exports even as its production costs were rising vis-à-vis its Asian rivals (Bernard and Ravenhill, 1995). The post-Plaza Accord appreciation of the yen was not immediately matched by the appreciation of the other Asian currencies.

Between 1985 and 1987, the yen appreciated by 40 percent (Das, 1996). Consequently, Asian exports to the United States continued to expand, and *pari passu* Japanese exports to Asian markets also grew. The structure of regional trade underwent a radical transformation. The Plaza Accord contributed to a new

---

[97] On September 22, 1895, the Group of Five (G-5) finance ministers and central bankers met at the Plaza Hotel in New York to accord recognition to the view that "recent shift in fundamental economic conditions . . . together with policy commitments for the future" had to be fully reflected in foreign exchange markets. The communiqué declared that in that international economic milieu "some further orderly appreciation of the main non-dollar currencies is desirable" and that an exchange rate policy should play a role in place of the *laissez faire*. The accord communiqué called for the appreciation of the yen and the deutsche mark, instead of the depreciation of the dollar. The Plaza communiqué had a substantial short-term impact over the foreign exchange markets and the dollar went into a steep decline, while the yen and deutsche mark began to appreciate, the former sharply (Das, 1993).

division of labor in Asia as well as a greater shift of the regional production locus toward the production networks (Bernard and Ravenhill, 1995; Das, 1996)[98]. The regional economic dynamism was such that the division of labor in the region enlarged to include the ASEAN-4 economies and China more than ever in the past. A wave of pan-Asian industrialization in high-technology industries expended into the ASEAN-4 and China. These economies had depreciated their currencies during this period. Consequently, not only their exports to the United States became more competitive but they also attracted more investments from Japan and the NIAEs. The ASEAN-4 economies and China soon started developing as export platforms in their own right to export to the United States and other industrial country markets. Closely related with the spatial enlargement of the triangular relations is the shift from the firm to the networks as the locus of production and innovative activities (EIU, 2004).

In the wake of the emerging regional production and investment trends, intra-regional trade expanded more rapidly than before. Since 1985 it grew at a rate roughly double that of the world trade. This growth rate of intra-regional trade was much higher than that in the other regions, particularly in the European Union (EU)[99] and North American Free Trade Area (NAFTA).[100] Evidence based on intra-industry trade in the region demonstrated that economic linkages or interdependence in the region strengthened considerably since the mid-1980s (Ng and Yeats, 2003).

The general direction of Asian economic regionalization and intra-regional trade over the preceding two decades is clear from the foregoing discussion. As the dynamic Asian economies had pursued outer-oriented economic development strategies, they proactively stimulated inward FDI flows. This included FDI from more industrialized Asian economies to the less industrialized ones. Together, they created complex regional economic ties among themselves as well as increased trade dependencies.

---

[98] Chapter 4 in Das (1996) presents a detailed account of the new division of labor and development of regional and sub-regional production networks in Asia.

[99] On December 1, 1991, agreement was reached in Maastricht on the Treaty on European Union, with a timetable for the Economic and Monetary Union (EMU). The European Single Market was completed on January 1, 1993. On November 1, 1993, the Maastricht Treaty came into force after Danes voted yes at the second try, and the EEC became the European Union (EU).

[100] NAFTA came into effect on January 1, 1994 and created the largest free trade area (FTA) in the world of that period. At the time of creation it covered some 360 million people and nearly $500 billion in yearly trade and investment. NAFTA maintained the tariff elimination schedule established by the Canada—U.S. free trade area (CUSFTA) for the bilateral trade between Canada and the United States. Both countries negotiated separate bilateral schedules with Mexico for the elimination of tariffs. However, the three member countries agreed to abolish tariffs and non-tariff barriers completely by 2009. NAFTA had an enormous demonstration effect in Latin America. In fact, it is said to have had a "domino effect."

Intra-regional trade started rising again in the late 1980s and early 1990s, reaching 49.7 percent in 1993 and 50.7 percent in 1997. In 1998, intra-trade declined to 44.6 percent of the total Asian trade (Das, 1993; Petri, 1994; WTO, 1995, 1999). This decline was normal because regional economies were languishing due to the 1997–98 Asian currency and financial crisis. In 1999, the five crisis-affected Asian economies made a swift V-shaped recovery, which led to the return of intra-regional trade. Growing exports accelerated demands for each other's imports, which in turn stimulated GDP growth. Therefore, expansion in intra-trade was considered both a cause—and effect—of rapid growth in the region during the post-crisis period (*The Economist,* 2000). The 2001 value of intra-regional trade in Asia was $722 billion, or 48.2 percent of total Asian merchandises trade. In 2002, intra-trade increased to $792 billion, but as a proportion of the total trade (48.9 percent) it was virtually stationary.[101]

3.2.3 Is trade growing more intra-regional?

Historically, intra-trade in Asia was well developed in the early decades of the twentieth century. Share of intra-trade in total trade in Asia was 45.5 percent in 1928 (WTO, 1995). It stabilized around 41 percent of all Asian trade in the 1950s. The above exposition provided a convincing evidence of brisk trade growth in Asia in the last quarter century. As for the directionality of trade, intra-regional trade grew at a brisker pace than Asia's trade with any other regional markets. While the larger Asian economies accounted for bulk of trade expansion, smaller ones were not left out of the process. Its direct consequence was an increase in market-led integration of the region. There were three basic causal factors supporting this trend, namely, unilateral trade liberalization by Asian economies, fulfillment of WTO commitments, and the slicing of value chain and creation of integrated production networks located in different Asian economies discussed in details in Section 3.7. Intra-regional trade was not only driven by growing demand but also by increased competitiveness of the regional economies (Das, 2004a; Kawai and Urata, 2002). According to recent calculations made by Urata (2004) intra-regional exports as a percentage of region's total exports for Asia were 40.1 percent in 1990 and 47.5 percent in 2001. For NAFTA the corresponding proportions were 41.4 percent and 54.6 percent, respectively, while for the EU they were 66.0 percent and 60.8 percent,

[101] For these statistics refer to the World Trade Organization, *International Trade Statistics 2002*. Table III.3 (published in July 2003), and the World Trade Organization, *International Trade Statistics 2003*. Table III.3 (published in June 2004), respectively.

respectively. The WTO also computes intra-regional trade for various regions. It put intra-regional trade for Asia at 48.2 percent for 2001 and at 48.9 percent for 2002.[102]

A good measure of Asia's intra-regional trade is intra-regional exports in the context of total world exports. This measure signifies the degree of importance of Asia's intra-regional trade vis-à-vis total world trade, or Asia's intra-regional exports as a share of total world exports. Petri (1993) was the first to use it and christened it as the absolute measure and was subsequently used by several researchers. When the absolute measure was utilized, it was found that over the decades of the 1980s and 1990s, in many sub-regional groupings intra-regional trade increased substantially, in some cases it nearly doubled. Between 1980 and 2000, ASEAN's intra-regional trade almost doubled, although it cannot be ignored that it started from a very small base. As share of world exports, intra-regional exports of ASEAN increased from 0.7 percent in 1980 to 0.9 percent in 1980 and 1.6 percent in 2000.

When the absolute measure was used for the APT economies, intra-regional trade was found to have an identical trend. It increased from 3.7 percent in 1980 to 4.6 percent in 1990 and 7.0 percent in 2000. If the APT is expanded to include Hong Kong SAR and Taiwan, (we shall call it "All Asia") intra-trade expansion trend strengthens. That is, it rose from 4.6 percent in 1980 to 7.8 percent in 1990 to 12.7 percent in 2000. In the APEC group of countries, which is essentially is an Asia-Pacific group, intra-trade has expanded, but not as much as for the so-called All Asia group. In 1980, intra-APEC trade was 19.1 percent of the total, in 1990 it jumped to 27.1 percent and further to 35.6 percent in 2000. When the performance of different Asian regional groupings is compared to other regional groupings like NAFTA[103] and the EU, we notice that NAFTA followed the same pattern as the various Asian groupings. Its intra-trade was 5.5 percent of the total trade in 1980, which rose to 6.8 percent in 1990 and 10.7 percent in 2000. That is, intra-trade nearly doubles over the period under consideration. However, the EU, one of the largest and oldest RIAs of the contemporary period, was an exception to this general trend. The intra-trade trend reversed after increasing from 24.4 to 29.5 percent between 1980 and 1990. In 2000, the level of intra-trade declined to 22.3 percent.[104]

Another equally important measure of Asia's intra-regional trade juxtaposes Asia's intra-regional exports against its own total exports, or as a share of

---

[102] The two WTO sources are (i) World Trade Organization. *International Trade Statistics*. 2003. Table III.3. Intra- and Inter-Regional Trade, 2001 and (ii) World Trade Organization. *International Trade Statistics*. 2004. Table III.3. Intra- and Inter-Regional Trade, 2002.

[103] Refer to footnote 100.

[104] Sakakibara and Yamakawa (2003) Chapter IV, Part II. Table 4.2.

Asia's total exports. This measure signifies the degree of importance of Asia's intra-regional trade relatively to its extra-regional trade. Petri (1993) called it the relative measure of intra-trade. As statistics in the following paragraph reveal, the trends in both the measures, that is, intra-trade share vis-à-vis the world trade on the one hand and Asia's intra-trade vis-à-vis Asia's own total trade on the other, were similar over the last two decades.

ASEAN's intra-trade vis-à-vis ASEAN's total trade was 18.6 percent in 1980. It rose to 23.1 percent in 2000. Similarly APT's intra-trade vis-à-vis APT's total trade was 29.5 percent in 1980; it increased to 32.0 percent in 2000. For All Asia the proportion of intra-trade vis-à-vis total trade rose from 33.8 percent to 46.3 percent over the same period. Likewise for the larger APEC forum it rose from 57.9 percent to 73.2 percent over the period under consideration. For NAFTA, the corresponding proportions were 33.6 percent and 55.7 percent, respectively. For the EU, which is the most integrated of these regional groupings, these proportions were found to be the highest. EU's intra-trade vis-à-vis EU's total trade was 60.8 percent in 1980, and it increased to 62.1 percent in 2000 (Sakakibara and Yamakawa, 2003).[105] These two measures, namely absolute and relative, of intra-trade demonstrate that over the 1980–2000 period the proportion of intra-trade in Asia increased both as a share of world export and as a share of Asia's total exports. Thus, the two measures lead to the same inference.

3.2.4 Intra-regional production networks

Trend toward becoming the so-called natural trading partners took several decades of intensive process of intra-regional trade and investment among the Asian economies. Changes in currency value configuration and evolution of economic complementarities buttressed this trend. In step with the emergence of these trends, production locus shifted from the firms to mutually supporting networks of regional production, which led to a new synergy in the industrial development. Asian economies were pioneers in this respect.[106] Regional production networks soon became a significant force driving the process of economic integration in East and Southeast Asia as well as of globalization. They went far beyond horizontal and vertical integration of production of the yonder years in Asia. The integration of Malaysia, Thailand and the Pearl River basin of China with Northeastern Asian production has been one of the most noteworthy

[105] Sakakibara and Yamakawa (2003) Chapter IV, Part II. Table 4.3.

[106] For a detailed account of international production networks in Asia, please refer to Borrus et al. (2000).

developments in the spatial organization of the Asian economy since the Plaza Accord (see Chapter 5, Section 5.7 for greater detail).

Supply chain slicing, an integral part of the integrated production networks, and its management is generally a complex process and varies from industry to industry and firm to firm. Over the years Asian firms successfully developed skills and acumen to manage them efficaciously. Unlike in the past when the supply chain was vertically integrated and managed by one firm, each stage of the chain could operate independently and efficiently managed by an individual firm. This firm was usually located in a different country from the firms that are producing and supplying components and parts. In the context of a supply chain, a supplier does not imply a firm that merely supplies one or more components in a manufacturing process. A supplier firm makes a much more complex contribution to the production process by way of providing technical solutions. These supplier-cum-partner firms can be large TNCs to small but highly competitive design and engineering firms. In many areas markets have become highly specialized and require customized products. Therefore, a supply chain network requires co-operation between firms on a regional, even global, basis (Organization for Economic Co-operation and Development [OECD], 2003).[107]

One of the most striking changes in regional production since the Plaza Agreement has been the rapid shift of much of Northeast Asia's low-end consumer electronics production first to Malaysia and subsequently to Thailand. Most prominent was the massive investment by the Japanese electronics industry in these two economies. A similar pattern was followed by Taiwanese and, to a lesser extent, Korean electronics investment in Malaysia and Thailand. This large infusion of investment in the electronics industry in Malaysia and Thailand led to transfer in a mere five years (1996–2000) of much of low-end, export-oriented consumer electronics assembly industry that had been built up in Japan, Korea and Taiwan since the 1950s. Northeast Asian investment in the ASEAN-4 economies brought a number of changes to the structure of production and exchange in the electronics industry in Asia.

During the late 1980s, the production networks began to spread to Guangdong and Fujian provinces in south China, and a borderless economy encompassing a much larger region with different comparative advantages began to emerge. This sub-region rapidly enlarged due to the complementarities that existed among the economies. It now includes Hong Kong SAR,[108] Macao, Taiwan, and Southern provinces of China like Guangdong, Hainan, Fujian,

---

107 Refer to Part III of OECD (2003) for details regarding supply chain management.

108 On July 1, 1997, Hong Kong was returned to the People's Republic of China and became a Special Administrative Region (SAR) of China.

Zhejiang and Shanghai. Geographically proximate regions possessing different resource endowments tended to develop close trade and investment ties, further intensifying the production networks. As Taiwan moved into high-technology industries and Hong Kong SAR moved toward[109] becoming a services economy, China was well placed to receive the "sunset" industries that were being phased out from both the NIAEs. This reduced the pain of phasing out of these sunset industries of Hong Kong SAR and Taiwan, and to a lesser extent in Korea and Singapore. In the process the sunset industries got a new lease of life through relocation and the pace of industrialization in China quickened because of their relocation. This was China's opportunity to move up the industrial value chain into high-technology products faster.

Early in 2001, the government in Taiwan was considering removing all investment value ceiling on projects intended for relocation to the mainland, but closed off certain "strategic industries" like high-end electronics. Consequently, both the intra-trade and production networking and mutual industrial dependence of the two economies were on the rise (Sender, 2001). Malaysia and Thailand also integrated with the southern part of China by developing close trade and investment links, followed by production networks. Together this sub-region of Asia has shown enormous dynamism and, therefore, it is bound to expand in size, level of sophistication, and scope of co-operation. A clarification is necessary here. When the so-called sunset industries were moving from the NIAEs to China, the latter was not the recipient of passé or outmoded industries having little present or future market. Hong Kong SAR and Taiwan transferred their entire computer hardware sector to mainland China by the early 1990s, which can hardly be called an outmoded industry. The NIAEs upgraded domestic ICT industry in textbook fashion, creating a new division of labor between manufacturing activities in mainland China on the one hand and Hong Kong SAR and Taiwan on the other (EIU, 2003).

The regionalization of production increased the momentum of integration of regional economies. It came to be organized in ways that made the logic of Kaname Akamatsu's age-old flying geese hypothesis (Akamatsu, 1961) seem relevant. Superficially, integration of production lent credence to the avian analogy, but emerging organizational and spatial changes in production paradigms actually undermined many of its key assumptions. Akamatsu's hypothesis had naively failed to grasp the complexities of technological progress and technology transfer. Also, it predated the product life cycle theory, which explained regionalization of production much more convincingly than the avian analogy. The life cycle theory "took individual products as disembodies from larger industrial structures, whereby the life cycle of any given product can be treated

[109] Intra-regional production networks in East and Southeast Asia have been studied by Hansen (2001); OECD (2002); Fukasaku and Kimura (2002) and Sakakibara and Yamakawa (2003).

in isolation from myriad of other products and the organizational foundations that initially spawned it" (Chen and Ku, 2000). The new trend of production networks was most conspicuous in the electronics industry. This industry provides the most revealing illustration of how production linkages in Asia operate. They are more complex than the trade and investment data describe them. These production linkages are not limited to the electronics industry but have become common in numerous industries.

Over the last quarter century, two virtuous circles of economic growth operated in East and Southeast Asia and they benefited from them immensely. Openness to trade and investment resulted in the first virtuous circle. This can be called the domestic virtuous circle. The second was a regional virtuous circle, which explains the diffusion of economic growth from one group of dynamic economies to another. The production networks created by Asian firms were an inherent part of the second virtuous circle. Together these virtuous circles reinforced each other, leading to brisk real GDP growth in the regional economy. It *prima facie* appeared counter-intuitive because increased networking among firms that were themselves competitors, is generally not expected (Borrus et al., 2000). However, it developed as a new trend and is at present successfully operating and synergizing the economies in Japan, the NIAEs, ASEAN-4 and China. The trade-creating effects of investment stand to logic in the context of dynamic networking firms. These are the newest trends in the regional economy. The end result is closer integration and increasingly cohesive economic ties and greater regionalization of the Asian economies.[110]

3.3 IMPACT OF OTHER RIAs ON THE ASIA-PACIFIC ECONOMIES

That the regionalism has been on the rise in the global economy is a widely-acknowledged fact. The evidence regarding the stock of completed regional integration agreements (RIAs), and the large number of RIAs planned or under negotiation is a testimony to the basic attraction of such agreements to virtually all 147 WTO members.[111] At the turn of the century, both globalism and regionalism came to coexist in the global economy. WTO members (as, previously, GATT contracting parties) are required to notify the regional integration agreements (RIAs) in which they participate. Some members are party to 20 or

[110] Refer to Das, 1996. Chapters 4 and 5 deal with this issue at great length and also provide relevant statistical data.

[111] As of July 2004, the WTO had 147 members and 31 countries had the observer status. Nepal, a least developed country (LDC), has joined the World Trade Organization, becoming its 147th member in April 2004. With such large membership, the WTO is almost a global institution.

more RIAs. In the 1948–94 period, the GATT received 124 notifications of RIAs (relating to trade in goods), and since the creation of the WTO (between January 1995 and October 2003) 149 regional agreements in trade in goods and services were notified to the WTO, which implies approximately 15 RIAs being formed annually. Not all RIAs notified in the last half century are still in force today. Many of the discontinued RIAs have, however, been superseded by re-designed agreements among the same signatories (Das, 2004a).

Total number of notified RIAs stood at 250 in March 2002 (WTO, 2002). According to the 2003 *Annual Report* of the WTO, 159 agreements were still in force in 2001, and in 2002 alone 20 additional RIAs were notified to the WTO. This brought total number of RIAs notified to the WTO by December 2002 to 177 (WTO, 2003). The upward surge in RIAs was most strongly felt in the Asia-Pacific region, where countries were long in favor of multilateral-only liberalization. Japan was one such country that became the latest RIA convert among the WTO members with the entry into force of its free-trade area (FTA) with Singapore in November 2002.

Trade and investment diversion would cause the Asian economies to lose out some of their export markets and FDI due to the presence of such a large number of RIAs in the global economy. Several scholars have devoted themselves to the issue of the impact of RIA formation over the Asian economies. In an extensive study, Frankel and Wei (1997) provided a comprehensive survey of various empirical studies done to reckon the effect of major RIAs on the Asian economies.[112] Studies of Canada—U.S. Free-Trade Area (CUSFTA) show a decline in trade with third-world countries in general (Braga et al., 1994; Cox and Harris, 1992). If anything, the developing Asian economies have more to lose from NAFTA because their labor-intensive manufactured products will lose some of the Canadian and U.S. markets to Mexico. Noland (1994) estimated that NAFTA could divert trade from the Korea, which could amount to 1 to 3 percent of total Korean exports. Similar trade diversions were to be experienced by the other NIAEs. A large part (almost two-thirds) of this estimated impact was to be in textiles, spinning and weaving sectors where Multifiber Arrangement (MFA) quotas were applicable. Hufbauer and Schott (1994) estimated that NAFTA could divert from Korea, and Taiwan manufactured exports worth $300 million annually that previously went to the United States. According to them, machinery and transport equipment sectors were to suffer largest loss of export markets. The range of estimates for effects on Southeast and South Asia were found to be similar by Hufbauer and Schott (1994). They estimated that Southeast and South Asian developing economies, excluding Korea and Taiwan, would lose $350 million in manufactured exports. Again,

[112] This section has benefited from the Frankel and Wei (1997) survey.

machinery and transport equipment sectors were to be the hardest hit sectors. The other two sectors that would be most adversely affected were clothing and consumer goods. Exports of primary products from these countries would also be adversely affected, to the extent of $100 million.

Safadi and Yeats (1993) examined the effects of NAFTA on the South Asian economies alone and inferred that trade diversion effects would be concentrated in textiles and apparel sectors of the South Asian economies. Although industrialized countries pledged under the Uruguay Round to phase out their textile quotas by 2005, the schedule is so heavily back-loaded that NAFTA could make a big difference to textiles trade of South Asian economies (Das, 2000b). These estimates of impact are not trivial, but are not particularly large either. Part of the reason was that the U.S. tariffs were low to begin with. They were slightly lower against some Mexican goods than against imports from other industrial economies under the GSP. Safadi and Yeats posited that it was due to this that the scope for both trade creation and trade diversion in the U.S. market was small.

The United States and other industrial economies have had low tariff barriers. Not the same can be said about non-tariff barriers (NTBs) and administrative protection measures like antidumping duties.[113] Exports from Canada and Mexico to the United States do not face many NTBs, although they are not out of reach for antidumping actions. This has turned out to be an important benefit of an RIA. However, NTBs do adversely affect Asian exports to the United States. This mode of trade diversion does seem to be a valid concern of the Asian economies. Another similar snag is created by the rules of origin (ROO). They can be interpreted in such a manner as to divert Asian auto exports to the United States. It would benefit Mexican exporters at the expense of those from Asia. There are distinct possibilities of trade diversion. Rapid growth in Mexico–U.S. trade since 1993 seemed consistent with these concerns.

FDI is another concern of the Asian economies because both CUSFTA and NAFTA include provisions to promote investment within the RIA. It is logical to assume that this could cause diversion of investment from Asian economies to Mexico. Although this was a general concern of the Asian economies, portfolio investment was considered especially vulnerable because it is fungible and mobile across counties. McCleery (1993) argued that investment diversion is a more serious impact of NAFTA than trade diversion. According to him it would have a more serious adverse impact over the Asian economies. He calculated that Indonesia would lose 4 to 5 percent of FDI to NAFTA, which would cause a 2.2-percent decline in GDP. Malaysia would lose 5 to 7 percent of FDI, which would cause a 1.4-percent decline in GDP. Singapore is to lose 2 to 3 percent of

[113] Non-tariff barriers (NTBs) include para-tariff measures, price control measures, financial measures, monopolistic measures and technical measures.

FDI, which in turn would cause a 1.3-percent decline in GDP. For Thailand the loss would be 4 to 5 percent, leading to a 1.0-percent decline in GDP. These numbers seem to be biased upwards. Other Asian economies, according to McCleery (1993), would be affected less than these ASEAN countries. Kreinen (1998) predicted that a significant amount of FDI might be diverted from ASEAN economies to Mexico in the following sectors: food, chemicals, textiles, metals, transport equipment, and electronics. U.S. FDI in Mexico started growing rapidly in 1993. In future, as its economy liberalizes further and becomes more productive, Mexico might start attracting Japanese investment as well.[114]

As a hemisphere-wide FTAA was proposed in 1994 during the Miami Summit of the countries in Latin America, Hufbauer and Schott (1994) estimated its impact. For each major commodity group, they calculated how much of the increased U.S. imports from Latin America would divert trade from other trading partners. Their estimates indicated $7.3 billion worth of diversion of exports from the NIAEs annually by 2002. They concluded that this was equal to 2.6 percent of the NIAEs' exports to the U.S. market in that year. They also subdivided trade diversion in various sectors and found that textiles and apparel would be affected most. Almost 40 percent of the diversion was concentrated in the textiles and apparel sectors. The category of leather and leather products was the next affected sector, followed by primary metals and sporting goods. As for the South Asian economies, they similarly found that this country group would suffer large trade diversions in textiles and apparel sectors as well as food products sectors. Their estimates of total diversion were substantive. They estimated it at $3.2 billion, or 2.8 percent of the projected exports to the U.S. market.

Studies of trade creation and trade diversion effects of the EU formation found that tread creation is five to seven times larger than trade diversion (Kreinen, 1982). As regards the impact of SEM on the Asian economies, studies show that the Australia, New Zealand, NIAEs would gain from it, while Japan would experience trade diversion due to diversion of its skill-intensive exports to the EU. Even in the 1980s, and especially after 1992, the Japanese auto industry was particularly hit by the spread of import quotas from France and Italy to the other EU members. Both Anderson (1993) and Gundlach et al. (1993) concluded that Japanese exports of photocopiers, electric scales, electric typewriters and semiconductors have also been affected due to ROO interpretation of the EU. As opposed to this they found that primary commodity exports of the Asian economies would not be diverted. This was essentially because the EU economies neither produce them nor have any close substitutes. In 1995, the EU was enlarged to include some of the former members of the European

[114] Results of these empirical studies are presented here in a cursory manner. Greater details of these studies are available in Frankel and Wei (1997). Researchers dealing with this issue are advised to consult this detailed survey. It is acknowledged that this section draws heavily on Frankel and Wei survey.

Free-trade area (EFTA), namely Austria, Finland and Sweden. This should have affected the skill-intensive exports of Japan, although no empirical estimates are presently available. This is not likely to be the situation when 2004 enlargement of the EU takes place. Labor-intensive exporters of Asia would naturally suffer the consequences and their labor-intensive exports would be diverted to the 10 new members joining the EU.

3.4 NEED FOR REGIONAL CO-OPERATION IN THE AFTERMATH OF THE CRISIS

As the Asian markets and economies are open, they are progressively becoming integrated through trade, investment and production networks. With increasing integration, their macroeconomic performance becomes closely linked and business cycles in the partner economies tend to become synchronized (Shin and Wang, 2003). That is, what happens in one economy impinges upon the trade partner neighboring economies. It was painfully demonstrated by the currency and financial crisis of 1997–98 and is fresh in everybody's memory. The contagion that spread affected several economies and as many as seven Asian economies contracted simultaneously in 1998 (Chapter 2, Section 2.8). This likelihood makes it imperative for the regional economies not to be indifferent to the macroeconomic and financial policies in the other economies as well as in the destabilizing events if they occur.

Although not all the crises lead to contagions, they are real and frequent and are considered a serious downside of financial globalization (Das, 2004b). Fundamental linkages between the economies are generally responsible for causing the contagion effect. There can be myriad channels for the crisis to spillover to the neighboring countries. This includes factors unrelated to fundamentals, such as herding behavior. De Gregorio and Valdes (2001) inferred that there was a strong neighborhood effect in the contagion that followed the Asian crisis. Trade links and similarity in pre-crisis growth also explained (albeit to a lesser extent) which countries suffered greater contagion.

Secondly, as intra-regional trade has accounted for almost half of the total trade in Asia and as many Asian economies compete with each other in the global market place, exchange rate policies in one country significantly influence the trade and economic growth in the other regional economies. Therefore, a mechanism for co-operation in exchange rate regime would potentially lead to a co-operative equilibrium benefiting the regional economies *en masse*. The alternative to this co-operative equilibrium is Nash non-co-operative equilibrium, which implies competitive currency depreciations.[115]

---

[115] For a succinct account of Nash non-co-operative equilibrium refer to Myerson (1999). It is widely considered a major breakthrough in economic thinking.

Third, the Asian crisis revealed that access to adequate liquidity could protect an individual economy when it was under pressure from speculators. There has been a perception among Asian policymakers that the existing multilateral mechanism for providing emergency liquidity did not serve Asian economies adequately when there was a pressing need of the liquidity. In addition, they felt that the liquidity provided by the IMF was inadequate, slow in disbursement and came with inappropriate conditionality, in the process sending wrong market signals and worsening the crisis situation. As reserves accumulation among the like-minded regional economies to avert a future crisis is an expensive process, the cooperating economies need to plan for and enhance macroeconomic and monetary co-operation among them. Designing pooling and disbursement mechanism both call for macroeconomic coordination (Das, 2003; de Brouwer, 2002).

3.5 IMPEDIMENTS TO REGIONALIZATION

Reasonably low logistics costs and high-quality infrastructure are among the essentials for the progress of regionalization. The two could be taken for the preconditions for regionalization. Higher logistics costs and a weak infrastructure effectively impede regionalization. In addition, for improving market access, promoting trade and enhancing competitive advantage in the regional market place, certain aspects of logistics needs to be paid extra attention. While trade growth was impressive in Asia, trade logistics, particularly transport systems did not keep pace with it in many economies. As economies in the other parts of the globe are working on it, Asian economies should also endeavor for logistics development for sustaining their competitive edge. In several Asian economies, higher logistics costs essentially stem from poor transport infrastructure, poorly developed transport and logistics services and slow and expensive bureaucratic procedures for imports and exports. A recent survey indicated the significance of having efficient ports for trade in terms of operational efficiency and document facilitation for competitiveness in trading operations (Wilson et al., 2002). Limao and Venables (2001) estimated that differences in infrastructure quality account for 40 percent of variation in transport costs in coastal Asian countries and 60 percent in landlocked countries, or landlocked areas in the countries.

Operational efficiency at entry or exit ports forms only one aspect of the connection between logistics and trade competitiveness. If one divides the cost of getting products from producers to their markets into its various segments, the largest cost is incurred in the land transport of exportables to the domestic port. It is frequently higher than the cost of processing within the port as well as maritime transport costs. Thus, in several Asian economies it is the improvement in land access that is required to be made cost efficient (Carruthers et al., 2003). Successful manufacturers, particularly those integrated into global production chains and integrated production networks, also need to have the shortest possible transit time, dependable delivery schedules, safe and proper handling of goods, certification of origin to fulfill the rules of origin (ROO) requirements and certification of product quality.

The survey conducted by Wilson et al. (2002) indicated that, for one, there are enormous differences in the quality of infrastructure and logistics in the Asian economies. These differences were directly related to the trade performance of the country in question. The more successful trader an economy was, the better logistics and infrastructure it had. Second, several Asian economies lagged behind in infrastructure development, logistics improvement and trade facilitation. The last named item includes customs clearance and regulatory administration. For instance, for China, as one moves inland the quantity of trade, and quality of transport infrastructure and logistics decline with the distance from the coast (Wei and Yi, 2001).

Carruthers and Bajpai (2002) plotted a graph between accessibility and logistics of the Asian economies on the x-axis and openness on the y-axis. The economies that had high accessibility with the world and good logistics were Singapore, Taiwan, Hong Kong SAR, Japan, Korea and coastal China, in that order. The next category of moderately poor logistics and accessibility included Malaysia, Thailand and the Philippines, in that order. The third category of poor logistics and accessibility included inland China, inland Thailand, Mindnao part of the Philippines, Vietnam and Indonesia. The third category of countries and areas also had the highest trade facilitation costs.

3.6 CONCLUSIONS AND SUMMARY

Notwithstanding the fact that the approximately half of the trade is presently intra-regional, the Asia-Pacific region was late in adopting regionalism in its institutionalized form. Progressively liberalizing trade and FDI regime underpinned market-led regionalization in Asia. The market expansion and regional integration that took place in Asia was both vertical and horizontal. First the NIAEs and then the other emerging market economies of Asia developed tiers of complex trade and manufacturing hierarchies. This occurred in association with the large flows of intra-regional investment into Southeast Asia and China. Over the preceding quarter century, Japan, Taiwan and Korea provided massive amounts of FDI to Southeast Asian economies and China, and in the process increased their commitments in these markets.

In the beginning of the twentieth century, intra-trade in Asia was well developed. During the early decades, intra-trade was close to half the total trade in Asia. It was dominated by Japan's colonial pattern of economic relations. After 1931, the Japanese colonial pattern of trade gave way to building independent industrial capacity outside Japan, essentially in China, Korea and Taiwan. This kind of economic relations between Japan and Asian economies led to significant intra-regional investment as well as development of regional transportation and communications infrastructure networks. Gradual development of Asian production networks supported mutually reinforcing trade and investment. The result was creation of complex regional economic ties among these economies as well as trade dependencies. Increasing trade dependence of Asia is clearly reflected in a simple measure, namely, intra-regional trade as a share of total trade of the region.

During the 1970s, a triangular production relationship had developed between Japan, the NIAEs and the United States, bringing the former two sets of economies closer together. Japan supplied the necessary components and technology to the NIAEs, which in turn produced and competitively marketed industrial products to the U.S. market. After the Plaza Accord in 1985, the currency value configuration changed. The dollar had reached a high against the yen in early 1985, which intensified imports from East and Southeast Asia into the U.S. market, and Japan was able to maintain its exports even as its production costs were rising vis-à-vis its Asian rivals. Changes in currency value configuration and economic complementaries buttressed this trend. Gradually production locus shifted from the firms to networks of regional production. Asian economies were pioneers in this respect. Production networks soon became a significant force driving the process of economic integration in East and Southeast Asia as well as of globalization. During the late 1980s, the production networks began to spread to Guangdong and Fujian provinces in south China, and a borderless economy encompassing a much larger region with different comparative advantages began to emerge.

Reasonably low logistics costs and high-quality infrastructure are among the essentials for the progress of regionalization. The two could be taken for the preconditions for regionalization. Higher logistics costs and a weak infrastructure effectively impede regionalization. There is a good deal of diversity in the quality of infrastructure and logistics. The economies that had high accessibility with the world and good logistics were Singapore, Taiwan, Hong Kong SAR, Japan, Korea and coastal China, in that order. The next category of moderately poor logistics and accessibility included Malaysia, Thailand and the Philippines, in that order. The third category of poor logistics and accessibility included inland China, inland Thailand, Mindnao part of the Philippines, Vietnam and Indonesia. The third category of countries and areas also had the highest trade facilitation costs.

REFERENCES

Akamatsu, K. 1961. "A theory of unbalanced growth in the world economy," *Weltwirtschaftliches Archiv.* Vol. 86. No. 1. pp. 56–58.

Anderson, K. 1993. "European integration in the 1990s: Implications for world trade and for Australia," in D.G. Mayes (ed) *External Implications of European Integration.* London: Harvester Wheatsheaf. pp. 120–148.

Beasley, W.G. 1987. *Japanese Imperialism, 1894–1945.* Oxford: Clarendon Press.

Bernard, M. and J. Ravenhill. 1995. "Beyond production cycles and flying geese: Regionalization, hierarchy, and industrialization of East Asia," *World Politics.* Vol. 47. January. pp. 171–209.

Borrus, M., D. Ernst and S. Haggard (eds). 2000. *International Production Networks in Asia.* London and New York: Routledge.

Braga, C., A. Primo, R. Safadi and A. Yeats. 1994, October. *NAFTA's Implications for East Asian Exports.* Washington, DC: World Bank. Policy Research Working Paper No. 1351.

Carruthers, R. and J.N. Bajpai. 2002. *Trends in Trade Logistics: An Asian Perspective.* Washington, DC: The World Bank. Transport Sector Unit. Working Paper No. 2.

Carruthers, R., J.N. Bajpai and D. Hummels. 2003. "Trade and logistics: An East Asian perspective," in K. Krumm and H.J. Kharas (eds) *East Asia Integrates: A Trade Policy Agenda for Shared Growth.* Washington, DC: The World Bank. pp. 117–139.

Chen, T. and Y.H. Ku. 2000. "Globalization of Taiwan's small firms: The role of Southeast Asia and China," paper presented in a symposium on *Experiences and Challenges of Economic Development in Southeast and East Asia,* Taipei. 20–21 October, 2000.

Cox, D. and R. Harris. 1992. "North American free trade and its implications for Canada: Results from a CGE model of North American trade," *World Economy.* Vol. 15. No. 1. pp. 31–44.

Credit Swiss First Boston (CSFB, December 15). 2000. *Emerging Market Quarterly: Asia Q1:2001.* Hong Kong CSFB.

Das, Dilip K. 1993. *The Yen Appreciation and the International Economy.* London: The Macmillan Press.

Das, Dilip K. 1996. *The Asia-Pacific Economy.* London: The Macmillan Press.

Das, Dilip K. 1998. "Changing comparative advantage and changing composition of Asian exports," *The World Economy.* Vol. 21. No. 1. January. pp. 121–140.

Das, Dilip K. 2000a. "Asian exports: The present predicament," in Dilip K. Das (ed) *Asian Exports.* Oxford: Oxford University Press. pp. 1–24.

Das, Dilip K. 2000b. "An action agenda for the next WTO round: A post-Seattle perspective," *The Journal of World Intellectual Property.* Vol. 3. No. 5. September. pp. 7370–7773.

Das, Dilip K. 2003. "Emerging market economies: Inevitability of volatility and contagion," *Journal of Asset Management.* Vol. 4. No. 3. pp. 199–216.

Das, Dilip K. 2004a. *Regionalism in Global Trade.* Northampton, MA: Edward Elgar.

Das, Dilip K. 2004b. *The Economic Dimensions of Globalization.* London: Palgrave Macmillan.

de Brouwer, G. 2002. "PECC survey of regional arrangements for financial co-operation," paper presented to PECC Finance Forum meeting in Honolulu, Hawai'i, August 12.

De Gregorio, J. and R.O. Valdes. 2001. "Crisis transmission: Evidence from the debt, Tequila and Asian flu crises," *World Bank Economic Review.* Vol. 15. No. 2. pp. 289–314.

The Economist. 2000. "Asian economies: Happy neighbors." August 26. p. 71.

The Economic Intelligence Unit (EIU). 2003, July. *Leaping Dragon, Trailing Tigers? Taiwan Hong Kong and the Challenge of Mainland China.* London: EIU.

The Economic Intelligence Unit (EIU). 2004. *China's Real GDP Forecast.* Available at: http://english.peopledaily.com.cn/200301/25/print20030125_110713.html.

Frankel, J.A. 1997. *Regional Trading Blocs in the World Economic System,* Washington, DC: Institute for International Economics.

Frankel, J.A. and S.J. Wei. 1997. "The New Regionalism and Asia: Impact and Options", N.P. Rao and A. Panagariya (eds) *The Global Trading System and Developing Asia*, Hong Kong. Oxford University Press. pp. 83–135.

Fukasaku, K. and F. Kimura. 2002. "Globalization and intra-firm trade: Further evidence," in P.J. Lloyd and H.H. Lee (eds) *Frontiers of Research in Intra-Industry Trade.* Basingstoke: Palgrave Macmillan. pp. 130–162.

Gundlach, E., U. Hiemenz, R. Langhammer, P. Langhammer and P. Nunnenkamp, 1993. "Regional integration in Europe and its impact on developing countries," in K. Ohno (ed) *Regional Integration and Its Impact on Developing Countries.* Tokyo: Institute of Developing Economies. pp. 134–158.

Hansen, G. 2001. *Should Countries Promote Foreign Direct Investment?* Geneva: United Nations Conference on Trade and Development. G-24. Discussion Paper Series No. 9.

Hufbauer, G. and J. Schott. 1994. "Regionalism in North America." in K. Ohno (ed) *Regional Integration and Its Impact on Developing Countries.* Tokyo: Institute of Developing Economies.

Ikenberry, J.G. 2000. "The political economy of Asia-Pacific regionalism," *East Asian Economic Perspective.* March. Vol. 2. pp. 35–61.

Kawai, M. and S. Urata. 2002. "Trade and foreign direct investment in East Asia," paper presented at the international conference on *Linkages in East Asia: Implications for Currency Regime and Policy Dialogue,* held in Seoul, September 12–13.

Kreinen, M. 1982. "Effect of EC enlargement on trade in manufactures," *Kyklos.* Heft 108. No.3. pp. 110–138.

Kreinen, M. 1998. "Multinationalism, regionalism, and their implications for Asia," paper presented at the Conference on Global Interdependence and Asia-Pacific Co-operation, Hong Kong, June 8–10.

Krueger, A.O. 2004. *Lessons From the Asian Crisis.* Keynote address at the SEACEN Meeting, in Colombo, Sri Lanka, February 12.

Lewis, J.D. and S. Robinson. 1996. *Partners or Predators? The Impact of Regional Trade Liberalization on Indonesia.* Washington, DC: The World Bank. Policy Research Working Paper No. 1626.

Limao, N. and A. Venables. 2001. "Infrastructure, geographical disadvantage, transport cost and trade," *The World Bank Economic Review.* Vol. 15. No. 2. pp. 451–471.

McCleery, R. 1993. "Modeling NAFTA: Macroeconomic effects," in K. Ohno (ed) *Regional Integration and Its Impact on Developing Countries.* Tokyo: Institute of Developing Economies. pp. 42–60.

Myerson, R.B. 1999. "Nash equilibrium and the history of economic theory," *The Journal of Economic Literature.* Vol. 36. No. 3. pp. 1067–1082.

Ng, F. and A. Yeats. 2003, June. *Major Trade Trends in Asia.* Washington, DC: The World Bank. World Bank Policy Research Working Paper 3084.

Noland, M. 1994. "Asia and the NAFTA," in Y. S. Kim and K. S. Oh (eds) *The US–Korea Economic Partnership.* U.K. Aldershot, and Brookfield, Vermont: Ashgate Publishers. pp. 134–148.

Organization for Economic Co-operation and Development (OECD). 2002. *Foreign Direct Investment for Development: Maximizing Benefits and Minimizing Costs.* Paris: OECD.

Organization for Economic Co-operation and Development (OECD). 2003. *Attracting International Investment for Development.* Paris: OECD.

Petri, P.A. 1993. *Regionalism and Rivalry: Japan and the United States in Pacific Asia.* Chicago: University of Chicago Press. pp. 21–52.

Petri, P. A. 1994. "The East Asian trading bloc: An analytical history," in R. Garnaut and P. Drysdale (eds) *Asia Pacific Regionalism: Readings in International Economic Relations.* Sydney: Harper Educational Publishers. pp.107–124.

Petri, P.A. 1997. "Measuring and comparing progress in APEC," *ASEAN Economic Bulletin.* Vol. 14. No. 1.

Safadi, R. and A. Yeats. 1993. The North American Free Trade Agreement: Its effect on South Asia. *Journal of Asian Economics.* Vol. 5. No. 2. pp. 197–216.

Sakakibara, E. and S. Yamakawa. 2003, June. *Regional Integration in East Asia: Challenges and Opportunities.* Part I and Part II. Washington, DC: Policy Research Working Paper Nos. 3078 and 3079.

Sender, H. 2001. "China steps up chip production," *The Asian Wall Street Journal.* January 10, p. N1–N2.

Shin, K. and Y. Wang. 2003. "Trade integration and business cycle: Synchronization in East Asia," *Asian Economic Papers.* Vol. 2. No. 3. pp. 1–29.

Urata, S. 2004. "Regional Economic Integration, Economic Growth and infrastructure in East Asia". Tokyo. Wased University. January. Available on the Internet at http://www.countryanalyticwork.net/CAW/Cawdoclib.nfs/0/AEC725C4F7D9241E85256E440058A724/$file/Manila+Wrkshop_SESSION+3_Urata.pdf. Access date June 12, 2004.

Wei, S.J. and W. Yi. 2001, March. *Globalization and Inequality: Evidence From China.* Cambridge, MA: National Bureau of Economic Research. NBER Working Paper No. 8611.

Wilson, J., C. Mann, Y.P. Woo, N. Assani and I. Choi. 2002. "Trade facilitation: A development perspective in the Asia Pacific region," paper prepared for the APEC conference, The World Bank Washington, DC.

World Trade Organization (WTO). 1995, March. *Regional and the World Trading Systems.* Geneva: WTO.

World Trade Organization (WTO). 1999. *Annual Report 1999.* Geneva: WTO.

World Trade Organization (WTO). 2002. "Regional Trade Integration under Transformation", Background paper prepared by the Trade Policy Review Division of the WTO for the conference on *The Changing Architecture of the Global Trading System*, organized by the World Trade Organization on 26 April, in Geneva.

World Trade Organization (WTO). 2003. *Annual Report 2003.* Geneva: WTO.

World Trade Organization (WTO). 2004, April 5. *World Trade 2003, Prospects For 2004.* Press Release. No. Press/373.

Chapter 4

CONTEMPORARY INITIATIVES IN INSTITUTIONALIZED REGIONAL INTEGRATION

4.1 REGIONAL INTEGRATION AND THE GLOBAL ECONOMY

The genesis of the notion of creating some kind of a formal regional grouping or economic community in Asia can be traced back to the Meiji era, in the mid-nineteenth century. Formal regionalism is the high light of this chapter. It aims at examining regional integration agreements (RIAs) and their economic impact on the Asian economies. Functionally, if somewhat loosely, a RIA could be defined as any agreement of preferential trade in which a set of trading partners reciprocally reduce trade barriers. The trading partners may or may not be contiguous or even close to each other. Page (2000) defined an RIA as a group of countries, which have "created a legal framework of co-operation covering an extensive economic relationship, with the intention that it will be of indefinite duration, and with the possibility foreseen that the region will economically evolve in the future."

Proliferation of RIA recorded a sharp rise in the 1990s. A total of 87 RIAs were notified to the GATT–WTO system during the 1990–99 period (Fukase and Martin, 2001). After the creation of the World Trade Organization (WTO), a spurt was noted in the RIA formulation. Between January 1995 and May 2004, 159 RIA were notified to the WTO. The process of RIA formation has recently gained a great deal of momentum. The period following the launch of the Doha Round of multilateral trade negotiations (MTNs)[116] has been prolific in terms

[116] The Doha Round of multilateral trade negotiations (MTNs) was launched following the Doha Ministerial Conference of the WTO, which was held during November 9–13, 2001.

of notifications of RIAs. By June 2004, a total of 211 RIAs of different kinds[117] were notified to the GATT–WTO system; the latest notification was that of the EU enlargement that took place in May 2004 (Das, 2004).

In 2004, four global tends were conspicuous in regional integration. First, economies that traditionally adhered to the principle of most-favored-nation (MFN) liberalization—that is, beyond the negotiated commitments they undertook under the aegis of the GATT and WTO, they preferred to reduce their tariff barriers only on a unilateral and non-discriminatory basis—are progressively changing their stance and adopting the concept of RIAs, which are based on the principle of discriminatory liberalization. Second, those economies that had affinity for and adhered to regionalism are increasingly seeking cross-regional and cross-continental partners at present. For instance, Republic of Korea (hereinafter Korea) entered into a free trade agreement (FTA) with Chile in April 2004. Third, mega-RIAs and plurilateral FTAs like the Free Trade Area of the Americas (FTAA), the Euro-Mediterranean Partnership Agreement (EMPA) and Euro-Mediterranean FTAs, which link large number of economies, are under formation. Fourth, a new, if excessive, fervor for bilateral FTAs has been noticed, which has enhanced after the culmination of the Fifth Ministerial Conference of the WTO without an agreement at Cancún, Mexico (Section 4.6).

As tariffs have declined worldwide, therefore the focus of contemporary FTAs has shifted toward other issues, including rules governing foreign direct investment (FDI), e-commerce regulations, trade in services, as well as trade facilitation issues like harmonization of technical standards, sanitary and phytosanitary (SPS) regulations, technical barriers to trade (TBTs) and streamlining of customs procedures. As alluded to in the preceding paragraph, several important traders like Australia, Japan, Republic of Korea, Mexico, New Zealand, Singapore and the United States (U.S.), had a history of sincere adherence of multilateralism and the MFN principle. However, that was past. After the failure of the Seattle Ministerial (1999) they began participating in RIAs. Of late, they have exhibited eagerness to sew up a web of bilateral free trade deals. They do not seem to have anything against RIAs or even bilateral trade agreements. Japan relied completely on the multilateral-only liberalization in the past, but it entered into a bilateral FTA with Singapore in November 2002 and was also actively pursuing preferential trade agreements with Korea and Mexico. Japan and Korea expected to use their bilateral trade agreements later on as a bridge to other free-trade constellations. Australia–Singapore

[117] A regional integration agreement (RIA) can be of a shallow variety, or it can be a deep integration. The former includes a preferential trade agreement (PTA), a free trade agreement (FTA) and a customs union (CU), while the latter includes a common market (CM) and an economic and monetary union (EMU).

FTA and services agreement of July 2003 were another importation illustration of the changing mindset in important trading economies (Das, 2004; WTO, 2003).

When tariff barriers are eliminated to create an RIA, share of imports from partner economies rises. Schiff and Winters (2003) made a before-and-after comparison and found that this observation holds for around 80 percent of the RIAs. "These results look like cause for celebration, for strong international trade performance is now generally accepted as one of the main determinants of economic prosperity. However, before breaking out the champagne we need to ask whether every increase in trade is desirable and whether these increases are actually due to regionalism." If exports from a constituent member of the RIA displace domestic output in the importing economy because once the tariff is eliminated the exporting partner's product becomes more competitive in the domestic market, the domestic economy benefits from two classical sources of gains from trade. First, real domestic resources are saved and production is diverted in the direction of comparative advantage of the economy. Second, domestic consumers benefit from lower, undistorted prices. This is trade creation and its impact is unambiguously favorable for the domestic economy. Further ahead in this chapter we shall see how various RIAs developed in Asia and what was their impact on the regional economy.

Forming an RIA naturally influences trade flows and their directionality and, therefore, production patterns in the economies that are constituent members of that RIA undergo alteration. Locations of production facilities in the constituent member countries are seriously influenced by RIA formation. As alluded to above, enlargement of national or "home" market by way of regional integration is another major economic impact of RIA formation over the domestic economy. An RIA per se is far from benign. Schiff and Winters (2003) remarked that, "A well crafted trade bloc can raise efficiency—and economic welfare—in its member countries by facilitating consumer choice and increasing the competition that producers face. Dropping tariff barriers enlarges markets and gives more efficient producers entry into countries where their prices had been inflated by duties and other trade barriers." Here the emphasis needs to be on well-crafted trading bloc.

To be sure, the fundamental benefit of an RIA is the larger regional market, which provides scale economies to firms, in turn leading to efficiency gains. Larger market also tends to attract greater investment, including more FDI. This argument applies *a fortiori* to the contemporary wave of new regionalism. Larger manufacturing and services sector projects for which market size matters become feasible for the first time due to the formation of an RIA. Dismantling of regional trade barriers also forces firms from different member countries into more intense competition with each other than it was feasible before the RIA was formed. This induces firms to make efficiency improvements and raise their level of total factor productivity (TFP). Thus, the immediate impact of enlarged markets is larger firms and enhanced competition.

Trade theory posited that trade liberalization enhances economic welfare by ushering in efficiency in the liberalizing economy. Trade policy liberalization undertaken to join an RIA takes an economy toward this objective, albeit a better motive would be to liberalize in a non-discriminatory manner, in keeping with the most-favored-nation (MFN) principle promoted by Article I of the WTO, Article II of the GATS and Article IV of the Trade-Related Aspects of Intellectual Property Rights (TRIPS) agreement. The language of Article I of GATT-1947 is subsumed in GATT-1994, which unequivocally states that, "With respect of customs duties and charges of any kind . . . any advantage, privilege, favor, or immunity granted by contracting party to any product originating in or destined for any other country shall be accorded immediately and unconditionally to the like product originating in or destined for the territories of all other contracting parties" (GATT, 1994).[118]

Neo-classical analysis would support this line of logic. As stated above, RIAs are widely considered the second best approach to trade liberalization. It is also well established that RIAs help in making a valuable contribution by giving early partial delivery of some of the benefits of liberalization, which can be expected from full MFN-consistent liberalization. However, Scollay (2000) has emphasized that this favorable impact of an RIA is subject to the proviso that adequate precaution is taken to ensure that trade diversion effects do not outweigh trade creation effects, and the dynamic gains arising from regional liberalization, which can include productivity gains stimulated by increased competition and exploitation of economies of scale made possible by access to a large market. RIAs also enable developing economies to phase in their integration into global markets.

The favorable impact of an RIA is conditional. The limiting condition is that RIAs are able to achieve a deeper degree of economic integration than the multilateral trading system. This is well within the realm of feasibility because RIAs usually entail neighboring like-minded countries. A smaller forum making negotiations on new trade issues, easier than a larger group of countries, has a fighting chance of working. A smaller group of like-minded neighboring countries also makes it possible to establish the necessary centralized institutions or

---

[118] In trade economics, the two expressions, namely, the GATT-1947 and the GATT-1994, are frequently used. The difference between the two is that that the latter is the revised version of the original GATT Agreement of 1947. The text of the Agreement was significantly revised and amended during the Uruguay Round and the new version was agreed upon in Marrakesh, Morocco. Apparently, the GATT-1994 reflected the outcome of the negotiations on issues relating to the interpretations of specific articles. In its renewed version, the GATT-1994 includes specific understandings with respect to GATT Articles, its obligations and provisions, plus the Marrakesh Protocol of GATT-1994.

federalizing policymaking and enforcement institutions. Economic theory suggests that RIAs can be so designed as to have favorable impact and be welfare improving, but in a real life situation "the necessary information, the incentives and the legal rights to manipulate the instruments of trade policy to guarantee such outcomes are missing."

Also, politically regions may well be more willing to agree to liberalization than individual economies. The post-war experience with the EEC confirms this observation. The Kennedy Round (1964–67) would not have taken-off without the EEC support. During that period, individual economies were reluctant to deepen their trade liberalization. France and Italy were resisting making any trade concession in the 1960s and Germany would not have made concessions in isolation from its close trading partners. However, as a group, EEC supported the Kennedy Round MTNs.

4.2 AGGLOMERATION OR CLUSTERING EFFECT

To be sure, the principle of comparative advantage is a force to reckon with in influencing the location and/or relocation decisions in an RIA. These decisions are also significantly driven by the agglomeration or clustering effect. Fujita et al. (1999) posited the concept of "cumulative causation," which implies that as clusters of manufacturing activity—or, say, economic activity in general—start to develop in a country and/or in an RIA, a spatial clustering or agglomeration of economic activity takes place assisting the location-specific development. The advantages of starting at a specific location provide an industry, or economic activity, a head start.

Age-old dictum is that in all economic activity, spatial clustering is all-pervasive. Why do towns and cities come into existence? It is because economic agents—consumers, producers, workers and capital owners—benefit from being in close proximity of each other. There is a strong symbiotic bond between them. A particular type of economic activity finds an appropriate location and creates a spatial cluster at that location. It has long been the story of industrialization, of which Detroit and Silicon Valley are two good contemporary examples. The banking activity is concentrated in the global financial centers like Wall Street in New York and the City in London for the same reasons. Numerous other industries provide examples of spatial clustering in one, or a few, locations.

Various centripetal forces that pull economic activity toward the spatial cluster are responsible for their creation. One of the most important centripetal forces is the knowledge spillovers and technological externalities that make it logical for firms to locate in the vicinity of each other. Second, availability of industrial skills and labor market pools encourage firms to be in a location where they are available readily, or where trained human resources are available and their skills can be augmented according to the specific needs of an individual firm at a reasonable cost. Third, the buyer-seller proximity is another important force pulling firms together in a specific location. Some firms produce inputs for the other firms and are vertically integrated with them. If the two sets of firms are close to each other, they both benefit from the proximity. In the theory of unbalanced growth, propounded by Albert O. Hirschman, this phenomenon was explained with the help of the "backward" or demand linkage and "forward" or supply linkage.[119] Fujita et al. (1999) formally established that these linkages create a positive interdependence between the location decisions of different firms and industries. This can give rise to the process of cumulative causation creating agglomeration of economic activity. Here the assumption is that the production activity has increasing return to scale.

The centripetal forces, when they operate at an aggregated level create backward linkages. That is, aggregate demand created by them strengthens the backward linkages drawing firms from different sectors into locations with large markets. At the aggregate level, agglomeration forces generate the need for a broad class of business activity and create a market demand for basic industrial infrastructure like financial and telecommunication services. There are real efficiency gains from spatial concentration. As opposed to this, centripetal forces can be spatially focused. Need and availability of highly specialized inputs or technologically narrow knowledge spillover operate to create clusters of narrowly defined industries or mere industrial sectors, rather than a broad manufacturing cluster. Creation of Silicon Valley is an excellent illustration of this kind of clustering. Conversely, congestion, pollution, rising prices of office space, land or other immobile factors of production pull a cluster in the opposite direction. Also, rising level of competition is another factor that can deter the spatial clustering process. Usually they strengthen after the cluster acquires a large size, and seems saturated.

Membership of an RIA affects the creation or expansion of spatial clusters. With such a membership, tariff and non-tariff barriers go down, or are eliminated. This makes forward and backward linkages stronger. Larger number of firms can participate in the creation of spatial clusters after the RIA formation. The opposite also holds; that is, an RIA makes it possible to supply goods to consumers from a small number of spatial clusters. This implies that forming an RIA tips the balance in favor of creation of larger agglomerations, until the centrifugal forces start operating in the opposite direction.

There is a strong possibility that formation of an RIA may generate more spatial concentration of sectors, rather than aggregate level industrial

---

119 Albert O. Hirschman propounded this theory in his book *The Strategy of Economic Growth,* published in 1958 by the Yale University Press, New Haven, Connecticut. Half a century ago, his theory became exceedingly popular among the academic and policymaking communities.

concentrations in the constituent member economies. For instance, industries in the United States are far more spatially concentrated than in Europe. This observation holds even after controlling for the distribution of population and manufacturing activity. Therefore, regional integration process in Europe could well advance agglomeration at the sectoral level. So far there is little evidence of relocation of industries in the EU on these lines, but if or when it happens it would result into considerable short-term adjustment costs for the European industrial sector. Industrial structure of member countries would change with relocation of industries. As there are real efficiency gains from spatial concentration, on balance there would be benefits from such industrial relocation and growth of spatial clusters. Sectoral agglomerations may also contribute to decrease in intra-RIA inequalities because each member country may attract industrial or services activity of one kind or the other.

One of the impacts of formation of an RIA could be a smaller number of large industrial agglomerations, which could deindustrialize some of the constituent members of an RIA and mark them as less favored regions. If this happens, some of the members of the RIA may grow and industrialize at the cost of others. Such an outcome is more plausible if manufacturing and services sectors are relatively small, that is, they account for a smaller share of the GDP. If the manufacturing sector is spatially limited to only a few locations, it is less likely to press against the supply constraints. It is also less likely to lead to rising prices of immobile factors like land. This is likely to take place at early stages of economic growth in a group of economies.[120]

4.2.1 Industrial and sectoral specialization in an RIA

As an RIA is created, inter- and intra-industry trade flows expand, and with that it is logical to expect that each member country's production structure would re-organized to exploit comparative advantage and possible benefits from spatial clustering of sectors. However, evidence from the EU reveals that regional integration resulted in only a modest increase in manufacturing specialization. Midelfart-Knarvik et al. (1999) computed measures of the difference between the industrial structures of the EU economies at the level of 36 different industrial sectors. They concluded that since 1970, all the EU economies except the Netherlands saw their industrial structures become more dissimilar and different from the other EU economies. That is, industrial structures of the EU economies were not becoming harmonized; if anything it was becoming dis-harmonized and specialized.

---

[120] See Venables (2002) for greater details. Also, refer to Midelfart-Knarvik and Overman (2002) for a discussion on the EU experiences in this regard.

The measures computed by Midelfart-Knarvik et al. (1999) were averaged over groups of countries according to the date of their accession to the EU. For the new entrants, it was observed that there was a more or less steady increase in the measures, which indicated that the industrial structure was becoming more dissimilar. Econometric analysis of these changing patterns of industrial and sectoral specialization indicated that it was largely in line with intra-EU comparative advantage. That is, labor-intensive and skilled-labor-intensive industries and sectors tended to relocate toward labor- and skilled-labor-abundant countries, and knowledge-intensive and R&D-intensive activities tended to relocate toward scientist-abundant countries (Midelfart-Knarvik and Overman, 2002). It should however be noted that reallocations in line with intra-EU comparative advantage are not necessarily salutary or welfare increasing, as they could result in trade diversion.

However, Venables and Winters (2003) contended that analysis at the level of countries, taking 36 industrial sectors, likely understates the degree of specialization that is taking place in the EU economies. At the level of narrow sectors, they believe that there is "evidence of increasing clustering of activity, and specialization is increasing at the sub-national as well as the national level." Despite this evidence of progress in clustering and specialization, it has been observed that the EU economies and regions remain very much less specialized than comparable size geographical units in the United States. Thus far, integration has not caused "specialization and clustering of activity to go as far as the U.S. experience suggests would be expected in a single country."

4.2.2 Foreign direct investment and RIAs

The FDI flows between countries are presently regulated by bilateral investment treaties (BITs). Approximately two thousand of them are in force, linking countries in all continents and at varying levels of development and stages of industrialization.[121] Typically, BITs are agreements with a "narrow" and specific purpose. Their objective is to remove barriers and uncertainty in the area of foreign investment. They are not made to encourage mutual investment between the two partners. In general, these bilateral treaties cover stipulations regarding admission and general treatment of investment, dispute settlement issues and other specific provisions. BITs defer to the domestic law of the home county, and the governments of the recipient country hold discretion to manage the sectors in which FDI is made. However, the United States has been more progressive than other investing countries in this regard and in most of its BITs insist on MFN and national treatment on the admission of investment (subject to explicit specific exceptions). Moreover, during the 1990s, when FDI assumed

[121] According to Heydon (2002), the precise number in 2000 was 1941.

a much more prominent role in development thinking, this approach began to find favor in other investing countries as well.

The BITs essentially call for fair and equitable treatment of FDI, security of ownership and freedom from unreasonable or discriminatory restrictions on the operation of investments. The MFN treatment in BITs implies that foreign investors should not be treated more favorably than are the partner country's residents, although, as in case of trade, this is subject to exceptions. In the context of RIAs, FDI from the RIA member countries is often treated more favorably. Dispute settlement provisions vary in BITs. However, most define arbitration procedures on the basis of international standards laid down by the organization established by World Bank Group. It is called International Center for Settlement of Investment Disputes (ICSID).

For the purpose of RIAs, the BITs have also been made into freestanding multi-country regional treaties. Agreement on Investment and Free Movement of Arab Capital among Arab Countries (of 1970) and the Colonia Protocol on the Promotion and Reciprocal Protection of Investment within Mercosur (of 1994) are two such treaties. A BIT can also form a part of an RIA. For example, the Andean Community, the EU, LAIA, NAFTA and Common Market for Eastern and Southern Africa (COMESA) all have elements of a BIT. Of these, the most far-reaching investment provisions are those of the EU. They had to be far-reaching because the EU was aimed at creating a Single Market, which includes movements of factors of production.

The United States also took initiative in the area of making the BIT concept regional, which is reflected in the NAFTA agreement. It contains a well-researched and innovative chapter on investment in NAFTA, notwithstanding the fact that it is only an FTA not a customs union (CU). This chapter has been admired and flatteringly imitated by other RIAs, particularly by the APEC and the Group-of-Three (G-3).[122] Some of the important features of NAFTA include (i) national treatment in establishment, (ii) MFN treatment in establishment and operations, (iii) a ban on new performance requirements, (iv) phasing out of old performance requirements and (v) a ban on expropriations except for public policy reasons on a non-discriminatory basis and with full compensation. This is a long list of provisions. Another innovation of NAFTA was to have extensive dispute settlement provisions, which include private action against recalcitrant host governments. Taking cue from the NAFTA, members of APEC agreed on a more extensive set of principles on intra-regional investment in 1994. However, these principles presently exist only on a non-binding basis.

Economies that suffer from low credibility of their policy regimes face aversion by foreign investors. If investors have noticed sudden policy shifts,

---

[122] The Group-of-Three (or G-3) Agreement was signed under the Enabling Clause of the GATT between Colombia, Mexico and Venezuela.

frequent changes in tariff rates, variations in tax incentives, a history of illiberal trade policy or instances of nationalization in the past, it is reasonable that that they would avoid investing in such an economy. Interest group driven governments and kleptocratic regimes also lead to low image in the global investment markets. In the backdrop of low credibility, when policy reforms are undertaken, their benefits may be slow to arrive because changing image in the global investment markets is a slow process. In such cases, RIAs can help improve the policy credibility of an economy. For policy reforms and changes to have a positive impact on investment, they must raise expected returns or lower costs. By anchoring such reforms through a binding commitment to an RIA, which is credible in it, the economy in question may improve its policy credibility in the global investment market place. In this regard, RIAs can set the norms. They can reward a good policy regime and reform measures in a constituent member economy. Conversely, they can punish the bad policy regimes and policy vicissitudes. If the latter target has to be achieved, the RIA partners must have the power, interest and commitment to enforce the necessary reforms. The partners need to be large enough, stable enough and have a sufficiently strong interest in the RIA to make it worth their while to discipline the target country (Fernandez, 1998).

Mexico's membership of NAFTA provided a considerable impetus to its policy reforms, tariff reduction and investment regulation liberalization. Its membership also seriously restrained the ability to raise tariffs and dismantle trade policy and investment reforms. That there was a sea change in its intellectual policy climate, which became obvious from the manner in which the 1994 financial crisis was handled. Its credibility in the global investment market enhanced considerably. With southern enlargement of the EU, risk premium on investment in the newly acceding economies declined markedly. Policy commitments by the EU governments reduced future uncertainty and induced additional investment and growth in the newly acceding economies. The same effect is likely to continue in the eight CEEC, Cyprus and Malta that signed the Accession Treaty with the EU in April 2003.[123]

4.2.3 Welfare implications

The economics of RIAs has been extensively researched, starting with the seminal contribution of Jacob Viner. The welfare impact of RIA is an issue, which has been the subject of ongoing debate since Viner's early analyses over a half century ago. Regional integration, when tariffs are prohibitively high so that economies are autarkic or nearly autarkic, raises the level of welfare of the regional trading blocs because trade diversion cannot take place. The other extreme is when the tariffs are zero or trade with non-partner countries

[123] This section draws on Chapter 4, Schiff and Winters (2003).

is free. Under these circumstances as well, regional integration among small economies would raise the welfare of the regional trading bloc. However, for any tariff levels between autarkic and zero, regional integration seems to have an ambiguous effect on welfare.[124]

Early research on welfare impact of RIA was stimulated by the integration experiment, taking place in Europe. In the Vinerian analysis trade creation and trade diversion were the two traditional tools for RIA analysis and were considered marvelous heuristic devises for illustrating the fundamental effects of RIAs. The age-old and well-known *static* Vinerian concept is that the trade creation effect benefits the partners of the RIA, while there is an unambiguous loss from trade diversion (Viner, 1950). These two seminal Vinerian concepts have proved to be central to the subsequent thinking and policy debate on regionalism. Viner's conclusions were that RIAs might predominantly be trade diverting and therefore welfare-reducing for the members. Therefore, the static theory essentially failed to yield universally applicable guidelines for policy application.

The welfare implications of regionalism or preferential trade policies in static economic theory are dependent upon the circumstances surrounding an individual RIA and the member economies. They are consistent with the theory of second-best in which the movements in the direction of Pareto-optimality are not always welfare-improving. Notwithstanding the long-lasting Vinerian concepts, some current researchers (see Winters, 1999) believe that except for the very simple case explored by Viner, the mapping from trade creation and trade diversion to economic welfare is treacherous. For example, *a la* Winters (1999) "pure trade diversion can be beneficial if its effect of lowering consumer prices is sufficiently important to welfare. The benefit of trade creation for a single country can be outweighed by the losses of tariff revenues on the pre-RIA volume of imports from the partner countries..." Thus, the results based on the trade creation and trade diversion concepts should be taken as indicative, not definitive. Trade creation for the RIA members indirectly affects the non-members or the rest of the world. Higher income inside the RIA would lead to greater consumption, parts of which will indeed be of goods and services produced outside the RIA. This benefits the non-members.

According to the maxims of the classical trade theory, welfare in the global economy is maximized if the number of RIAs is one, or if the global economy is one large RIA. This amounts to free global trade. By the same token global welfare is also maximized if the membership of RIA is large. This would stand for zero or near zero optimal tariffs, so that the effect is close to free trade. With the increase in the number of RIAs, economic welfare must first decline, reach a minimum, and then rise again. De Melo and Panagariya (1992) posited that if one starts from one RIA in the world or from a free trade scenario, and divides the world into two RIAs, there is trade diversion due to a positive tariff

---

[124] See, for instance, Viner (1950); Meade (1955); Lipsey (1960) and Arndt (1969).

on extra-bloc imports. This should lead to a decline in global welfare. Next, if the world is divided into three RIAs, the optimal tariff declines; however, each bloc becomes smaller. The former leads to trade creation, while the latter to trade diversion. Thus, the net welfare effect would remain somewhat unclear.

Measured static welfare effects of regional integration tend to be ambiguous in sign and small in size. This led proponents of regional integration to bring in refinement and switch attention from the old stylized static approach to dynamic effects of RIA. They believed that the latter were likely to be positive and large (Cernat, 2001; Hoekman et al., 1998). In earlier exposition we have seen that RIAs can lead to dynamic benefits through economies of scale for small economies having small markets and through the effect of enhanced competition. These effects can enhance welfare only if market forces determine which firms expand and which contract and phase out.

Another source of dynamic benefit in an RIA is the incentive for knowledge and transfer of technology, which may favorably affect the rate of GDP growth. This kind of dynamic benefits may be large in an RIA between developing and industrial economies, and may not exist in one between developing economies. The probabilities of RIAs generating economies of scale and competitive gains under imperfectly competitive market structures are high. This would be another beneficial effect, leading to welfare gains. However, these benefits would potentially double if RIAs also stimulate investment. RIAs can potentially increase FDI flows, both from the more developed members of the RIA and from the rest of the world. In addition, locating (or relocating) of industry among member countries would be logically affected in a manner that enhances growth, and eventually welfare (Hoekman et al., 1998).

RIAs and trade liberalization on preferential basis does not necessarily have to be benign in itself. Membership of an RIA does not suspend the ordinary laws of economics. That mere membership of an RIA does not necessarily ensure welfare gains is obvious from the EU membership of Greece and Ireland. The latter became a part of the then EEC in 1973, with per capita GDP level of 62 percent of the EU average, measured in purchasing-poser parity (PPP) terms. In 2002, Ireland's per capital GDP was 21 percent above the EU average. In contrast, Greece joined the then EEC in 1981. Between then and 2002, the ratio of per capital GDP to the EU average has risen little. Welfare implications of EU membership for Greece were virtually zero (EIU, 2003).

Numerous studies have empirically examined the welfare effects of RIAs (Laird, 1997; Schiff, 1999; Rutherford and Martinez, 2000). Their conclusions convincingly demonstrated that RIAs could be welfare-enhancing *but only* under certain conditions. When they are welfare-enhancing, welfare gains are greater (i) the higher the trade barriers being reduced, (ii) the higher the share of pre-existing trade between the partners, (iii) the larger the trade partner, (iv) the more diversified the partner countries' economies are, and (v) the more closely the partners' domestic prices resemble world prices. Riezman (1999) analyzed the strategic interactions between trading blocs in a computable general equilibrium (CGE) model, and concluded that when RIAs are of more or less equal size they are welfare-enhancing. If the RIAs are of unequal size, their impact is the opposite.

There are not many studies that provide a comprehensive general equilibrium examination of similarities and dissimilarities across different kinds of RIAs, like customs unions (CUs) and FTAs. Kose and Riezman (1999) tried to fill this gap by constructing a simple model for studying various types of preferential trade agreements. Along with other variables, they analyzed the welfare implications of two kinds of RIAs, namely, the CUs and FTAs. Their results indicated that on welfare grounds, FTAs are better than CUs for the global economy as a whole. However, member economies benefit more in a CU than in an FTA. Decomposition of welfare effect indicated that a major proportion of the welfare gains in both member and non-member countries are explained by the volume of trade effect for the CUs and FTAs. This implies that having free market access is the most significant benefit of participating in RIAs. In the CUs, the terms of trade effects generate relatively large welfare gains because members of a CU determine their CET rates. Conversely, members of an FTA do not coordinate their trade policies, which diminish their market power, which in turn results in welfare losses. These losses are also associated with the terms of trade effect in the FTA.

The principal objective of an RIA is wider market access. The welfare gains to the members of RIAs also result from the same improved market access. The above-cited empirical studies show that these welfare gains would be greaterwith the increasing partners' share in home trade. These studies also concluded that home price effect (sum of consumer surplus and producer surplus) would also be larger with increasing market access of the RIA partners. Effect on non-members' welfare is a function of the level of common external tariff (CET) of the RIA. At the overall level, taking the rest of the world as a single region, the CET that reflects the minimum tariffs of the RIA would not harm non-members' welfare. However, at the country level the RIA formation with CET of minimum tariffs would benefit some countries, while harm others. Which effect will be greater for an RIA—trade creation or trade diversion—will depend upon the sizes of the economies (as proxied by their GDPs) forming the RIA and the relative similarities and competitiveness among them. There can be no categorical answer in this regard. These effects will necessarily vary for each RIA (Laird, 1997; Schiff, 1999; Rutherford and Martinez, 2000).

The constituent members of RIA are the mutual trading partners. The size of the trading partner generally takes on a great deal of significance in an RIA. A large partner economy, for a given tariff rate, can be a source of several benefits. Foremost, a large partner is more likely to satisfy the home country's import demand at the world prices. Second, the home country is likely to gain more on its exports to the large partner because a large partner would continue to import from the rest of the world even after the formation of the RIA. Since the partner has a tariff on imports from the rest of the world, the home country is more likely to obtain an improvement in its terms of trade by selling to the partner at the higher tariff-inclusive price (Michaely, 1998; Schiff, 1999). Structural complementarity in trade is another important factor affecting welfare. An RIA as an entity would be better off in welfare terms if each country imports what the other exports. This, indeed, is a hypothetical situation. What is feasible is that a large proportion of import of one partner is also a large proportion of exports of the other partner, in turn leading to large welfare gains for both the constituent members.

Which member incurs welfare losses and which one gains from an RIA has been a moot issue. The comparative advantage of member countries, relative to the rest of the world, provides a basis for predicting who gains and who loses. Using two-by-two Recardian model, Venables (2002) concluded that typically the country in the RIA that has comparative advantage most different from the world average is the most at risk from trade diversion. Thus, if a group of low-income countries form an RIA, there will be a tendency for the lowest income members to suffer real income loss due to trade diversion. As opposed to this, if an RIA includes a high-income country, then lower income members are likely to converge with the high-income partner[125]. That RIAs with higher income countries are likely to lead to convergence of income level is a valuable inference for the policy mandarins.

Following Harris and Cox (1986) and Smith and Venables (1988), large literature has emerged in which the RIAs are treated as operating in an imperfectly competitively world. These empirical studies delved into the changes in the nature of competition due to the creation of RIA. As an economy becomes a member of an RIA, the immediate effect on the domestic firms is that their market enlarges and the special privileges provided by the domestic government decline or disappear. Competition from the firms from the member countries reduces the hold of the domestic firms on the domestic market. This generates both gains and losses. The new, post-RIA situation would redistribute rents in the larger market.

There is a distinct possibility of beneficial dynamic effects of an RIA. A good illustration of which is the well-known and widely cited Cecchini Report (1988), which calculated that by 2000 the GDP in the EU economies would rise on the order of 2.5 percent to 6.5 percent as a result of the Single European

[125] Here a high-income country means one that has relatively higher per capita income relative to other members of the RIA as well as to the world average. Venables (2002) came up with these conclusions.

Market (SEM) initiative. Higher real income in the EU would raise imports from all trading partners. Assuming elasticity of import demand to be about 2, exports from Asia to EU would go up at least 5 percent. This positive effect should be netted against the negative effects of trade diversion. However, the dynamic estimates are usually considered uncertain. Yet, it is widely believed in the business community that the 2004 enlargement of the EU would result in spreading financial and macroeconomic "stability and prosperity across a large swathe of Europe's heartland."[126]

At the turn of the century, a large number of RIAs and the multilateral trading systems coexist. As regards, how RIAs affect the global trading system is a difficult proposition to assess. Serious efforts to study this have been made in the past. Opinions on this issue vary widely and researchers and policymakers need to continue examining this issue. One such effort was made by Schill (1996). After synthesizing the conflicting viewpoints, he concluded that the effect on the multilateral system would depend on the structure of the RIA. Whether an RIA facilitates or impedes global free trade essentially depends upon whether procedures for joining it are liberal, whether it satisfies WTO regulations and whether it is accompanied by some degree of trade liberalization of the members' trade regimes. In short, the effect of an RIA on the global trading system would depend upon the terms of the agreement. Clear policy guidelines in this regard are not available because the terms of every RIA and the rationale behind establishing them have differed throughout history (Sager, 1997). RIAs established for different reasons would have varied effects on global trade flows.

Similarly, using both gravity model and simulation using computable general equilibrium (CGE) model to make welfare estimates, Gilbert et al. (2001) examined the potential welfare effects of RIAs in the Asia-Pacific region. Although both the techniques are quite different, they can offer insight into areas where the other is commonly used. Thus, the CGE model can be used to consider the effect of existing arrangements through back-casting the models. Similarly, the gravity models are often used for predicting the consequences of the proposed agreements by searching for pre-existing trends that might portend to "natural" trading partners. Gilbert et al. (2001) concluded that both the techniques suggested that there might be "significant welfare gains" from the RIA proposed in the Asia-Pacific region. The welfare gains were found to be the largest (i) when the RIA had diverse members, and (ii) when the RIA is large having many members. Interestingly, welfare benefits of liberalization within the Asia-Pacific region on an MFN basis were found to be substantially greater than on a preferential basis. The simulation results indicated that even when

---

[126] Over 90 percent of the senior European business executives surveyed in July 2003 by the Economic Intelligence unit were of this opinion. See *Europe Enlarged: Understanding the Impact,* July 2003.

RIAs had substantial net benefits for the member economies, they managed to impose a substantial cost on non-members, both within the Asia-Pacific region and to the rest of the world.

4.3 INSTITUTIONALIZED REGIONAL ECONOMIC INTEGRATION

At this stage, regionalization needs to be distinguished from regionalism. As alluded to in Chapter 3, Section 3.1, regionalization implies market-driven increase in economic interdependence that occurs through expansion of trade, investment, technology and human migration flows without any formal framework of co-operation. Conversely, regionalism stands for a formal, government-led, economic co-operation arrangement between two or more economies, not necessarily geographically contiguous. The purpose of both the arrangements is mutual support for economic growth through the expansion of trade and investment as well as other mutually agreed genre of collaboration.

Some purposeful and structured regional institutions were established during the latter half of the last century. They were created in the immediate World War II period and some Asian countries participated in each one of them. Although these groupings no longer exist and they merely have limited historical significance, they have had some influence on the one that do exist at present. Regional trade, investment and economic integration were not in the agenda of the early country grouping of this genus. The motivating factors behind these regional groupings included social, cultural, military, anti-communism, and security issues, or several of them together. None of them survived because of "territorial disputes, the preference of nationalism over regionalism, racial tensions, ideological animosity, and complete mutual distrust" (Sakakibara and Yamakawa, 2003). Notwithstanding the failure of these early endeavors toward regional co-operation, Asian countries did feel the need of developing some kind of institutionalized regional groupings to cope with the divisive issues and political tensions in the face of first departure of Britain from the region. The debacle in Vietnam and the U.S. departure from Asia had a large regional impact over the Asia-Pacific countries. They began to plan for the emerging geopolitical situation. For the first time, Australia and New Zealand began to feel that their place is with their Asian neighbors. Expanding economic influence of Japan since the early 1960s that made several Asian countries uncomfortable and various sub-regional disputes in Asia made it necessary for the region to have some kind of a functional economic-political Asian forum (Sakakibara and Yamakawa, 2003). The early formal groupings that had some semblance of regionalism were listed by Tongzon (1998). These country groupings included the following:

1. Southeast Asian Treaty Organization (SEATO), 1954–77
2. Asia and Pacific Council (ASPAC), 1966–73
3. Association of Southeast Asia (ASA), 1961–63
4. MAPHILINDO, 1963–64

Two of the early initiatives made in the direction of institutionalized regionalism were the Association of Southeast Asian Nations (ASEAN) in 1967 and the 1970 Korean (Republic of) proposal for an Asian Common Market (ACM). The latter had well-defined economic motives but did not receive enough regional support and failed to take off. Asian economies did not follow a distinct or purposeful strategy of regionalism or institutionalized regionalization during the early post-World War II era. This was opposite of the strategy of the Western European economies, which promoted regionalism earnestly since the early 1950s. However, belatedly regionalism did emerge in Asia.

4.3.1 Formation of ASEAN

The first wave of contemporary regionalism began with the signing of the Treaty of Rome in 1957, and the formation of the European Economic Commission (EEC). Economic and financial globalization that began in the last quarter of the preceding century had an enormous impact on global public policy. Somewhat belatedly, the ASEAN was formed in Asia. Five Asian economies (Indonesia, Malaysia, the Philippines, Singapore and Thailand) signed the Bangkok Declaration in 1967 forming the ASEAN, a political and strategic organization.[127]

The Bangkok Declaration had seven principal policy planks of which the first was "to accelerate economic growth, social progress and cultural development of the region" and the other six were similar socio-economic objectives reinforcing the first. Notwithstanding the declared objectives, it was widely acknowledged that the ASEAN came into being for essentially political and strategic reasons. During the 1960s, the five founding members had several unresolved disputes and tensions among themselves. Its formation suited all the founding members' erstwhile needs. For instance, such a regional body was needed to foster harmonious relations between Indonesia and Malaysia, to bring together Thailand and other non-communist states of Southeast Asia, to provide a forum for debating the Philippines' claim of North Borneo and finally ensure Singapore's claim to continue to exist as an independent city state.

---

[127] The ASEAN was established on August 8, 1967 in Bangkok by the five original member countries, namely, Indonesia, Malaysia, the Philippines, Singapore and Thailand. The precise dates of accession of the other members are as follows: Brunei Darussalam joined on January 8, 1984, Vietnam on July 28, 1995, Laos and Myanmar on July 23, 1997 and Cambodia on April 30, 1999.

Owing to outstanding disputes and differences between the founding members, the first ASEAN charter thoughtfully emphasized on the principles like accommodation for each other's views, consensus in decision-making and non-interference in the domestic affairs of the members on the one hand, and accommodating the needs of members at different levels of economic development on the other. This approach was christened "the ASEAN-way." To be sure, the ASEAN-way contributed to stability of the region. However, one direct outcome of the consensus building in its decision-making process was inhibited economic co-operation among the members.

For over a decade-and-a-half other Southeast Asian nations eschewed ASEAN, although the membership was open to them. In 1984, Brunei Darussalam became the sixth member. Vietnam, Lao PDR, Myanmar, and Cambodia joined during the 1995–99 period. In 2000, the ASEAN region had a population of approximately 500 million, a gross domestic product of $737 billion, and a total trade of $720 billion. Seen from the vantage point of the early 21st century, progress of ASEAN in achieving its declared economic objectives was far from rapid. As explained below, in the initial stages it was nix, but in the latter half of the 1990s it began to evolve into ASEAN-Plus-Three (APT) and institutionalized regional co-operation progressed.[128] Often a comparison is drawn between the achievements of the ASEAN and the EEC. To be sure, the institutional growth of ASEAN has been much slower. The EEC turned into a Single Market and then an economic union, called the European Union (EU) in 36 years. In 2003, the ASEAN also turned 36, but it was a long way from becoming an economic union, although the ASEAN Free Trade Area (AFTA) was formed.

At the outset, the Southeast Asian nations thought that both global and regional geopolitical *mise-en-scene* was undergoing a significant and irreversible transformation and they needed to collaborate to deal with it in a unified manner. Although there was a desire to unify in their response to the new challenges in five founding members, it had to be in such a fashion that their national interests were conserved and not given a second priority. They perceived the need for economic alignment and recognized its potential benefits, but were not clear regarding their own plan of action. Therefore, ASEAN's economic consequences, during the initial phase, were not noteworthy and it concentrated completely on its political objectives. In the Fourth ASEAN Ministerial Meeting in 1971, the issue of setting up of a common market was broached for the first time. It was resented and summarily rejected by Indonesia, which believed that regional integration was not what the founding members of ASEAN had visualized. In its rejection of the common market proposal, Indonesia emphasized

---

[128] The ASEAN-Plus-Three (APT) grouping comprises the 10 members of ASEAN, plus China, Korea and Japan.

that regional economic co-operation and economic integration are two different commodities, and that ASEAN's objective was the former.

In order to meet the stated objective of regional economic co-operation, the following industrial co-operation initiatives were attempted: (i) ASEAN Industrial Projects (1976), (ii) ASEAN Preferential Trading Arrangement (1977) and (iii) ASEAN Industrial Complementation (1981). By way of these trade and industrial projects ASEAN aspired to facilitate regional economic co-operation and industrialization. Other than the advantage of market size, it was believed that the region would benefit from economic complementarities as well as in the use of skilled labor resources. In the textbook manner, larger regional markets were to allow scale economies in manufacturing sector. They were also expected to underpin the comparative advantage of each regional economy through expansion of trade volume under a preferential trade agreement (PTA). It was believed that the final outcome would be enhanced intra-regional trade and investment. Although the concepts were rational, all these early proposals and initiatives were largely unsuccessful. Problems related to implementation, financing and those of involving the private sector put paid to these initiatives. In addition, they were not based on a comprehensive plan but were of ad hoc and piecemeal patchy in nature. For these reasons early initiatives of economic co-operation failed.

The Bali summit of 1976 marked a breaking point, when the Declaration of ASEAN Concord was signed, which gave ASEAN a tilt toward economic co-operation. Regional production and trade, particularly trade in basic commodities and energy, were made part of the agenda. For the first time, establishment of a PTA was made into a long-term objective. Under a PTA, trading partners give each other partial preferences in terms of preferential tariff rates.

4.3.2 Formation of ASEAN free trade area

During the late 1980s and early 1990s, the global economy was again experiencing a surge in regionalism, which was christened the "second" wave of regionalism. Once again, the EEC took lead in this regard. The growth rate of intra-European Community trade was uneven in the mid-1980s. The rapid increase that had characterized the early stages of integration had lost steam by this time. It was around this period that the seeds of the "second" wave of regionalism were sown. Members of the EEC hatched their Single Market Program (SMP) in 1986. The SMP was to be completed by 1992, and the plan was called the EC-92.[129] Soon thereafter, the North American Free Trade Area (NAFTA)

---

[129] On December 1, 1991, agreement was reached in Maastricht on the Treaty on European Union, with a timetable for the Economic and Monetary Union (EMU). The European Single Market was completed on January 1, 1993. On November 1, 1993, the Maastricht Treaty came

was created in 1994, which was another momentous event and led to a "domino effect" of renewed interest in and creation of RIAs. In addition, progress in multilateral trade negotiations (MTNs) in the Uruguay Round (1986–94) was exceedingly slow and then it came close to complete collapse. Its deadline for completion had to be moved forward again and again (Das, 2004).

During the second wave, not only the number of regional integration arrangements (RIAs) being negotiated increased exponentially but also their scope and geographical reach broadened. The EU and NAFTA were frequently being used as prototypes by economies forming RIAs. Furthermore, RIAs began to be concluded between non-contiguous, non-regional countries. Cross-regional arrangements increased in number and the term "regional" began to appear an incongruity. Greater regional economic integration was frequently taken up as one of the principal objectives of the RIA, which implied deepening of intra-regional trade. Deep integration, as opposed to shallow integration, goes beyond border protection measures, that is, beyond liberalization of tariffs and non-tariff barriers (NTBs). It includes expansion of mutual foreign direct investment (FDI) and harmonization of commercial regulations, standards and practices (Das, 2004).[130]

As indicated in Section 4.1, a rapid clip expansion of RIAs, and deepening of many of them, occurred in the global economy after 1990. It caused ASEAN members concern regarding their future export markets. Discussions regarding the formation of an ASEAN Free Trade Area (AFTA) had begun in 1991 and the ASEAN countries agreed in principle on it. After considerable hesitation to join broader regional forum, ASEAN members agreed to join the Asia-Pacific Economic Co-operation (APEC) forum. This reflected their belief that ASEAN may be a narrow grouping in a rapidly globalizing world economy. The ASEAN economies did not intend to lose their identity and swallowed by APEC. Therefore, the ASEAN members felt it necessary to move fast on the formation of AFTA and to further ensure the ASEAN's economic role in the regional and global economy.

As a response to rising level of regionalization in the global economy and stark uncertainty on the multilateral trading front, AFTA was launched in 1992. In the formation of the EU Single Market in 1993 and NAFTA in 1994 the ASEAN members further saw possibility of a loss of important global markets. Also, FDI from these two large RIAs could be redirected to the member countries instead of coming toward the ASEAN economies. Therefore, AFTA's reciprocal tariff reduction program was re-scheduled. Originally it was to be

---

into force after Danes voted favorably at the second try, and the EEC became the European Union (EU).

[130] Refer to Chapter 3 of Das (2004) for greater details regarding the "second" of "new" wave of regionalism in the global economy.

completed by 2008, but later on it was brought forward to 2003 (see Section 4.3.3). The AFTA was subsequently broadened significantly to include some of the so-called Singapore issues, particularly trade facilitation between the ASEAN economies through harmonization of customs procedures.[131] A framework agreement for liberalizing trade in services and harmonization of standards was also included to eliminate the technical barriers of trade (TBT) among the ASEAN countries (Ariff, 2000). An ASEAN Investment Area (AIA) was agreed and endorsed by the members.

By 1999, the AFTA agreement was ratified by all the ten members. Regional "economic integration" was formally mentioned for the first time in December 1998 during the preparation of the Hanoi Plan of Action (HPA). The HPA was formulated immediately after the Asian crisis (1997–98) and covered six years between 1999 and 2004. Its objectives included restoring confidence, regenerating economic growth and promoting regional financial stability by maintaining sound macroeconomic and financial policies as well as strengthening financial system and capital markets enhanced by closer consultations, so as to avoid future economic and financial disturbances. The HPA laid a lot of emphasis on greater economic integration, so much so that the objectives of the action agenda for the six-year period looked too ambitious to be achieved.

Furthermore, by 2003 the APT economies had had seven annual meetings for modalities of joining the ASEAN as members. Negotiations with the People's Republic of China (hereinafter China) began in 2002, while with Japan were completed in 2003 (see Chapter 3, Section 3.2.1). The flip side of the coin is that these 13 Asian economies have been feeling the pressure to move toward institutionalized arrangements like the EU in the foreseeable future. In the wake of the Asian currency and financial crisis, particularly during the early 2000s, the Asian economies grew more determined to move toward formal and institutionalized regional co-operation than ever before.

4.3.3 Common effective preferential tariff framework

When ASEAN was established, trade among the founding members was insignificant. Estimates for the 1967 and the early 1970s showed that the share of intra-ASEAN trade in the total trade of the member countries ranged between 12 and 15 percent. Thus, some of the earliest economic co-operation schemes of ASEAN were aimed at addressing this situation. Therefore a Preferential Trade Area (PTA) was proposed during the Declaration of ASEAN Concord

[131] The Singapore issues are (i) trade and foreign investment, (ii) trade and competition, (iii) transparency in government procurement and (iv) trade facilitation. They are referred to as the Singapore issues because they were raised for the first time by the industrial economies during the Singapore Ministerial Conference in 1996.

in 1976, which accorded tariff preferences for trade among ASEAN member economies. Ten years later, in 1987 an Enhanced PTA Program was adopted at the Third ASEAN Summit in Manila to give further impetus to intra-ASEAN trade. However, the PTA proposition did not yield desirable and tangible results.

The Framework Agreement on Enhancing Economic Co-operation was adopted at the Fourth ASEAN Summit in Singapore in 1992, which included a schedule for launching an ASEAN Free Trade Area or AFTA. The strategic objective of AFTA was to increase the ASEAN region's competitive advantage as a single production unit. A Common Effective Preferential Tariff (CEPT) framework was devised for trade liberalization among the six ASEAN members in 1992. Initially the CEPT stipulated that tariff on all manufactured products that meet a 40 percent ASEAN content precondition, and on processed agricultural products, would be slashed to 0 to 5 percent within a decade-and-a-half. As alluded to in the preceding section, this schedule had to be truncated because of two reasons. First, because of the completion of the Uruguay Round in 1994 and, second, because of APEC's declaration of the Bogor initiatives. AFTA decided to achieve the target of 0 to 5 percent tariffs by 2003 for the ASEAN-6 economies. It was further moved to 2002 for all but a few products. The members that were at a lower level of economic growth were given more time to reach this level of tariff liberalization. For Vietnam, which acquired membership in 1995, the deadline was scheduled at 2006, for Lao PRR and Myanmar it was 2008 and for Cambodia 2010.

The CEPT framework comprised four lists of tradable products, namely, the Inclusion List (IL), the Temporary Exclusion List (TEL), the Sensitive List (SL) and the General Exception List (GEL). The IL was sub-divided into the normal track and the fast track. Tariffs for the goods on the normal list were to be slashed to 0 to 5 percent by 2002, while for those on the fast track had to be reduced to the same level by 2000. When the CEPT was conceived, the average tariff level for the goods on the IL was expected to decline from 12.76 percent in 1993 to 2.68 percent in 2003.

As the name indicates, the TEL comprised the products for which tariff liberalization was consciously, if temporarily, delayed. Trade liberalization in agricultural products is always a challenging task. An important decision was taken in 1994 in this regard and the agricultural products were brought under CEPT. Unprocessed agricultural products were placed on the SL, which were not due for tariff liberalization until 2010. In accordance with Article XX of the GATT-1994, a certain number of items were put on the GEL, which were permanently excluded from tariff reduction. Under the CEPT framework, in 2001, 55,680 tariff lines in the IL were included in the liberalization program. This was 85 percent of the total ASEAN tariff lines. The 2001 liberalization program also include 8,660 lines in TEL, which was 13 percent of all the tariff lines, and 823 tariff lines in the GEL, which was 1.3 percent of the total. Of the SL, 360 tariff lines or 0.6 percent of the total tariff lines were included in the liberalization program. It was planned that by 2010, the five original ASEAN signatories and Brunei Darussalam, would achieve zero tariffs in all their intra-ASEAN imports. This period has been extended to 2015 for the four new members, which are at a lower level of economic development.[132]

The conceptualization of the CEPT framework enabled ASEAN members to achieve real progress in the area of economic co-operation. It turned out to be a substantial improvement over the earlier PTA notion, which did not yield many results because it was open-ended, without time boundaries. Probability of the PTA plan delivering goods in this regard was slim to none. Under this plan, the tariff lines to be liberalized were a voluntary decision of the PTA members. In addition, members tended to pad their inclusion lists.[133] While NTB liberalization was included in the PTA, it was not paid much attention. Conversely, the CEPT framework had time boundaries for liberalization measures. Under this framework member countries granted each other concessions on a reciprocal basis in each tariff line—as is customary in a regional trading agreement (RTA). A member county can expect to receive tariff concession only in those products in which it is willing to liberalize its own domestic market. This system encourages each member to offer concessions in as many tariff lines as possible, thereby quickening the pace of trade liberalization in all the member economies. Also, member countries were required to eliminate quantitative restrictions and NTBs for products on which they received concessions within five years. In order to eliminate the possibility of padding of the inclusion lists, the CEPT framework classified the inclusion on a sectoral basis but exclusions on a disaggregated level (Chia, 1997, 2002; Sakakibara and Yamakawa, 2003).

4.3.4 Impact of common effective preferential tariff

To determine whether AFTA would result in benefits to the member economies, several computable general equilibrium (CGE) exercises were conducted. The CGE model is frequently used to quantify the cost and benefits of various kinds of regional integration agreements (RIAs). It is an efficient method of simulating and thereby quantifying how simultaneously slashing tariffs and NTBs in a preferential or nondiscriminatory manner affects economy wide variables, including quantities of goods and services produced, consumed and traded, exchange rate and prices. This exercise addresses the static costs and benefits of forming an RIA.

---

[132] For greater details see Fukase and Martin (2001), Tan (2000), Tay (2000) and Sakakibara and Yamakawa, 2003.

[133] According to one story, Indonesia offered to cut tariff on imports of snow ploughs from the ASEAN members.

The simulation results of an early CGE model exercise done by DeRosa (1995) to quantify the benefits of AFTA for the five founding members of ASEAN economies concluded that trade creation does take place under AFTA.[134] The simulation exercise indicated that RIA formation increased intra-RIA and trade with the rest-of-the-world (ROW) to almost the same level. Intra-ASEAN-5 trade was found to increase by $2.9 billion, while trade of the ASEAN-5 with the ROW increased by $2.4 billion. As opposed to this, under the most-favored-nation (MFN) liberalization scenario, intra-ASEAN-5 trade expansion was small at $1.7 billion, but trade expansion with the ROW was much larger, at $9.1 billion. The reason why the trade expansion under MFN trade liberalization with the ROW was so large was the enormous difference in comparative advantage with the ROW, in particular with the matured industrial economies. These results were buttressed by another CGE exercise of the same period conducted by Lewis and Robinson (1996) who confirmed that the MFN liberalization in the ASEAN-5 economies resulted in much larger gains in trade and economic welfare than did the RIA formation among this group of economies.

A recent CGE simulation by Fukase and Martin (2001) quantified the effect of AFTA on the four new ASEAN members. Due to serious data constraints different types of CGE models were used for different countries. Like the older CGE simulation exercises, Fukase and Martin (2001) assessed cost and benefit of AFTA creation and on an extended MFN liberalization basis for each one of the four new members. Their estimates revealed that Cambodia benefited very little through AFTA because trade diversion offsets the benefits of trade liberalization. Lao PDR benefited more than Cambodia because of the positive effect on its exports to ASEAN, particularly that of wood products. Benefits to Myanmar were small because its tariffs are low. It recorded minor gains in terms of trade. Likewise, Vietnam benefited very little because its trade volume with the other ASEAN members was small. Its agricultural sector benefited through access to ASEAN markets. Thus, all the four new members were favorably affected, although the effects were relatively small (Sakakibara and Yamakawa, 2003).

4.3.5 ASEAN's contribution to regional integration

This institutional initiative is justly credited for rendering stability and regional integration in Southeast Asia. The ASEAN-way did make a contribution to the sub-regional stability. ASEAN's acceptance of regional integration within the global economic context was another favorable feature that contributed to sub-regional growth. ASEAN was born with a "soft" institutional structure

[134] The sixth member, Brunei Darussalam, was excluded because of scanty data availability.

because it was necessary for its birth and survival. Soft institutionalism is considered an ASEAN invention. With the passage of time its principles of non-interference and non-confrontational were found to be out of synch in the complex and rapidly globalizing world economy. Therefore, time has come for it to embrace a structured and rule-based institutional system of other cognate regional bodies.

This institutional initiative is justly castigated for slow movement and for remaining inactive when there was a need for taking decisive measures and show result. Critics pointed out that for inordinate periods ASEAN remained ineffectual, bureaucratic, indecisive and unable to deal with the regional problems. Progress toward regional integration was belated due to framework agreements, work programs and myriad of plans. These programs sounded good but stayed more on paper than were acted upon efficaciously and seldom produce tangible results. Thus far, the economic co-operation in the ASEAN has been confined to encouraging intra-regional trade and investment. After the launch of the AFTA, intra-ASEAN trade grew in absolute as well as relative terms. To be sure, success in this area was necessary, but it was not sufficient for regional economic integration. ASEAN needs to move beyond these immediate objectives.

Although being small economies with small trade volumes, it is not in the interest of ASEAN economies to increase their trade with the other ASEAN economies at the expense of the third country. Their global trade and investment links continue to remain highly valuable to them. However, a recent study commissioned by the ASEAN secretariat and conducted by MacKinsey & Co. revealed that, institutionally, ASEAN failed in lowering the cost of production in order to become competitive in the global market place.[135] ASEAN's competitive advantage as an integrated production area did not increase over the years. To be sure, ASEAN economies have benefited from global investment, but global investors did not consider this sub-region a prime destination for foreign direct investment (FDI) because of its small size and fragmentation, varying product standards from country to country effectively creating technical barriers to trade (TBTs) and slow customs clearance procedures. Its northern neighbor China offered a far more attractive alternative to the global investors that did the ASEAN. In view of this, ASEAN needs to aim at deeper economic integration—of the common market or economic and monetary union variety—and liberalize the region for free movement of goods, services and factors of production in the short-term. Deeper integration is sure to increase ASEAN's global trade and investment volumes and enhance capacity for international negotiations.

---

[135] This study was conducted in November 2002 and cited by Sakakibara and Yamakawa (2003) in Chapter 3.

For an almost four-decade-old institution, ASEAN does not have many achievements to its credit. Time has come to assign national sovereignty considerations a second place to sub-regional progress in the ASEAN group of countries and make conscious endeavors to move from an FTA to deeper integration, indicated above. Secondly, it needs to be borne in mind that the diminutive benefits of ASEAN took an inordinate length of time in coming and are likely to taper off in the foreseeable future even if ASEAN moves toward deeper integration. Joining the APEC forum as a core group has enhanced ASEAN's global significance. Also, the APT is evolving into a meaningful extension of ASEAN. If it succeeds in coming into being as a formal grouping in Asia, it would be in the interest of ASEAN to continue within APT framework as a sub-group. Unlike the APEC, the APT has the advantage of an Asian identity. If the new configuration thrives it would not only be a positive move but also has better prospects of growing into a viable regional institution (Soesastro and Morrison, 2001; and Wain, 2002).

4.3.6 ASEAN economic community 2020

The 2003 targets in the area of trade liberalization, that is bringing tariffs down to 0 to 5 percent, were achieved by the ASEAN-6. Therefore, during the Ninth ASEAN Summit of 2003, Declaration of ASEAN Concord II (also known as the Bali Concord II), at the insistence of the Government of Singapore it was decided that "ASEAN shall continue its efforts to ensure closer and mutually beneficial integration among its member states and among their peoples. . . "[136] The new target that was endorsed was to establish both a single market and a single production base by 2020, so as to enhance ASEAN's credibility and economic weight in the Asian and global economies. The new framework was named the ASEAN Economic Community (AEC). This was the vision of an integrated common market, albeit a clear plan was to be prepared.

At the time of the Bali Concord II, ASEAN members were concerned about the increasing level of integration in NAFTA, expansion of the EU membership to 25, and the formation of the hemispheric free trade area called the Free Trade Area of the Americas (FTAA), which had 34 members, stretching from Alaska to Antarctica. In the backdrop of these global realities, greater planned economic integration and creation of an AEC became an imperative. Perception of a threat from vertiginously growing Chinese economy was considered the second motivation behind the AEC proposal (Hew, 2003). In order to stay a competitive region vis-à-vis China and face the challenges of globalization, the ASEAN would need to restructure and integrate the member economies. It

[136] The ASEAN members concluded their Ninth Summit in October 7–8, 2003, at the resort island of Bali in Indonesia.

was expected that an integrated ASEAN would benefit from creation of a sub-regional market, global trends in trade, FDI flows, manufacturing and creating integrated production networks. It was also expected to command a bigger voice in the international fora, particularly in the WTO. Therefore, ASEAN leaders declared accelerated regional integration in 11 priority sectors, which were identified by the High Level Task Force (HLTF). A deadline of 2010 was decided for integration in these sectors in April 2004 (Reyes, 2004).

Although global economy is markedly different today than what it was in the 1950s, the prototype of the European Economic Community (EEC) can still have some relevant lessons for the ASEAN economies. The EEC evolved into a fully integrated common market between 1957 and 1993, and became the European Union (EU). It is so far the most successful example of regional integration. Although there were differences, the member economies successfully overcame them. Their political determination and shared vision for the common good helped them do that. The ASEAN members would do well to replicate these attitudes if they wish to attain their objective of forming an AEC.

As the ASEAN members differ considerably in terms of the stage of economic development, forming customs union (CU) or an economic and monetary union (EMU) like the EU by 2020 may not be a plausible target. It would be difficult for all the ASEAN members to have common external tariffs vis-à-vis the non-members. However, the AEC can be realistically planned as an FTA-Plus, that is, a free trade area and some elements of a common market, like free movement of factors of production. This is not a daunting goal because some of the building blocks have been in place. The following current programs would provide an impetus to the formation of AEC: AFTA, AIA and the ASEAN Framework Agreement on Services (AFAS). Together they would make the AEC the next rung on the economic integration ladder (Hew, 2003).

4.4 ASEAN-PLUS-THREE GROUPING

A succession of proposals of creating vehicles for Asian regional co-operation has emerged, and the APT is the latest in that series. Since the early 1990s, attempts have been afoot to expand the ASEAN to include the other larger Asian economies. The first attempt in this direction was Malaysia's proposal for an East Asian Economic Group (EAEG), which was to be composed of the ASEAN-6[137] and China, Japan, Korea, Hong Kong and Taiwan. After

[137] It excluded the four new members of ASEAN, namely, Cambodia, Lao PDR, Myanmar and Vietnam.

some deliberations and debates the proposal was mutated into a caucus, which was to operate within the APEC forum. It was accordingly re-named as the East Asian Economic Caucus (EAEC). Even with this change, the EAEC failed to gain enthusiastic participation among the member economies. Australia and the United States vehemently criticized the concept of the caucus formation and strongly supported the APEC in lieu of the EAEC, because it was thought that a broad-based forum would bring greater benefits to Asia. Consequently, the EAEC concept remained inert and behind the scene.

The ASEAN-Plus-Three (APT) concept was initiated in the latter half of the 1990s. The APT has an Asian identity and could well become the kernel for a future EU-like regional structure, an Asian Community. The intellectual predecessor of this concept could be traced back to the Asianitic school that emerged in Japan, toward the end of the nineteenth century. The emergence of this so-called "school of the East" or *toyoshi* was the consequence of a reactionary movement conceived by Japanese scholars who were averse to Japan's turning away from China. This group rejected the imported Western liberalism of the Meiji era (1868–1912)[138] and West's understanding and interpretation of the East and its economic history (Iida, 1997; Okfen, 2003). During this period, Japan saw itself as the natural leader of Asia but its ideas never held sway in Asia and could not persuade the other Asian economies. Similarly Chinese and Korean concepts of Pan-Asianism never spread to the rest of Asia. The concept could not be developed further in the twentieth century because of discontinuity caused by wars, colonization and decolonization.

Initially Taiwan was also to be included in the APT group, but political reasons kept it out. After two years of behind-the-scene diplomacy, in 1997, at the ASEAN Summit in Kuala Lumpur, the 13 APT heads of the government met for the first time and the APT concept was formally accepted. In this summit the Plus-Three countries (China, Japan and Korea) were invited by the ASEAN. Of the three, China was most enthusiastic supporter of the APT concept, and emphasized having an annual summit of APT. Thus, the APT evolved as a firm, resilient and long-lasting concept of ASEAN extension, one to which neither the regional economies nor Australia and the United States had any aversion. The formation of APT received a stimulus from the Asian currency and financial crisis and the disenchantment of the Asian policymakers with the role of the supranational institutions during the crisis (Das, 2000, 2003). The APT group had its first meeting in December 1997, when the crisis was still battering the regional economies. Although Asian crisis was not a long one but a deep one,

[138] With the Meiji Restoration in 1867–68, the Tokugawa era ended. The emperor Meiji was moved from Kyoto to Tokyo, which became the new capital. His imperial power was restored. The actual political power was transferred from the Tokugawa Bakufu into the hands of a small group of nobles and former samurai.

the APT concept caught on and gained strength after the recovery had set in. The crisis is regarded as the most competing motivation behind catalyzing regional integration endeavors.[139]

The APT began as an informal group and thus far has no secretariat of its own. It continued to meet annually at the initiative and invitation of the ASEAN. For seven years between 1997 and 2003, the APT economies have had annual meetings for determining the modalities for the Plus-Three entrants joining the ASEAN as full-fledged members. Negotiations with China in this regard began in 2002, while those with Japan were completed in 2003. Although the APT process was initiated and driven by ASEAN, its agenda was generally determined by the larger Plus-Three economies. By early 2000s, the formal activities of ATP had expanded and included periodic meetings of finance, trade and foreign ministers of these 13 Asian countries.

The APT made meaningful contribution to regional co-operation in the financial and monetary areas during the post-Asian crisis period through the Chiang Mai Initiative (CMI) of May 2000. The momentum given by the CMI is further strengthening the regional co-operation and the APT is likely to go beyond mere financial and monetary co-operation. Recent debates in the economic and financial media portend to the fact that APT may be the stepping stone to the return to the old idea of forming the Asian Economic Bloc, a *mutatis mutandis* facsimile of the EU. The concept is not considered far-fetched because the APT comprises economies of Northeast and Southeast Asia and includes the three most dynamic economies, two of which are the largest in the region. Japan (exporting $542 billion worth of goods and services in 2003) is the second largest global economy and the third largest trading economy, which makes its co-operation with the ASEAN economies invaluable. China was the fourth largest exporter of merchandise, exporting $483 billion worth of goods and services in 2003, and Korea exporting $225 billion worth of goods and services in 2004 (WTO, 2004).

Japan had had long-standing prominence in the region as an investor and a large market destination for Asian exports. China's membership of the APT is of considerable significance as well, because over the last two decades it has emerged as the largest trading economy among the developing economies, and its competitive potential was causing the ASEAN economies serious concern in the early 2000s. Therefore, its institutional co-operation in the framework of the APT was being considered valuable. Korea is an important newly industrializing economy known for its dynamic growth. It is also a member of the Organization for Economic Co-operation and Development (OECD), a substantial trader

[139] Reading through the speeches of the ASEAN leaders one gets the impression that their dissatisfaction with the way the Asian crisis was handled by the supranational institution provided a strong motivation for forming the APT.

(12th largest trader in 2003) and a significant investor in the other regional economies.[140]

In the early 2000s, formation of the APT grouping grew more important than in the past because of several internal and external problems of ASEAN. Following the events of September 11, 2001, some non-economic factors have created tensions among the ASEAN countries, which included the Muslim revivalism and tensions between the moderate and radical Muslims. Secondly, addition of the four new members to ASEAN has turned it into a two-tier country grouping, having two divergent mentalities, outlooks and expectations.[141] Serious differences between the six older and four newer members have surfaced, making ASEAN look like an organization that is incohesive. Thirdly, the ASEAN economies have not totally recovered from the Asian crisis and are at a loss regarding their future direction. They lack vision, drive and leadership, giving an impression that ASEAN may grow into a rudderless ship.

As alluded to above, China's rapid clip growth posed a threat in trade and investment areas. ASEAN faces a growing competitiveness gap with China in terms of production, exports and on return on investment (ROI). Economic problems and uncertainty in Japan during the decade of 1990s and the early 2000s also affected ASEAN badly. It is under this set of circumstances that ASEAN is apprehensive of becoming marginalized and, therefore, sees the APT grouping as its savior (Cheow, 2002). ASEAN's fear of marginalization has been compounded by the clear preference of Japanese firms and transnational corporations (TNCs) for investment in China. Participating in a larger Asian entity, the ASEAN economies see several tangible advantages, namely, larger regional market size, economic synergy created by production networks, vast expansion of foreign exchange reserves, possibility of a larger international clout and possibility of an EU-like convergence for growth in the short-term for at least the higher-income ASEAN economies. For turning APT into an EU-like formal regional group the potential members need political commitment and a strong drive for integrating their markets. There can be no short cuts to this approach.

4.4.1 Exploring the future potential

In keeping with the Japanese principle of *Kaizen*[142], in each of the ASEAN annual meetings since 1997 progress was made toward enhancing regional cooperation. In the 2001 summit, ASEAN members and China announced their

---

[140] The source of these statistical data is Appendix Tables 1 and 3 in *World Trade 2003, Prospects For 2004*. World Trade Organization. Press Release. No. Press/373. April, 5, 2004.

[141] The four new members that joined ASEAN last were Cambodia, Lao PDR, Myanmar and Vietnam.

[142] *Kaizen* in Japanese means gradual, orderly and continuous improvement.

intention of making APT into an FTA before 2011 and proposed that negotiations should be launched forthwith. A general consensus on the concept of a FTA evolved and possibilities of setting up an APT Secretariat short-term were discussed. China displayed the maximum support and enthusiasm for the FTA proposal and by proposing an FTA between ASEAN and China it provided a proof of its sincerity. It was agreed by both the partners that negotiations for the ASEAN-China FTA should be so launched that the FTA could be inaugurated in 2010.

Inter-government dialogues and consultations on APT FTA increased markedly and Asian regionalism began evolving. As regards the shape of this FTA, it is a matter of conjecture, but if it does evolve as planned it would be a significant development in the area of regional and global integration. That APT FTA would subsequently join the European Union (EU) and Free Trade Area of the Americas (FTAA) is not a far-fetched idea. The APT grouping and the FTA are getting support from the potential members by default also, because they view the other two regional groupings APEC (discussed below in Section 4.5) and ASEAN as sluggish and feeble in terms of producing concrete results for the dynamic Asian economies. Despite early activity, the APEC did not live up to its promise. After increasing its membership to 10, ASEAN has increased disagreements among the members, which have been discussed above. In the early 2000s, both these grouping were being perceived as semi-stagnant by the APT economies.

Indications are that the APT is gradually but purposefully developing as a large FTA covering the 13 Asian economies and a key regional body in the foreseeable future. Taking this concept further, Cheow (2002) proposed a China-led APT model for Asia, whose focus would be the large and rapidly growing Chinese domestic market. According to this model the ASEAN, Korean and Japanese economies would dovetail their manufacturing and services sectors into the Chinese market and locate appropriate niches. The result would be evolution of a new regional division of labor, creation of expanded production networks, which in turn would stimulate novel outsourcing patterns and more flexible supply chain management. Alternatively, since 1994 Japan has been fighting a strong deflationary trend, and therefore the APT can adopt a Japan-led model of Asian growth, which would reflate and stimulate the Japanese economy in an APT framework.

4.5 ASIA-PACIFIC ECONOMIC CO-OPERATION FORUM

An atypical regional institution, the Asia-Pacific Economic Co-operation (APEC) forum, was launched at a ministerial meeting in November 1989. It began as an informal dialogue group of 12 Pacific Rim economies. It now considers itself a "formal institution" with a permanent secretariat located in Singapore; yet it is not formal in the sense the EU is and still has a loose structure. Its founding 12 members were Australia, New Zealand, the United States, Canada, Japan, Korea, Thailand, Malaysia, Indonesia, the Philippines, Singapore and Brunei Darussalam. Since its inception, nine more countries joined, bringing the membership to 21. In 1991, APEC admitted China, Taiwan (admitted as Chinese Taipei), and Hong Kong; together the three are called greater China. Mexico and Papua New Guinea joined in 1993; Chile in 1994, and Peru, Russia and Vietnam in 1998. This list of 21 members indicates that APEC is a multilateral forum encompassing the Pacific Rim, as opposed to exclusively Asian economies. APEC has grown into a major regional grouping with virtually all important Asian economies as its members. In addition to the member economies, the APEC forum covered three functioning FTAs, namely, the Australia New Zealand Closer Economic Relations (ANZCER), the AFTA and the NAFTA.

The APEC provides a forum for ministerial level discussion and co-operation on a range of economic issues including trade, investment, technology transfer, and transportation. A new member assumes the chairmanship of the forum every year. All the members submit items to be included in the next year's agenda to the country chairing APEC. Finally, the agenda is chosen from these submissions. This mechanism wards off any possibility of large member economies dominating the agenda. The APEC forum considers this as one of its strengths. To give importance to ASEAN members, APEC secretariat is located in Singapore and its annual meetings are alternated between ASEAN countries and non-ASEAN countries. Decision-making in APEC forum is based on Asian style consensus forming. It considers itself the principal vehicle for promoting open trade and practicable economic co-operation. Its goal is to advance Asia-Pacific economic activity and sense of community among the 21 member economies. The APEC Business Advisory Council (ABAC) is the private sector arm of the APEC forum.

A unique feature of APEC was its adoption of the open regionalism. It is not a new concept and was pioneered by Australia and New Zealand, while forming ANZCER. Open regionalism refers to plurilateral agreements that are non-exclusive and open to new members to join, implying that open regionalism promotes trade liberalization without discrimination against non-members. The primary condition of open regionalism is that plurilateral initiatives be fully consistent with Article XXIV of the GATT-1947, which prohibits an increase in average external barriers. Beyond that, it requires that plurilateral agreements not restrain members from pursuing additional liberalization with non-members either on a reciprocal basis or unilaterally. Because member countries are able to choose their external tariffs unilaterally, open regional agreements are less likely to develop into competing bargaining trade blocs. Finally, the principle of open regionalism promotes and facilitates external liberalization, meaning trade with non-member economies outside the RIA.

The essential element of open regionalism is that economies grouped in to form RIAs can regard RIAs as complementary as well as supplementary to multilateralism. They need not necessarily be antithetical to multilateralism. By following both regional and multilateral approaches simultaneously, the pace of liberalization of global trading system can be made brisker. This two-pronged approach to trade liberalization is the polar opposite of "fortress-Europe" kind of regionalism and can achieve greater gains for those willing to proceed faster and at the same time put pressure on the multilateral negotiations to perform better and deliver tangible results in a reasonable time. This is essentially the so-called "building bloc" argument buttressing the formation of RIAs, for the ultimate purpose of multilateral trade liberalization.

The Bogor Declaration of 1994 called for the adoption of objective of "free and open trade in Asia-Pacific by 2010 for developed member economies and 2020 for developing ones" through autonomous MFN tariff reductions. Next year the Osaka Action Agenda provided soft guidelines for reaching this target. They were called the trade and investment liberalization and facilitation (TILF) guidelines. Members were asked to reveal their tariff reduction programs and take other trade-enhancing and business-facilitating measures under the Individual Action Plans (IAPs), which were non-binding. Members were expected to review each other's progress made under the implementation of IAPs.

Another key feature that sets the APEC forum apart from other regional bodies is its commitment to business facilitation and the regular involvement of the private sector in a wide range of APEC activities. The Osaka Action Agenda (of 1995) conceived of "three pillars," namely, liberalization of foreign-investment-related regulation among the APEC economies and opening of more sectors for foreign investment. The second pillar was business facilitation or removing procedural impediments to trade. The third pillar was "co-operation in economic and technical areas" (Section 4.5.2) and capacity building, which involves making institutions more effective. Liberalization of domestic markets directly impinges upon and strengthens regional institutions. As noted ahead (Section 4.5.1), good deal of efforts were devoted to institution-building by the member economies. Owing to dissatisfactory progress in the implementation of IAPs, the IAP review requirement was made formal in 1996, and members were asked to submit the their progress reports in IAPs for general scrutiny. The first formal submissions were made in 1997. Although the reviews were far from rigorous, it was observed that IAPs had not advanced significantly.

Culmination of the Fifth Ministerial Conference of the WTO without an agreement at Cancún, Mexico, had little element of surprise for the cognoscenti in the area of international trade.[143] The Third Ministerial Conference of the

[143] Thus far five Ministerial Conferences of the World Trade Organization have taken place. They are: Singapore (December 9–13, 1996), Geneva (May 18–20, 1998), Seattle (November 3 to December 3, 1999, Doha (November 9–13, 2001) and Cancún (September 10–14, 2003).

WTO in Seattle in 1999 had also ended in a debacle, and it was believed that the APEC members had contributed to it by not arriving at an agreement on the agenda (Das, 2001). While APEC members looked forward to a successful Ministerial Conference in Cancún, variations in their stands on several important issues again persisted. Following the failure in Cancún, at the Fifteenth Ministerial Meeting of the APEC, held in Bangkok, Thailand, in October 2003, the concerned APEC members not only strongly supported the objectives of the Doha Round of multilateral trade negotiations (MTNs), which was driven by Doha Development Agenda (DDA), but also reaffirmed their commitment to multilateral trade and investment liberalization. They reiterated their belief that "DDA offers the potential for real gains for all economies, particularly developing economies, in the areas of agricultural reform, improved market access for goods and services and improvement of trade disciplines. We lent our strong support for continuing the valuable work done at the Cancun Ministerial Conference to advance the DDA." While the APEC members reaffirmed their support and primacy to the multilateral trading system, they agreed, "that for global free trade to flourish, regional and bilateral free trade agreements must be consistent with WTO principles, advance WTO objectives and contribute to the Bogor goals." APEC's formal stand on the DDA was to "press for an ambitious and balanced outcome to the DDA, reiterating that the development dimension is at its core." As for the intra-APEC activity, members supported work with the ABAC and the business community to continue to implement the Shanghai Accord, which included the reduction of transaction costs by 5 percent by the year 2006.

4.5.1 Consequences of trade and investment liberalization

To compute the progress made in the IAP process, four recent studies developed scorecards. Their results are not comparable because they used different time periods and measured different variables. First, tariffs and non-tariff measures (NTMs), services, investment standards and conformance, customs procedures, intellectual property rights, competition policy, government procurement procedures, deregulation, rules of origin (ROO), dispute mediation and business mobility were studied for 18 of the 21 member countries by Yamazawa and Urata (2000). Due to sparse data Peru, Russia and Vietnam were excluded. Yamazawa and Urata (2000) measured commitments of members as Uruguay Round-Plus-Alpha, denoted by *a* and found that the value of *a* was small for many of the APEC economies. The IAP reviews in 1997 and 1998 revealed inadequate progress in commitment to trade and investment liberalization because most members wanted to wait for the outcome of the Seattle Ministerial (held in 1999) of the WTO. In 12 of the 18 member economies for which the study was conducted, trade and investment liberalization did take place (Yamazawa and Urata, 2000).

Secondly, the Trade Policy Forum of the Pacific Economic Co-operation Council (PECC) also delved into the progress made by the APEC members toward trade and investment liberalization (Trewin and Azis, 2000). It concluded that simple average tariffs declined from 11 to 7 percent in the member economies over the 1995–98 period but increased in 1999. This increase in tariffs was due to change in the method of measuring them following the implementation of the recommendations of the Uruguay Round of MTNs. Tariffs on agricultural products, which came under NTBs in the past, began to be counted in with the other tariffs, increasing the average level of tariffs. Therefore, the increase observed for 1999 did not reflect increase in general trade protection. The third study measured fall in tariff rates from 12 percent in 1995 to 8 percent in 2000 (DFAT, 2001). It reckoned that APEC economies lowered average tariff rates by one third, from 12 percent to 7 percent between 1994 and 2003 (ABAC, 2003). Unlike these studies, the fourth MITI (2001) focused on tariff decline for a longer (1988–2001) period and reported tariff declines for the individual Asian members of APEC. The standard deviation in members' tariff fell from 30 percent in 1995 to 10 percent in 1999 (Trewin and Azis, 2000). Lower dispersion in tariffs tends to lead to less distortion in the economy, resulting in welfare gains. However, tariff decline was found to be uneven across sectors, and there is still a high incidence of tariffs in several of them, particularly in food, beverages and tobacco, agriculture, textiles and apparel and fishing. There were still numerous tariff peaks or "spikes" in the APEC economies.[144]

The Economic Committee of APEC conducted an impact study in 1999, and concluded that if only static gains are taken into account, trade liberalization and facilitation measures expanded the annual GDP for the APEC economies by $75 billion in 1998 (at 1997 dollar value and prices), which was 0.4 percent of the regional GDP. This regional income gain was in addition to the annual income gain created by the implementation of the Uruguay Round commitments. If dynamic effects are included APEC member's gains rise to between $90 billion and $105 billion (APEC, 1999). When the static gains were disaggregated, it was found that real income gains attributable to trade facilitation were greater than from trade liberalization measures. Of the estimated 0.4 percent gain in the APEC GDP, 0.25 percent originated from trade facilitation and 0.16 percent from trade liberalization. That is, of the $75 billion annual gains mentioned above, $46 billion came from trade facilitation alone, which includes measures that reduce the unit cost of trading. In terms of specific policy actions these measures include streamlining customs procedures, curtailing documentation and duplication in documentation, aligning domestic standards with international standards and removing technical barriers to trade (TBT), establishing mutual

---

144 Tariff peaks or "spikes" are relatively high tariffs amidst generally low tariff levels. For the industrial economies, tariff rates of 15 percent and above are considered as tariff spikes.

recognition arrangements (MRAs) in telecommunication and other sectors and enhancing business mobility through business travel cards.

According to the 2003 estimates of the APEC Business Advisory Council (ABAC), over the 1994–2003 period, APEC trade and investment liberalization resulted in reducing absolute poverty by a third in the Asia-Pacific region, lifting 165 million people out of poverty.It also succeeded in creating 195 million jobs and generating 70 percent of the global economic growth.[145] According to this assessment, APEC achieved the following over the 1995–2001 period: (1) Trade between the APEC members increased 113 percent to over $2.5 trillion and foreign direct investment (FDI) grew by 210 percent; (2) APEC further took important measures to facilitate business in areas such as streamlining of custom procedures, immigration, aligning domestic standards and conformance to international standards, and many other areas that have resulted in cost savings, efficiency gains, and economic growth; (3) APEC members also engaged in capacity building to ensure that everyone can fully participate in and benefit from trade liberalization and economic growth; and (4) between 1998 and 2002, APEC engaged in 984 capacity-building projects in areas such as developing human capital; developing stable, safe and efficient capital markets; strengthening economic infrastructure; harnessing technologies for the future; promoting environmentally sustainable development; and encouraging the growth of small and medium industries.[146]

Not all the credit of tariff reduction in Asian economies goes to APEC and the TILF program. A lot of it goes to unilateral trade and investment liberalization endeavors of these economies, the GATT–WTO system, which includes implementation of the recommendations of the Uruguay Round, economic and financial restructuring programs of the International Monetary Fund (IMF) and the World Bank, AFTA's CEPT process and lastly the WTO accession of China in November 2001.

4.5.2 Economic and technical co-operation

In the beginning of Section 4.5, we noted that the third pillar of the Osaka Action Agenda was the economic and technical co-operation (Ecotech). Addition of the third pillar occurred after disagreements and a long debate among the members. The original proposal came from Indonesia, which was opposed by both developing and industrial country members of APEC. First, it was believed that addition of the third pillar would amount to a distraction

---

145 The APEC Business Advisory Council (ABAC) released a paper entitled "The First Decade Since Bogor: A Business Assessment on APEC's Progress" on October 21, 2003, in Bangkok, Thailand, This report is available on the Internet at http://www.apecsec.org.sg/apec/news_media/fact_sheets/biz_assessment_of.html

146 Ibid.

from the principal objectives of trade and investment liberalization and facilitation. As economic and technical co-operation was not properly defined, its real intent was open to imagination and interpretation. While industrial economies saw it as laying down the foundation for future requests for economic assistance for development, developing economies thought of it as a way of building institutional capacity. The Manila Declaration of 1996 attempted to clarify that future demand for "foreign aid" was not the intention of the economic and technical co-operation. The intention behind this proposal was that members should benefit from the pool of expertise, technological knowledge and information available in the APEC economies (Elek and Soesastro, 2000).

Even after this clarification, the Ecotech did not take off to a good start. Typically, an Ecotech project was to be launched by a member with its own resources. It was to be coordinated in the APEC countries by the sponsoring member, and only partially supported by the APEC. This was called the "pet project" syndrome. The Manila Declaration attempted to make it goal-oriented and with measurable criteria. It was proposed that under the Ecotech, members should (a) develop human capital, (b) develop stable, safe and efficient capital markets, (c) strengthen economic infrastructure, (d) harness technologies for the future, (e) safeguard the quality of life through environmentally sound growth, and (f) develop and strengthen the dynamism of small and medium enterprises (Elek and Soesastro, 2000).

4.5.3 APEC's contribution to regional integration

Although not overwhelming, the APEC forum made some economic contribution to the integration of the Asia-Pacific region. According to APEC (1999) computations, the impact of liberalization endeavors by the APEC was one fourth of the total impact of implementation of trade liberalization under the Uruguay Round. It needs to be recalled that the Uruguay Round was the most comprehensive round of multilateral trade negotiations (MTNs), covering the largest ever number of issues covered in any MTN before and after. It took 123 contracting parties (CPs) of the GATT seven years (1996–94) to complete (Das, 2001). Consequently, its eventual impact on the global trade was substantial. It brought about weighted tariff reduction of 38 percent.[147]

The APEC forum has many economies that are complementary to the ASEAN group. It comprises a continuum of economies at different stages of economic growth and with different factor endowments, some of them being knowledge- and capital-intensive, while others being labor-intensive. It was stated in Section 4.2 that when the constituent members of an RIA

---

[147] In particular refer to Chapter 2, of Das (2001).

are at varying levels of economic development, that is, when RIAs are formed between developing, emerging market and industrial economies, they are known to promote technology transfers from the high-income, mature industrialized economies to the lower-income, less-developed constituent members. Therefore, possibility of enhancing such technology transfer motivates developing economies to form RIAs with the emerging market and mature industrial economies. Although the mechanisms of technology transfer are neither clear nor fully understood, an important body of literature argues that it is promoted through trade flows. It was also brought home in Section 4.2 that when members of an RIA are at varying levels of economic development, their knowledge accumulation also varies. Knowledge is an international public good and could be transferred to other RIA member economies through trade, FDI and scientific exchanges, affecting their growth, which is a vital imperative for development.

The APEC International Assessment Network (AIAN), which is a collaborative, independent project among participating APEC Study Centers (ASCs), to assess the execution of APEC initiatives, issued its first report in 2001. While it acknowledged many accomplishments, it made numerous recommendations for improvements in APEC operations and organization. The most important ones address the following areas: (a) IAP commitments must be specific, concrete and measurable, (b) members should be held responsible for their IAP commitments, (c) the APEC secretariat is weak and need to be strengthened with high-caliber professionals having long-term assignments and commitments, (d) APEC should consciously integrate financial and developmental issues and (e) members should encourage academics and researchers to collaborate and integrate.

The AIAN report draws attention to the soft institutionalism of APEC, which was rendered essential because of its "blend of idealism and realism." One of the disadvantages of soft institutionalism is that trade and economic integration agreements under APEC cannot be made binding. The AIAN report also concluded that as an institution, APEC lacks capability to monitor and evaluate its crucial work programs (Feinberg and Ye, 2001). APEC ministers agreed to these findings of the AIAN report and agreed to creating a new system that strengthened the peer review of the IAPs to enhance objectivity and transparency. Accordingly, the peer review process was expanded, made formal by appointment of a review team for each IAP exercise. An independent expert was appointed for conducting in-country research in the pre-specified areas. Japan and Mexico were the first to volunteer for the new review process. The reposts were published by APEC in the third quarter of 2002. Although the new review system was a definite move forward, it is to be seen how many more members volunteer for such peer reviews (APEC, 2002).

4.6 BILATERAL TRADE AGREEMENTS

As alluded to in Section 4.1, since the 1999 debacle in Seattle, many important traders in the Asia-Pacific region that traditionally espoused multilateralism and promoted MFN liberalization changed track and turned to bilateral trade agreements (BTAs), also known as the "new age" trade liberalization. Australia, China, Hong Kong SAR,[148] Japan, Korea, New Zealand, Singapore and Taiwan have added the regional card to their trade policy repertoire and are energetically entering into a variety of BTAs. They are of different kinds, trade and economic framework agreements, PTAs, FTAs, agreements in services in trade and WTO-Plus agreements (Das, 2001, 2004).

In the beginning of 2004, over 40 BTAs were either formally proposed, or were at various stages of negotiations, or were signed in the Asia-Pacific region. In June 2000, the United States and Vietnam signed a BTA. In October 2003, Australia signed the Australia–China Trade and Economic Framework Agreement and Australia–Thailand FTA. Beginning in March 2003, several rounds of meeting had taken place to create the Australia–U.S. FTA. Japan–Singapore and Singapore–U.S. BTAs were also consummated in 2003. Both of these were WTO-Plus. Korea had signed an FTA with Chile. Other than these, a good number of BTAs were either formally proposed or their negotiation process was underway. (i) China took initiative and formally proposed bilateral trade negotiations with Hong Kong SAR, Macao and Malaysia. (ii) China also proposed an FTA with the ASEAN. (iii) Hong Kong SAR proposed such agreements to Macao and New Zealand; the latter is under advanced negotiations. (iv) Japan proposed for creating an FTA with Canada and the Philippines and was seriously studying bilateral trade agreements with Chile, Korea, Malaysia, Mexico and Thailand. (v) Korea and Chile consummated a BTA in early 2004, and Korea also proposed an FTA to Peru and was studying plans to have bilateral agreements with Australia, Mexico, New Zealand, Singapore, Thailand and the United States. (vi) Malaysia made formal proposals to Japan and the Unites States. (vii) The Philippines made a similar proposal to the United States. (viii) Singapore's negotiations with Canada, India, Korea, Mexico, New Zealand were in progress and it was also negotiating with the European Free Trade Area (EFTA)[149] and the EU. (ix) Taiwan had proposed to Costa Rica, Japan, Panama, Singapore and the United States, while its negotiations with New Zealand broke down, resulting in New Zealand's withdrawal from the table. (x) Thailand was negotiating with Australia, Japan, Korea and New Zealand.

---

[148] Hong Kong is the special administrative region of China and is referred to as Hong Kong SAR.

[149] Iceland, Liechtenstein, Norway and Switzerland are the members of the European Free Trade Area (EFTA).

Spurt in the bilateral agreements in the Asia-Pacific economies was due to the concern regarding the spread of regionalism in the other parts of the globe. Asian economies apprehended that their trade would be adversely affected if they fail to negotiate parallel agreements. In some Asian economies, particularly in Korea and Japan, pressure for negotiating bilateral agreements came from the private sector. *Keidanren* (the Japanese Federation of Economic and Business Organizations) noted that while Europe and the United States exported to Mexico at zero tariff rates, Japanese exports faced an average duty of 16 percent. The timing of such a large number of bilateral agreements in Asia-Pacific can be explained by what is being perceived as the slow progress in trade and investment liberalization under the aegis of both AFTA and the APEC. In addition, members of AFTA wanted to exclude several crucial areas of trade from the liberalization program (Ravenhill, 2003).

Another motivation why bilateral agreements were springing forward was the lesson learned from the EU, which made clever use of a loophole in Article XXIV of GATT-1994. The vagueness of Article XXIV, Para 8, of GATT-1994 permits delaying or avoiding structural adjustments in the least efficient sectors of the domestic economy. That is, it allows trade liberalization without political costs. In its bilateral agreements with Mexico and South Africa, the EU excluded many important agricultural products. This was a new precedent set up by the EU, the largest trading bloc in the global economy. The justification given by the EU was that it has not excluded all agricultural products, and that the bilateral agreement covers 90 percent of the existing traded products, therefore, it is not violating the WTO norms.

East Asian economies, particularly *Keidanren,* followed this precedent while negotiating bilateral agreements, and the other Asian economies followed suit. Like the EU, their defensive argument ran as follows that while it is desirable "to liberalize as much trade as possible," ambiguity in Article XXIV of GATT-1994 permits the trade partners to exclude "sensitive" items or sectors from the liberalization schedule. This helps in maximizing the political gains from the bilateral trading agreements. While finalizing its agreement with Singapore, Japan adhered to this line of logic and some of the sensitive products that Singapore exported in the agriculture sector, like cut flowers, goldfish, were not included in the liberalization schedule. Likewise, in its proposal for bilateral trade agreement with Chile and Mexico, Korea clearly noted that it has no intention of exposing its agricultural sector to further competition from Chile and Mexico, and that this sector was kept out of the agreement. In Taiwan's proposal to Singapore, a good number of textiles and apparel items have been kept out of the bilateral agreement to protect the domestic textiles and apparel industries (*Keidanren,* 2000; Ravenhill, 2003).[150]

---

[150] Refer to Ravenhill (2003) for details regarding the learning value of the EU practices for the Asia economies.

4.7 SUMMARY AND CONCLUSION

The RIAs are widely considered the second best approach to trade liberalization. A surge was noted in the RIA formulation after the creation of the WTO. Forming an RIA naturally influences trade flows and their directionality and, therefore, production patterns in the economies that are constituent members of that RIA undergo alteration. An RIA is not benign in itself. It could be welfare-enhancing *but only* under certain conditions. The welfare impact of RIA is an issue, which has been the subject of ongoing debate since Viner's early analyses over a half century ago. The age-old and well-known *static* Vinerian concept is that the trade creation effect benefits the partners of the RIA, while there is an unambiguous loss from trade diversion. RIAs often lead to dynamic benefits through economies of scale for small economies having small markets and through the effect of enhanced competition. These effects can enhance welfare only if market forces determine which firms expand and which contract and phase out.

The ASEAN was one of the first RIA formed in Asia that has survived and expanded since its creation. At the time of its creation, it did not have many economic objectives. Consensus building in its decision-making process was one of its strategies, which inhibited economic co-operation among the members. The Bali Concord of 1976 marked a breaking point, which gave ASEAN a tilt toward economic co-operation. A rapid clip expansion of RIAs, and deepening of many of them, occurred in the global economy after 1990. It caused ASEAN members concern regarding their future export markets. Discussions regarding the formation of an ASEAN Free Trade Area (AFTA) had begun in 1991 and the ASEAN countries agreed in principle on it. After considerable hesitation to join broader regional forum, ASEAN members also agreed to join the Asia-Pacific Economic Co-operation (APEC) forum. This reflected their belief that ASEAN may be a narrow grouping in a rapidly globalizing world economy. During the ASEAN Summit of 2003, Declaration of ASEAN Concord II, also known as the Bali Concord II, it was decided that ASEAN shall continue its efforts to ensure closer and mutually beneficial integration among its member states and among their peoples. The new target that was endorsed was to establish both a single market and a single production base by 2020, so as to enhance ASEAN's credibility and economic weight in the Asian and global economies.

The ASEAN-Plus-Three (APT) concept was born in the latter half of the 1990s. It could well be the kernel for a future EU-like regional structure. Japan had had long-standing prominence in Asia as an investor and a large market destination for Asian exports. China's membership of the APT is of considerable significance as well, because over the last two decades it has emerged as the largest trading economy among the developing economies, and its competitive potential was causing the ASEAN economies serious concern in the early 2000s. Therefore, its institutional co-operation in the framework of the APT was being considered valuable. Korea is an important newly industrialized economy known for its dynamic growth. It is also a member of the Organization for Economic Co-operation and Development (OECD), a substantial trader and a significant investor in the other regional economies. Although Asian crisis was not a long one but a deep one, the APT notion caught on and gained strength after it. The APT made meaningful contribution to regional co-operation in the financial and monetary areas during the post-Asian crisis period through the Chiang Mai Initiative (CMI) of May 2000.

An atypical regional institution, the Asia-Pacific Economic Co-operation (APEC) forum was launched at a ministerial meeting in November 1989. It began as an informal dialogue group of 12 Pacific Rim, as opposed to Asian economies. It grew into a major regional grouping with virtually all important Asian economies as its members. At the time of creation, APEC covered several functioning free-trade areas, including (i) the Australia New Zealand Closer Economic Relations (ANZCER), (ii) the AFTA and (iii) the NAFTA. Its current membership is 21. A unique feature of APEC was its adoption of the open regionalism. It is not a new concept and was pioneered by Australia and New Zealand, while forming ANZCER. Another key feature that sets the APEC forum apart from other regional bodies is its commitment to business facilitation and the regular involvement of the private sector in a wide range of APEC activities. The Bogor Declaration of 1994 called for the adoption of objective of free and open trade in Asia-Pacific by 2010 for developed member economies and by 2020 for developing ones, through autonomous MFN tariff reductions. Next year the Osaka Action Agenda provided soft guidelines for reaching this target.

Since the 1999 debacle in Seattle, many important traders in the Asia-Pacific region that traditionally espoused and promoted most-favored-nation (MFN) liberalization changed track and turned to bilateral trade agreements, also known as the "new age" trade liberalization. Australia, China, Hong Kong SAR, Japan, Korea, New Zealand, Singapore and Taiwan have added the regional card to their trade policy repertoire and are energetically entering into a variety of bilateral trade agreements. They are of different kinds: trade and economic framework agreements, PTAs, FTAs, and WTO-Plus agreements. During the early 2000s, over 40 bilateral trade agreements were either formally proposed, or were at various stages of negotiations, or were signed in the Asia-Pacific region.

REFERENCES

APEC Business Advisory Council (ABSC). 2003. *The First Decade Since Bogor: A Business Assessment on APE's Progress*. APEC (Asia-Pacific Economic Co-operation) Forum Singapore. Bangkok, Thailand, October 21, 2003.

Ariff, M. 2000. "Trade, investment and interdependence," in S.S. Tay, J. Estanislao and H. Soesastro (eds.) *A New ASEAN in A New Millennium*. Jakarta: Center for Strategic International Studies. pp. 110–133.

Arndt, S. 1969. "Customs Union and theory of tariffs," *American Economic Review*. Vol. 59. No. 1. pp. 108–118.

Asia-Pacific Economic Co-operation (APEC). 1999, September. *Assessing APEC Trade Liberalization and Facilitation*. Singapore: APAC Secretariat. APEC Economic Committee.

Asia-Pacific Economic Co-operation (APEC). 2002, August. *APEC Strengthens Peer Review Process for Achieving Open Trade and Investment*. Singapore. Media Release 21.

Association of Southeast Asian Nations (ASEAN). 2000. *Approved AICO Applications*. Jakarta: ASEAN Secretariat. Available at: http://www. aseansec.org/menu.asp?action=4&content=9. Accessed May 10.

Cecchini, P. 1998. *1992, The European Challenge: The Benefits of a Single Market*. London: Aldershot and Hants Publishers.

Cernat, L. 2001. *Assessing Regional Trade Agreement: Are South-South RTAs More Trade Diverting?* Geneva: United Nations Conference on Trade and Development. Study Series. No. 16.

Cheow, E.T.C. 2002. "Economic and monetary co-operation in Asia: An ASEAN perspective," paper presented at the Euro-Asia Conference organized by the Japan Center of International Finance, Tokyo, May 23–24.

Chia, S.Y. 1997, October 29. *ASEAN: 30 Years of Existence and Challenges Ahead*. Seoul: Korea Institute for International Economic Policy.

Chia, S.Y. 2002. "East Asian regionalism," paper presented at the conference on *East Asian Co-operation: Progress and Future Agenda*, organized by the Institute of Asia-Pacific Studies and Center for APEC and East Asian Co-operation, Beijing, August 22–23.

Das, Dilip K. 2000, December. *Asian Crisis: Distilling Critical Lessons*. Geneva: United Nations Conference on Trade and Development (UNCTAD). Discussion Paper No. 152. 33 pp.

Das, Dilip K. 2001. *The Global Trading System at Crossroads*. London and New York: Routledge.

Das, Dilip K. 2003. "Emerging market economies: Inevitability of volatility and contagion," *Journal of Asset Management*. Vol. 4. No. 3. pp. 199–216.

Das, Dilip K. 2004. *Regionalism in Global Trade: Turning Kaleidoscope*. Northampton, MA: Edward Elgar.

De Melo, J. and A. Panagariya. 1992. *The New Regionalism in Trade Policy*. London: Center for Economic Policy Research.

Department of Foreign Affairs and International Trade (DFAT). 2001. *APEC Progress on Tariffs: Implications for a New Agenda*. Canberra: Commonwealth of Australia.

DeRosa, D.A. 1995, September. *Regional Trading Arrangements Among Developing Countries: The ASEAN Example*. Research Report 103. Washington, DC: International Food Policy Research Institute.

The Economist Intelligence Unit (EIU). 2003, July. *Europe Enlarged: Understanding the Impact*. London: EIU.

Elek, A. and H. Soesastro. 2000. "Ecotech at the heart of the APEC: Capacity building in Asia-Pacific," in I. Yamazawa (ed) *Asia-Pacific Economic Co-operation: Challenges and Tasks for the Twenty-First Century*. London and New York: Routledge. pp. 218–254.

Evans, D. 1998. *Options for Regional Integration in Southern Africa*. Sussex: Institute of Development Studies. IDS Working Paper No. 94.

Feinberg, R.E. and Z. Ye. 2001. *Assessing APEC's Progress; Trade, Ecotech and Institutions*. Singapore: Institute of Southeast Asian Studies.

Fujita, N., P. Krugman and A.J. Venables. 1999. *The Spatial Economy: Cities, Regions, and International Trade.* Cambridge, MA: The MIT Press.

Fukase, E. and W. Martin. 2001. *Free Trade Area Membership as a Stepping Stone to Development: The Case of ASEAN.* Washington, DC: The World Bank. Policy Research Working Paper No. 421.

General Agreement on Tariffs and Trade (GATT). 1994. *The Results of the Uruguay Round of Multilateral Trade Negotiations: the Legal Text. Geneva.*

Gilbert, J., R. Scollay and B. Bora. 2001. *Assessing Regional Trading Arrangements in the Asia-Pacific.* Geneva: United Nations Conference on Trade and Development. Policy Series. No. 15.

Harris, R. and D. Cox. 1986. "Quantitative assessment of the economic impact on Canada of sectoral free trade with the United States," *Canadian Journal of Economics.* Vol. 19. No. 2. pp. 377–394.

Heydon, K. 2002. "RIA market access and regulatory provisions," paper presented at the conference on *The Changing Architecture of the Global Trading System,* organized by the World Trade Organization, Geneva, April 26.

Hew, D. 2003, June 16. *Towards an ASEAN Economic Community by 2020: Vision or Reality?* Viewpoints. Singapore: Institute for Southeast Asian Studies.

Hoekman, B.M., M. Schiff and L.A. Winters. 1998. *Regionalism and Development: Main Message From Recent World Bank Research.* Washington, DC: The World Bank. (mimeo)

Iida, Y. 1997. "Fleeing the West, making Asia home: Transposition of the otherness in Japanese Pan-Asianism," *Alternatives.* Vol. 22. No. 3. pp. 409–432.

Keidanren, 2000. *Urgent Call for Active Promotion of Free Trade Agreements.* Tokyo. Available at: http://asia.neww.yahoo.com. Keidanren. or.jp.english/policy/2000/003/proposal.html.

Kose, M. A. and R. Riezman.1999, October. *Understanding the Welfare Implications of Preferential Trade Agreements.* Coventry, Warwick, UK. The Center for the Study of Globalization and Regionalization. University of Warwick. CSGR Working Paper No. 45/99.

Laird, S. 1997, September. "Mercosur: Objectives and achievements," paper presented at the Third annual World Bank Conference on *Development in Latin America and the Caribbean,* Montevideo, Uruguay, September 11–12, 1997.

Lipsey, R. 1960. "The theory of Customs Unions: A general survey," *Economic Journal.* Vol. 10. No. 2. pp. 498–513.

Meade, J.E. 1955. *The Theory of Customs Union.* Amsterdam, North Holland.

Michaely, M. 1998. "Partners to a preferential trade agreement: Implications of varying size," *Journal of International Economics.* Vol. 46. No. 1. pp. 73–85.

Midelfart-Knarvik, K.-H., H.G. Overman, S. Redding and A.J. Venables 1999. *The Location of Industry in Europe.* London: Center for Economic Policy Research.

Midelfart-Knarvik, K.-H. and H.G. Overman. 2002. "Delocation and European integration: Is structural spending justified?" *Economic Policy.* Vol. 35. No. 2. pp. 321–359.

Ministry of International Trade and Industry (MITI). 2001. *White Paper on International Trade 2001: External Economic Policy Challenges in the 21st Century.* Tokyo.

Nagarajan, N. 1998. "On the evidence for trade diversion in MERCOSUR," *Integration and Trade.* Vol. 2. No. 6. pp. 3–30.

Okfen, N. 2003. June. *Towards An East Asian Community? What ASEM and APEC Can Tell Us.* University of Warwick. Center for the Study of Globalization and Regionalization. Houndmills, Basingstoke, Hampshire, UK. CSGR Working Paper No. 117/03.

Page, S. 2000. *Regionalism among Developing Countries.* London: The Macmillan Press.

Ravenhill, J. 2003, June. "The move to preferential trade in the Western Pacific Rim," *Asia-Pacific Issues.* No. 69. Honolulu. Hawai'i. East-West Center.

Reyes, A.R. 2004. "ASEAN: A Single Market and Production Base". *The Jakarta Times.* 14 June. p. 10.

Riezman, R. 1999, October. *Can Bilateral Trade Agreements Help Induce Free Trade?* Coventry, Warwick, UK. The Center for the Study of Globalization and Regionalization. University of Warwick. CSGR Working Paper No. 44/99.

Rutherford, T.F. and J. Martinez. 2000, June. "Welfare effects of regional trade integration of Central American and Caribbean nations with NAFTA and MERCOSUR," *The World Economy.* Vol. 4. pp. 799–825.

Sager, M.A. 1997. "Regional trade agreements: Their role and the economic impact on trade flows," *The World Economy.* Vol. 20. No. 1. pp. 239–273.

Sakakibara, E. and S. Yamakawa. 2003, June. *Regional Integration in East Asia: Challenges and Opportunities.* Part I and Part II. Washington, DC: Policy Research Working Paper Nos. 3078 and 3079.

Schiff, M. 1999, August. *Will the Real "Natural Trading Partner" Please Stand Up?* Washington, DC: World Bank. Policy Research Working Paper No. 2161.

Schiff, M. and L.A. Winters. 2003. *Regional Integration and Development.* New York: Oxford University Press.

Schill, M. 1996, October. *Small is Beautiful.* Washington, DC: World Bank. Working Paper No. 1668.

Scollay, R. 2000. "CER: Future Developments", in D. Robertson (ed) *AFTA-CER: A Way Forward*?, Melbourne. Melbourne Business School. pp. 68–90.

Smith, M. and A.J. Venables. 1988. "Completing the internal market in European community: Some industry simulations," *European Economic Review.* Vol. 32. No. 8. pp. 1501–1525.

Soesastro, H. and C.E. Morrison. 2001. "Rethinking the ASEAN formula," in *East Asia and the International System.* A Report to The Trilateral Commission. New York, Paris, Tokyo. pp. 57–75.

Tan, G. 2000. *ASEAN Economic Development and Co-operation.* Singapore: Times Academic Press.

Tay, S.S. 2000. "Institutions and processes: Dilemmas and possibilities," in S.S. Tay, J. Estanislao and H. Soesastro (eds) *A New ASEAN in a New Millennium.* Jakarta: Center for Strategic International Studies. pp. 3–24.

Tongzon, J.L. 1998. *The Economies of Southeast Asia: Growth and Development of ASEAN Economies.* Cheltenham, UK: Edgar Elgar.

Trewin, R. and M. Azis. 2000. *Updated Impediments Report: Measuring Tariff-Related Impediments.* Trade Policy Forum. Pacific Economic Co-operation Council.

Venables, A.J. 2002. *Winners and Losers From Regional Integration Agreements.* Available at: http://econ.lse.ac.uk/staff/ajv/research_material.html#regint. Accessed September 10, 2003.

Venables, A.J. in press. "Regional integration agreements: A force for convergence or divergence?" *The Economic Journal.*

Venables, A.J. and L.A. Winters. 2003. *Economic Integration in the Americas: European Perspectives.* London School of Economics, London (unpublished manuscript)

Viner, J. 1950. *The Customs Union Issue.* New York: Carnegie Endowment for International Peace.

Wain, B. 2002. "Outgoing chief says lack of integration puts off foreign investors," *The Asian Wall Street Journal.* 05 November. p. A3.

Winters, L.A. 1999. "Regionalism for developing countries: Assessing costs and benefits," in J. Burki, G. Perry and S. Calvo (eds) *Trade: Towards Open Regionalism.* Washington, DC: The World Bank. pp. 141–185.

World Trade Organization. (WTO). 2002. "Regional trade integration under transformation," background paper prepared by the Trade Policy Review Division of the WTO for the conference on *The Changing Architecture of the Global Trading System,* organized by the World Trade Organization, Geneva, April 26.

World Trade Organization. (WTO). 2003, November 14. *A Changing Landscape of RTAs*. Geneva: WTO.

World Trade Organization (WTO). 2004, April 5. *World Trade 2003, Prospects For 2004*. Press Release. No. Press/373.

Yamazawa, I. and S. Urata. 2000. "Trade and investment liberalization and facilitation," in I. Yamazawa (ed) *Asia Pacific Economic Co-operation: Challenges and Tasks for the Twenty-First Century.* London and New York: Routledge. pp. 57–97.

Chapter 5

TRADE, COMPETITIVENESS AND FOREIGN INVESTMENT AND THE LINKAGES AMONG THEM

5.1 OUTER-ORIENTATION: THE STRATEGIC STANCE

The conventional wisdom of the 1990s is that growth prospects for developing countries are greatly enhanced if they adopt an outer-oriented strategy and fairly uniform incentives—primarily through the exchange rate—for production, which includes production for exporting and import competing goods.[151] Outer-orientation *inter alia* comprises strategies followed in the area of trade, investment and exchange rate. The chosen policy framework in these imperative policy areas can determine whether an economy would succeed in climbing on to the high growth trajectory, or would settle for a low-level equilibrium for an inordinate period. Policies and growth experiences of dynamic Asian economies in these areas are widely considered valuable for the developing economies.

Economists have debated for decades whether there is a positive link between openness to trade and investment, or liberalization of policy stance on the one hand, and economic performance on the other. Although there is no consensus, it is widely agreed that outer-orientation or liberalization of trade and investment regimes spurs efficiency gains and promotes real GDP growth (Section 5.2). Both trade and foreign direct investment (FDI) are regarded as facilitators of growth and development. They individually have a direct bearing on GDP growth, and concurrently have an indirect impact through their linkages. However, establishing a causal link has not been possible. In addition, evidence

---

[151] For a recent analysis of the concept of outer-orientation refer to Krueger (1997).

at the microeconomic level points in the same direction. Asian firms that either were export-oriented or had foreign partnership of some ilk were found to be far more productive than the totally domestic-oriented firms. Productivity differences of 40 percent were found between the two sets of firms in Indonesia and the Philippines, and 15 to 20 percent in Thailand and the Republic of Korea (hereinafter Korea) (Hallward-Driemeier et al., 2002).

Although Japan, the four newly industrialized Asian economies (NIAEs)[152] followed by the ASEAN-4[153] traditionally epitomize the success of outer-oriented development strategy, the People's Republic of China (hereinafter China) has been the most successful recent case (see Chapter 2, Section 2.5.1). During the decade of the 1990s, China's exports to and market share in the mature industrial economies expanded appreciably. Over the preceding four decades, Asia established itself as the most dynamic trading region of the world. Statistical data in Section 5.2 underpins this assertion.

5.1.1 Adopting outer-orientation

Different Asian economies adopted outer-orientation at different points in time. As stated in Chapter 2, Japan provided lead in the adoption of this strategy in Asia. The safe time point for its adoption can be taken as late 1940s. Sachs and Warner (1995) determined the time points for adoption of different Asian economies. According to their reckoning, Hong Kong and Thailand were almost always open economies without high tariff and non-tariff barriers (NTBs). Malaysia and Taiwan adopted outer-orientation in 1963, while Singapore in 1964, Korea in 1968, Indonesia in 1970, China in 1978 and the Philippines in 1988. These economies continued liberalization of their trade and investment regimes with the passage of time, albeit the pace varied in every one of them.

As Japan pioneered the outer-oriented growth strategy, its success on the export front was phenomenal in the 1950s and 1960s, eventually turning it into the first Asian economy to develop into a mature industrial economy (Chapter 2, Section 2.4). The NIAEs was the first major group (Hong Kong should be excluded) that tread Japan's path of outer-orientation and export-induced success in the 1960s. Their economic growth trailed Japan by 15 to 20 years. They also achieved astonishingly rapid growth, and by early 1990s succeeded in achieving the living standards that were comparable to the industrial economies. In 1997, they were grouped with the high-income countries by the World Bank. To be sure, significant differences among them persist. The next country group that began to adopt outer-oriented strategy in the 1970s or later was the ASEAN-4. The

[152] Hong Kong SAR, Korea (Republic of), Singapore and Taiwan.

[153] ASEAN stands for the Association of Southeast Asian Nations. Indonesia, Malaysia, the Philippines and Thailand are called the ASEAN-4 group of countries.

group recorded impressive growth rates in the 1980s and the 1990s, and three of its members were classified as the emerging market economies (EMEs). Individual differences existed, and continue, in this group as well. The most significant case is that of Indonesia, whose petroleum reserves and OPEC membership set it apart from the other three economies. It also kept the level of protection higher than the other three members of the group. Their rapid growth was essentially based on reliance on their export markets, although less so than that of the NIAEs. One striking difference between the two country groups is the ASEAN-4 was more resource rich than the NIAEs (Krueger, 2000).

The last to adopt the outer-oriented strategy was the Philippines, while China was the second last. Although China's contemporary success in global trade after the adoption of outer-orientation strategy has been widely discussed and incessantly analyzed in the academe, when annual rate of export growth in constant dollars for the other successful Asian economies is compared, China's growth rate does not appear out of line. For instance, over the 1954–81 period Japan's annual average export growth rate averaged 14.2 percent. For Korea, during the 1960–95 period it was 21.5 percent, while for Malaysia over the 1968–96 period it was 10.2 percent. For the four NIAEs it averaged 13.1 percent for the 1966–97 period. Against this backdrop, China's export growth rate of 11.9 percent for the 1978–2002 fails to appear exceptionally remarkable or excessively favorable (Prasad and Rambaugh, 2003). China was not a trailblazer but merely followed the Asian tradition of outer-orientation, and kept up with its energetic neighbors in trade performance.

For the purpose of adopting outer-oriented strategy, tariffs and NTBs are brought steadily down, and obstructions in the way of capital inflows are removed. One standard measure of trade policy liberalization is the ratio of trade to GDP, where trade includes both exports and imports. On an average, the trade to GDP ratio is higher for the East and Southeast Asian economies (65.6 percent) than that for the Economic and Monetary Union (EMU)[154] economies (56.3 percent) and the NAFTA members. That said, there is a significant diversity in this ratio for the Asian economies. As Hong Kong SAR and Singapore have been long-standing and successful *entrepot*, this ratio is the highest for them. It is relatively lower for China because it was an autarky until 1978 and stated liberalizing its economy only after that time point. Cambodia and Lao PDR are also at the lower end, reflecting the slower and recent opening of their economies.

The value of import tariff revenues earned by an economy is another indicator used for measuring the degree of openness in trade. It has been reduced

---

[154] The Agreement in Maastricht was signed on a Treaty on European Union on December 10, 1991. It included a timetable for Economic and Monetary Union. On January 1, 1993, the European Single Market was completed. On November 1, 1993, the Maastricht Treaty came into force, and the EEC became the European Union (EU).

considerably over the decade of the 1990s, largely owing to the effects of regional integration agreements (RIAs) and the post-Uruguay Round multilateral trade liberalization. In 1990s, import tariff revenues earned by the Asian economies were much higher than those for the EMU economies and the members of NAFTA. Hong Kong SAR, Japan and Singapore were the exceptions in this regard, where import tariff revenues were low. Higher tariff revenues reflected Asia's developing country status as well as early liberalization of trade policy regime in the other two country groups. Although the European Economic Community (EEC) became the European Union (EU) in 1993 after the Treaty of Maastrischt and NAFTA were launched in January 1994, the EU and NAFTA were liberalizing their trade regime for a while. Compared to them, Asian economies were late and slower in liberalizing. However, the statistics for 2000 show that in a short time-span the tariff revenues for the Asian economies had fallen sharply. Progress toward ASEAN Free Trade Area (AFTA), the Bogor Declaration (1994) of liberalizing trade in stages for the Asia-Pacific Economic Co-operation (APEC) forum members, and rapid trade liberalization in China for the purpose of acceding to the World Trade Organization (WTO) led to rapidly reducing the trade barriers in Asia. Average tariff rates in primary and manufactured products in China declined from 41 percent in 1992 to 16.3 percent in 2000. China acceded to the WTO in 2001.

5.1.2 Global capital flows

Volume of private capital flows from the global markets to an economy reflects, first, the degree of openness of the economy, second its domestic investment climate and, third, its credibility and creditworthiness in the world of global finance. Liberalization endeavors in developing and transitional economies, when they stay the course, lead to a qualitative transformation in the economies that undertake them. This qualitative transformation in turn enables them to integrate with the global economy and take advantage from global factor movements, in particular capital flows. These economies have been christened the EMEs.[155] An indispensable condition for an EME is its sustained ability to

[155] What are the emerging market economies? Other than the rapid endogenous growth endeavors, respect of property rights and respect of human rights are some of the basic prerequisites of becoming an emerging market economy. The national government should offer protection to property and human rights of both, the citizens of the country and the non-residents alike. An indispensable condition for an emerging-market economy is its sustained ability to attract global capital inflows. Only an assurance of protection of property rights will attract global investors to a potential emerging market economy. Thus, protection of property rights is a fundamental, non-negotiable, condition, which an economy needs to meet before embarking on its road to

attract global capital.[156] These inflows, as a percentage of the GDP, for Asia have remained low. In 2000, this proportion was as low as 13.3 percent. The comparable percentage for the EMU economies was 49.3 percent. As 2000 was a post-Asian crisis year, its effects on the global capital inflows to Asia are obvious. In addition, in several Asian economies financial market development has been slow and is a long way from the EMU countries.

A noteworthy relationship between FDI and trade was observed in the economies that follow outer-oriented liberalized policy regime. FDI has followed trade in Asia. This relationship was not unidirectional because at the next stage of growth, trade followed foreign investment. Both trade and investment stimulated integration of Asian economies. One recent study has generalized this relationship and concluded that first trade expansion leads to FDI, and then the relationship is reversed and FDI leads to trade expansion (UNCTAD, 2001). However, emergence of international and regional production networks have put the veracity of this inter-relationship in doubt. Additional benefits of FDI include more rapid growth in the recipient economy, upward movement on the industrialization ladder, and its integration with the regional and global economies (OECD, 2002). The dynamic Asian economies bear witness to this trend (Das, 1996a, 1997).

Outer-orientation of strategy is necessary, although not sufficient, for FDI inflows. Factors that attract FDI have varied from period to period. In the present global economic *mise-en-scene,* creating an enabling environment for the inflows of FDI in the domestic economy requires certain level of development in the areas of education, technology and physical and financial infrastructure. Furthermore, FDI flows have not been observed to take the direction of economies that have not attained a certain level of macroeconomic, exchange rate and socio-political stability, institutional development and policy predictability, efficient and equitable tax administration, capital market development and most importantly created a liberal trade and financial policy regime. This calls for proactive pragmatic changes in several policy areas by the host country government. Many Asian economies, particularly the EMEs of Asia, succeeded in creating this enabling environment and are reaping the benefits of brisk FDI inflows. When economies fail to maintain this policy milieu, FDI is known to

---

becoming an emerging market economy. So far there is little agreement on the country count. In the industrial economies the emerging market economies were thought of as the newly industrialized economies (NIEs) and some middle-income developing countries. The latter group included those countries in which governments and firms are creditworthy enough from the perspective of global investors to successfully borrow from the global capital markets and/or attract institutional portfolio investment. Different international institutions include slightly different sets of countries in this category (Das, 2004a).

[156] See Das (2004a), particularly Chapter 2.

exit. One case in point is Indonesia after 1997; FDI stock has been depleting because of economic and socio-political uncertainties.

Since the early 1970s, FDI has grown so much that it became a defining feature of both Asian and global economies. In the aftermath of the 1982 debt crisis, bank lending to the developing economies had dried up. Many developing economies saw FDI as a stable source of development finance and began to liberalize and modulate their domestic policies to attract it. Development of the concept of bilateral investment treaties (BITs), prescriptions from multilateral development banks and positive evidence from developing countries that had liberalized their economies for FDI inflows created an appropriate enabling environment for the rapid FDI inflows. They were also underpinned by contemporary wave of globalization of the world economy (Das, 2004a).

The share of FDI in global capital flows to developing economies increased from 24 percent in 1990 to 60 percent in 2000. Between 1973 and 1995, global FDI flows increased over 12 times, while trade flows increased over 8.5 times. Between 1995 and 2000, global FDI flows increased 40.3 times, while global trade flows increased 1.2 times.[157] Thus, long-term growth rate of FDI has been much higher than that of international trade. The FDI flows increased from $209 billion in 1990 to $1.27 trillion in 2000. In 2001 FDI recorded precipitous declines of 40.9 percent and in 2002 another decline of 21.0 percent. In 2002, FDI flows stood at $651 billion (UNCTAD, 2003a).

The transnational corporations (TNCs) have been the foremost source of global FDI. Based on a survey of 500 TNCs, EIU (2004) has projected a rebound in the FDI flows in 2004 and 2005. Strengthening global economic recovery and a pick-up in fixed capital spending, as well as improved confidence with regard to mergers and acquisitions (M&As), would underpin the recovery in global FDI flows. Other reasons for expecting growth in FDI over the medium-term include the ongoing global trend toward better business environments (as measured by the EIU's cross-country business environment rankings), including ever more open policies toward FDI; progress in regional integration; technological change and the search for competitively priced skills; sharper global competition pushing companies to seek lower cost destinations; and opportunities in emerging markets.

In response to the growing importance of FDI in the global economy and international economic relations, the international policy framework for FDI was needed to be strengthened and endeavors were made to transmute it in accordance with the changing needs of the global economy in the early 1990s. The composition of FDI flows changed during the 1990s from largely "greenfield"

---

[157] Over this period global FDI flows soared from $25 billion to $315 billion, while trade flows rose from $575 billion to $4,900 billion. In 2000, the global FDI was $1.27 trillion and global trade was $6.18 trillion.

investment to M&As, which led to increased integration among economies. However, the M&A-related FDI steadily declined after 2000.

5.1.3 Role played by TNCs

The TNCs are attracted by outer-oriented strategy in the host economy. The additional capital made available by the investing TNCs helps in increasing exports by raising investment levels in the promising sectors, that is, sectors having comparative advantage. Inflows of FDI from large TNCs are acknowledged to bring in technology, managerial skills and training opportunities for the domestic workforce. Technology diffusion to broader domestic manufacturing and business sectors takes place through legion of channels. However, researchers concur that the most important source of technological spillover are vertical linkages between TNCs and local suppliers in the host economy (OECD, 2003). Foreign-owned enterprises and TNCs commonly provide their suppliers with technical assistance, training, blueprints and other information to raise the quality of their final product.

Besides, investing TNCs help in market expansion for the domestic firms and facilitate their access to the regional and global markets. The resources and market access that TNCs make available to the host country complement host country's own resources and "can provide some of the missing elements for greater competitiveness" (UNCTAD, 2002). As competitiveness of the host economy enhances, its capability of earning foreign exchange—which has myriad usages for an emerging market or developing economy—also increases. It was observed in the Asian economies that rising export competitiveness moved the host economy to a higher plateau of development, meaning thereby, from primary extractive industries, low-technology and less capital-intensive sectors, and further on to high-technology, export-oriented industries and products. Furthermore, the host economy is able to benefit from dynamic effects of FDI by realizing scale economies through accessing larger and more diverse markets.[158] Competitive assets provided by the TNCs for export-oriented production in the host economy are often firm-specific and are difficult for firms in the emerging market and developing economies to acquire independently, without external assistance or interaction (World Economic Forum [WEF], 2002).

The impact of TNC operations and investment over the global GDP and economic welfare has been a subject of numerous empirical studies. Some of their conclusions point in the same direction and indicate that (i) the relationship between FDI and global GDP growth is positive, (ii) as the affiliates embed themselves in the host economy, FDI operations create skilled jobs, increase

---

[158] Refer to UNCTAD (2002), Chapter 6, for an extensive discussion of improved competitiveness that TNC operation can enable in a host economy.

local value-added and a suppliers' networks, (iii) technology transfer is another real benefit, (iv) affiliates contributes to both real income growth through efficiency and productivity in the host economy and (v) the principal channel for this contribution is through increase in total factor productivity (TFP), which fundamentally entails an increase in efficiency of the resource utilization. Urata (2001) convincingly demonstrated that these results apply to Asian economies as well. These empirical studies do not concur on all aspects of FDI. They disagree regarding the magnitude of FDI's contribution to real income growth and productivity in the host economy. Another important point of disagreement was that while some of them concluded that FDI "crowds out" domestic investment, others reached the opposite inference.

Owing to these TNC benefits, many EMEs and developing economies devised incentive packages, or improved the existing ones, during the 1990s. Notwithstanding what was said in the preceding paragraph, benefits of TNC cannot be taken for granted. There can be situations in which TNC operations may not have a salutary effect in the host economy. For instance, if the TNC operations focus only on the static comparative advantage of the host economy, numerous dynamic benefits associated with export-oriented TNC subsidiaries may not materialize at all in the host economy. In such a case "dynamic comparative advantage may not be developed, local value-added may not be increased, and affiliates may not embed themselves in the local economy by building linkages to the domestic entrepreneurial community" (UNCTAD, 2002). The common dynamic benefits like training of labor and transfer of technology also may not materialize. In addition, as the competition to attract TNC investment has intensified, the costs of wooing them may be too high and the benefits may not be commensurate to the costs for the host economy.

5.1.4 Interaction between trade and FDI

Whether trade and FDI interact to initiate a mutually reinforcing virtuous circle or not has been analyzed in the recent period for the Asian economies. Multilateral organizations demonstrated special interest in delving into the trade and FDI link.[159] This inter-relationship has high economic significance and is important per se. The developmental implications of this link have become an overarching concern for policy mandarins. So has its effect on employment,

[159] Particularly the Organization for Economic Co-operation and Development (OECD), United Nations Conference on Trade and Development (UNCTAD) and the World Trade Organization (WTO) devoted a great deal of time and resources to producing several empirical studies and Working Group reports on trade—FDI nexus. Three influential, albeit somewhat dated, studies on trade—FDI nexus were conducted in 1996. They were: (1) *Investment, Trade and International Policy Arrangements,* UNCTAD (1996a) (2) *World Investment Report*, UNCTAD (1996b) and (3) the *1996 Annual Report* of the World Trade Organization.

environment, competition, innovation and technology transfer. The Asian experience demonstrated that there is nothing simple and direct about this interrelationship. It tended to show variation with product, sector and the set of economies. It was also found to vary with the kind of FDI and the level of economic growth of the host economies.

As set out in the preceding chapters, Asian economies, particularly the EMEs, went a long way in liberalizing their trade and foreign investment policy regimes, particularly during the 1980s and 1990s. Liberalization was a part and parcel of the outer-oriented strategy of development, and it strengthened the trade–FDI linkage in the dynamic Asian economies. As the regional economic integration progressed in Asia, the significance of intra-regional trade and FDI nexus further intensified. Evolution of integrated production networks was one of the direct outcomes of trade–FDI nexus.[160] This strategy has both intra-regional and global elements, which are essential for continued growth of the regional economy. Although these issues were touched upon in a fleeting manner in another context in Chapter 3, they are the principal focus of Section 5.7 in this chapter.

5.2 TRADE PERFORMANCE

Several policy measures and macroeconomic factors that were crucial to GDP growth in Japan were subsequently found in the NIAEs, ASEAN-4 and lastly in China. Consequently, if GDP growth rates of these countries and sub-groups are plotted on a logarithmic scale, they tend to show parallel trends. However, majority of these economies began their exports from a low level. As evident from the foregoing exposition, trade recorded a phenomenal growth in Asia. Over the 1980–2000 period, exports soared sixfold and imports fivefold. Although during the decade of the 1990s, trade growth in Asia was slower than that in the 1980s, trade still managed to double during this decade. In 2000, Asian exports touched $2,153 billion. After a slight decline in 2001 to $1,905 billion, they rose to $2037 billion in 2002.[161] In 2003, Asia recorded merchandise trade expansion of 11 percent in real terms, more than twice as fast as the average growth rate (4.5 percent) of the world merchandise trade.[162]

Asian trade statistics has a low base effect. China is the most recent and notable example of this low base effect. In the mid-1970s, China's exports were

---

[160] The basic concept of integrated international production was propounded by UNCTAD in 1993. Refer to UNCTAD, 1993 as well as UNCTAD, 1999.

[161] World Trade Organization. 2004. *International Trade Statistics*. Geneva. May. 2004. Table III 1.

[162] World Trade Organization (WTO). 2004. *World Trade 2003, Prospects For 2004*. Press Release. No. Press/373. 5 April .

around $7 billion. When the "open-door policy" was launched in 1979, exports were still a paltry $12.6 billion. The economy opened itself at an unpropitious period because global recession in the early 1980s followed by a weak recovery reduced import demand in the industrial economies for China's exports. Also, China was a latecomer to the club of successful Asian exporters; it was not accorded the favorable treatment that the NIAEs and the ASEAN-4 economies enjoyed under the Generalized System of Preferences (GSP), when they had launched their trade-induced growth programs. Nevertheless, the recent statistics for China reflect a radical change in the structure of its economy, macroeconomic management and growth performance.

Using nominal and constant dollar trade figures, Das (2000c) showed that trade in Asian economies grew much faster on average than the rate of global trade expansion. Using quinquennial growth rates of exports growth, Das (2000c) led to the same conclusion. In Chapter 2, Section 2.2, we saw that several dynamic Asian economies have grown into globally significant traders and have important places on the WTO league table of leading traders. Owing to the successful trade performance the dynamic Asian economies have become a significant, if not conspicuous, group in their own right in the global economy, accounting for a quarter of multilateral trade. The total share of the ten dynamic Asian economies in the world exports was 25.1 percent in 2002 and 25.5 percent in 2003. This made their global export share much larger than that of Germany (10.0 percent) and the United States (9.7 percent), the two largest individual trading economies in the world (WTO, 2004). This implies that the ten dynamic Asian economies as a group have a significance presence, credence and influence in the multilateral trading system.[163] The share of China in the world exports did not begin to rise until 1980, but thereafter it recorded a vigorous increase. Between 1980 and 1990 it more than doubled to 1.9 percent of total multilateral exports. Between 1990 and 1997, it almost doubled again to 3.3 percent. In 2003, it was 5.9 percent of the total multilateral exports, not much less than that of Japan (6.3 percent), the third largest treading economy in the world. According to the 2003 statistics, Japan and China are the third and fourth largest exporters in the world.

5.2.1 Trade and economic growth nexus

There is a sizeable body of literature that attributes brisk growth in Asia to successful structural transformation due to trend in export performance.

[163] The largest of the ten exporters was Japan accounting for 6.3 percent of the global exports in 2003, followed by China which accounted for 5.9 percent. The other exporters were ranked in the following order: Hong Kong SAR, Korea, Taiwan, Singapore, Malaysia, Thailand, Indonesia and the Philippines.

Quite a few studies highlighted various beneficial static and dynamic aspects of the trade-growth nexus in a stylized manner. The logic included greater capacity utilization in the economy, resource allocation in line with the comparative advantage, exploitation of scale economies, technological upgradation first at micro- and then macroeconomic levels and efficient management procedures leading to higher GDP growth rate.[164] Many of these take place due to competitive pressure from abroad. These studies imply that since there are substantial differences in productivity in export-oriented firms and industries and domestically oriented ones (noted in Section 5.1), economies that are dominated by the former benefited from higher growth rates. These studies treated trade as a locomotive of growth and industrial competitiveness.

Trend in export growth portends to a long-term trend in an economy's foreign exchange earnings. Export earnings increase when the terms of trade turn favorable, and fall when they turn unfavorable. This is a transitory effect on exports and is not taken to imply any long-term trend because as soon as the business cycle turns, both export and GDP growth plummet. Therefore, we take only the export growth stemming from "reasonably efficient set of incentives" as well as induced by other factors as a long-term trend in export expansion (Krueger, 2000). By incentives we mean equal incentives for producers to spend domestic resources on earning a unit of foreign exchange, or for producing for the domestic market. They do *not* imply differential rewards for production for exports and for domestic production. Where discriminatory ad hoc incentives are provided for export promotion, first the strategy is not sustainable, and second, it does not spawn a long-term trend in export expansion and GDP growth rate. Besides, such ad hoc export incentives are not WTO-consistent.

Export as an engine of growth was considered the new orthodoxy in economics; but some later studies questioned this hypothesis and expressed skepticism due to two reasons. First, in the trade-growth nexus causality could not be established in an unequivocal manner and the statistical link at best remained weak. Second, when endogenous growth models were used, the hypothesis that export played a role in GDP growth was not convincingly proven. Several studies disagreed with the hypothesis, while others found the link tenuous.[165] Besides, empirical studies exploring cross-country evidence concluded that per capita growth rates had little correlation with the export/GDP ratios, once the regression included other important variables, such as savings, investment in plant and equipment and rate of technology absorption.

---

164 See among others Balassa (1978), Krueger (1980 and 1995), Feder (1982), Balasa and Williamson (1990), Edwards (1992 and 1993) and Dollar (1993). Also, refer to the survey of this literature by Bhagwati and Srinivasan (1999) on this issue.

165 See, for instance, Kormendi and Meguire (1985), Grossman and Helpman (1991), Young (1991), and Levine and Renelt (1992).

The post-war Asian economic history provides evidence of benefits from successful trade expansion. The regression results of Fukuda and Toya (1995) concluded that the effect of export growth on the GDP growth rate of dynamic Asian economies was significantly positive. Their rejection of the empirical studies that came up with ambiguous conclusions regarding the trade-growth nexus was based on data problems and choice of inappropriate dummy variables. What was convincing in their assertion was that the standard endogenous growth model was not applicable to Asian economies of the latter half of the 1980s and early 1990s, because of the post-Plaza accord (see Chapter 2, Section 2.4) currency configuration. It led to dramatic increases in the demand for exports of manufactured goods from the dynamic Asian economies. The big demand pull contributed to rapid GDP growth without following the sequential steps prescribed by the endogenous growth models. During this period, many dynamic Asian economies sustained export growth rates of 20 percent and even higher. Several of them had agriculturally based economies or were exporters of textiles and apparel. Rapid trade expansion provided them with an opportunity to climb up the technological ladder and become exporters of sophisticated manufactured lines of products. The bottom line in this long enduring debate is that the belief that "there is a positive and significant relationship between more rapid and sustained export growth on the one hand and more rapid and continuing GDP growth on the other" is seldom questioned (Dollar, 1993). Rapid clip trade expansion is associated with speedy industrialization. The prestigious World Bank study of the Asian "miracle" identified trade as the key element in the high performance of the dynamic Asian economies.[166]

Trade expansion in the dynamic Asian economies progressed *pari passu* with expansion in the size of the GDP cake, structural transformation and maturing economic institutions.[167] As these economies moved up their growth trajectories, the product mix continued to change. In Section 5.5.3, we shall see how the proportion of exports of manufactures in total exports from the Asian economies increased steadily. Exports from the dynamic Asian economies diversified away from resource- and labor-intensive products to high-technology manufacturing products.

5.2.2 Export deceleration and the Asian crisis

As seen above, export expansion became a vitally important policy instrument of Asian economic growth. By 1990, external demand had become one of

---

[166] Several noted trade and development scholars had contributed to this study. It was cited in Chapter 1. Its title is *The East Asian Miracle: Economic Growth and Public Policy*.

[167] Confirmation of this is provided by the five country case studies in *Asian Export,* edited by Dilip K. Das, published by the Oxford University Press in 2000 (Das, 2000a).

the most important sectors of the dynamic Asian economies. As a locomotive for growth, exports began to have a profound impact on their economic performance. Many Asian economies had moved up the growth and industrialization ladder and became successful exporters of several high technology products, particularly information technology (IT)-related products like computer hardware, semiconductor and integrated circuits (ICs). They began to compete with the mature industrial economies. As the Asian economies imported intermediate inputs, parts and components from Japan and other industrial economies for their export products, their sensitivity to real exchange variations increased markedly. Using regression analysis, Ito (2000) established that this pattern of production and export increased the sensitivity of Asian economies' real exchange rates to movements in both the dollar and the yen.

Beginning mid-1996 export growth rates in the dynamic Asian economies began to plummet from around 20 percent to single digits in the ANIEs and were decelerated to less than half in the ASEAN-4 economies. The deceleration was most striking in Thailand, where deceleration in export growth rate took place from 25 percent to minus 1 percent during this period. The next worst case was Korea where it decelerated from 30 percent to 4 percent. The question whether this transition to low export growth rates was a structural and permanent feature or a cyclical one began to be asked in various national, regional and international fora. The deceleration in this vital sector became one of the primary causal factors behind the Asian crisis (Das, 1996b).

There were several reasons behind the deceleration. First, exchange rate in several Asian economies was appreciating, as many of them had pegged their exchange rates to the dollar. As stability in their nominal exchange rates was the objective of the policymakers, having a dollar peg seemed logical to them. Under this circumstance, if the domestic inflation rate is higher than that in the United States, real currency appreciation is the direct result. Second, 1996 saw an abrupt decline in the global export growth rate. This decline from cyclical peak in 1995 was the largest in 15 years—in dollar terms the deceleration was from 20 percent in 1995 to 4 percent in 1996. Third, on the one hand Japan was an important trade partner of the Asian economies. On the other hand Asian economies competed with Japan in the global market place. Although Asian economies had achieved stability in exchange rate vis-à-vis the dollar, it did not mean that their real effective exchange rate (REER) became stable. The yen depreciated by over 50 percent between January 1995 and June 1996, which was christened the yen shock. Slowdown in global export growth compounded with the negative impact of the yen shock. Asian exports in the global market, as well as in the Japanese market, lost considerable competitiveness in several product lines and suffered enormously.

The Asian economies also received serious sectoral shocks. During the 1995–97 period commodity and oil prices plummeted. What was worse was that a recession in the global electronics and information technology (IT) sectors began in 1996. Prices in the semiconductor and computer-related hardware products recorded a precipitous decline due to overwhelming overcapacity. This is considered the trigger behind the 1966 deceleration. Semiconductor industry in Korea and Malaysia and integrated circuit (IC) sector in Thailand suffered the worst from the declining global prices. Several Asian economies, particularly Korea, Malaysia, Taiwan and Thailand, had large parts of their exports concentrated in the IT sector. Korea was particularly hard hit when the 16-MB DRAM chips, which accounted for a large share of electronics exports, fell from a peak of $150 per unit to $10 between 1995 and 1997. Such a precipitous price recession caused massive terms of trade losses for the Asian economies. Prices of labor-intensive manufactures, such as textiles and apparel, were also unsteady during this period. These factors coalesced to trigger the 1996 deceleration in Asian exports, which in turn eased Asian economies on toward the crisis.

Existence of large intra-regional trade exacerbated the situation. The Japanese economy was in the doldrums and was underperforming since 1990; consequently its import demand had substantially weakened. As it was an important trading partner of several Asian economies, it had a damaging impact on their exports. Decline in the performance of one economy had a multiplier effect on others and the various economic shocks were amplified to have a pernicious effect over the regional economy (Das, 2000b).

5.2.3 Emerging trade triangle

China's vertiginous economic growth and trade expansion in a short time span became a development of great consequences both for Asia and for the global economy, which in turn made it essential to redefine China's economic relationship with the neighboring Asian and its other large global partners. The initial reaction of neighboring Asia to China's rapid growth, trade expansion and fast growing FDI stock was defensive, and was widely discussed in the financial press. They saw a formidable competitor looming uncomfortably large in the areas of trade and FDI. This apprehension, if is carried far, may "undermine both regional and global multilateralism and retard the progress of trade-induced growth in the region" (Ronald-Holst, 2002). A careful scrutiny would reveal that this newly evolving situation would usher in not only threats but also opportunities.

The long-term economic relations and trade pattern were simulated by Ronald-Holst (2002) with the help of a multi-country dynamic forecasting model. This modeling framework had traditional neoclassical roots and was a eighteen country/region, eight sector global CGE model, calibrated over a period of 24 years between 1987 and 2010. This model made product differentiation and captured the pervasive phenomenon of intra-industry trade, where an economy is both an importer and exporter of similar goods. The results indicated that while regional economies will be required to make adjustments, benefits would likely outweigh costs if the neighboring economies adopt flexible and accommodating trade policies. An important conclusion of this modeling exercise was that as a large and rapidly growing economy, China would have two immediate influences over the region. First, it would intensify export competition among the regional economies in a wide array of product lines, justifying the threatening giant image of China. Second, China's long-term growth trajectory would make it a leading Asian importer. It should open unprecedented market opportunities for the neighboring Asian exporters, in turn leading to acceleration of their export growth. In fact, this has already materialized (refer to Section 5.9 also). As China's domestic economy is still emerging, this aspect is seldom noted and discussed among the Asian policymakers. With such rapid real GDP growth and trade expansion, China should reasonably emerge as a future source economy of FDI in Asia. Overtures of this trend already exist and have been discussed below (see Section 5.6.1).

China emerged as a major engine for intra-regional trade in 2002. This trend accelerated in 2003, and involved most of developing Asian economies as well. The dynamic economies in East Asia and Southeast Asia benefited most from the strong increase in China's imports. In 2003, China became the single largest export market for the East Asian economies while for Southeast Asian ones, China's share in total exports became sizable. Exports from Asian economies to China were spurred by its strong economic growth, acceleration in export growth, stable exchange rate and the integrated production networks of which China became an integral part. Ronald-Holst's (2002) simulation exercise concluded that by 2020 China would be Asia's largest trading nation and "its growth over the intervening period will dramatically change the regional economy." It should, however, be noted that in 2003 China ($438.4 billion) was not far behind Japan ($471.9 billion) in terms of merchandise exports. Japan's exports were merely 7.6 percent higher than that of China. The simulation exercise estimated that by 2010 China would be Asia's largest exporter, while it would be the largest importer earlier, by 2005. The time line in the simulation went a trifle off the mark because WTO (2004) statistics indicated that in 2003 China *was* the largest importer ($412.8 billion) in Asia and the third largest in the world, accounting for 5.3 percent of world imports. Japan stood in the second place ($383.3 billion) in Asia and sixth in the global economy, accounting for 4.9 percent of the global imports.

This evolving scenario also pointed to the growth of a trade triangle in Asia, whose three angles would be China, Asian economies and the mature industrial economies of the EU and North America. China is likely to run a substantial structural trade surplus with the mature industrial economies, while a structural deficit of almost equal magnitude with the Asian economies. This implies that

China would be an important export market for the Asian economies in the near future. Thus viewed, the ultimate benefits of China's success on the trade front would be passed on to its Asian neighbors in the form of significant rise in their exports to China. This leads one to the rational conclusion that China's economic success should be seen by the other Asian economies as a boon, not a bane. If the present growth trajectories persist, China would logically be the future locomotive of growth for Asia, which should be seen as a propitious development.

5.3 GROWING COHESION IN TRADING PATTERN

Other than the trade volume, trading pattern among the Asian economies evolved both regionally and globally during the decades of the 1980s and 1990s. This evolutionary process transformed the trading pattern discernibly. The simplest measure of trade is its dollar value. The value-related data are easily available, and provide one of the many ways of analyzing the evolution of current trading pattern in Asia as well as its changing paradigms. Using the International Monetary Fund (IMF) statistics, Sakakibara and Yamakawa (2003) tabulated average trade shares for the 1998–2000 period for the Asian economies.[168] This table reflected both intra-regional and extra-regional trade as well as transformations in it.[169] The tabulation revealed that with the exception of the smallest nations, which were also small traders, all Asian economies had a significant amount of trade with the European Union (EU)[170] and the United States, the two largest global traders. Their trade with the EU and the United States ranged between 10 and 30 percent of the total trade of these economies. The shares of intra-regional trade, or proportion of trade with ASEAN, of these economies were even larger. The smaller Asian economies had larger shares of intra-trade than the larger Asian economies. If trade with ASEAN-Plus-Three (APT)[171] economies is considered instead of that with ASEAN, the shares of trade for all countries rise significantly. The rationale of this rise is essentially addition of trade with Japan, which has been an important trading partner of

---

[168] International Monetary Fund. *Direction of Trade Statistics,* Washington, DC. Various issues.

[169] See Sakakibara and Yamakawa (2003), Table 4.1.

[170] On December 1, 1991, agreement was reached in Maastricht on the Treaty on European Union, with a timetable for the Economic and Monetary Union (EMU). The European Single Market was completed on January 1, 1993. On November 1, 1993, the Maastricht Treaty came into force after Danes voted yes at the second try, and the European Economic Community (EEC) became the European Union (EU).

[171] The ten ASEAN members are Brunei Darussalam, Cambodia, Indonesia, Lao PDR, Malaysia, Myanmar, the Philippines, Singapore, Thailand and Vietnam. The addition of the following three countries makes the ASEAN-Plus-Three (APT) grouping: China, Japan and Korea.

all Asian economies. Hong Kong SAR was an exception to this because its large trade with China pushed up the level of its trade with the ATP group of economies.

For analyzing the changes in the directionality of trade, trade statistics for the ASEAN group of economies, China and Japan were plotted for the 1980 and 2000 period by Sakakibara and Yamakawa (2003). Again, the IMF trade statistics were used for this purpose. Several interesting outcomes became evident. Japan was given its appropriate importance because what happened to Japan's trading pattern was important for the other Asian economies, because it was the only mature industrial economy of the region and was closely related to it by way of trade, investment and technology transfer. For the ASEAN group of economies, Japan was an important trading partner in 1980. However, with the passage of time its importance declined markedly. The share of imports from Japan dropped from 23 percent in 1980 to 16 percent in 2000. Share of exports to Japan also fell from 30 percent in 1980 to 13 percent in 2000. As the ASEAN-4 economies[172] were severely mauled by the Asian crisis, their imports were negatively impacted. But the post-crisis decline in imports from Japan was greater (37 percent between 1996 and 1998) than decline in ASEAN's total imports (26 percent over the same period).

ASEAN exports to Japan increased in absolute value between 1980 and 2000, but this growth did not keep pace with ASEAN's export growth, which increased sixfold in two decades to $432 billion in 2000. The importance of ASEAN's trade with the EU and the United States did not change appreciably since 1990, and the trade with Japan declined, as in 2000 ASEAN share of exports to Japan fell below those to the EU and the United States. As regards ASEAN's imports, the proportions of imports from the EU and Japan declined but those from the United States virtually remained unchanged.

As for the intra-ASEAN trade, there was an appreciable rise, particularly after 1990. Intra-ASEAN imports soared 10 percentage points between 1990 and 2000, from 16.4 percent of the total to 26.5 percent. This proportion was much higher than that of Japan (16 percent), the EU (11 percent) and the United States (14 percent). Unlike imports, intra-ASEAN export growth was slow. They rose by a mere 3 percent, to 23 percent of the total in 2000. Yet, this proportion was larger than that of the United States (20 percent), the EU (15 percent) and Japan (15 percent).

Japan's pattern of trade share also transformed discernibly. Among the broad trends that have emerged are decline in the proportion of trade with the EU and the United States and rising trade with the ASEAN region and China. The United States continues to be Japan's most prominent trading partner, accounting for 19 percent of Japan's imports and 30 percent of exports in 2000. Between 1980

[172] The ASEAN-4 group comprises Indonesia, Malaysia, the Philippines and Thailand.

and 2000, imports from China grew with a steep pace, tripling in value between 1990 and 2000. At $34 billion they were 14 percent of Japan's total imports. They were larger than imports from the EU (12 percent) and came close to those from the ASEAN (16 percent). However, Japan's exports to China have not shown a large increase since 1990, and are still 6 percent of the total.

At the defining moment in China's recent economic history, when the "open door" policy was adopted (1978), Japan was its closest trading partner accounting for over a quarter of its total trade. Since this point in time, China's trade has increased and diversified dramatically. By 2002, it became a significant trading economy, the fourth largest trader in the world. Although Japan continues to be the larges source of imports, its proportion of imports declined from 27 percent of the total in 1980 to 14 percent in 1990. It increased marginally, to 16 percent, in 2000. The same trend was mirrored by imports from the EU and the United States, which declined sharply over the 1980–2000 period. They were 12 percent and 8 percent of the total, respectively, in 2000. These declines were made up by sharp increase in China's imports from the ASEAN economies and Korea. By 2000, the two together accounted for almost a quarter of total Chinese imports. On the export side, the United States became the closest partner accounting for 27 percent of Chinese exports in 2000. For the EU and Japan the corresponding proportion was 14 percent each. For the EU this proportion was an improvement over the 1990 level, when the share of Chinese exports was only 9 percent of the total exports, while that of Japan it was14 percent. This implies that over the decade of the 1990s, the proportion of Chinese exports to Japan remained stationary. The Japanese economy suffered from four successive recessions during this period. These statistics show a complete reversal of the trend since 1980, when China's exports to the United States were only a small (5 percent) proportion of the total and those to Japan were the largest (22 percent). This reflects progressively closer economic relationship between China and the United States. It also reflects the fact that TNCs from the United States and EU have been increasingly moving their manufacturing activity to China and exporting to the rest of the world from their Chinese bases.[173]

Over the years the product composition of intra-regional trade in Asia grew increasingly concentrated. The largest 30 export products accounted for over half of the total intra-regional trade in 2003. Four large sub-sectors accounted for 38 percent of it. They were office machinery, telecommunication equipment, electronics and textile and apparel. Rapid expansion of integrated production networks, which also entails trade in parts, components and partially assembled goods, contributed most to increasing product concentration (refer to

[173] This part draws on Sakakibara and Yamakawa (2003) Chapter IV, Part II. The statistical data cited in this section also come from the same source.

Section 5.7). As China became an active player in regional production-sharing networks, it successfully located important niches in production-sharing, which resulted in an increase of $20 billion in exports of parts and components over the 1996–2001 period. Likewise, other smaller Asian economies have succeeded in locating their own niches. Japan has emerged as the economy that originates about a third of all integrated production network activity in the region and is a major participant in the exports of parts, components and partially assembled products. Intra-regional trade in Asia has also grown mutually complementary. At the present stage, the degree of complementarity is comparable to that in the EU (of original 6)[174] and NAFTA (Krumm and Kharas, 2003; Ng and Yeats, 2003). The three low-income economies (Cambodia, Lao PDR and Vietnam) of the APT group have not integrated well with the dynamic Asian economies and have also remained so far out of the production-sharing networks.

5.4 COMPETITIVENESS IN GLOBAL MARKET PLACE

Competitiveness is considered a vital variable for firms as well as economies. The micro- and macroeconomic aspects of competitiveness are also important to the dynamic Asian economies. Their importance snowballed during the mid-1990s. Competitiveness began to be treated as if it is one of the essential and elemental sources of growth like savings, investment, openness, trade and technology—or a newest elixir of economic growth. One reason for the abrupt rise in the significance of competitiveness was the total factor productivity (TFP) studies conducted during this period, which inferred that dynamic Asia's economic growth was essentially factor input- or accumulation-based (Chapter 2, Section 2.6). These results were widely noted and caused a good deal of concern among the policy mandarins.

Factors like macroeconomic policy structure, intensifying regionalization and globalization, absorption of technology and advancement in R&D, management skills and corporate governance impinge upon competitiveness at the micro- and macroeconomic levels, which in turn are influenced by the knowledge base of the economy. These factors have brought into focus a whole new range of challenges, and opportunities, for the Asian firms as well as the public policy community, whose eagerness for enhancement of competitiveness is manifested by their investment of resources in creating councils, committees and writing white papers on this vital issue. The Asian crisis rendered

---

[174] The European Economic Community Treaty, also known as the Treaty of Rome, was signed on March 25, 1957 between the following six countries: Belgium, France, Germany, Italy, Luxembourg, the Netherlands. These six were called the Common Market countries.

new urgency to harnessing globalization, technology, management skills and competitiveness for rapid growth and stability.

5.4.1 Quantifying competitiveness

In common parlance, competitiveness is understood as the ability to compete with rivals. The concept has applicability to a firm, an industrial sector, an industry or even an economy. A competitive firm or economy is expected to out-compete its counterpart. However, competitiveness at firm level and that at macroeconomic level are markedly different from each other. Labor productivity and other economic indicators are frequently used for quantifying competitiveness at the national level. If long-term national competitiveness is associated with labor productivity, the argument can be further developed as follows: the vital variable for achieving the long-term competitiveness is growth in productivity in an economy (Krugman, 1996). Another perspective regarding competitiveness is that national competitiveness should be determined by price competitiveness, which makes REER and unit labor cost (ULC) important measures of national competitiveness (McCombie and Thirlwall, 1994; Turner and Golub 1997). When general statements of competitiveness are made, people commonly think of the latter, that is, the price competitiveness. For instance, when China is referred to as a competitive economy in the global market place, it is taken to mean that its currency is undervalued, the wages are lower than that of the neighboring economies and labor productivity is virtually the same or higher. This would help make the Chinese products competitive in the global market place and it would be able to out-compete the other Asian economies.

Quantification of national-level competitiveness with the help of abovementioned variables is not a simple and straightforward exercise. There are several problems with the computations of labor productivity, REER, and ULC. For one, reliable data series on wages and productivity for constructing ULCs are difficult to come by *a fortiori* in the developing economies. Second, for making inter-country comparisons of ULCs one needs to translate the costs in individual countries into a common currency, which poses problems. Third, rise in ULC in an economy should lead to a logical decline in the competitiveness in the global market place, but empirical evidence paradoxically shows that market share of exports and their relative unit costs or prices of exports from industrial economies tended to move together. This is called the Kaldor paradox (Fagerberg, 1996). Fourth, the non-price factors play a significant role. It is possible for the REER or ULC to rise in tandem with strong economic performance. If firms in a country become more successful in terms of non-price competitiveness because they are innovative, flexible, produce high-quality goods, then the REER would logically strengthen. Finally, both the REER or ULC measures can be calculated in different ways, potentially leading to different results (Asian Development Bank [ADB], 2003).

To see how the Asian economies have performed on the various competitiveness rankings in the world, let us examine the principal competitiveness indexes. The concept of a competitiveness index has been an attractive and useful one and since 1979 the World Economic Forum (WEF) began publishing an annual *Global Competitiveness Report.*[175] Its methodology went on changing, evolving and improving from year to year, bringing in marginal improvements as it went along. The *Global Competitiveness Report* computes two sets of competitiveness indices: the growth competitiveness index (GCI) developed by Jeffrey D. Sachs of Columbia University and the business competitiveness index (BCI) developed by Michael Porter of Harvard University. The two indexes are based on hard data compiled by the WEF in its annual Executive Opinion Survey (EOS). One improvement that was brought about in 2003–04 was increasing the number of country coverage from 80 to 102.

The GCI is based on three broad criteria: the macroeconomic environment, the quality of public institutions and technological base of the economy. It quantifies the growth potential of the economies it covers. In the GCI ranking for 2003–04 only a small number of dynamic Asian economies were near the top. Taiwan had the 5th place and Singapore the 6th. Other economies with high rankings included Japan was 11th, Korea 18th. However, Hong Kong SAR was 24th, Malaysia was 29th, Thailand was 32nd and China was ranked 44th, not pride of places (WEF, 2004).

While the macroeconomic policies and environment determine the growth potential of an economy, goods and services are essentially created at the microeconomic level. With this in perspective, the BCI is computed on the basis of firm data. An economy cannot be competitive until the firms operating in it have high productivity. The microeconomic foundation of productivity in an economy is based on the following inter-related variables: the sophistication with which the domestic firms and foreign subsidiaries operate and the quality of microeconomic environment. As the operations of domestic firms are intertwined with the national business environment, Executive Opinion Survey [EOS] is an important element of the BCI computation, and so are skill levels of the labor force, information availability, efficiency of the government system and presence/absence of rent-seeking tendencies, R&D institutions, suppliers' networks, and domestic competitive pressure on firms, which determines the domestic

---

[175] *The Global Competitiveness Report,* published by the World Economic Forum annually, since 1979, provides an authoritative and thorough assessment of the comparative strengths and weaknesses of 102 industrialized, emerging market and developing economies. It is the leading cross-country comparison of data and information relating to computation of economic competitiveness and growth, both at micro- and macroeconomic level.

business environment. In the BCI rankings, no Asian economy was near the top; Singapore stood 8th, Japan 13th, and Taiwan 16th. Other dynamic Asian economies were not placed very high, for instance, Hong Kong SAR was 19th, Korea 23rd, Malaysia 26th and China 46th (WEF, 2004). Thus not many dynamic Asian economies were able to acquire high rankings in the global BCI rankings either. Majority of them turned apathetic in the two competitiveness reckonings.

Let us pull the related strands together. First, as indicated earlier, the TFP studies of the mid-1990s concluded that real growth in the dynamic Asian economies was factor input-based (Chapter 2, Section 2.6). First, the increase in TFP was minimal. Second, the two fairly trustworthy competitiveness indexes did not assign majority of the dynamic Asian economies high spots in the competitiveness rankings. Third, in the backdrop of these findings it would appear completely paradoxical that the dynamic Asian economies have continued to record high export growth rates in real terms year after year. In terms of performance in the global markets they also did better than other country groups (Section 5.2.2). The second and third assertions lend support to the first contention that rapid growth, including trade expansion, in Asia has been more accumulation-based than productivity-, efficiency- and competitiveness-based.

5.4.2 Strengthening competitiveness

The Asian economic and financial crisis adversely affected the potential to compete in the regional economies. In the post-crisis *mise-en-scene,* Asian firms need to vitalize their competitive strength more than in the past. To this end, the firms that are well integrated in the production networks and exposed to global competition would finally emerge as profitable, competitive and resilient, while those that are not may not survive the harsh winds of regional and global competition. In the current environment of regionalization and globalization, firms need to maximize their returns by participating in the production networks as well as developing their own differential products and niche markets because the alternative to that is marginalization, even extinction. By working in and around the production networks firms they can realize their technological potential. Therefore, Asian firms need to move toward technology and skill-intensive modes of production, leaving behind the factor-intensive mode of the past.

Secondly, it is important for the Asian firms to move up the value chain by "relying more on the productivity-enhancing innovations based on science and technology" for their principal source of growth (Yusuf, 2003). Future competitiveness would be squarely based on the innovative capability in manufacturing and services sectors. To be sure, Asian economies were served well by input-based growth, but without a constant run of innovations, enhancing TFP and competitiveness would be difficult at this stage of growth in the dynamic Asian economies.

The basic *modus operandi* for raising the level of innovativeness is to develop stronger institutions, better macroeconomic policies and closer regional coordination. Asian firm have been following Japan in enhancing their innovation systems, but it was so far done in a small way. These systems not only need to be strengthened but also need to be fine-tuned. To this end, as discussed below, a mélange of public and private sector initiatives is essential. There is an imperious need of adopting appropriate strategies in the following three areas, namely, development of a tertiary educational system that focuses on science and technology, strong R&D networks and equally strong information and communication technology (ICT) networks. Past experience shows that innovation that enhances economic competitiveness is likely to occur in a few major industrial clusters and cities that have strong research capabilities and infrastructure (Yusuf and Evenett, 2003).

Stern and Stiglitz (1997) posited that the process of strengthening innovation and competitiveness, at the economy level, in the manner indicated in the preceding paragraph requires a joint and coordinated endeavor between the governments and the markets. Asian firms cannot possibly improve their competitiveness and productivity in a non-competitive domestic business environment, where appropriate institutions are weak or non-existent, where the role of government is unclearly understood and where there is inadequate investment in technological infrastructure and R&D institutions. Matured industrial economies that have achieved high level of competitiveness in the global market place succeeded by devoting a good deal of resources to the development of their technological infrastructure and R&D institutions.

In the initial stages when economies endeavor to improve their competitiveness, a direct and strong macro—micro link is required to be developed. The general institutional infrastructure created by the government has a direct bearing on how firms succeed in developing their entrepreneurial and technological capabilities. The collaboration of state and market consists of a series of sequential tasks and responsibilities for each one of them. This is particularly relevant in the context of EMEs and developing economies, where both markets and institutions are poorly developed. While the scope for government intervention may be greater in developing countries, government capacity to intervene may be limited. The O-Ring theory of economic development posits that developing a partnership between state and market must be a synchronized process (Crafts and Venables, 2001; Kremer, 1993). In the process of enhancing competitiveness, the tasks undertaken by the government and the market complement each other, and the smallest failure of one component puts the quality and efficiency of the entire system at risk. Experiences of firms in the mature industrial economies demonstrate that at later stages, the significance of the macro–micro link declines and firms can acquire cutting edge competitiveness on their own momentum (DeBrouwer, 2002).

5.4.3 Liberalized policy stance and competitiveness

Adoption of outer-oriented growth strategy, which *inter alia* led to entry of TNCs, in turn impinged on the competitiveness of Asian firms, economies and eventually exports to the global market place. In Section 5.4.1, we learned that on the global competitiveness indexes, dynamic Asian economies did not earn high places, implying that the improvement brought about by the TNC operations was significant, albeit barely enough. In this section we shall examine how competitive the dynamic Asian economies were in the global market place. The World Bank (2003) used COMTRADE data to compute (i) export growth, (ii) export demand growth and (iii) growth in competitiveness over the 1981–2001 period for different country groups. The results show that for the 1981–91 period exports from East and Southeast Asia grew by 232 percent. In comparison, global exports grew by 115 percent over the same period. At 124 percent, demand for exports from Asia grew faster than the world average. It was largely the enhanced competitiveness that raised exports by 109 percentage points relative to overall market growth.

According to the World Bank (2003) South Asian economies experienced significant improvement in competitiveness for the decade of 1981–90, which accounted for additional 70-percentage point export growth for this country group. Exports grew by 199 percent while export demand for South Asia grew by 129 percent. In contrast to Asia, Europe, Central Asia, the Middle East and North Africa lost export competitiveness over the same period.

For the following decade of 1991–2001, East and Southeast Asia recorded an export growth of 139 percent against the backdrop of world average of 68 percent. Export demand grew by 75 percent and competitiveness by 64 percent. The world averages for the latter two indicators are not available, but Europe and Central Asian economies performed better than the East and Southeast Asian economies during this decade. As a group, industrial economies showed a small loss of competitiveness for the decades of 1981–90 and 1991–2001. During the first decade the loss was 16 percent, while during the second decade it rose to 22 percent.[176] Thus, according to this study, export performance of the dynamic Asian economies was stellar during the two decades under study. This statement holds both in absolute terms and relative terms. This occurred despite the fact that the Asian economies did not succeed in acquiring high places on the global competitiveness ranking tables.

The share of manufactures in total Asian exports rose sharply between 1981 and 2001. By this time, in the East and Southeast Asian economies manufactured exports accounted for almost 90 percent of the total exports, although the rising

---

[176] See World Bank (2003), Table 2.2, p. 74.

tide of exports did not lift all boats. In the East and Southeast Asian economies export of manufactured products started rising from a high base, over 60 percent of the total exports. Several Asian economies did not participate is this export success, while others participated partially. In the South Asian economies the share of manufactures was around 50 percent of the total in 1981, and by 2001 it rose to 80 percent (WB, 2003). A decomposition of recent export growth rate by level of technology indicated that, as a generalization, many of Asian economies were gaining ground in higher technology exports. High-technology export products increased at the highest rate from China and India between 1981 and 2001; their average annual growth rate was 36 percent. In the electronics sector, corresponding growth rate was 20 percent.

In Section 5.7 below, we shall see that Asian economies developed and benefited from the regional and global production-sharing networks. A good deal of growth in high-technology exports was due to the creation of these networks. Participation in these networks enhances competitiveness at microeconomic level. In an integrated production network, labor-intensive stages are completed in the labor-abundant countries, while knowledge-intensive stages are performed in a matured, technologically advanced and knowledge-abundant economy (Deardorff, 2001; Hummels et al., 2001). Importance of production-sharing doubled for India between 1981 and 2001, albeit it had started from a low base. Similarly, in China it started from a much higher base than that in India, and it nearly doubled over the period under consideration. It is believed that statistics underestimate production-sharing in China, which had established a strong tradition of using imported inputs for producing exportables in the manufacturing sector under the coastal development strategy (discussed in Chapter 2, Section 2.5). Exports based on imported intermediate products accounted for half the total exports in China (Ianchovichina, 2003). This strategy was further intensified after 1987, when duty-free access to imported intermediate products was extended to a much wider range of exportable products than in the past. Singapore is another such example where the economy is much more integrated into regional and global vertical specialization.

Liberalizing the external sector of the economy for trade and FDI and to global integration are known to have a dynamic effect over the economy and enhance the competitiveness through both micro- and macroeconomic channels (Das, 2004c). Advances in information and communication technology (ICT), improvements in transportation technology, declining tariffs and NTBs and lowering barriers to foreign investment *inter alia* have supported the contemporary wave of globalization, which began in the 1980s. The preceding quarter century saw a great deal of liberalization in global trade and investment flows (Das, 2004c). Particularly, during the decade of the 1990s, FDI grew dramatically in the global economy bringing in additional capital to the developing economies, including the Asian economies—augmenting capital per worker. In the East and Southeast Asian economies capital per worker annually increased one-and-a-half times that in the industrial economies (WB, 2003). These developments as well as FDI flows favorably affected competitiveness at the microeconomic level. Besides, FDI is known to bring in technological and managerial know-how.[177]

While liberalization of external sector partially explains export volume success of the dynamic Asian economies, it did not succeed in improving the place of these economies on the two global competitiveness indexes (Section 4.5.1). The Asian EMEs liberalized their capital account for the non-FDI financial flows as well. It is believed that these economies were ill-prepared to cope with the resulting capital volatility resulting from the non-FDI financial flows. Asian crisis put paid to the hyper growth of Asia, and seriously discouraged private investment from the global financial market. So much so that the crisis-affected Asian economies suffered from reversal of global capital flows. However, during the post-crisis period Asian economies did not retract and continued to adhere to their liberalized policy stance (Das, 2000, 2001c).

5.5 REGIONAL TRENDS IN FDI

The dynamic Asian economies consciously strive to come to an appropriate policy mix that would maximize benefits of FDI to host economy. They succeeded in spawning the enabling environment for FDI. In addition, they recorded brisk growth, which attracted global investors, which in turn further facilitated their rapid growth. FDI growth increased substantially during the last two decades. One reason was liberalization of policies, removal of restrictions and conscious implementation of policies to attract FDI inflows. Net FDI inflows to Asia did not follow the global trend. They languished during and after the Asian crisis, reaching a nadir of $44 billion in 2000. A slow rise began in 2001 when the net FDI flows were $48 billion. They rose to $55 billion in 2002 and $57 billion in 2003.[178] Favored FDI destinations changed in the decade of 1990s. Indonesia, which was one of the favored destinations in the early 1990s, dropped from the scene completely because of its domestic socio-political and economic uncertainties. India and Vietnam, which were not favored destinations in the early 1990s became that in the late 1990s and early 2000s. Malaysia, a preferred destination of the early 1990s because of its consistently open strategy for FDI flows, was overtaken by Hong Kong SAR, Singapore, Korea and Thailand in the latter part of the decade.

[177] Refer to World Bank (2003), Chapter 2.

[178] Statistics used here come from the *Global Development Finance 2004*. Refer to Chapter 3, Table 3.1.

Net FDI inflows to Asia were not evenly spread but tended to be heavily concentrated. Throughout the decade of the 1990s, China remained the highest FDI recipient in Asia as well as in the developing world. The top 10 recipients in Asia accounted for 97 percent of total net FDI inflows to the region in 2002, while the top 3 for 81 percent of the total. According to UNCTAD (2003a), the largest recipient amongst the top ten recipients in Asia was China, which received 57.7 percent of the total FDI in 2002. Hong Kong SAR was second largest recipient accounting for 15.0 percent. The other large recipients, in descending order, were Singapore (8.4 percent), India (3.8 percent), Malaysia (3.5 percent), Kazakhstan (2.8 percent), Korea (2.2 percent), Taiwan (1.6 percent), Vietnam (1.3 percent) and the Philippines (1.2 percent). The appearance of Kazakhstan on the FDI list was a surprise. It has lately become a popular destination because of large interest of foreign investors in the development of hydrocarbons.

Asia attracted $144 billion in fresh FDI commitments (as opposed to net FDI inflows) in 2000, which was a 44 percent increase over 1999. As noted in the preceding paragraph, China and Hong Kong SAR have been the two largest recipients of FDI in the contemporary period. In 2000 Hong Kong SAR received $64 billion, which followed Hong Kong SAR recovery from the crisis and economic restructuring measures. The other reason for receiving such a large FDI was M&As in the ICT sector and increasing importance of Hong Kong SAR as the hub of global business. For once, Hong Kong SAR displaced China from its high perch, as the recipient of largest FDI in Asia; in 2001 its FDI receipt was reduced to half. China received $50 billion in 2001, much larger than Hong Kong. FDI flows to the ASEAN-4 economies hit a plateau, essentially because divestment from Indonesia continued. Intra-regional investment in Asia has grown considerably. China held the maximum promise for the Japanese firms and TNCs. Another noteworthy feature of the contemporary period was that Malaysia and Thailand emerged as the largest investors in the Greater Mekong Sub-region (Cambodia, Lao PDR and Vietnam). China, Korea and Taiwan were also substantial investors in this sub-region.

Japan's has traditionally been a significant source of FDI for the other Asian economies; its outward investment grew by 21 percent, to $38 billion in 2001. Oddly enough, it grew in the background of declining domestic investment. According to a 2002 survey of the Japan Bank of International Co-operation (JBIC), it is expected to go on rising in the short-term (JBIC, 2002).[179] A large proportion (72 percent) of the Japanese TNCs was planning to increase their outward investment over the next three years. The same survey reported this proportion to be 21 percent in 1999 and 55 percent in 2000. East and Southeast Asia continued to steadily attract Japanese FDI in manufacturing activities.

[179] The sample size of this survey was 792 Japanese manufacturing companies, which had minimum of three affiliates. It was conducted in July 2001.

In 2001, Asian economies accounted for 20 percent of Japan's total FDI. The reasons for large investment in Asia were Japan's high wages and high prices of business services, which were discussed in Chapter 2, Section 2.4. Because of pressure for cost reduction, electrical and electronics sectors had to be relocated in the Asian economies. Japanese TNCs have been increasing their investment in China. In 2001, China successfully attracted 30 percent of the total Japanese FDI flows to Asia. Rise in FDI to China was at the cost of the ASEAN-4 economies, where Japanese FDI declined. Even before China's WTO accession in 2001, it was the most attractive destination for the Japanese TNCs (JBIC, 2002). Japan accounted for around 30 percent of total FDI stock in Thailand and 25 percent in Malaysia. These countries are eying increasing flows to China with growing apprehension and consternation (Section 5.6.3).

FDI commitments (not net FDI flows) plummeted in Asia from $144 billion in 2000 to $102 billion in 2001. A good part of this decline was caused by an over 60 percent drop in FDI flows to Hong Kong SAR, which was the recipient of massive inflows in 2000. Despite the fall, the share of Asian economies in global FDI flows increased from 9 percent in 2000 to 14 percent in 2001. Individual Asian economies performed unevenly and the concentration of FDI persisted. China had lost its high perch to Hong Kong SAR in 2000, but regained in 2001.

Although FDI flows to the dynamic economies of Northeast Asia declined, Hong Kong SAR's status as the business hub for the region was not affected and continued to be strengthened. By the end of 2001, 3,237 TNCs had set up their regional offices there, with 944 TNCs having their regional headquarters in Hong Kong SAR. Korea received two-thirds less FDI ($3 billion) in 2001 than in 2000. Opposed to this performance, Taiwan received $4 billion in 2001, which was a historical high. Accession to the WTO (in November 2001) made Taiwan more attractive to international investors and helped FDI inflows to Taiwan.[180] A dominant part of FDI was attracted by financial services sector.

FDI inflows to Southeast Asian economies tended to stagnate at $13 billion. Divestment from Indonesia, alluded to earlier in this section, continued. In 2001, divestment was $3 billion. Likewise FDI receipts by Malaysia also stagnated and the new set of incentives failed to reverse the trend. Conversely, inflows to the Philippines increased considerably between 2000 and 2001, while those to Singapore recorded an increase of 59 percent, to $9 billion. However, this level was still below the peak of $11 billion reached by Singapore in 1997. The economy has suffered because of erosion in competitiveness in the ICT sector vis-à-vis its neighbors. Having accepted this fact, Singapore is trying to make biomedical sciences and biotechnology as the focus of future growth in FDI.

---

[180] Although this fact draws little attention, one day after China became a member Taiwan also acceded to the WTO.

Concerted endeavors to improve the infrastructure are also underway. Likewise, between 2000 and 2001, FDI increased by a billion dollar in Thailand, to $3.8 billion. It is also well below its peak level reached in 1998. Thailand has continued to strengthen its position as the most attractive Asian location for the TNCs in auto industry. Several major automakers and component manufacturers, including BMW, Honda, Land Rover, Toyota and Ishiwawajima-Harima, announced expansion or entry plans in Thailand. Albeit belatedly, Vietnam is turning a page in its economic relations with the other regional and global economies and trying to emerge as a host FDI economy of significance. It has strengthened its Bilateral Trade Agreement (BTA) with the United States , which has improved its prospects of attracting FDI.[181] A WTO Working Party was formed to process its membership to the WTO. When it does become a member, it would help in stimulating its FDI inflows (Anderson and Norheim, 1993).

5.5.1 Medium-term prospects

According to the EIU (2004) survey and projections (cited in Section 5.1.2) Asian countries would be the principal beneficiaries of the expected upturn in FDI. The EIU survey results indicated that the EMEs of Asia would be among the most important beneficiaries of the FDI rebound, with China continuing to be the top recipient. India is also projected to become very attractive to global investors; its attraction would expand beyond being a profitable destination for outsourcing.

The survey confirmed China as the leading destination for investment on most criteria. The large investing firms and TNCs, which sought new consumer and corporate markets and were sensitive to labor cost, found China most attractive. It was also found a favorable location for R&D activities, second to the Euro Zone. Similarly, investing firms rated it high for outsourcing, second to India. Notwithstanding the fact that the economy is overheated, investor confidence in China remained undiminished. Its attraction reached across industries: manufacturing and services sector companies (including IT and financial services firms) are equally attracted by the country's rapid growth and low-cost environment.

An unusual observation emerged regarding India, which traditionally was not regarded as a successful FDI attracting economy, albeit it became highly successful in outsourcing business. The medium-term scenario for India has improved. The EIU (2004) projections show that it would attract an increasing amount of FDI because of its recent commitments to investment-friendly

---

[181] On June 13, 2000, pursuant to the requirements of the Trade Act of 1974, the United States and Vietnam signed an "Agreement Between the United States of America and the Socialist Republic of Vietnam on Trade Relations."

policies. India's technology revolution has also been noted by global investors, with companies from a range of industries—including IT and financial services—citing India as the world's top target for R&D investments. The country also offers attractive new consumer markets, and better opportunities than other large EMEs for business partnerships.

5.5.2 Outward FDI flows

Japan's outward FDI was discussed above, in Section 5.5. As Asian EMEs progressed on the path of industrialization and economic growth, they also began to invest in the other economies. They became significant outward investors and by the end of 2000 accounted for four fifths of total outward FDI by developing countries. Over the decade of 1990s, TNCs owned by overseas Chinese as well as Korean *chaebol* were two major forces of outward FDI from Asia.[182] A large part of outward FDI from Asia essentially comprised FDI from Asian economies to other Asian economies. To a limited extent, Asian economies are also known to invest in Australia, Europe and North America.

In 1980, Asia (excluding Japan) was the most important region in the developing world from the perspective of outward FDI stock. The book value of Asian outward FDI stock exceeded Japan's outward FDI stock for the first time in 1997. The net outward FDI flows declined after the Asian crisis and were down to $32 billion in 2001, lowest since the crisis. However, by 2002, the FDI stock of Asian economies was double that of Japan.[183] A distinctive feature of outward FDI from Asia was the shift in the mode of investment from new assets or "greenfield" FDI to acquisitions of existing assets (or M&As), which accounted for approximately 80 percent of the total Asian FDI outflows. This change in the composition of FDI and growing proportion of M&As was a trend that established itself in the 1990s. It was established by the Asian economies undertaking extensive privatization of public enterprises. Using annual data for the period 1987–2001, Calderón et al. (2004) found that that higher M&As trend is typically followed by higher greenfield investment.

Hong Kong SAR, has traditionally been the largest source of FDI among the Asian economies, excluding Japan. Recent steep fall in outward investment

---

[182] *Chaebol* are conglomerates of many companies clustered around one holding company. The parent company is usually controlled by one family. In 2000, the 40 top *chaebol* grouped a total of 671 separate companies. The companies hold shares in each other. Korea must be easily the most prosperous industrial country to have such a concentration of the economy: the top four super-*chaebol* have sales that account for 40–45 percent of Korea's GNP. *Chaebol* are styled after Japanese *keiretsu,* which are centered on one large financial institution or bank. The *chaebol* do not have their own financial institutions. Also, unlike *keiretsu,* which integrate vertically in the same industry, Chaebol tend to spread across industries.

[183] Refer to Chapters 1 and 4 of UNCTAD (2003a) for more details.

from Asia was caused by a sharp decline in the outward FDI from Hong Kong SAR. Its net outward FDI declined from $59 billion in 2000 to $9 billion in 2001. Conversely, due to two large M&As deals, net outflows from Singapore doubled in 2001. FDI from Taiwan, which has also been a large investor in Southeast Asian economies and China, declined by 18 percent in 2001. The industries that attracted Taiwan's FDI in China shifted from labor-intensive industries in the 1980s to high-technology, and knowledge-intensive (computers, electronics and electronic components) industrial sectors in the late 1990s. This trend is likely to strengthen in the near future because of two reasons. First, it is likely that there would be a further easing of restrictions on investment in China and in Taiwan and, second, both the economies are now WTO members. Korean outward FDI declined in the post-crisis period. Its FDI in Asia was halved between 2000 and 2001 (to $2.6 billion) because Korean *chaebol* and TNCs sold off many of their subsidiaries in the non-core sectors in the other Asian economies. Their foreign assets had gone on declining since the late 1990s.

Chinese firms have been expanding abroad rapidly, and China increasingly became a source of outward FDI. Although outflows were erratic, China's average annual outward FDI grew from $0.4 billion in the 1980s to $2.3 billion in 1990s, adding up to $35 billion in book value of stock at the end of 2002. Chinese TNCs invested not only in the neighboring Asian economies but also globally. The important sectors that attracted Chinese investment include trade, transportation, resource exploration, tourism and manufacturing (UNCTAD, 2003b). China is likely to grow into a reasonable sized outward investor in the medium-term.

Large Chinese state-owned enterprises (SOEs) took lead in making FDI. Their foreign assets were worth $30 billion in 2001, had 20,000 foreign employees and their total sales were $33 billion. In 2001 and early 2002, SOEs invested $7 billion in natural resources and services sectors. Chinese government is easing restrictions on outward FDI flows and proactively encouraging investment in the neighboring Asian economies. Large accumulation of foreign exchange reserves and pressure on fixed currency regime are the two principal motivations behind government's increasing interest in outward FDI (WB, 2004). Non-SOE Chinese firms also began following the SOEs in making investments abroad—again a large proportion in Asia. Majority of them were medium-sized TNCs. The leading non-SOE Chinese TNCs include Huawei Technologies, Wanxiang Group and Zheng Tai Group. Together these three Groups have 56 foreign subsidiaries, majority of which are in the neighboring Asian economies (Zhan and Ge, 2002).[184]

---

[184] This section is based on UNCTAD (2002) Chapter 3 and UNCTAD (2003a) Chapter 4. Statistical data presented here come from the same sources.

5.5.3 Centripetal forces in China

China has been highly successful in attracting FDI over the recent period. Over the 1990s, it emerged as a large destination of regional and global FDI, somewhat destabilizing the other Asian FDI destination economies in the process (Eckholm and Kahn, 2002). The reason was China's Special Economic Zone (SEZ) and coastal economic zone strategies. Decision makers in the public policy community proactively created an enabling environment for the inflows of FDI in the domestic economy, which were essentially located in the coastal areas of the eastern and the southern provinces of China. As alluded to earlier in this chapter, along with liberalization of external sector, it requires certain level of development in the area of education, technology and infrastructure, including financial infrastructure. During the 1990–95 quinquennium, average annual FDI flows to China were $19 billion. They soared to $40 billion in 1996. Statistics presented in Section 5.6 revealed that China succeeded in attracting the largest share of regional FDI.

Growth rate of net FDI decelerated somewhat between 1998 and 2000. After three years of relatively slow growth, China received $46.8 billion in 2001. This momentum continued in the aftermath of the WTO accession, and in 2002 China received $53 billion. China continued to retain its high perch and be Asia's and the developing world's largest recipient of FDI. It was also the recipient of the second highest of FDI in the world. That FDI played a prominent role in the Chinese economy is well recognized (Chapter 2, Section 2.5.1). In 2001, FDI accounted for 23 percent of the total value-added in the industrial sector. They also generated 18 percent of the domestic tax revenue and were responsible for 48 percent of Chinese exports (MOFTEC, 2001). According to the statistics released by the Ministry of Commerce, China approved more than 41,000 new foreign-invested firms in 2003, a 20 percent rise over 2002. This led to an FDI inflow of $53 billion in 2003. This performance was the consequence of China's ongoing economic liberalization and structural reforms, and efforts to bring domestic regulations in line with international standards. The manufacturing industry continued to be the star performer, garnering 70 percent of the total FDI. Electronics, telecom equipment, chemicals and machinery were the most important sectors in the manufacturing industry in 2003; Chinese economists saw this trend to continue in the near future (BT, 2004).[185]

The flip side of the coin is that at $30 per capita, China receives much less FDI than other comparable developing countries, such as Brazil, where per capita FDI was $195. A great deal of credit for China's recent success goes to its adopting and meticulously following "open door" policy or the Deng

---

185 The Beijing Times (BT). "China's Foreign Investment Hits $53 Billion". Thursday, January 15, 2004. p.1.

doctrine.[186] However, in the 25 years since China opened the door to foreign investment, much of the spending has been concentrated in low-technology, labor-intensive manufacturing projects, not to say that high-technology industries were excluded. Electronics and telecom are among the favored high-technology sectors. A relatively low share of FDI has come from the world's most prolific group of investors. Historically, Organization for Economic Co-operation and Development (OECD) member countries have been the largest investing group in the world. To be sure, during the recent period a good deal of FDI stock in China was built by Japan, which was not a large investor in the past. In addition, large part of the FDI flows to China still originated from the other Asian economies. The present challenge faced by China is to develop a more transparent business environment and business policies with a clear legal and regulatory framework. It should help attract higher-quality, long-term investments from the West European and North American economies in high-technology, capital-intensive industries (OECD, 2003).

After initial skepticism FDI from the large Japanese firms and TNCs to China began to rise in the early 1990s. The JBIC (2002) survey mentioned in Section 5.2 revealed that between 1993 and 2001, manufacturing bases of Japanese TNCs in China rose from 100 to almost 700. Although at 1000, in 2001, the corresponding number was higher in the ASEAN-4 countries, the pace of investment in China shows that this number may become higher for China in the short-term. It was noted earlier that the Japanese TNCs regarded investment benefits in China greater than in ASEAN-4 economies and gradually it became the most favored destination of Japanese FDI (JBIC, 2002). In the early 2000s, while Thailand, Malaysia and Vietnam were ranked high in the survey of Japanese TNCs as destination countries, they remained below China in rankings. Several Japanese TNCs were planning relocating their manufacturing

---

[186] At the Third Plenary Session of the 11th Central Committee of the Chinese Communist Party (CCP) in December 1978, the People's Republic of China adopted its "open door" strategy. This became famous as the Deng doctrine as Deng Xiaoping was the intellectual father of this liberal economic strategy. This marked a turning point in the Chinese economic performance and economic history. The economy grew with a healthy clip through the 1980s and 1990s. Gross domestic product (GDP) increased by 10 percent per annum in real terms over the 1980–2000 period. In a short period of two decades China economically transformed itself. Between 1978 and 2000, the GDP grew almost fivefold, per capita income quadrupled, and 270 million Chinese were lifted out of absolute poverty (*The Economist,* 2001). In 1990, China's GDP was $378.8 billion and per capita GDP was $341.60. A decade later, in 2000 GDP reached $1,080 billion, while per capita GDP rose to $853.40. China successfully became the manufacturing storehouse of the global economy. In doing so, it turned from a near autarky to the fourth largest merchandise exporter in the world, accounting for 6.6 percent ($325.6 billion) of merchandise exports in 2002. In addition, throughout the decade of the 1990s China was pre-empting the largest amount of net FDI among the developing economies. In 2000, it lost its high perch for one year to Hong Kong SAR, but in 2001 it regained its lost position.

facilities from Japan to China, while a good number of them were even considering relocating from the ASEAN-4, Hong Kong and Taiwan to China.[187] The JETRO (2001) survey reported that the Japanese TNCs found better advantages in the areas of market growth, production costs and labor supply in China.

FDI statistics from UNCTAD (2002) show that since the mid-1990s, the share of China in total FDI to Asia has grown at the cost of ASEAN economies. During the 1990–95 period ASEAN's average annual share of inflows to Asia was 38 percent. In 2001 it declined to 14 percent. Conversely, China's average annual share during the 1990–95 period was 44 percent per annum. It peaked at 51 percent in 1998, fell for the subsequent two years, and then it rose again to 49 percent in 2001. It soared to 57.7 percent of the total FDI flows in Asia in 2002. That China has enormous "pull" force is obvious. Low labor cost and relatively higher labor productivity were two of the principal pull forces for the TNCs in the industrial economies (Das, 2001a).

5.5.4 Is China eating ASEAN's lunch?

The ASEAN-4 economies succeeded in attracting FDI easily in the 1980s due to early adoption of liberalization measures and a high degree of openness. Their consistent domestic macroeconomic policy improvements, global economic environment and proactive participation in the integrated production networks were the other facilitating factors. Both regional and global competition for FDI intensified during the 1990s. Besides, after the Asian crisis the ASEAN-4 economies were slow to regain their position as attractive destination economies. By 2001, the Philippines was the only ASEAN economy in which FDI inflows reached the peak level of the pre-crisis period.

In 1992 global FDI flows to China surpassed those to the ASEAN-4 economies, which caused good deal of consternation in these economies. Competition to attract FDI became intense. The ASEAN-4 economies could not entice the investors away from China. FDI flows in the ASEAN-4 economies peaked in 1997. Since then they took a downward trend, FDI statistics show that in 1990, three fifths of global FDI flows to Asia went to the ASEAN-4 economies and one-fifth to China. The situation in 2000 was that two-fifths went to China, while the ASEAN-4 received only one-fifth. The share of ASEAN-4 in global FDI sharply declined between 1990 and 2000. Two of the principal reasons of decline were continued divestment in Indonesia and Malaysia losing its attractiveness to investors.

Electronics industry and its various sub-sectors had developed into significant sectors in Malaysia. The electronics and electrical equipment sector

---

[187] See Lardy (2002) for the evolving FDI trend and JETRO (2001) for the results of the TNC survey.

in Malaysia was considered highly attractive until the early 1990s. However, in 2001, this industry in Malaysia received merely $0.55 billion, as against $4 billion in the preceding two years. It is believed that Malaysia lost these FDI inflows to China. In 2001, the number of FDI proposals submitted to the Malaysian government in electronics and electrical equipment sector dropped to a third of the 2000 level (Eckholm and Kahn, 2002). As opposed to this, for China in the technology-intensive areas, which included electronics and electrical equipment sector, the share of foreign affiliates increased from 59 percent in 1996 to 81 percent in 2000, a 22 percentage point increase in a short time span. Example of the export of electronic circuits (ICs) is a telling one in this regard. TNC affiliates in China were the major exporters of it. Their share of exports increased from 78 percent of the total in 1996 to 93 percent in 2000. Intel and Samsung subsidiaries are the largest exporters of ICs from China (Sakakibara and Yamakawa, 2003).

Japan was consistently the largest investor in the ASEAN-4 economies until the late-1980s. As the preference of the Japanese firms and TNCs changed in the early 1990s, as set out above, they began to prefer China for its low labor and production costs and other sound economic reasons. The JBIC (2002) results were discussed above, which revealed that the number of manufacturing bases of the Japanese firms was going to rise in China and decline in the ASEAN-4 economies. China's popularity with the Japanese firms went on increasing and by 1997 it became the favored location for relocating labor-intensive manufacturing activity. Thus, bulk of FDI decline in the ASEAN-4 group was caused by declining FDI by the Japanese large firms and TNCs. Their preference for China grew so strong that in 2000 Japan did not figure among the top ten external investors in the ASEAN-4 economies.

The Chinese Diaspora spread in Hong Kong SAR, Malaysia, Singapore, Taiwan and Thailand has continued to be a strong investing community for China. Besides, GDP growth rate trend in the host economy has been an important determinant of FDI flows. Continued strong growth performance and WTO accession is likely to further divert FDI flows from the ASEAN-4 to China. As physical infrastructure improves in China, the ASEAN-4 countries would begin to appear even less attractive to the global investing community than they do at present. Therefore, reversal of this trend in the short- or medium-term is not on the cards. If China is eating ASEAN-4's lunch, the rationale is to be found on both the sides, that is, the ASEAN-4 becoming less attractive destinations and contemporaneously China growing more suitable and profitable.

There is some light at the end of the tunnel for the ASEAN-4 economies. Some TNCs that have large investments in China apprehended over exposure and, therefore, tried to divert their new FDI to the ASEAN-4 economies as a risk balancing measure. Some of them have gone even to Vietnam for the same reason. Secondly, Chinese SOEs and private firms have begun investing in the

ASEAN-4 economies. At this stage anecdotal evidence on this count abounds. For instance, CNOOC, which is an SOE in offshore oil business has acquired stakes in a large Indonesian oil company (Rajan, 2003). On the trade front, exports from the ASEAN-4 economies to the rapidly growing Chinese market would increase rapidly, which should cushion the shock of declining FDI. In fact, it has been pointed out in Section 5.9 that during the 1990s they increased by 50 percent. This trend is likely to strengthen in the future and mitigate the loss of ASEAN-4 economies.

5.6 INTEGRATED PRODUCTION NETWORKS AND REFINEMENT OF COMPARATIVE ADVANTAGE

Integrated production networks are not a new-fangled phenomenon. Trade statistics revealed that they have existed since the early 1960s. Far above average growth rates in trade in components and partially assembled manufactured goods reflected the growth of integrated production networks. In its most recent form, production-sharing arrangements entail development of specialized labor-intensive activities in a vertically integrated manufacturing industry. Although numerous examples exist, a good example is manufacture of semiconductors, valves, turners and the like, which are assembled for the TNCs in Malaysia and the Philippines. This issue was touched upon in a cursory manner in Chapter 3, Sector 3.2.4.

The two research projects undertaken by UNCTAD (1996a and 1996b) inferred that the relationship between trade and FDI was linear, with investment substituting for trade as firms increase their commitment to international markets. However, with the passage of time this relationship grew less linear and the two variables began to be determined by the same set of external and domestic factors. By "slicing the value chain" TNCs and large companies in the industrial economies increasingly began to integrate their regional and global production. Creating such production networks is the latest production trend in the world economy. Internationalization of manufacturing process enables several firms located in different countries to participate in different stages of fabrication of a specific product. As the TNCs are involved in the integrated production networks in a significant manner, intra-firm exports to and from subsidiaries of TNCs increased from 37 percent of their total trade in 1970 to 60 percent in 1993. Intra-firm trade was found to be one third of the total global trade by the mid-1990s. TNCs' exports to third parties accounted for another one-third. Thus, only a third of the total global exports were found to be non-TNC exports.[188]

---

[188] WTO (1996) buttressed these inferences.

From the perspective of the Asian economies, the production networks, or integrated international production, turned out to be a momentous development. They opened a new vista of opportunity for the Asian economies. We have noted above that there has been a strong upward trend in intra-firm and intra-TNC trade. The integration of production has moved forward from simple to complex stages. Economies now tend to attract those TNC functions and manufacturing operations in which they have comparative advantage. To that extent integrated production has further refined the classical principle of comparative advantage. Myriad co-operative business arrangements were being established to create extensive and intensive integration across national borders. Several Asian economies began to proactively participate and benefit from this production trend.

5.6.1 Need for integrated production networks

Global competition in general, and in the export-oriented sectors in particular, has been intensifying because of growing number of competing firms and the entry of newcomers. In addition, while global consumers crave for variety and choice, their insistence on low prices has been a constant. Therefore, large firms and TNCs were forced to think up their strategic reaction to face the challenge of intensifying competition and consumers' expectation of reasonably priced products. There was little uniformity in this strategy. It necessarily varied according to industry, technology level and the firm or TNC in question. The response to the competitive pressure also varied according to how a firm or TNC perceived its competitive advantages at different stages of the global value chain. For instance, in a high-technology sector the competitive advantage of a TNC lay in its technological prowess as well as in its R&D and innovation capabilities. Most industry leader TNCs tried to keep their core competitive advantage in-house, shrouded in secrecy. This is as true as a generalization could be because differences were commonly observed in the strategy of two industry leaders.[189]

Evidence is available to show that in many large firms and TNCs non-core functions, particularly the labor-intensive manufacturing operations and production processes, or assembly of less technologically intensive parts, are frequently outsourced to low-cost locations. The consequence is enormous cost savings, which is one of the largest motivating factors for the firms and TNCs endeavoring to create integrated production networks. The other benefits of outsourcing and production networks include enhanced competitiveness and enlengthening of product life cycle. This leads to spurt in trade in parts,

[189] An excellent illustration is in telecom industry, where Nokia and Ericsson seem to follow different strategies for facing the competitive challenge. The former focuses more on in-house production of mobile phones, while Ericsson has gone to the other extreme and has completely outsourced it.

components and partially assembled products, which does not always have to be intra-firm trade. Increase in global outsourcing by companies in the industrial economies has been one of the drivers of globalization of manufacturing activity, and business in general.

5.6.2 Splitting the value chain

As alluded to above, slicing of the manufacturing value chain opened a wealth of opportunities for the Asian economies. They began to benefit from the transfer of several non-core processes and component manufacturing in which they had a comparative advantage. To cash in on this new trend, the TNCs as well as other large firms in the industrial economies carefully set up semi-permanent integrated production networks for many parts of their manufacturing operations and functions. This corporate strategy demands that the TNCs or the large firms create an optimal configuration of their production process, which is usually created by them after experimentation and trial and error. The optimal production network is geographically spread to such locations that not only create cost advantage but also lead to access to third markets. Locations that can provide efficient and cost-effective labor and services benefit from global slicing of value chain.

For the reasons given in the preceding section, the logistical organization of product distribution is also outsourced by many TNCs. The extreme form of outsourcing phenomenon is contract manufacturing, which entails outsourcing of the entire production process and product line. This trend in outsourcing has increased the significance and scale of the suppliers' operations in Asia. With the passage of time the global value chains would be more finely sliced into "specialized functional and geographical elements" (UNCTAD, 2002).[190] Dynamic Asian economies need to remain vigilant in spotting and exploiting these opportunities.

5.6.3 Expanding opportunities

Several Asian economies have accumulated a good deal of experience in the global outsourcing and integrated production networks. Across numerous industrial and services sectors, large firms and TNCs in Japan, the United States and other industrialized economies extend their supply chains to China, Korea, ASEAN-4 economies and India.[191] Although it is difficult to provide statistics in

---

[190] Refer to UNCTAD (2002), Chapter 5, for greater details.

[191] Asia is not the only region that has benefited from global outsourcing by TNCs and large companies in the industrial economies, but supply chains are being extended to many other emerging market economies, particularly those of Eastern Europe.

this regard, in the recent past EMEs of Asia in general, and China in particular, have begun to figure prominently in it. Firms in these economies have adopted and adapted to process in a dexterous manner. They have benefited a great deal from the transfer of several non-core processes or component manufacturing as well as global outsourcing. Supply chain management has emerged as a new science. When individual firms become part of a supply chain, they need to have, and provide, independent process development capabilities. They also need to develop abilities to perform a wide range of value-added functions, which are commonly associated with the manufacturing process of which they are a part.[192]

Japan has an exclusive place in the integrated production networks in Asia. Due to high wage structure and high prices of business services, a lot of manufacturing activity was forced to migrate to Asia, which raised concern regarding the "hollowing out" of the industrial sector (Chapter 2, Section 2.4). However, a small number of Japanese manufacturing firms (such as Canon and Toyota) have managed to stay in Japan by developing integrated manufacturing networks that are far more sophisticated and complex than their rivals have so far devised. Such firms have learned to protect their trade secrets and core processes that made them competitive in the past (*The Economist*, 2004).

On the one hand, transfer of non-core processes to China and other Asian destinations has been eliminating white-collar jobs in the mature industrial economies. On the other hand, firms in several Asian economies have skillfully developed their acumen and resources to be trustworthy links in the supply chains. They are competitively manufacturing parts and sub-assemblies for firms in the industrial economies and performing large swaths of manufacturing activities for them. Consequently, they are being branded as villains that are responsible for creating unemployment—or slowing down job creation—in the industrial economies by the politicians and popular press.

There is an unseemly dimension of supply chain extending to Asian economies. Often lowering the prices of the final products cannot be achieved without further lowering the low wages as well as accepting poor physical working conditions along the supply chain. Firms along the supply chain compete fiercely. Factories in the special economic zones (SEZs) of China and in Indonesia are being undercut by Filipino and Vietnamese suppliers, who in turn are looking over their shoulders at Bangladesh and Mongolia, where both wages and prices are still lower.

---

[192] In this section only fundamentals of international production networks have been introduced. There has been a great deal of scholarly interest in this issue and, therefore, there is a large volume of recent literature on the theme of FDI and expanding integrated production networks. Refer to recent research on this theme like Arndt and Kierzkowski (2001), Birkinshaw (2001), Humphrey and Schmitz (2001), Mathews (2001), Mortimore (2000) and Zhan and Ge (2002).

The recent regionalization trend in Asia is strengthened by—and in turn strengthens—integrated production networks. It is a circular, mutually reinforcing, relationship. The reason is that these networks call for numerous trade offs and collaboration among firms, managers and governments. In addition, as comparative advantage changes and industries and services relocate, economies need to co-operate in handling the related tensions and conflicts. If economies are like-minded, as many Asian economies are, or are members of a regional integration agreement (RIA), they stand a better chance of handling these tensions and would be able to cooperate and resolve the intricate issues better. Regional rules can also be set up under the RIA to ensure that the national benefit objectives and regional interest stay aligned. Thus, regionalization can support globalization.

5.7 OUTSOURCING IN ICT AND BUSINESS-PROCESS SERVICES

In the same streak as creation of production networks, a great many opportunities have been created by outsourcing, or off-shoring, in computer hardware, information and communications technology (ICT) as well as business-process outsourcing (BPO). India's ICT and software exports became competitive and successful since the mid-1980s. The reason was its well-educated, English-speaking, inexpensive and young labor force. As alluded to in Chapter 2 (Section 2.5.2) outsourcing falls squarely under the rubric of global trade in services and, therefore, comes under the General Agreement on Trade in Services (GATS). Primarily, it covers trade in the following two categories: (i) ICT services or computer-enabled services and (ii) BPO.

Software development, data processing, database services, ICT support services broadly come under the first category. BPO is defined by Mattoo and Wunsch (2004) as "a contractual service to completely manage, deliver and operate one or more information-technology-intensive business-processes and functions." BPO covers all the services that come under customer interaction services, back-office operations and independent professional and business services. These services do not correspond to any existing statistical classification and are, therefore, difficult to quantify with any degree of precision. Although a wealth of anecdotal evidence is available, no reliable data set exists so far. To be sure, broad, if imprecise, estimates can be made using the IMF data on trade in services.

Although boundaries between many of these traded services are hard to draw, trade in ICT services and the BPO has been expanding fast in some Asian economies. It has recorded the most dynamic growth since the mid-1990s. While the OECD economies dominate trade in outsourcing of business services, some developing economies, including India and China,[193] essentially in that order, recorded a much faster growth rate in expansion of trade in these services since the mid-1990s.[194] Outsourcing of non-core business process allows significant reduction in labor costs, and leads to 15–25 percent in productivity gains (Mattoo and Wunsch, 2004). Outsourcing operations benefit business firms as well as have notable global welfare implications. Globalization, which *inter alia* includes advancing global division of labor, stimulates remarkable efficiency gains. According to the estimates made by Prudential, the British insurance giant, off-shoring some of its customer services to India enabled it to make an annual saving of $26.2 million and create 1000 jobs in India. For GlaxoSmithKline, a pharmaceutical leviathan, this saving was 35 percent of its total annual ICT budget. General Electric saved $350 million annually through its Indian ICT operation, which employed 18,000 strong ICT and software professionals (Mattoo and Wunsch, 2004).[195]

In Asia, India has emerged as an unchallenged leader in the exports of ICT-enabled services, software exports as well as in a large array of BPO. The intrusive and ineffectual government did not get an opportunity to interfere in the ICT-related businesses, and they expanded at an impressive pace. For instance, by resolving the Y2K-related problems in the industrial economies, Indian software firms were able to earn $2.5 billion. Growth of Indian ICT industry in 2002 was 29 percent, faster than growth of ICT anywhere in the world. During the same year, growth in export of ICT-enabled services was 65 percent. Growth in BPO services was also much faster than the industry average. Almost half of the Fortune-500 corporations outsource their software requirements to India. Comparative advantage of countries like India will neither be static nor limited to standard back-office services. Other Asian economies having the identical combination of well-educated and inexpensive labor are sure to move into this market. China and Vietnam are known to have lower labor costs than India and have moved into ICT-enabled services and BPO business. As Indian wages rise in these sectors, India's loss would be the gain of China and Vietnam. The choice for Indian services suppliers would then be to move into higher value-added analytical tasks and leave the low-cost commercial services operations for China and Vietnam.

---

[193] According to a Silicon Valley wit, IC stands for Indian and Chinese, not for integrated circuits.

[194] The other emerging market and developing economies in the fray are Barbados, Brazil, Bulgaria, Dominica, Israel, the Mauritius, Mexico and Nicaragua. Several of these economies, albeit not all, recorded high growth rates in their exports of ICT-enabled services and a whole array of BPO business.

[195] In an interview on Lou Dobbs Tonight, CNN's premier business and economic news program, on March 9, 2004, three CEOs of U.S. software firms, who outsourced their software programming to India, reported that they found Indian software superior in quality and 40 to 50 percent less expensive than the software produced by U.S. software firms.

5.7.1 Igniting protectionism: squaring the circle

It is being increasingly believed that outsourcing has led to loss of white-collar jobs and "hollowing out" of several traditional industrial sectors, igniting protectionist sentiment in some industrial economies, particularly in the United States. China and India are frequently, if erroneously, blamed by politicians and popular press in the United States for taking away a large number of jobs and making the U.S. economic recovery of 2003–04 a jobless one. The unemployment rate in the U.S. remained obstinately high at 5.6 percent until mid-2004. For over two centuries, politicians have poorly understood the gains from trade. A strong public opinion emerged in the United States against outsourcing of white-collar jobs as well as integrated production networks in different parts of Asia, particularly in China and India. Imposition of quantitative restrictions and other trade barriers seemed a comprehensible probability.

Technological advancements in ICT are turning what was once a segmented global labor market into an integrated whole. These advances have created a global pool of workers, who compete with each other, causing downward pressure on wages. This trend began with the manufacturing sector in the 1990s, and now it is advancing toward services sector. This evolving global trend brought workers in the globalizing economies together and a global labor competition was its final consequence. Labor markets in former socialist economies of Eastern Europe and Soviet Union, China, India and Mexico became participants in this globalized labor market. This trend in globalization of labor market is there to stay. Globalized competition in the ICT sector has been particularly strong. Polaski (2004) cited estimates made by Gartner, a forecasting and consultancy firm in ICT, which predicted that 25 percent of IT jobs would relocate from the industrial economies to developing countries by 2010.

Phobia of expanding unemployment in the outsourcing industrial economies is ill-founded. If anything, this trend is having a favorable impact over the labor markets in the mature industrial economies. R.J. Samuelson contended that, "These companies (TNCs) *do* shut U.S. plants. They *are* growing abroad. Indeed, foreign-job increases are higher in percentage terms, because they start from a smaller base. But numerically, job growth is still greater in the United States. From 1992 to 2002, U.S. multinationals added about five American jobs for every three foreign jobs. Perhaps these companies succeed simultaneously at home and abroad. But expansion abroad—motivated by low wages or closeness to growing foreign markets—may also create U.S. jobs, concludes Matthew Slaughter of Tuck School of Business, Dartmouth University, in a study for the Coalition for Fair International Taxation, a group of multinational firms" (Samuelson, 2004). This argument applies to outsourcing as well. As the possibility of protectionist barriers is strong, one way of squaring this circle is the ongoing Doha Round of multilateral trade negotiations. This round is driven by the Doha Development Agenda (DDA) and can be utilized as an opportunity to pre-empt the rising protectionism in trade in services, covering both the trade in ICT services and in the BPOs. This is an apt opportunity for promoting and consolidating comprehensive commitments on freeing trade in services under the GATS. Commitments on market access and national treatment are sure to forestall discrimination against outsourcing and foreign provider of services.[196]

5.8 CHINA'S WTO ACCESSION AND ITS REGIONAL RAMIFICATIONS

In the Fourth Ministerial Conference, held in Doha, Qatar, in November 2001, China, one of the original contracting parties (CPs) of the GATT, acceded to the WTO. The long-drawn accession process commenced in July 1986 and lasted for over 15 years, a record worthy of the Guinness Book (Das, 2001a, 2001b). With WTO accession China became a formal part of one of the important institutions of the global economic governance. In its long preparation for acceding to the WTO, China liberalized its domestic trade policies by reducing tariff rates from an average of 40 percent in the early 1990s to 12 percent in 2002, with further reduction scheduled for the foreseeable future. The post-accession domestic and external liberalization would redefine China's regional trade and economic relations in way that are beginning to be understood. Even before the WTO accession, China was perceived as a strong competitor in the global market place by the other regional economies as well as a powerful magnet for FDI.

As it has emerged as a formidable competitor in the export of a large array of products and in attracting FDI to its huge market, China's accession will have profound implications for Asian economies. However, nowhere the impact will be as large as in China's domestic economy. Two immediate implications of accession would be as follows: First, the pace of regionalization—and for that matter globalization—of Chinese economy would intensify. Therefore, China's export to and imports from the region can be logically expected to escalate. Given its long-term growth trajectory, it would soon become a larger export market for its Asian neighbors. In Section 5.2.3, I have said that this has come to pass and in 2003 China became the largest importing economy in Asia. Furthermore, China's FDI inflows and outflows would upsurge for the same reason. Second, following the accession China is sure to compete with its Asian neighbors more effectively and aggressively in the third-country markets in a broad spectrum of products, and in the process affect the competitive advantage as

---

[196] For greater details refer to particular ITC (2000), WTO (2001) and Mattoo and Wunsch (2004).

well as comparative advantage of the neighboring economies. This "threatening giant" imagery of China was also discussed in Section 5.2.3. While China's Asian neighbors are aware of the possibility of increased access to the large and fast growing Chinese markets, they are daunted by the competition that China would offer in the third-country markets. The threatening giant image dominates their thinking. As China is still in an early stage of implementing its outer-oriented economic strategy, China the awesome competitor has drawn far more attention from policy mandarins in the Asian economies than China providing a larger future market for their exports.

A foretaste of what would be the future, post-accession, impact was taking place in the decade of the 1990s. For instance, expanding Chinese domestic market led to increase in exports from the four NIAEs as well as from the smaller ASEAN-4 economies. The ASEAN-4 members increased their exports to China by 390 percent during the decade of 1990s. Their share in China's imports soared by 50 percent, from 6 percent to 9 percent. WTO accession would further increase regional as well as global exports to the large Chinese market. In the services sector China has committed to substantial trade liberalization in its accession package. It is obliged to provide national treatment to foreign services firms as well as liberalize domestic market for services, which would result in a large increase in trade in services. Similarly, in the manufacturing sector Chinese tariffs on an average would decline from 13.3 percent in 2001 to 6.8 percent in 2010, the end of implementation period. This would not only increase imports further but also encourage restructuring of the domestic manufacturing sector. High-end manufacturing and automobile are sure to be affected by rationalization and restructuring. Agricultural imports are also expected to grow substantially, albeit protection on many products is to decline only modestly (Huang and Rozelle, 2002). There should also be an indirect favorable effect on Asian exports. That is, increased exports to China would fuel import demand in the Asian economies. As intra-regional trade in Asia is large, this in turn should increase the exports of their neighboring trading partners.

Owing to the complexity of the exercise, assessing the impact of accession through the channels indicated above is possible through a computable general equilibrium (CGE) modeling. Also, partial equilibrium studies a suitable method to assess the impact on different regional economies and groupings. A CGE model comprises a system of simultaneous equations that simulate price-directed interactions between firms and households in commodity and factor markets. The roles played by governments, trade partners and capital markets are also taken into account. The CGE model covers economy-wide resource allocation, production and income determination.

A CGE modeling exercise by Ianchovichina and Martin (2001) projected increases in the Chinese imports by product groups. According to these projections, the following product groups would record increases in import due to the WTO accession: oilseeds, meat and livestock, dairy, other foods, beverages and tobacco, wood and paper, metals, electronics and other manufactures. The textiles and apparel sector was projected to have the largest increases in its imports. Both the direct and indirect effects on trade will add up to have a significant impact on regional trade and integration pattern.

Asian economies having similar comparative advantage as China would face China's competitive exports in the global market place. The ASEAN-4 economies compete with China in a large array of labor-intensive product groups, higher value-added manufactures and high-technology products such as semiconductors and other IT and computer parts and components. China succeeded in competing down unit prices in many of these products. Contrary to the experiences of these economies, which have been feeling the Chinese presence in the global market, the exporters from NIAEs managed to maintain their market shares in Japan and the U.S. markets. In Japan, this group managed to enlarge its market share. China did expand its market share in some product groups, but it was at the expense of the U.S. exporters.

Results of the large CGE modeling exercises concur (cited above) that on balance China's accession would benefit Japan and the four NIAEs. All these countries export capital goods to China. As their exports rise, they would see an improvement in their terms-of-trade and balance of payments (bop). This trend had begun before the accession. China's expanding garment industry would raise the textiles production in the region, although garment industry in many smaller economies may be forced to face stiff Chinese competition. China's demand for intermediate goods is expected to drive export demand in numerous product groups upward in the neighboring Asian economies. This category includes metals and petrochemicals from Korea; electronics and high-technology manufactures from Singapore and light manufactures, petrochemicals, machinery, equipment and electronics from Taiwan. In electronics, China is expected to source its inputs from countries that have benefited from the largest tariff reduction, like India and the United States. In the automobile sector, China's plans for restructuring and rationalization would make the sector become efficient and competitive in the region, which in turn would make China enter the export market in autos in the short- or medium-term. This possibility may promote reorganization of automobile industry in the medium-term in Asia.[197]

On balance, the ASEAN-4 economies would have a mixed impact of accession. On the one hand China's large markets would present an opportunity for export expansion from this country group; on the other hand some sector specific

---

[197] See Ianchovichina et al.(2003), Ianchovichina and Walmsley (2002), Wang (2002) and Ianchovichina and Martin (2001). All these CGE modeling exercises came up with similar results.

adjustment will be made necessary in these economies. Agro-processing, electronics, machinery and equipment sectors and professional services and tourism are sure to benefit in the ASEAN-4, while textiles and apparel sector would have to face increasing competition. In Indonesia and Thailand, many product lines directly compete with Chinese exports in the global market place and would feel competitive heat.[198]

The large CGE modeling exercise by Ronald-Holst (2002) (Section 5.2.3) came to several notable conclusions on the above-mentioned lines, with far reaching implications for China's neighboring economies. One of the valuable results related to China becoming a large importer before becoming a larger exporter and was discussed in Section 5.2.3. This implied that between the threats and opportunities presented by the WTO accession, opportunity would take precedence over the threat of being crowded out of the export markets. Ronald-Holst (2002) also concluded that by 2020 China would have a large structural deficit with the neighboring Asian economies. This conclusion has enormous policy implications for the Asian economies. How well they adjust to the changing regional and global economic scenario would essentially depend upon their own policy flexibility and readiness to adjust. They need not assume that China's competitive exports would drive them out of their established export markets and erode their trading potential. In addition, by 2020 China would be Japan's largest trading partner, exceeding trade with all other bilateral trade destinations. This would develop as a large opportunity for Japan, that is, if Japanese policymakers are prepared to adopt the required changes in policy orientation focusing on a shift from traditional OECD markets to the fastest growing consumer society next door.

5.9 SUMMARY AND CONCLUSION

Evidence is available both at macro- and microeconomic levels to show that outer-orientation directly facilitates trade expansion and FDI inflows, and indirectly GDP growth. They individually have a direct bearing on GDP growth, and concurrently have an indirect impact through their linkages. Although Japan, the four NIAEs, followed by the ASEAN-4 traditionally epitomize the success of outer-oriented development strategy, China is the most successful recent case. Creating a policy framework for a successful trading regime and for enabling environment for the FDI inflows in the domestic economy requires certain level of development in the areas of education, technology and physical and financial infrastructure. Furthermore, FDI flows have not been observed to take the direction of economies that have not attained a certain level of macroeconomic,

198 Ibid.

exchange rate and socio-political stability, institutional development and policy predictability, efficient and equitable tax administration, capital market development and most importantly a liberal trade and financial policy regime. This calls for proactive pragmatic changes in several policy areas by the host country government. Many Asian economies, particularly the EMEs of Asia, succeeded in creating this enabling environment and are reaping the benefits of energetic FDI inflows.

The TNCs, a major source of global FDI, are attracted by outer-oriented strategy. The additional capital made available by the investing TNCs help in increasing exports by raising investment levels in the promising sectors, that is, sectors having comparative advantage. As evident from the foregoing exposition, trade recorded a phenomenal growth in Asia. Over the 1980–2000 period, exports soared sixfold and imports fivefold. Although during the decade of the 1990s, trade growth in Asia was slower than that in the 1980s, trade still managed to double during this decade.

Many Asian economies had moved up the growth and industrialization ladder and became successful exporters of several high-technology products, particularly IT-related products like computer hardware, semiconductor and ICs. They began to compete with the mature industrial economies. As the Asian economies imported intermediate inputs, parts and components from Japan and other industrial economies for their export products, their sensitivity to real exchange variations increased. Beginning mid-1996 export growth rates in the dynamic Asian economies began to plummet from around 20 percent to single digits in the ANIEs and were reduced to less than half in the ASEAN-4 economies. The deceleration in this vital sector became one of the primary causal factors behind the Asian crisis.

The dynamic economies in East Asia and Southeast Asia benefited most from the strong increase in China's imports. In 2003, China became the single largest export market for East Asia while for Southeast Asian economies, China's share in total exports became sizable. Exports from Asian economies to China were spurred by its strong economic growth, stable exchange rate and the integrated production networks, of which China is an integral part. Historically, intra-trade in Asia was well developed in the early decades of the twentieth century.

Various indicators of intra-regional trade reveal that over the decades of the 1980s and 1990s, in many sub-regional groupings intra-trade increased substantially. There has been a strong upward trend in intra-firm and intra-TNC trade.

Two fairly trustworthy competitiveness indexes did not assign majority of the dynamic Asian economies high spots. In this backdrop, it would appear completely paradoxical that the dynamic Asian economies have continued to record high export growth rate in real terms year after year. In terms of performance in the global markets they also did better than other country groups. This lends support to the hypothesis that rapid growth, including trade expansion, in Asia has been more accumulation-based than productivity-, efficiency- and competitiveness-based.

Since the early 1970s, FDI has grown so much that it became a defining feature of both Asian and global economies. Due to brisk real GDP growth Asia attracted a good deal of FDI, which in turn further facilitated its rapid growth. FDI growth increased substantially during the recent decades. Net FDI inflows to Asia tended to be heavily concentrated. Throughout the decade of the 1990s, China remained the highest FDI recipient in Asia as well as in the developing world. The top 10 recipients in Asia accounted for 97 percent of total net FDI inflows to the region in 2002, while the top 3 for 81 percent of the total. Over the 1990s, China emerged as a large destination of regional and global FDI, somewhat destabilizing the other Asian economies in the process. Conversely, FDI flows to ASEAN stagnated and then went into a decline.

Trade statistics revealed that integrated production networks have existed in Asia since the 1960s. Far above average growth rates in trade in components and partially assembled manufactured goods reflected the growth of integrated production networks. In its most recent form, production-sharing arrangements entail development of specialized labor-intensive activities in a vertically integrated manufacturing industry. From the perspective of the Asian economies, the production networks turned out to be a highly significant development. They opened a new vista of opportunity for the Asian economies. Several Asian economies have begun to figure prominently in the global outsourcing and integrated production networks, with China being one of the most important players. Across numerous industrial and services sectors, large firms in the industrialized economies and TNCs extend their supply chains to China, Korea, ASEAN-4 economies and India.

The recent regionalization trend in Asia is strengthened by—and in turn strengthens—integrated production networks. It is a circular, mutually reinforcing, relationship. The reason is that these networks call for numerous trade offs and collaboration among firms, managers and governments. In the same streak as creation of production networks, a great many opportunities have been created by outsourcing in computer hardware, information and communications technology (ICT) as well as in business process outsourcing (BPO). India's ICT and software exports became competitive and successful since the mid-1980s.

REFERENCES

Anderson, K. and H. Norheim. 1993. "History, geography and regional economic integration," in K. Anderson and R. Blackhurst (eds) *Regional Integration and the Global Trading System*. Hertfordshire, UK: Harvester Wheatsheaf. pp. 19–51.

Arndt, S.W. and H. Kierzkowski. (eds) 2001. *Fragmentation: New Production Patterns in the World Economy.* Oxford: Oxford University Press.

The Asian Development Bank (ADB). 2003. *Asian Development Outlook 2003.* Hong Kong: Oxford University Press.

Balassa, B. 1978. "Exports and economic growth: Further evidence," *Journal of Development Economics.* Vol. 5. No. 1. pp. 181–189.

Balasa, B. and J. Williamson. 1990. *Adjusting to Success: Balance of Payments Policies in the East Asian Economies.* Washington, DC: Institute of International Economics.

The Beijing Times (BT). 2004. "China's foreign investment hits $53 billion," Thursday. January 15. p. 1.

Bhagwati, J.N. and T.N. Srinivasan. 1999. *Outward Orientation and Economic Development: Are Revisionists Right?.* Available at: http://www.columbia.edu/~jb38/Krueger.pdf. Accessed September 17.

Birkinshaw, J. 2001. "Strategy and management in MNEs subsidiaries," in A.M. Rugman and T. Brewer (eds) *Oxford Handbook of International Business.* Oxford: Oxford University Press. pp. 134–160.

Calderón, C., S. Loayza and L. Servén. 2004, January. *Greenfield Foreign Direct Investment and Mergers and Acquisitions: Feedback and Macroeconomic Effects.* Washington, DC: The World Bank. Working Paper 3192.

Crafts, N. and A. Venables. 2001. *Globalization in History: A Geographical Perspective.* London: Center for Economic Policy Research. CEPR Discussion Paper. 3079.

Das, Dilip K.1996a. *The Asia-Pacific Economy,* London, UK: The Macmillan Press; New York: St. Martin's Press.

Das, Dilip K. 1996b. "Asian exports, not so bad," *The Asian Wall Street Journal.* September 5.

Das, Dilip K. 1997 *The Future of Asian Exports.* Singapore and London: Financial Times Business.

Das, Dilip K. 2000a. "Asian exports: The present predicament," in Dilip K. Das (ed) *Asian Exports.* Oxford: Oxford University Press. pp. 1–24.

Das, Dilip K. 2000b. "Rejuvenating Asian exports," in Dilip K. Das (ed) *Asian Exports.* Oxford: Oxford University Press. pp. 383–412.

Das, Dilip K. 2000c, December. *Asian Crisis: Distilling Critical Lessons.* Geneva: United Nations Conference on Trade and Development (UNCTAD). Discussion Paper No. 152.

Das, Dilip K. 2001a "Liberalization efforts in China and accession to the World Trade Organization," *The Journal of World Investment.* December. Vol. 10. No. 6. pp 44–75.

Das, Dilip K. 2001b. *China's Accession to the World Trade Organization: Issues and Implications.* Canberra: Asia Pacific School of Economics and Management. Australian National University. Working Paper No. EA01-1. Available at: http://ncdsnet.anu.edu.au. Accessed March 20, 2003.

Das, Dilip K. 2001c, January. "Stimulants to capital inflows into emerging markets and the recent role of speculators," *Journal of International Development.* Vol. 22. No. 1. pp. 26–56.

Das, Dilip K. 2004a. *Financial Globalization and the Emerging Market Economies.* London and New York: Routledge.

Das, Dilip K. 2004b. *Regionalism in Global Trade.* Boston, MA: Edward Elgar.

Das, 2004c. *The Economic Dimensions of Globalization.* Houndmills, Hampshire, UK: Palgrave Macmillan.

Deardorff, A. 2001. "International provision of tyrade services, trade and fragmentation," *Review of International Economics.* Vol. 9. No. 2. pp. 233–248.

DeBrouwer, G. 2002. "Does a formal common-basket peg in East Asia make economic sense?" in G. DeBrouwer (ed) *Financial Markets and Policies in East Asia.* London and New York: Routledge.

Dollar, D. 1993. "Outward-oriented developing countries really do grow more rapidly: Evidence from 95 LDCs," *Economic Development and Cultural Change.* Vol. 40. No. 3. pp. 523–544.
Eckholm, E. and J. Kahn. 2002. "Asia worries about growth of China's economic power," *The New York Times.* November 24. p. 10.
The Economic Intelligence Unit (EIU). 2004, June. *World Investment Prospects.* London: EIU.
Edwards, S. 1992. Trade orientation, distortion and growth in developing countries," *Journal of Development Economics.* Vol. 39. No. 1. pp. 31–57.
Edwards, S. 1993. "Openness, trade liberalization and growth in developing countries," *Journal of Economic Literature.* Vol. 31. No. 3. pp. 1358–1303.
The Economist. 2001. "Enter the Dragon." March 10. pp. 21–24.
The Economist. 2004. "Still Made in Japan." April 10. pp. 57–59.
Fagerberg, J. 1996. "Technology and competitiveness," *Oxford Review of Economic Policy.* Vol. 12. No.3. pp. 39–51.
Feder, G. 1982. "On exports and economic growth," *Journal of Development Economics.* Vol. 12. No. 1. pp. 59–74.
Frankel, J.A. 1997. *Regional Trading Bloc in the World Economic System.* Washington, DC: Institute for International Economics.
Fukuda, S. and H. Toya. 1995. "The conditional convergence in East Asian countries: The role of exports for economic growth, " in T. Ito and A. O. Krueger (eds.) *Growth Theories in Light of the East Asian Experience.* Chicago: University of Chicago Press. pp. 178—200.
Goto, J. and M. Kawai. 2001. "Macroeconomic interdependence in East Asia," paper presented at the *International Conference in on Economic Interdependence: Shaping Asia-Pacific in the 21st Century*, jointly organized by the Institute for International Monetary Affairs, the IMF and the World Bank, Tokyo, March 22–23.
Hallward-Driemeier, M., G. Iarossi and K.L. Sokoloff. 2002, October. *Export and Manufacturing Productivity in East Asia: A Comparative analysis with Firm Level Data.* Cambridge, MA: National Bureau of Economic Research. NBER Working Paper No. W8894.
Huang, J. and S. Rozelle. 2002. "The Nature of distortions to agriculture in China and implications of WTO accession," paper presented at the Seminar on *The WTO Accession, Policy Reforms and Poverty Reduction in China*, organized by the World Bank and held in Beijing, June 28–29.
Hummels, D., J. Ishii and K.M. Yi. 2001. "The nature and growth of vertical specialization in world trade," *Journal of International Economics.* Vol. 54. No. 1. pp. 75–96.
Humphrey, J. and H. Schmitz. 2001. "Governance in global value chain," *IDS Bulletin.* Vol. 32. No. 3. pp. 112–138.
Ianchovichina, E., S. Suthiwart-Narueput and M. Zhao. 2003. "Regional impact of China's WTO accession," in K. Krumm and H. J. Kharas (eds) *East Asia Integrates: A Trade Policy Agenda for Shared Growth.* Washington, DC: The World Bank. pp. 57–79.
Ianchovichina, E. and W. Martin. 2001. "Trade liberalization in China's accession to the World Trade Organization," *Journal of Economic Integration.* Vol. 15. No. 4. pp. 421–445.
Ianchovichina, E. 2003. *Economic Impact of China's Accession to the WTO.* Washington, DC: The World Bank.
Ianchovichina, E. and T. Walmsley. 2002. *Regional Impact of China's Accession.* Washington, DC: The World Bank.
International Trade Center (ITC). 2000, October. *Offshore Back-Office Operations: Supplying Support Services to Global Markets*. Geneva: ITC.
Ito, T. 2000. "Principal causes of Asian export deceleration," in Dilip K. Das (ed) *Asian Exports.* Oxford: Oxford University Press. pp. 75–114.

Japan Bank of International Co-operation (JBIC). 2002. "JBIC FY 2001 Survey: The outlook of Japanese foreign direct investment," *Journal of the Research Institute of Development and Finance*. No. 9. January. pp. 4–38.

Japan External Trade Organization (JETRO). 2001, October. *Japanese Investment in China*. Tokyo: JETRO.

Kormendi, R.C. and P.G. Meguire. 1985. "Macroeconomic determinants of growth: Cross-country evidence," *Journal of Monetary Economics*. Vol. 16. No. 1. pp. 141–163.

Kremer, M. 1993. "The O-Ring Theory of economic development," *Quarterly Journal of Economics*. Vol. 106. No. 3. pp. 551–575.

Krueger, A.O. 2000. "Factors affecting export growth and performance and the Asian case," in Dilip K. Das (ed) *Asian Exports*. Oxford: Oxford University Press. pp. 25–74.

Krueger, A.O. 1980. "Trade policy as an input to development," *American Economic Review*. Papers and Proceedings. Vol. 70. No. 4. pp. 288–292.

Krueger, A.O. 1997, January. *Trade Policy and Economic Development: How We Learn?* Cambridge, MA: National Bureau of Economic Research. NBER Working Paper No. W5895.

Krueger, A.O. 1995. "East Asian experience and endogenous growth theory," in T. Ito and A.O. Krueger (eds) *Growth Theories in the Light of East Asian Experience*. Chicago: University of Chicago Press.

Krugman, P. 1996. *Pop-Internationalism*. Cambridge, MA: The MIT Press.

Krumm, K. and H.J. Kharas. 2003. *East Asia Integrates: A Trade Policy Agenda for Shared Growth*. Washington, DC: The World Bank.

Lardy, N. R. 2002. *Integrating China into the Global Economy*. Washington, DC: Brookings Institution Press.

Levine, R. and D. Renelt. 1992. "A sensitivity analysis of cross-country growth regression," *American Economic Review*. Vol. 82. pp. 942–963.

Mathews, J. A. 2001. *Dragon Multinationals: A New Model of Global Growth*. New York: Oxford University Press.

Mattoo, A. and S. Wunsch. 2004, March. *Preempting Protectionism in Services: The WTO and Outsourcing*. Washington, DC: The World Bank. Policy Research Working Paper No. 3237.

McCombie, J.S.L. and A.P. Thirlwall. 1994. *Economic Growth and Balance of Payments Constraints*. New York: St. Martin's Press.

Mortimore, M. 2000. "Corporate strategies for FDI in the context of New Economic model," *World Development*. Vol. 28. No. 9. pp. 1611–1626.

Ministry of Foreign Trade and Economic Co-operation (MOFTEC). 2001. *Foreign Trade Statistics*, Beijing: MOFTEC.

Ng, F. and Yeats. 2003. *Major Trade Trends in East Asia*. Washington, DC: The World Bank.

Organization for Economic Co-operation and Development (OECD). 2002, October. "Foreign direct investment for development: Maximizing benefits, minimizing costs," *OECD Policy Brief*.

Organization for Economic Co-operation and Development (OECD). 2003. *Investment Policy Review of China—Progress and Reform Challenges*. Paris: OECD.

Polaski, S. 2004. "Job Anxiety is Real—and it is Global". *Policy Brief*. Washington DC. Carnegie Endowment. May 30.

Prasad, E. and T. Rambaugh. 2003. "Beyond the Great Wall," *Finance and Development*. December 2003. pp. 46–51.

Rajan, R.S. 2003. *Emergence of China as an Economic Power: What Does it Imply for Southeast Asia?* Adelaide: School of Economics. University of Adelaide. Available at: http://www.economics.adelaide.edu.au/staff/rrajan/unpub/PRCASEAN-1.pdf. Accessed June 30.

Rajan, R.S. and R. Sen. 2002, April. *The Japan-Singapore "New-Age" Partnership Agreement: Background, Motivation and Implications*. Singapore: Institute of Policy Studies. IPS Working Paper No. 13.

Ronald-Holst, D. 2002, October. *An Overview of PRC's Emergence and East Asian Trade Patterns to 2020.* Tokyo: ADB Institute. Research Paper Series. No. 44.

Sachs, J. and A. Warner. 1995. "Economic reforms and the process of global integration," *Brookings Papers on Economic Activity.* No. 1. pp. 1–118.

Sakakibara, E. and S. Yamakawa. 2003, June. *Regional Integration in East Asia: Challenges and Opportunities*. Part I and Part II. Washington, DC: Policy Research Working Paper Nos. 3078 and 3079.

Samuelson, R.S. 2004. "Keeping US jobs at home," *The Washington Post.* April 28. p. A21.

Stern, N. and J. Stigllitz. 1997, April 20. *A Framework for a Development Strategy in a Market Economy: Objectives, Scope, Institutions and Instruments.* London: European Bank for Reconstruction and Development. Working Paper .

Turner, A.G. and S.S. Golub. 1997, November. *Towards a System of Multilateral Unit Labor Cost-Based Competitiveness Indicators for Advanced, Developing, and Transition Countries.* Washington, DC: International Monetary Fund. IMF Working Paper WP/97/151.

United Nations Conference on Trade and Development (UNCTAD). 1993. *World Investment Report: Transnational Corporations and Integrated Production.* Geneva and New York: UNCTAD.

United Nations Conference on Trade and Development (UNCTAD). 1996a. *Investment, Trade and International Policy Arrangements.* Geneva and New York: UNCTAD.

United Nations Conference on Trade and Development (UNCTAD). 1996b. *World Investment Report.* Geneva and New York: UNCTAD.

United Nations Conference on Trade and Development (UNCTAD). 1999. *World Investment Report.* Geneva and New York: UNCTAD.

United Nations Conference on Trade and Development (UNCTAD). 2001. *World Investment Report: Promoting Linkages.* Geneva and New York: UNCTAD.

United Nations Conference on Trade and Development (UNCTAD). 2002. *World Investment Report: Transnational Corporations and Export Competitiveness.* Geneva and New York: UNCTAD.

United Nations Conference on Trade and Development (UNCTAD). 2003a. *World Investment Report.* Geneva and New York: UNCTAD.

United Nations Conference on Trade and Development (UNCTAD). 2003b. *China: An Emerging FDI Outward Investor: A Research Note.* Geneva and New York: UNCTAD. Available at: http://r0.unctad.org/en/subsites/dite/fdistats_files/pdfs/China_Researchnote.pdf. Accessed January 24, 2004.

United States Trade Representative (USTR). 2002. *NAFTA at Eight: A Foundation for Economic Growth.* Available at: http://www.ustr.gov/naftareport/nafta8_brochure_eng.pdf.

Urata, S. 2001. "Emergence of FDI-trade nexus and economic growth in East Asia," J.E. Stiglitz (ed.) *Rethinking the East Asian Miracle.* New York: Oxford University Press. pp. 409–459.

Wang, Z. 2002. "WTO accession, Greater China free trade area and economic eelations across the Taiwan Strait," paper presented at the *Fifth Conference on Global Economic Analysis,* held in Taipei, June 5–6.

The World Bank (WB). 2003. *Global Economic Prospects 2004.* Washington, DC: The World Bank.

The World Bank (WB). 2004. *Global Development Finance 2004.* Washington, DC: The World Bank.

World Economic Forum (WEF). 2004. *Global Competitiveness Report 2003–2004*. New York and Oxford: Oxford University Press.

World Economic Forum (WEF). 2002. *Global Competitiveness Report 2001–2002*. New York and Oxford: Oxford University Press.

World Trade Organization (WTO). 2001. *Market Access: Unfinished Business. Post Uruguay Round Inventories and Issues*. Geneva: Economic research and Analysis Division.

World Trade Organization (WTO). 2004, April 5. *World Trade 2003, Prospects For 2004*. Press Release. No. Press/373.

World Trade Organization (WTO). 1996. *Annual Report 1996*. Geneva, Switzerland: WTO.

Yamazawa, I., A. Hirata and K. Yokota. 1991. "Evolving patterns of comparative advantage in the Pacific economies," in M. A. Ariff (ed) *The Pacific Economy: Growth and External Stability*. Sydney, Australia: Allen and Unwin. pp. 213–232.

Yusuf, S. 2003. *Innovation is Key to Asia's Growth*. New York: Oxford University Press.

Yusuf, S. and S. Evenett. 2003. *Can East Asia Compete? Innovation For Global Markets*. New York: Oxford University Press.

Zhan, X.J. and S. Ge. 2002. "Multilateral framework for investment and its implications for China," *Journal of World Economy and Policy*. Vol. 4. No. 2. pp. 12–21.

Chapter 6

FINANCIAL SECTOR DEVELOPMENT

Structure, Institutions and Markets

6.1 FINANCIAL SECTOR: CHINK IN THE ASIAN ARMOR

Financial sector development has enormous significance for economic growth. Researchers have been attracted to studying this relationship for a long time. Consequently, there is a surfeit of literature on this issue. There is no scarcity of disagreement among various studies; however, a recent survey of this literature brought Levine (1997) to a tentative conclusion that theoretical reasoning and empirical evidence does portend to a direct link between financial sector development and economic growth. More recent studies were more positive regarding this causal link. They firmly concluded that this link is empirically valid and that financial sector developments improve the lot of the poorer segments of the society and improve income distribution thereof (Honohan, 2004). The causal link between finance and growth is the most striking empirical macroeconomic relationship uncovered in the 1990s.

The structure of financial market directly influences financial sector development. A secure foundation of well-functioning financial institutions and markets contribute to stable growth performance. Narrowly defined, the structure of financial market in an economy depends upon the degree to which it has a bank-based or capital market-based financial system. In the former case, it is the banking system that is responsible for fulfilling the credit needs of firms and individuals. In the latter case, firms largely rely on the financial markets and securities—bond and equity—for their credit needs. Corporate entities directly access the bond markets, where there are numerous investors that are willing to diversify their asset portfolios.

The three factors that essentially determine what kind of financial systems an economy is likely to have are stage of economic development, information asymmetry associate with extending credit and techniques to cope with it and the state of legal infrastructure. There is little possibility of one kind of financial system existing at the complete exclusion of the other. The bank-dominated and market-dominated, or securitized financial structure, universally coexist—with usually one dominating the other. In economies where they coexist, the competition between the two keeps the financial system efficient. The process of competing renders them vigorous and the two systems make each other stronger.

Asian economies need a strong, well-regulated financial sector, which is a crucial element in a sustainable domestic financial policy framework. Krueger (2004) noted that it implies that markets should be successfully able to address difficult issues "such as non-performing loans (NPLs), capital adequacy, and effective supervision. Financial institutions need the appropriate incentives to develop the skills required to assess and manage credit risk and returns. Effective bankruptcy laws—that strike the right balance between creditors' and debtors' rights—need to be in place.... Going beyond bankruptcy, countries need to have a legal and institutional framework that respects and protects property rights, upholds the rule of law, and combats corruption."

Like the rest of the economic development, financial development in Asia was far from uniform. Likewise, financial markets, institutions and systems are highly uneven in their degree of development, quality of performance, financial depth and strength. In many Asian economies they were and continue to be fragile, underdeveloped, unsophisticated and shallow. The financial sector is often called the Achilles' heel of the Asian economies. Weakness in this sector impeded economic efficiency and made Asian economies vulnerable to external shocks. Inefficiency of the financial sector was widely considered an important causal factor behind the financial turmoil of 1997–98. A long litany of fundamental deficiencies persisted in the financial sector and corporate governance of Asian economies during the pre-crisis period (Das, 2001). This included unsound risk management practices, inefficient banking regulations, lax and inept prudential and supervisory norms, poor disclosure practices and weak and old-fashioned corporate governance. Accounting and auditing standards were woefully below the international norms.

In case of foreign currency loans, on the eve of the Asian crisis financial sector acutely suffered from what became known as the "double mismatch," that is, mismatch in terms of both maturity and currency. The proportion of hard-currency short-term loans in several economies was inordinately high, which in turn contributed to financial instability. In this regard Thailand, where the crisis started, was a conspicuous case. Furthermore, inflexible exchange rate mechanism led to misalignment in exchange rate, rendering economies vulnerable to speculative attacks. Close relationships between corporations and banks further undermined the weak prudential safeguards that were institutionalized. The corporate legal framework had serious inadequacies in that it did not, or poorly, supported the rights of minority shareholders and frequently condoned corporate malfeasance. Although Asian crisis did not directly affect the Peoples' Republic of China (hereinafter China) and Japan, banks in China and Japan are overburdened with non-crisis-related NPLs, causing sclerosis in the financial sector.

The crisis situation ended and a swift V-shaped recovery set in 1998. Since the recovery began, efforts have been afoot to remedy many of the financial sector deficiencies. There has been some degree of success. The flip side of the coin is that a good deal remains to be accomplished in the financial sector restructuring and reforms. A quinquennium after the recovery began, in the five crisis-affected Asian economies, banks and corporations are still struggling with weak balance sheets, which undermine growth opportunities (Chapter 2, Section 2.7).[199] It is no coincidence that those economies that have been more rigorous in carrying out financial sector reforms after the crisis enjoyed better GDP growth performance. Secondly, in many economies there is a need to put in place effective bankruptcy laws, and improve prudential oversight and governance in the capital markets. Until this is accomplished, Asian economies would be far from having an open and competitive financial environment, which is needed for fostering sustainable growth. Third, concerted endeavors are needed to deepen financial markets, and to extend the number and variety of instruments available. Fourth, Asian economies need to rapidly shift toward equity and bond financing, because it would reduce the heavy reliance on the banking sector. Creating equity and bond markets would improve the assessment and management of credit risk and help in the creation of a thriving financial market.

6.2 THE QUALITY CONTINUUM

In terms of the quality of the financial infrastructure, a continuum exists in Asia. Financial and institutional development in some Asian economies is as sophisticated as those in the mature industrial economies, while others fall in the middle ground and a third group having a weak financial infrastructure comes at the bottom. de Brouwer and Corbett (2003) pointed out to the prolonged concurrent coexistence of developed and underdeveloped financial markets and institutions in the region. While Japan, Hong Kong SAR, Singapore and Taiwan can be considered to be meeting the international norms in many areas of performance, Republic of Korea (hereinafter Korea), Malaysia and Thailand

[199] They were Indonesia, Korea, Malaysia, the Philippines and Thailand.

rank below the top three. China, Indonesia and the Philippines are considered to be poor performers from the international standards. The onward march of globalization is increasing the competitive pressure. Financial markets in many Asian economies, particularly those from Southeast Asia, are not able to face the competitive pressure from outside the region as well as from inside the region. In addition, during the decade of the 1990s and the early 2000, the Japanese financial sector suffered from weaknesses in banking, insurance and pension fund areas. It was unable to remedy these long-standing weaknesses.

Four key factors are indispensable for the financial sector to be efficient and well functioning, namely, (i) an efficacious legal framework, (ii) reliable accounting and disclosure norms, (iii) efficient clearing and settlement process and (iv) reliable and easily accessible information system. Using these four key indicators, Herring and Chatusripitak (2000) prepared a quality index and rated Asian economies on a 0 to 10 scale. As a frame of reference, the United Kingdom (U.K.) and United States (U.S.) financial systems were also rated on the same scale, using the same indicators. Their ranking process confirmed what was stated in the preceding paragraph. Hong Kong SAR (7.75), Japan (8.67) and Singapore (7.58) had the most efficient financial infrastructure and institutions, almost comparable to the U.K. (8.93) and the United States (8.99). Taiwan (7.50) was not rated as high as the top three, but its rating was close to them. As opposed to these, rating of other Asian economies was poor. For instance, Indonesia (3.52), Korea (6.73), Malaysia (6.55), the Philippines (4.14) and Thailand (6.50) stood lower or much lower on the same 0 to 10 scale. These quality indicators also took into account contract realization, lack of corruption, bureaucratic quality, accounting standards and press freedom.

Sovereign debt rating agencies like Standard and Poors (S&P) and Moody's rate the creditworthiness and the quality of financial markets on a scale ranging from the highest AAA to the lowest C. They facilitate the analysis and dissemination of information on a borrower's or an insurer's financial standing. They are perceived to be over-dependent on quantitative models. Their ratings are a dynamic phenomenon, and financial structure is only a small part of it. For instance, a large NPL overhand brought down the sovereign credit rating of Japan. These rating agencies continually rate the economies, and depending upon the changing circumstances economies are given higher or lower ratings to direct the global investment institutions. Usually in Asia, these agencies put the three developed financial markets (Japan, Hong Kong SAR and Singapore) at or near the upper end of the scale as high-quality financial markets, on a par with the U.K. and the United States. The emerging markets economies fall substantially below the industrial economy quality, and therefore loan spreads on them are higher. Usually, Taiwan, Korea, Malaysia and Thailand fall in the middle of the scale of the sovereign debt rating agencies, whereas the Philippines comes low on the rating scale and Indonesia has been rated as unstable.

One silver lining behind the cloud of Asian crisis was that it exposed the limitations of the financial markets and institutions in the region. In the post-crisis period, the debate on the structure of financial market and its inadequacies acquired added importance. A consensus has emerged on the necessity of a strong domestic financial system. In particular, deliberations on developing domestic-currency corporate bond market intensified because they were highly underdeveloped. Whether a better developed and strengthened corporate bond markets would reduce the probability of another crisis in Asia remains a moot point. The second related post-crisis issue was improvement and strengthening of legal and regulatory framework. It was hoped that this would not only reinforce the existing financial structure but also emphasize its future development. Trying to directly fortify the financial structure while ignoring legal, information and enforcement mechanism is indubitably a recipe for failure (Harwood, 2000).

6.3 FINANCIAL MARKET STRUCTURE AND COUNTRY CLASSIFICATION

As a rule of thumb, developing economies are more dependent on the bank-based financial system than a market-based, securitized one. This is essentially because the former is easier to develop and expand than the latter. The second reason for inadequate development of the securitized financial system is inefficient and deficient information and legal systems, which are endemic in the developing economies. The Asian economies are no exception to this generalization. Their financial system was not only bank-dominated but was characterized as "repressive" in the early stages of development. In a repressive financial system, for one, credit allocation was controlled and directed by the government. Second, the monetary authority determined interest rates on both deposits and loans. Third, they are kept below the market clearing rates. In many Asian economies, particularly in Japan and the NIAEs, financial repression was premised on the development strategy that used finance as a potent and pragmatic instrument of industrial policy (see Chapter 2). It helped these economies achieve multiple objectives like fulfilling long-term financial needs of the so-called "winner" or strategic industries and favored firms and projects, promoting exports and strengthening the industrial infrastructure. During the early stages of growth, several Asian economies used financial repression with enormous success, but it cannot be a long-term strategy.

Using different indicators, several recent studies have attempted to classify the market structures of the Asian economies. Shirai (2001a) computed total external finances raised by firms by sources for the United States as a benchmark and compared them to the same indicator in the Asian economies for the 1990–99 period. The securities markets played a conceivably predominant role in the United States. Data showed that almost 70 percent of the finances were raised by firms from the equity market and close to 18 percent through the issuance of bonds. The banking sector was responsible for merely 12 percent of the total finances raised by corporations. As opposed to this, in many Asian economies, bank loans and equities were the principal instruments of raising finance, while securities markets were not important channels of financial intermediation. As several Asian economies have relatively less developed financial structures, this observation applies squarely to them. In case of Thailand, Indonesia and China bank loans were the largest source of credit and the banks overwhelmingly dominated the financial sector, while Singapore, Malaysia and the Philippines were relatively more reliant on equity markets. All the three sources of finance were active in Korea. Bank loans and securities market both played an important role, with bank loans supplying the largest proportion of funds to the Korean firms. Bank financing varied between 30 percent of the total external financing in Malaysia and Singapore to 70 percent in Thailand and 80 percent in China.

Instead of the United Kingdom or the United States, Japan's financial structure resembles that of the other Asian economies, where the securities markets dominate. The financial structure in Japan resembles that of Germany, where banks play the most predominant role. Bank claims in Japan and Germany are usually large, in the vicinity of 130 percent of the GDP. In most of the Asian economies, corporate bond markets were highly underdeveloped until the Asian crisis. In Korea they were relatively larger than in the other Asian economies because of the presence of the *chaebol*.[200]

The stance that the financial market structure in Asia was and continues to be bank dominated did not go unchallenged by several recent studies. For instance, Demirguc-Kunt and Levine (2001) constructed a conglomerate financial structure index for the 1990s. They took into consideration the size, activity and efficiency of the financial systems to determine the relative importance of banks and securitized capital markets in the Asian economies. Their empirical assessment of financial market structure first separated sample economies as developed and industrialized and ranked them into bank-based and market-based systems. The next step was computation of a structure index of markets. The structure index placed each sample country on the continuum running from bank-based to market-based system. The results were opposite of what was stated so far. According to this index many Asian economies were found to be more market-based than bank-based. The Philippines, Thailand, Korea, Singapore, Hong Kong SAR and Malaysia fell in this category. Interestingly, Hong Kong SAR (2.10) and Malaysia (2.93) were found to have higher value of structure index than the United States (1.96) and Switzerland (2.03). The

---

[200] What are *chaebol* has been explained in Chapter 5.

value of structure index should be interpreted carefully. Although the value of structure index for Hong Kong SAR and Malaysia is high because their stock markets are active and large, their stock market development and activity is high relative to their own banking sectors, and not relative to the level of stock market development in other countries. By the same token, the Philippines was classified as having a market-based financial system because its banking sector is small, underdeveloped and not very active, and not because its stock markets are large and highly developed. The explanation that Demirguc-Kunt and Levine (2001) provided for classifying Korea as having a market-based financial system is not only because Korean equity market is active and efficient but also because the non-banking institutions play a substantial role in the financial market. Their role is as substantial as that of the banks.

6.4 CARRYING OUT FINANCIAL MARKET DEVELOPMENT

Inadequacies and limitations of the financial sector were considered one of the prime causal factors that caused the Asian crisis (Chapter 7, Section 7.1). In its aftermath, while eagerness to dilute the dominance of banking sector was rational, Asian economies also needed to strengthen their post-crisis, NPL-weakened, domestic banking system. The five crisis-affected Asian economies launched restructuring of the financial sector. At an early stage, unilaterally as well as under the direction of the IMF steps were taken to recapitalize banks, write off NPLs and transfer bad debt off the books to loan restructuring and asset management institutions. Although banking sector was out of the woods by mid-2004, it took a great deal of resources, astute planning and good judgment.

Another channel of bringing in improvements in the financial sector was further globalization of Asian banking sector. It took place during the 1980s and 1990s and indubitably Asian economies benefited from it. It should be noted that the globalization of banking sector is distinguished from its internationalization.[201] The post-crisis environment could be conducive to promote further globalization and thereby strengthening of banking sector in Asia, as it did in thevadjust Latin American economies after the *Tequila* crisis.[202] But

[201] Globalization of banking is distinguished from internationalization of banking. The principal difference is in the manner in which a bank finances its foreign assets. An international bank uses funds raised in the domestic market to finance its claims on borrowers in the foreign markets. As opposed to this, a global bank uses funds raised in the foreign markets to finance its claims on borrowers in the same foreign markets.

unlike Latin American economies, Asian economies began to record significant current account surpluses soon after the crisis. As international liabilities in Asia were not rising, pressure to globalize the banking sector has not been acute. In case of China, one of the conditions of World Trade Organization (WTO) accession was to liberalize the domestic banking sector and open it to foreign banks. This included opening the local currency banking business as well. Chinese banking sector is sure to come in the ambit of globalized finance in the short-term, although this cannot be said about the other Asian economies (McCauley et al., 2002).

Development of capital markets for raising securitized finances by the firms was the best-known alternative for strengthening as well as deepening the financial sector. Having variant sources of finance provides an opportunity to firms to balance debt and equity in their financial structure. Creating such variations in sources of credit helps firms in maintaining a manageable degree of leverage and reduces the impact of shock received through a particular channel of financing. A well-developed and active corporate bond market can also function as a warning mechanism as well as an exit mechanism. Likewise, an active domestic equity market can provide an effective cushion against currency and interest-rate shocks. Given the significance of their development, bond markets and equity markets in Asia are the focus of Section 6.7 through Section 6.9, respectively.

6.5 BANKING SECTOR

There are region-wide variations in the ownership pattern of banks. No two economies have similarities in this regard. Although banks with widely held ownership are most common in Asia, there are banks that are not widely held but controlled by families of important industrialists, banks owned by unlisted firms and individuals and public sector banks. Thus controlling shareholdings in the banking sector varies from bank to bank. Family owned banks dominate the ownership only in the Philippines, while the state-owned banks overwhelmingly dominate the banking sector in China because of its socialist heritage. Toward the end of 2003, China prepared plans to allow as many as two of its four state-owned banks to launch initial public offerings of their stock domestically and abroad during the next several years, a step that could stimulate an overhaul of the nation's NPL-ridden banking sector (WSJ, 2003). To replenish their

[202] The *Tequila* crisis started in Mexico in December 1994 and had a strong contagion effect, including neighborhood effect. The contagion effect transmitted the crisis to several large and small Latin American economies. The neighborhood effect is one of the channels of transmission of a crisis. See Das (2003) for a discussion on various channels that transmit a financial and economic crisis.

NPL-weakened capital bases, options like issuing substandard debenture, using pre-tax profit to write off dead loans and transferring non-performing loans to a professional entity are to be allowed to the state-owned banks. These measures should reduce public ownership of the banking sector in China. In several Asian economies government ownership of banks increased after the crisis due to reform and restructuring efforts, albeit the range in this regard is wide. The highest was in Indonesia (72 percent) in 2000 and the lowest in Malaysia (18 percent). Korea (58 percent) and Thailand (30 percent) fell between these two extremes (Kawai, 2002). By international standards, asset ownership share of foreign banks continued to remain small in the Asian economies.

The ownership structure influences the banking performance. Generally, public ownership is associated with low levels of systemic efficiency, and high price banking services, but it holds only as a generalization. According to the Asian Bankers' Association (ABA) survey (2003), profitability of family-owned banks was higher in Hong Kong SAR, Singapore, Korea and Taiwan than that of the widely held banks. The government-owned banks were the most profitable in Brunei Darussalam, China, Malaysia, Thailand and Vietnam.[203] Foreign ownership is associated with a high degree of operational efficiency.

High concentration of banking assets was not one of the characteristics of banks, but after the post-crisis restructuring, which entailed measures like bank closures, mergers and recapitalization, asset concentration was found to increase markedly in several economies. There are no serious adverse policy implications of asset concentration. It would *prima facie* appear that high concentration of assets would thwart competition, but theoretical and empirical arguments suggest that the benefit of efficiency and scale-economies created by asset concentration may offset higher cost of banking operations.

As it dominated the financial sector, banking industry was appallingly blighted by the Asian crisis. The post-crisis reforms efforts in banking began to show some results by early 2004. Lending was growing, profits in the banking industry began to return and the capital base seemed to be adequate. Bankers tried to instill better risk management practices and reduced their dependence on corporate lending by turning toward financing to small businesses and consumer finance. Regulators became more vigilant than ever in the past. They forced banks to consolidate; consequently Malaysia has two commercial banks, Singapore has three, and Thailand four. Governments were forced

---

[203] The Asian Banker's Association (ABA) survey entitled "The Regulatory and Business Environment for Risk Management Practices in the Banking Sector of APEC Economies" was conducted in collaboration with the Pacific Economic Co-operation Council (PECC), and the Chinese Taipei Pacific Economic Co-operation Committee (CTPECC). The results of the ABA survey were circulated at the Second Annual Conference of PECC Finance Forum, held in Hua Hin, Thailand, on July 8 and 9, 2003.

to takeover banks during the crisis. The resale of these stakes led to a wave of cross-border takeovers in Asia. Singapore- and Hong Kong-based banks, healthiest in the region, were snapping up stakes in the regional banks (*The Economist*, 2004a). The flip side of this coin is that governments still meddle in the financial decision-making, legal systems are not up to the mark and often bank balance sheets are not what they seem. Problems persist because financial restructuring in several Asian economies, particularly those in Southeast Asia, progressed with a slow pace.

6.5.1 Ascertaining the dominance

The dominance of the banking sector in the financial sector can be easily established statistically. Endo (2001) calculated the proportion of external financing in the Asian firms from different sources as a percentage of the GDP to show a heavy reliance on bank loans in Asia. For instance, Indonesia (68.9 percent of GDP), Korea (82.5 percent), Malaysia (104.1 percent) and Thailand (127.8 percent) had the highest reliance on bank lending. Only Malaysia was an exception in this regard, having much greater reliance (137 percent of GDP) on equity markets, which was not different from that in the industrial economies like the United States and the United Kingdom.

Outstanding bank loans are another useful measure for calculation whether banks dominate the financial structure or not. Banks overwhelmingly dominate the financial sector in China. Measured as a percentage of GDP, outstanding bank loans for the 1990–99 period were 99 percent of the GDP in China, the highest proportion in the region (Shirai, 2001a; see Chart 1a). Thailand (92 percent) and Malaysia (80 percent) came next, in that order. Using yet another measure, that is, outstanding bank loans as a percentage of total external finance, China again comes at the top with 85 percent for the 1990–99 period, followed by Thailand (70 percent), Indonesia (63 percent), Korea (45 perecent) and the Philippines (40 percent) (Shirai, 2001a; see Chart 1c).

The share of outstanding bank loan in total external finance of corporations, which had increased steadily before the crisis, began to decline during the post-crisis period. This was indicative of the fact that securitized capital markets became relatively more important and active as a source of finance after the crisis. However, absolute size of the bank loan did not decline, implying that banks have continued to be an important source of finance.

Dominance of the banking sector, both on asset and liability side, has been a long-term trend in the Asian financial markets. They were the principal source of corporate finance and an overwhelming part of household assets were held with them as deposits. The financial market structure has evolved away from this trend. During the crisis, banking sector found itself undercapitalized owing to sizeable NPLs and was struggling for recapitalization. Therefore, during the immediate post-crisis period corporate bond issuance increased, particularly in the five severely crisis-affected economies. Between 1997 and 2000 bond issuance nearly doubled in these economies, increasing from $68 billion to $130 billion (IMF, 2001). The largest amount of corporate bond issuance took place in Korea, followed by Malaysia and Thailand. This growth of the corporate bond market was forced by the Asian crisis and it somewhat moderated the overwhelming dominance of banks in the financial structure.

6.5.2 Foreign banks

If foreign-owned banks are defined as fully owned branches and majority-owned subsidiaries, foreign ownership in Asia has historically had a low profile. This holds both in absolute sense and relatively. Presence of foreign banks in the emerging market economies (EMEs) has increased substantially, particularly in the 1990s. However, the dynamic economies of Asia remained an exception to this general trend. In 1999, assets under foreign control were 52.3 percent of the total assets in the EMEs of Central and Eastern Europe, and 25.0 percent in the EMEs of Latin America. In Asia the corresponding proportion was a paltry 6.3 percent (Montgomery, 2003). Mathieson and Roldos (2001) computed foreign banks' participation in the EMEs using three different methods. They also inferred that the percentage of financial assets under foreign control in the Asian EMEs were well below those in the other EMEs.

Ownership in the banking sector is another measure of foreign banks' presence in an economy. According to the ABA survey (2003), in the two international financial centers, Hong Kong SAR and Singapore, foreign banks' ownership in the banking sector was 48 percent and 71 percent, respectively in 2003. Their case was an exception. The corresponding proportion in Japan was 6 percent, Indonesia 11 percent, Korea 5 percent, the Philippines 15 percent, Taiwan 4 percent and Thailand 11 percent. Although participation and presence of foreign banks in Asia increased after the crisis, they continue to remain far below the averages for the EMEs in the other regions.

The reason behind such low presence of foreign bank branches, scanty ownership in the banking sector and low ownership of assets was the legacy of stringent regulations in this regard. Until recently, dynamic Asian economies had formal, and often informal, restrictions on the entry of foreign banks. Some of them banned them completely. In other economies foreign banks' entry was *de jure* free and unrestricted but the entering foreign banks found that there was a difference between the principle and practice. The authorities were uncomfortable about their presence. When foreign banks tried entering by way of minority holdings and joint ventures, their reception was cold and barriers were created. Indeed there were some exceptions. Korea illustrates this point well, wherein principle monetary authorities did not prevent the entry but in practice they very openly did. The exception was the Koran Bank, which was a collaborative endeavor between the Bank of America and some domestic banks.

China did not participate in the ABA (2003) survey, but foreign ownership in China is exceedingly low, although it is expected to gradually enlarge after it acceded to the WTO in 2001. The ABA Survey (2003) revealed that foreign-owned banks were generally more profitable than domestically owned banks were. They recorded higher profit rates in Brunei, Darussalam, Indonesia, Malaysia, the Philippines, Thailand and Vietnam than in Hong Kong SAR, Korea, Singapore, and Taiwan. There has been some anxiety in Asia about entry of foreign banks causing loss of control over monetary policy and sovereignty. However, if the domestic supervision is in place, loss of control to foreigners would be very difficult. Likewise, risk of losing sovereignty is grossly overstated. If anything, foreign banks bring in financial skills, technology and expand the exposure of the domestic market, which is essential for developing links with the rapidly integrating global economy.

An important reason behind low foreign ownership of assets in the banking sector is that the policymakers did not see evidence of foreign banks achieving the vital objectives of growth and stabilization. The proponents of the presence of foreign banks in Asia argue that as they are a source of much needed capital and help in creating an efficient and vibrant financial system with a wide range of financial services, therefore, they should be welcome in the Asian economies. The opponents disagree and contend that foreign participation can have a potentially pernicious influence over the financial sector. The Asian crisis testifies to this fact. During the Asian crisis, and the financial and currency crises in the EMEs that occurred after that, it was observed that the financial crisis followed on the heels of financial liberalization. Therefore, there is a good deal of skepticism regarding opening up of the banking system in Asia to foreign participation. The entry of foreign banks amounts to de facto liberalizing the capital account, which in turn may become a source of destability in the domestic financial market and the banking sector, and so Asian central banks have voted against the large presence of foreign banks. Thus, lack of support for foreign banks in the policymaking community is not without reason.

6.5.3 Non-performing loans

A large proportion of bank loans turning into NPLs is sure to have insidious influence over the financial intermediation process as well as on investment and GDP growth rates. Excessive NPLs are a serious and problematical issue for the balance sheet of the loaning bank because, for one, the asset side of the balance sheet is adversely affected and, second, the income statement is weakened because loan loss provisions have to be made or increased due to NPLs. A portfolio of impaired assets and plunging income coalesce to make it impossible for the bank to extend fresh credit, resulting in deceleration in credit growth in the economy, and even a credit crunch. NPLs limit financial intermediation, followed by investment in the economy. If the NPLs are not resolved properly, they also become a source of moral hazard for the lending banks and borrowers. Burden of NPLs becomes a large monetary and fiscal liability (ADB, 2004). Sizeable NPLs accumulated during the Asian crisis worsened the unhealthy banking and financial situation in the five affected economies.

In the post-crisis period, the NPL situation has gradually improved. A great deal of bad debts has been taken off the banks' balance sheets by the centralized asset management companies (AMCs) set up by the central banking authorities, and the capital base of the affected banks was strengthened with public resources. Although initially NPLs remained high, their level fell slowly but steadily. de Brouwer and Corbett (2003) compiled NPL statistics from different sources and reported that for Malaysia they declined from 15 percent in end-1999 to 10.7 percent at the end of 2001. Indonesia was the worst case where the NPLs fell from 56.3 percent at the end of 2000 to 49.8 percent at the end of 2001, and for Korea they declined from 13.9 percent at the end of 2000 to 9.9 percent at the end of 2001. By the first quarter of 2004, the NPLs had declined further. For instance, in Korea they were at the lowest (less than 3 percent) level in the region. In Indonesia they had come down to 5 percent and in Malaysia, the Philippines and Thailand they had declined to a low level (*The Economist,* 2004a).

In China and Japan, banks held large NPLs and they have been a serious financial problem for a while. Although correct statistics are not available, private sector estimates for these two economies are twice that of the officially publicized NPL figures. Japan's NPLs were a legacy of the bubble era, the latter half of the 1980s. Although they remained at a menacingly high level all through the 1990s and early 2000s, by mid-2004 their level had declined considerably (refer to Chapter 2, Section 2.4). For the fiscal year that ended in March 2004, major banking groups posted a fall in NPLs: Mitsubishi Tokyo Financial Group posted a fall from 5.3 percent to 2.9 percent, Sumitomo Mitsui Financial Group from 8.4 percent to 5.0 percent and Mizuho Group from 6.4 percent to 4.4 percent (*The Economist,* 2004b).

China's NPL problem, which was not related to the Asian crisis, was a systemic problem and concentrated in the state-owned commercial banks as a result of the "transfer to loans" scheme, which was launched in the 1980s. This scheme aimed at routing state budgetary allocations to SOEs through the banking system. As a consequence, the financial system's vulnerability in China became increasingly evident in the late 1990s. The four major state-owned commercial banks—Bank of China, China Construction Bank, Industrial and Commercial Bank of China and Agricultural Bank of China—were beleaguered by lack of corporate governance, high NPL ratio and low capital adequacy ratio. Central bank figures show that the "big four" had outstanding NPL amounting to 1.99 trillion renminbi yuan ($239.76 billion) at the end of last September 2003. That is, 26 percent of all loans were NPLs. The political leadership was aware of the poor state of affairs. Premier Wen Jiabao, in his annual state-of-the-nation address, remarked that China needs to "accelerate the reform of the wholly state-owned commercial banks." Slow pace of banking and financial reforms has been widely criticized. In March 2004, China announced opening of its banking business in all places and all currencies to foreign banks by 2006.

As opposed to this, banking and financial sector in Hong Kong SAR and Singapore did not suffer from large Naples, and was the first to rebound from the effects of the financial crisis. By early 2000, there was a marked improvement in it. Banks in Hong Kong SAR and Singapore not only continued to be healthy but also helped other regional banks in their restructuring and by acquiring stakes in them.

6.6 INTERMEDIATE FINANCIAL STRUCTURE

Asian financial system during the post-crisis era of necessity developed into an "intermediate financial structure," which covers the middle ground between a bank-based and a securitized financial structure (Shirai, 2001b).[204] As the banks had traditionally dominated the financial scenario, they developed trust and reputation and had the information advantage in the domestic economy. Therefore, they should be equipped for their post-crisis role. They can launch into a new role of issuers, investors, underwriters, developers, brokers and guarantors in the fledgling corporate bond market during the post-crisis period. This would be the beginning of a healthy and much-needed trend, one that adapts to the demand of a period. That is, on the one hand the banking sector can help develop healthy bond markets, and on the other as the bond markets become a significant substitute for bank loans. If developments take place in this sequence, banks can carve out a complementary niche for themselves. The final result would be a strong, diversified and competitive financial sector, which would be more crisis resistant than the one that existed.

The intermediate financial structure can be visualized as operating on the following lines. Large and reputable banks can issue short- and medium-term—or one to five years—debentures. Given that Asian economies have traditionally been high savers, this should be an undemanding task. Recall that the region enjoys a global creditor status. However, a psychological barrier is natural because investors may not like to diversify their investment portfolios, as they are accustomed to safe and liquid banking. This barrier is small and not insurmountable

---

[204] Shirai (2001a) provides a detailed discussion on intermediate financial structure and the regulatory framework necessary for it.

in the medium-term. The short- and medium-term debentures can be easily converted into long-term financial resources by the banks. These long-term resources can be utilized in serving the needs of corporate entities.

The next meaningful step can be taken by the central banks by indirectly supporting these debentures. They can use them in open market operations. The debentures can also be qualified for central bank's discount window, which in turn would increase liquidity and boost investor confidence in the bank debentures. Such support from the central banks can make the debentures an acceptable payment reserve asset for commercial banks, which depend so highly on central bank borrowings. Shirai (2001b) has drawn a comparison to the post-war financial development in Japan, where long-term credit banks played a pivotal role during the shift in industrial structure from the light to heavy and high-technology industries. They played the role of venture capitalists, carefully screened the new ventures and evaluated them keeping the future demand forecast in sight. During this period bank debentures were in use.

Banks' endeavors and support in developing securities markets is a two-way street because it benefits them also. As domestic banking sector and capital accounts in the Asian economies have liberalized, the competition has intensified and the banking sector has been facing a decline in revenues and profitability. If the banks can extend their old loaning relationship with their clients by underwriting their securities, they will be able to generate more profits in the form of fees. Due to their old relationship with the clients, it would come easily to them because they have proprietary information regarding the old clients and have enjoyed the privilege of monitoring their past performance. Second, due to their market reputation and proprietary information advantages, banks would be able to handle issuance of securities expertly and with no trouble compared to the non-bank financing companies. The reputation of the bank contributes to investor confidence, and is generally instrumental in rapid purchase of securities. Third, through their branch network, banks can handle the securities business relatively easily. Fourth, the underwriting costs would be lower for the banks than for the non-bank financial companies, leading to the possibility of further investment growth for the firm issuing securities. Fifth, development of long-term credit banks would minimize maturity mismatches and provide long-term credit to domestic firms through the bond markets. Lastly, large Asian banks can set up subsidiaries for their securities business. This structural extension is an easy-to-establish profitable option for the Asian banks.

6.7 BOND MARKETS

That financial structure in Asia needs to be transformed in the post-crisis period is well acknowledged. There are several economic and financial benefits of active domestic currency sovereign bond and corporate bond markets. First, their most significant contribution is in diversifying the sources of finance and reducing the conventional reliance on the domestic banks, which was badly needed in several Asian economies. Second, local currency bond markets are instrumental in determining and locking in interest rates in the financial markets. Third, they can be important means of reducing an economy's vulnerability to maturity risk, exchange rate risk, "sudden stop" in access to global capital markets and "sudden reversals" of global capital market inflow, which was observed during the Asian crisis. Local currency bonds provide a cushion against the "hot money," or the volatility in global capital inflows. In so doing, they help in creating a financial environment that is appropriate for crisis prevention (Das, 2003). Fourth, creating and strengthening domestic currency bond markets indirectly improves corporate governance by developing a "credit culture." It promotes enhancement of transparency in financial institutions and corporate world through stringent information disclosure requirements. Fifth, bond markets engender and stimulate opportunities for risk-pooling and risk-sharing for both the sides, borrowers and lenders. This ushers in improvements in the efficiency of resource allocation through market-determined interest rates. They also provide access to longer-term finance for larger projects. This is what banks do not prefer to handle. Lastly, corporate bond markets intensify competition in the domestic financial markets and help in bringing down interest rates (Harwood, 2000; Lian, 2002).

For central banks, bond markets are a multiple utility instrument. Their basic use is in issuance of sovereign bonds for funding the budget deficits in a non-inflationary manner, which enhances the effectiveness of monetary policy. Central banks frequently use government or sovereign bond markets for the implementation of monetary policy. They function as the agents of the government in various aspects of the management of government debt. Also, bond markets are needed for sterilizing the capital inflows from the global capital markets. Asian economies were the recipients of substantial sum of global capital until mid-1997. Sale of sovereign bonds is an easy and risk-free method of sterilizing the external capital inflows.[205] Basically central banks are responsible for the stability of the financial system as well as supervision, clearance and settlement systems of the sovereign bond markets.

6.7.1 Bond market developments in the pre-crisis period

The traditional reasons for tenuous domestic currency bond markets were not only the preference of both borrowers and lenders for bank intermediation, but also little need for sovereign debt due to conventional Asian aversion to

---

[205] In the absence of bond markets, central banks can sterilize external financial flows with the help of short-term debt instruments, but this is not the ideal manner of sterilization because it raises short-term interest rates and leads to financial sector distortion.

fiscal deficits. In the pre-crisis period, Asian economies saw little utility of having large domestic currency bond markets. As alluded to Section 6.2, in the pre-crisis era, Korea was the leader in creating bond markets, particularly the corporate bond market. This was largely due to the presence of the large number of *chaebol,* or business conglomerates. Issuance of corporate bonds began in Korea much earlier than in other Asian economies. Ssanyong Cement issued the first convertible corporate bonds in 1963. After a slow initial period, the bond issuance pace picked up in the 1970s. The investment trust companies (ITCs) grew during the1990s and with that grew the bond issuance activity. They were active non-bank financial firms and their purchase of corporate bonds accounted for almost 80 percent of the financing activity of non-bank financial firms over this period. By 1997, the outstanding bond issuance was 20 percent of the GDP in Korea. Owing to the crisis, outstanding bond issuance rose to 25 percent of GDP in 1998 (Kim and Park, 2002). Daewoo, the third largest *chaebol,* filed for chapter 11 in mid-1999, giving corporate bond market a near-fatal jolt. Several ITCs collapsed and since then investor confidence has evaporated. After the Daewoo bankruptcy, only very high quality bonds could be floated in Korea (Turner, 2002).

In Thailand, the Securities and Exchange Act was enacted in 1992, which allowed listed companies to issue corporate bonds for the first time. Since then corporate bond issuance expanded a little bit, although the market size remained small. In 1999, there was a spurt in bond issuance because several blue-chip companies entered the market to augment their financial resources. Liquidity has tended to improve. But the bond market size continued to be small. In Indonesia, corporate bond market did not exist until 1987 because of stringent regulations. Since then several reforms measures were implemented, but in comparison to Korea, Malaysia and Thailand, the size of the corporate bond market in Indonesia remained much smaller. Throughout the 1990s, outstanding bond issuance stagnated to around 5 percent of the GDP. The highly underdeveloped state of these markets did not change much (Shirai, 2001a). The small corporate bond markets are not known for brisk secondary market activity. There were two reasons for it. First, investors tended to hold their bonds until maturity. Tax and interest rate policies encourage this proclivity. Second, when banks invested in the short-term bonds, they held them until maturity to avoid maturity mismatches.

As regards the maturity profile, Asian bond markets displayed a heavy concentration toward short- and medium-term. Korea was an exception in this regard, where maturity profile did not change after the Asian crisis. The three-year maturity bonds were the most popular before the crisis, and remained so after that. In the other Asian economies, the penchant for short-maturity became more intensive during the post-crisis period. This was largely due to a lack of confidence in the viability of the corporations and information asymmetry. Declining maturity also reflected a general lack of investor confidence in this segment of the market. The issuing firms accepted it comfortably because of lower interest rates of the short-term bonds.

6.7.2 Bond market developments in the post-crisis period

Following the Asian crisis, the banking sector was excoriated for not function in an efficacious manner, contributing to the crisis (Ohno, 1999). While policymakers cannot avert every crisis, they can indeed learn lesson from the previous one to minimize the probability of the next one. Time has arrived to initiate the required changes in the financial structure. Wide consensuses on a pressing need to diversify it, reduce reliance on bank credit and develop domestic currency bond markets as an alternative source of external finance followed. Policymakers logically inferred that broad and deep domestic bond markets would serve to reduce financial vulnerability of banks and corporations to sudden shifts in risk perception on the part of the global investors.

In the post-crisis environment, financing of large budget deficits and recapitalization of banks created a pressing need for capital, which in turn created a need for developing local sovereign bond markets. As the banks were facing serious difficulties after the crisis in extending credit, causing severe credit crunch, creating, expanding and strengthening bond markets were given a priority to minimize the plausibility of the crisis to reoccur any time in the near future. It was accepted as an important financial strategy in the region.

When firms are able to sell domestic currency bonds to raise long-term capital, their need for entering the foreign bond markets for this purpose would decline. Consequently, the risk of a double mismatch (noted in Section 6.1) would be eliminated. The domestic currency bond markets in the Asian economies were poorly developed. This applied to both sovereign bonds and *a fortiori* to corporate bond markets. Japan and Singapore were the only two exceptions to this generalization.

Creating or expanding corporate bond market is a difficult, complex and time-consuming process.[206] Many Asian economies do not have the ability and wherewithal to create them. Attitudinal problems further complicate the process. The credit culture, noted above, is an intangible but crucial facet of the financial culture of an economy. It reflects the maturity of the financial markets. Developing the required attitude and credit culture needed for the bond markets, particularly corporate bond markets, in a developing economy is a time-consuming process. Therefore, in many Asian economies these corporate bond markets may not be created without long delays, or may not be created at all (Sakakibara and Yamakawa, 2003). It has been observed that equity markets

[206] See Harwood (2000) for a detailed discussion on the requirement for creating a well-functioning corporate bond market.

Table 6.1. Bond Issuance (In millions of $)

Country	1998	1999	2000	2001	2002	2003
1. China	1,794	1,060	1,771	1,342	603	2,034
2. Hong Kong	725	7,125	7,059	10,459	1,951	1,451
3. Indonesia	0	0	0	125	375	609
4. Korea	5,084	4,906	7,653	7,756	6,706	11,531
5. Malaysia	NA	2,062	1,420	2,150	1,880	963
6. The Philip	1,890	4,751	2,467	1,842	4,774	3,730
7. Singapore	1,500	2,147	2,339	8,665	562	2,702
8. Taiwan	1,041	475	1,698	2,152	5,481	8,940
9. Thailand	300	794	0	279	48	3,000
Total	12,335	23,321	24,306	35,770	22,348	32,259
Percentage of total financing	39.19%	43.81%	29.23%	55.19%	42.52%	NA

Source: International Monetary Fund. *Global Financial Stability Report.* 2004. April. (various issues)

tend to burgeon in economies that fail to create bond markets due to an underdeveloped financial infrastructure and credit culture. The reason is the structures of the two markets. While bond markets promise repayment of principle and interest, equity claims promise repayment of a prorated profit share and a vote in important corporate decisions. In addition, in an underdeveloped financial institutional environment, pricing a bond is a daunting task. It is intricate and complicated how to set an interest rate that can compensate for the opportunity cost, default risk, inflation and liquidity risks. The idiosyncratic features of a bond, like a call option or sinking fund, make this task more problematic.

The endeavors of the Asian governments in developing their bond markets are reflected in the growth of size of their debt security issuance (see Table 6.1). Until 2001, Hong Kong SAR, Korea, Singapore and Taiwan recorded sharp increases in their bond issuance activity, but a decline set in in 2002. As a proportion of total external financing (which includes syndicated loans, bond issuance and equity issuance), bond issuance peaked in 2001. The amount of bond issuance approximately doubled between 1998 and 2001. Due to the concern regarding terrorism and continued recession in the global economy bond issuance activity dropped from $35.7 billion to $22.3 billion in 2002. In 2003, there was a spurt again to $32.2 billion. Korea and Taiwan recorded substantial increases.

Despite limitations (see Section 6.5.3) domestic currency bond markets in Asian economies picked up some pace and the financial structure in the Asian economies has gradually begun to transform. In 1997, the domestic bond markets in Asia (excluding Japan) were the source of less than 3 percent of the funds raised by domestic corporate entities. By 2001, the corresponding proportion soared to 38 percent of the total domestic financing. Malaysia, followed by Korea, expanded their bond markets significantly. Measured as a percentage of GDP, the volume of the Malaysian bond market was 51 percent of the GDP while in Korea it was 28 percent in 2001. The volume of bond markets was $150 billion in Asia by 2001. This led to diversification of financial structure and the absolute dominance of banks declined. Excessive reliance of firms on the banking sector yielded to an increasing use of securitized markets, although secondary market liquidity continues to remain an unresolved issue. Bond markets caught up with banks, which had lent $180 billion in 2001 (Tran and Roldos, 2003).) There have been several noteworthy improvements, but "Asia remains heavily dependent on bank financing" (IMF, 2004).

By 2004, some regional initiatives were taken, which included creation of Asian Bond Market Initiative (ABMI) by the Asia-Pacific Economic Co-operation (APEC) forum. It is a broad umbrella covering many areas of domestic bond market development. The ABMI focused on resolving some of the supply-side impediments that exist in Asian economies, to make Asian bond markets more accessible to the Asian issuers (IMF, 2004). The other objective of the ABMI is to strengthen market infrastructure for domestic and regional bond market development.

6.7.3 Market limitations

Many Asian economies began developing their sovereign and corporate bond markets in the post-crisis period. Even in the economies that had always run budget surpluses, like Hong Kong SAR and Singapore, government began issuing securities—complete with a benchmark yield curve—so that a liquid government bond market can be created. Indubitably there was a marked diversity in the endeavors made by Asian economies for developing bond market during the post-crisis era. Their overall development was far from vigorous. There were several clearly comprehensible reasons for plodding progress. Poorly developed sovereign bond market made it difficult to establish benchmark yield curves, which are necessary for pricing the corporate bonds.

To be sure, some Asian governments did succeed in establishing the benchmark yield curves because of a spurt in sovereign bond issuance. However, it is uncertain that government would continue to issue sovereign bonds once fiscal deficits have tapered off to a low level. Second, in most Asian economies the issuer base is small because there are too few large issuers, too few non-financial firms, size of the issues is small and maturities range between short- and medium-term. Third, many potentially issuing corporations still prefer bank loans and equity markets as liquid and safe sources of capital. Corporations also tend to shun corporate bond markets because of strict rules and regulations for listing and issuing. Fourth, institutional investors are small in many Asian economies and secondary markets are illiquid. Lastly, some Asian central banks continue to have a reluctant, even grudging attitude, toward bond markets because they see corporate bond market development as a direct challenge to their authority. They fear that active and efficient corporate bond markets will undermine their authority over monetary policy (Shirai, 2001a; World Bank, 2002).

The buy-and-hold tendency of Asian investors reduces liquidity in the secondary market and retards the rapid growth in the bond markets. It also leaves little for the retail investors in the corporate bond markets. This has resulted in a small and inactive investor base in many economies, which in turn causes pricing inefficiency in the bond markets. Corporate bond markets in Indonesia, Korea and Thailand suffer from the buy-and-hold tendency excessively (IMF, 2001).

Many Asian bond markets have remained illiquid, particularly for corporate bonds. They continue to remain segmented and insulated from each other. In China, this kind of market segmentation exists between bond markets in the same country. Furthermore, segmentation persists between investors, instruments and trading mechanisms. International investors who try to invest in local currency bond markets in Asian economies are discouraged by the high cost of hedging exchange risk. Complete lack of regional standardization and harmony in bond contracts, underwriting, clearing and settlement procedures further make Asian bond markets an unappealing alternative. Until progress in regional standardization in these areas is made, regional bond markets are likely to remain underdeveloped.

6.7.4 Market and institutional upgrading

Although Wong and Ho (2003) considered the recent improvements in the Asian bond markets nothing short of "remarkable," other analysts were not so enthusiastic toward them. Korea, Malaysia and Thailand took several tangible measures toward improving the corporate bond markets, particularly in the area of strengthening financial market infrastructure and the establishment of benchmark yield curves. These economies also opened up their corporate bond markets for the non-resident investors. However, some of the obvious areas that call for considerable improvement are corporate governance, bankruptcy laws, and disclosure requirements (IMF, 2001; Park, 2001).

Cost of bond issuance in Malaysia fell below that of bank loans and in recent years it became a larger source of funds for the corporate sector than the banking sector. All major *chaebol* took to corporate bond issuance in Korea. These bonds were guaranteed by banks and placed with the ITCs owned by the banks. The Hong Kong Monetary Authority (HKMA) took many concrete measures in this regard. All the three Asian governments proactively took measures to improve the bond market infrastructure by establishing a network of primary dealers and establishing trading, clearing and settlement systems. Secondary market activity picked up considerably during 2002 in Malaysia, while in Korea it picked up most strongly (Tran and Roldos, 2003).

Notwithstanding the efforts and progress made during the post-crisis period, majority of Asian bond markets still remain underdeveloped when measured by the yardstick of matured financial markets. Second, there is a large variation in them in terms of the depth, size, liquidity and sophistication. The reason is that the contemporary system of bond markets calls for adoption of international best practices in many inter-related areas, which mutually reinforce each other. If and when Asian economies succeed in doing so, the final result would be efficiently and effortlessly functioning bond markets. Third, a reasonable size investor base, essentially comprising financial institutions, is indispensable, and so are legal, regulatory and supervision frameworks, market infrastructure, and supporting markets, like repo market[207] and derivatives. If this system is not established as a whole, weak links can create enormous inefficiency, wastefulness and disorganization. Consequently, investors may move away and borrowers may look for alternative sources of finance. Concerted endeavors were made in these areas during the post-crisis period. Asian governments not only issued sovereign bonds but also motivated institutional investors to invest in marketable debt securities. Legal reforms were undertaken and weak spots in institutional infrastructure were strengthened. Bond trading and clearing mechanisms were underpinned. Three International Financial Institutions (IFIs), namely, the International Monetary Fund, the World Bank and the Asian Development Bank promoted establishment of domestic currency bond markets in Asia. They prepared and published guidelines on how to establish bond markets (ADB, 1999; IMF/WB, 2001).

---

[207] The term "repo" is a shortened form of repurchase. In repo transactions, securities are exchanged for cash with an agreement to repurchase the securities at a pre-determined future date. The securities serve as collateral for what is effectively a cash loan and, conversely, the cash serves as collateral for a securities loan. There are several types of transactions with essentially equivalent economic functions—standard repurchase agreements, sell/buy-backs and securities lending—that are defined as repos. A key distinguishing feature of repos is that they can be used either to obtain funds or to obtain securities. This latter feature is valuable to market participants because it allows them to obtain the securities they need to meet other contractual obligations, such as to make delivery for a futures contract. In addition, repos can be used for leverage, to fund long positions in securities and to fund short positions for hedging interest rate risks. As repos are short-maturity collateralized instruments, repo markets have strong linkages with securities markets, derivatives markets and other short-term markets such as inter-bank and money markets. Repos are useful to central banks both as a monetary policy instrument and as a source of information on market expectations. Repos are attractive as a monetary policy instrument because they carry a low credit risk while serving as a flexible instrument for liquidity management. In addition, they can serve as an effective mechanism for signaling the stance of monetary policy. Repos have been widely used as a monetary policy instrument among European central banks and with the start of EMU in January 1999, the Eurosystem adopted repos as a key instrument.

6.8 REGIONAL BOND MARKET

Creation of a regional bond market was another concept that was being debated in various regional fora after the crisis. The second phase of the New Miyazawa Initiative (NMI) was launched in May 1999, which also envisioned development of domestic corporate bond markets in the dynamic Asian economies. They in turn were intended to be the precursor to the development of a regional bond market. It would *inter alia* be more cost efficient than domestic corporate bond markets and also serve those Asian economies that are not able to establish their own bond markets because of the numerous difficulties involved. A regional bond market would provide an opportunity for diversification for the sources of finance, for utilization of the large accumulation of regional savings, and by way of cross-border flow of finances integrate the regional economy (APF, 2001; Kuroda, 2001; Kobayashi, 2001).

Various frameworks of how the NMI could support the creation of regional bond market were debated. Some alternatives were based on support through the Japan Bank of International Co-operation (JBIC)[208], guarantee mechanism or interest rate subsidy for the bonds issued by Asian economies and possible establishment of an international guarantee institution for the Asian economies. However, these initiatives did not go beyond debating stage. A regional bond market creation has so far not made tangible progress. None of the important financial markets in the region, namely, Hong Kong SAR, Singapore and Tokyo, have shown any discernible momentum in this regard originating from the NMI deliberations.

Creating a regional bond market entails the same set of complexities as a domestic bond market creation does (see Section 6.6.3). The supporting institutional needs of a regional bond market, like that of a domestic bond market, are regional credit-rating agencies, regional clearinghouse to support its operations. A mechanism for cross-border borrowing and lending of securities needs to be installed and properly honed for efficient operations. Disclosure laws and information dissemination practices regarding Asian corporations are also needed to be standardized. The business culture in Asia would need to shift toward easy and rapid communication between public sector bodies and private sector enterprises. In addition, a dominant Asian currency with wide acceptability in the region is required to function as the key currency in the regional market.

Although Tokyo may be taken as a prime candidate for the development of a regional bond market, it has several shortcomings. First, it is not considered international enough and, second, there are deficiencies in institutional

[208] The Japan Bank for International Co-operation (JBIC) was created by merging the Export-Import Bank of Japan (JEXIM) and the Overseas Economic Co-operation Fund (OECF).

infrastructure. Hong Kong SAR, Singapore and Bangkok have challenged Tokyo's candidacy and are eager and competent rivals. If instead of Asia, the Asia-Pacific region is considered, Sydney is also a rival financial center for the creation of a regional bond market. However, because of its location its claim is far from compelling. The physical location debate is somewhat spurious because in the contemporary financial markets, physical marketplace or particular market locations are of secondary significance. A bond market serves the functions of originating, underwriting, listing, trading and settlement of debt securities. Of these, the first four functions are performed electronically, in cyber space, without the need of a physical marketplace. The fifth function of settlement can be done in a market that allows free flows of cross-border capital. To this end, Japan, Hong Kong SAR and Singapore are equally good locations and, therefore, are equally suitable.

The issue of developing an Asian Bond Market was taken up for further deliberation in February 2003 by the ASEAN-Plus-Three (APT) economies.[209] The enthusiastic Ministry of Finance (MoF) in Japan took initiative and drew up the basic profile of a regional bond market and the other APT members agreed to cooperate and create a regional bond market in Tokyo. The fundamental thinking behind the acceptance of the concept of the Asian Bond Market was that Asia is a net saving surplus region, which makes it a credit surplus region as well. Asian economies have been a major investor in the U.S. Treasury Bonds. In the first quarter of 2004, the estimated holdings of Asian central banks were $1 trillion in the U.S. Treasury Bonds (Day and Choi, 2004). It was decided that the Asian saving surplus should first be utilized at home and minimize the probability of recurrence of another crisis. The APT economies decided that the regional bond market would actively cater for the sovereign bonds and corporate bonds of Asian enterprises. An active asset-backed securities (ABS)[210] market would be developed in the short-term. The regional market could not only deal in bonds denominated in domestic and foreign currencies but also in currency baskets. To this end, development of related regional financial infrastructure, including settlement system, rating agencies and rules concerning transactions, has been proposed by the APT economies (AWSJ, 2003).

In 2003, a regional initiative was taken and the Asian Bond Fund (ABF) was created by the Executive's Meeting of East Asia Pacific Central Banks

---

209 The ten ASEAN members are Brunei Darussalam, Cambodia, Indonesia, Lao PDR, Malaysia, Myanmar, the Philippines, Singapore, Thailand and Vietnam. The three economies making it the ASEAN-Plus-Three (APT) are China, Japan and Korea.

210 Asset-backed securities (ABS) are bonds that represent pools of loans of similar types, duration and interest rates. By selling their loans to ABS packagers, the original lenders recover cash quickly, enabling them to make more loans. The asset-backed securities market has grown as different types of loans are securitized and sold in the investment markets.

(EMEAP).[211] This initiative worked at both demand and supply sides of the creation of a regional bond market. The Asian Bond Fund—I was announced in June 2003 "to channel resources held by Asian economies back into the region" (IMF, 2004). The ABF-I had an initial funding of $1 billion contributed by the members of the EMEAP. This was earmarked for investment in the dollar denominated sovereign or quasi-sovereign bonds issued by eight members of the EMEAP. Japan, Australia and New Zealand were the non-borrowing members. The Bank for International Settlements (BIS) co-operative in this endeavor and the ABF-I was passively managed by the BIS Asset Management Group. At the time of the launch of the dollar ABF-I, plans were announced to examine the feasibility of extending the ABF concept to include bonds denominated in regional currencies. It was believed that this follow-up initiative would further strengthen, broaden and deepen the bond markets in the region (McCauley, 2003b). Accordingly, launching of ABF-II was under negotiation in mid-2004. It was intended for investment in the local currency sovereign and quasi-sovereign bonds of the participating economies.

6.8.1 Facilitating market growth

Experience suggests that demand for the bonds determines whether the regional bond market would be successful or not. An inadequate demand for bonds leads either to stagnation of the market or to its decline and closure. Wong and Ho (2003) contended that for averting such a prospect, sovereign and corporate bonds issued must be of good quality and so attractive that investors like to invest in them. Two mechanisms can contribute to this objective and facilitate establishment and expansion of the regional bond market. Credit guarantees and securitization are two important means of making the bonds appealing to domestic and international investors. To this end, institutional support is essential.

Lack of credit rating of Asian bonds has curtailed their market size and has been a serious impediment to their growth. International credit-rating agencies do not take interest in Asian bonds. They have been inactive in Asia because of the inadequate demand for Asian bonds as well as lack of information about them and the issuers. A way out is having Asian bond rating agencies to do the job, but developing them is essentially a time-consuming process. Institutional investors dominate the investors in the bond markets. This category includes central banks, supranational organizations, insurance companies, multilateral organizations, mutual funds, pension funds, banks and non-bank financial institutions. Their interest is restricted to bonds having safe and stable returns,

---

211 The eleven members of EMEAP are Australia, China, Hong Kong SAR, Indonesia, Japan, Korea, Malaysia, New Zealand, the Philippines, Singapore and Thailand.

which is provided by investment-grade debt securities, as opposed to high-yield speculative grade debt securities. The lower end of credit-rating scale for the investment-grade securities in Moody's system is Baa while in S&P system it is BBB. If there are independent Asian credit-rating agencies, which actively rate and publicize ratings of Asian debt securities, it will facilitate the task of investment managers and the investment flows of institutional investors in Asian bonds would logically rise, resulting in swift development of Asian Bond Market.

The market reality is that Asian corporate bonds find it difficult to earn investment-grade credit rating. This has been a serious obstacle. The country of domicile of the corporation has a large influence on the credit rating of its bonds. In the Moody's system, Japan, Singapore and Taiwan earn the sovereign debt rating of AA or above and manage to remain at the top. China, Hong Kong SAR, Macao and Korea come next with A rating, while other Asian economies have B-or related ratings. If the sovereign debt rating of a country is at the bottom of rung of investment grade, its corporations do not get investment-grade rating. Bond issuance of corporation from such countries is sold as high-yield speculative grade, a category shunned by institutional investors. While Malaysia is a borderline investment-grade case and has Baa rating, Indonesia, the Philippines and Vietnam have not qualified so far.

The old practice of credit guarantee or insurance can make corporate bonds appealing for the investors. The U.S. Municipal bond market had initiated this practice. Credit guarantee is an efficient manner of enhancing the quality of corporate bonds and a small number of Asian insurance companies are in the business of credit insurance. Under the credit guarantee scheme, the primary risk is borne by the insurers, but they reduce it by over-collateralizing it. Other channels of reducing the risk are diversification, reinsurance and securitization. The premium changed by the insurance company has a direct bearing on their perception of risk involved (Wong and Ho, 2003).

6.8.2 Managing foreign exchange reserves to support bond markets

As discussed in Chapter 7 (Section 7.7), in the post-crisis period Asian economies accumulated foreign exchange reserves, which were "more than half the global total" (McCauley, 2003a). Excessive market intervention by Asian central banks during 2002–03 raised their level of foreign exchange reserves by 33 percent, to \$1.9 trillion by the end of 2003, most of which were held in dollars. Largest increases in reserves were recorded by China and Japan. Consequently by the end of first quarter of 2004, Asian central banks owned around one quarter of all U.S. Treasury bills, worth close to \$1 trillion (*The*

Economist, 2004c).With soaring volume of reserves, the need for a range of investment products *pari passu* grew in the region. With falling interest rates in major global markets, Asian central banks began to diversify and move reserves away from the low-yielding Group-of-Three (G-3) government securities.[212] In their diversification endeavors, Asian central banks displayed a clear preference for long-duration instruments.

During the post-crisis period, the BIS have been helpful to the Asian economies in managing their foreign exchange reserves. It offered returns on investment which was between those available on the G-3 sovereign instruments and those on private investments, which carry higher credit risks. This was a successful strategy and the BIS succeeded in attracting a good deal of business from the Asian central banks, leading to opening a Regional Treasury in its Asia and Pacific Regional Office in October 2000. This office operates during the same time zone as the Asian central banks (Aizenmann and Marion, 2002). Regional presence has turned out to be a sound idea for the BIS. By 2003, Asian central banks' placements with the BIS represented the largest single source of liability for any region.

After establishing its regional presence in Hong Kong SAR, the BIS developed its product line in accordance with the needs of the Asian central banks. In so doing, the BIS provided medium-term instruments with enhanced returns, which were more in line with the growing trend and expectations. As stated above (Section 6.7), in collaboration with the EMEAP a $1 billion ABF-I was launched in June 2003. The launch of ABF-I as well as the plan for ABF-II, both were a part of the strategy of adapting the product line suitable to the Asian central banks' needs (EMEAP, 2003). The BIS is engaged in these endeavors with the expectation of creating and strengthening the regional bond market with the help of the region's foreign exchange reserves.

6.9 EQUITY MARKETS

It has been set out that developing and strengthening bond markets entails difficulties and is an intricate, time-consuming process (Section 6.6). Establishing or expanding equity markets is relatively less so. Presently 10 major active equity markets operate in the dynamic Asian economies, namely, Bangkok, Shanghai and Shenzhen in China,[213] Hong Kong SAR, Jakarta, Kuala Lumpur, Manila, Seoul, Singapore, Taipei and Tokyo. Other than these, there

---

[212] The G-3 securities means the U.S. Treasury securities, and the German government and Japanese government securities.

[213] The Government legalized the trading of stocks by establishing the Shanghai Stock Exchange in December 1990 and Shenzhen Stock Exchange in July 1991.

are secondary markets in Malaysia (called the Secondary Board), the Surabaya Exchange in Indonesia, and the SESDAQ and CLOB exchanges in Singapore. Some of these equity markets also deal in fixed income instruments. Vietnam has an over-the-counter (OTC) exchange in Ho Chi Minh City.

The two universal measures of equity market are market capitalization and trading volume. If they are used to size up the various Asian markets, Tokyo comes at the top. It is also the third largest equity market globally, after New York and London. In absolute terms, Hong Kong SAR and Taipei are respectable size markets, while Seoul and Singapore are smaller. From the perspective of market capitalization and trading volumes these equity markets can be ranked as Hong Kong SAR, Taipei, Seoul and Singapore, strictly in that order. Other markets in Asia are small in terms of capitalization and trading volume (Freeman, 2000; Freeman and Bartels, 2000).

Market capitalization as a percentage of GDP is a standard measure of size. This measure also yields similar results. Wilson (2002) used this measure and reported that in 2000, the size of the Hong Kong SAR market was 337 percent of the GDP, and that of Singapore 262 percent. Malaysia came third with 165 percent, followed by Taiwan at 120 percent of the GDP. Korea and Sydney were smaller equity markets with market capitalization of 66 percent and 36 percent of the GDP, respectively. China with 8 percent of the GDP had a very small-sized equity market.

Aggregate market capitalization in the region had steadily increased until the eve of Asian crisis. This is known as "equitization" of the economy. Liquidity in the stock markets increased steadily but it was not comparable to those in the mature markets. Only Taiwan was an exception in this regard. It is an important indicator because it is a crucial determinant in county or regional indexes, which in turn help fund managers and brokerage houses in determining their asset portfolios. Asian equity markets performed largely in line with the major U.S. markets. They had their own performance indexes, which followed the trend set by the Dow Jones Composite, NYSE Composite and S&P 500 indices. They were regarded as important indices and quoted daily on electronic stock market reports and by financial media.

Equity markets are known for their sectoral biases. Asian equity markets are known to be biased toward stocks from banks, finance companies and property developers. Stocks from media companies, technology and new-economy-oriented companies are poorly represented in the Southeast Asian economies. However, these sectors have a significant presence in the NIAEs. Following the financial crisis, both domestic and foreign investors withdrew their capital from the asset class and the region. Some contrarian investors tried to buy in slumping equity markets to build a cheap Asian equity portfolio but those trying to exit far outnumbered them (Freeman, 2000; Freeman and Bartels, 2000). Aggregate capitalization figures in the Asian equity markets declined significantly.

The outflow of global capital during the crisis was led by sharp reversal of bank loans and portfolio investments. To be sure, there were notable rallies in the last quarter of 1998 and the first quarter of 1999, and there was a recovery in portfolio investment flows in 1999, but the pre-crisis level remained remote. Because of uncertainties in the global economy over the next two years, private portfolio flows to Asia declined again. In addition, the situation in 2001 was worsened by the bursting of the bubble in the information and communication technology (ICT) sector and the non-economic factors, like events of September 11 in the United States.

As the banks were heavily NPL-ridden, equity markets played an active role in the post-crisis period. Their significance in the post-crisis period increased considerably. Their role in financial restructuring of corporate sector was vital, although it was supported by other financial channels as well. In Indonesia and Thailand corporate restructuring was supported by the equity markets to the maximum degree. The other sources of finance remained relatively inactive in these two economies.

Although the performance of the Asian equity markets was mixed during the post-crisis period because they were buffeted by global economic, non-economic and financial events, by the early 2000s, these markets began to perform better than the financial markets in the other regions. They also became accessible to non-resident investors. According to Standard and Poors' (S&P) data, Asia accounted for 10 percent of the global market capitalization in 2002. Japan overwhelmingly dominated it and accounted for 70 percent of the total regional capitalization. While Japan has been waning, Korea recorded the largest increase in stock market index over the preceding five years.[214] However, Asian equity markets have not recovered in a robust manner. Serious efficiency and microstructure problems persisted. They included problems related to market size, number of listed stocks, extent of foreign listings and trading hours.[215] The United States, Japan and the United Kingdom, in that order, have been the long-established and time-honored global leaders in terms of capitalization, listed stocks and market turnover. Contrary to them, Asian equity markets continue to have a narrow investor base, their savings systems are restricted, small and underdeveloped mutual funds, and highly regulated asset management industry. Role of the insurance companies in the capital market is also limited. Although Asian equity markets are open to non-resident investors, they have a lower proportion of foreign stocks listed on their bourses. Even in Japan the proportion of foreign stock listings are substantially lower than those in the United States and the U.K. markets. Hong Kong SAR and Singapore have the highest proportion of foreign listings, while Indonesia, Malaysia, Thailand and Taiwan have

---

214 Source S&P Global 1200 Index, Standard and Poors 2002 Review of Global Indices.

215 See de Brouwer and Corbett (2003) and de Brouwer (2003).

virtually none. Asian markets also suffer from an acute sectoral imbalance, with disproportionate dominance of financial and real-estate firms.[216]

6.9.1 Origin of equity markets in China

Although Chinese constitution lifted ban on private business activity in 1982, the State Council did not issue the preliminary regulations for private sector business activity until 1988. Legalizing trade in stocks was the next move and the Shanghai stock market was established in December 1990, and the one at Shenzhen in July 1991. The so-called B-shares were issued next year to attract non-residents and provide them with a legal channel for investing in China. The domestically listed firms issued only A-shares. The same firm can issue both A-shares and B-shares, which is an unusual characteristic of the Chinese stock market.

Development of company and securities law was initially left to the local authorities of these regions because national securities law was not enacted. Thinking related to creating a market economy was gaining momentum. In this economic milieu, the 14th National Congress of the Chinese Communist Party proposed development of a socialist market economy in 1992, which entailed distancing the SOEs from the government and making their operations independent of the state. The State Council Securities Commission (SCSC) and the China Securities and Regulatory Commission (CSRC), the executive branch of the SCSC, were established in October 1992. SCSC determines the overall national policies regarding the securities markets. Since their establishment the equity markets recorded rapid growth. The number of domestically listed firms in 2000 was 1,088 (Gordon and Li, 1999; Shirai, 2002).

In the preceding section we noted that the size of the equity market in China is small. The number of listed firms was much smaller than that in India, Japan and the United States, but greater than those in Korea, Singapore and Thailand. These statistics are misleading for China, because 60 percent of the shares are those of SOEs and are non-tradable. They inflate the value of the ratio of equity market capitalization to GDP. A better indicator is the ratio of negotiable market capitalization to GDP, which recorded only a moderate rise between 1992 and 2000.

The number of investors increased rapidly; therefore, demand for A-shares remained high. They were traded at a substantially higher premium than the identical B-shares. Shirai (2002) computed the price-earning-ratio (PER) of the A-shares for the 1996–2000 period and found them in the 30 to 50 percent range, which is higher than Japan, Korea, Thailand, the United Kingdom and the United States. Such high price differentials accelerated speculation in the equity markets.

---

[216] Ibid.

6.10 RISK MANAGEMENT

It has been alluded to earlier (Section 6.1) during the pre-crisis period financial markets in Asia suffered from unsound risk management practices, lax and inept prudential and supervisory norms and lackadaisical disclosure practices. Consequently, the financial systems functioned in an inefficient manner and became one of the biggest constraints on the real economy. During the crisis these systemic weaknesses and their pernicious effects came to the surface. Therefore, serious efforts were initiated to mitigate these flagrant flaws, which were condoned before. Conventional wisdom is that development and diffusion of codes and standards of sound practices like prudential and supervisory norms begin in the real sector first, and then spread to the financial sector. That is, there is a relationship of diffusion and adoption of codes and standards of good practices with the level of economic development. At an early stage they apply to the real sector. Subsequently, as development proceeds they spread to the financial sector. This does not imply a shift of emphasis from the real to the financial sector. It is merely the result of acknowledging that the financial sector is an instrument of economic growth and integration.

The process of creation and diffusion of financial regulations has undergone discernible transformation over the last half century. Both governmental and non-governmental institutions conventionally set rules for the financial sector. The latter category includes technical bodies and supervisory authorities. Initially, governmental organizations and bodies used to lay down the regulations for co-operation among economies. This applied to both bilateral and multilateral co-operation. However, since the seventies non-governmental institutions began to lead the governmental institutions in the area of financial co-operation. Initiatives by technical and professional bodies increasingly began to pave the ground for action by the authorities. The first such initiative taken by a non-governmental technical body was the Basle Committee of Banking Supervisions (BCBS) created in 1975, in the aftermath of the Herstatt Bank collapse (June 1974) in Germany, which had global repercussions.[217] The basic objective of the BCBS was to underpin the supervision and coordination of banks that have widely spread international operations so that Herstatt-like crisis did not reoccur.

After the supervision process evolved, the legal and regulatory instruments also underwent a transformation. Initially, governments entered into treaties,

---

[217] The collapse of Herstatt Bank in June 1974 had global repercussions. It rippled globally throughout the international banking system for good reasons. The debacle severely undermined the fundamental building block of commerce, that is, the integrity of the payment system. A chain is only as strong as its weakest link, and bank payment systems are integrally linked to one another through necessary clearing and settlement processes that enable bank liabilities to circulate as currency.

which entailed long-drawn negotiations and ratification by parliaments. This process was not only slow and inefficient but also incompatible with the need of the contemporary world of finance, which functioned and moved at a rapid pace in developing new financial instruments. Therefore, non-governmental bodies were born to create codes, standards and rules of acceptable behavior. These frameworks of regulations were different from the traditional treaties and were intended to shape the common behavior without changing the legal frameworks. At the global level, since the mid-1980s several non-institutional informal groups like G-3, G-5 (which grew into G-7, and subsequently G-8), G-10, G-20, G-22 and G-30 were created from time to time. They all exist and are functioning productively and efficiently, making meaningful contribution. Successful existence of these groups reflects the contributions they made to productive international co-operation in the area of international finance. The process of creation of new regulatory framework as well as harmonization took a markedly different route from that of the past.[218]

There are variegated modes of regulatory harmonization. Forming a monetary union is one oft-utilized government-induced mode. Regulatory harmonization has also worked in those parts of the globe where one or more large and successful economies have exerted gravitational pull for the neighboring economies. In such cases, the large economy works as a catalyst and initiates the process of regulatory alignment for the other economies to follow. The experiences of regions that have followed these modes demonstrated that adopting the principle of minimum harmonization reduced the difficulties of creating a top-down harmonization system. This principle has had immense utility for the global financial integration in the recent past. In addition, market mechanism has made a great deal of contribution by successfully developing and enforcing financial standards through reputational disciplines. These market-determined standards are set and maintained by large dominant institutions that have long-established reputations. The principle of minimum harmonization and the reputationally induced disciplines have been the most important pillars of the current episode of financial globalization. These two principles have played a greater role than the standards and codes of financial regulation (Jordan and Lubrano, 2002).

These two principles became instantly popular for the following reasons. First, together these principles reflect both regulatory discipline and functionality of a market. Little wonder they appealed to both market regulators and market players. Second, their generality made them attractive to economies with different economic history and levels of economic growth. Third, the most important trait of these two principles was their conceptual simplicity.

---

[218] Refer to Jordan and Majnoni (2002) and Jordan and Lubrano (2002) for more detailed discussion of these issues.

It should be noted that these two principles did not present a novel approach. They were part of a system of law that followed the practice of having norms that did not have the binding force of legislation.[219] Such conventions have been christened "soft law" due to the lack of a codified procedure for their definition and enforcement (Giovanoli, 2001). In national legal systems, soft law amounted to adoption of codes of best practices prevalent at an international level and accepted by a group of large countries. They are non-binding and voluntary in nature and referred to as "codes of conduct," "guidelines" or "recommendations."[220]

In 1998, the BCBS created what became known as "the Basle 1988 Accord," also called "the New Basle Capital Accord" (BCBS, 2001). It is perhaps the best illustration of developing a set of highly successful financial standards during the recent period (Barth et al., 2001; Powell, 2003). Although they were designed for the internationally active banks in the G-10 economies, by early 2003 more than a hundred countries claimed adherence to the New Basel Capital Accord. Some central banks apply these standards to all banks. The first set of proposals under the Basle New Accord was published in January 2001. The final version was published in July 2002 for implementation by 2006 (BCBS, 2002). The new set of proposals made considerable advances "in linking risk and regulatory capital for internationally active banks, especially for their corporate loan book." The implementation of this accord in the G-10 economies would indeed affect the cost of capital in the emerging market economies. The accord essentially takes an internal rating-based (IRB) approach. Indubitably the IRB approach should lead to significant changes in capital requirements and spreads for the banks that lend to the emerging market economies. The accord has proposed that for the purpose of sovereign lending, internationally active banks should develop internal ratings according to an S&P or Moody's scale and capital charges should be levied according to the corresponding weights assigned by the standard approach.

According to the ABA (2003) survey, many banks in Asia, excluding those in Japan, face serious challenges in their efforts to improve risk management practices to the level required by the New Basle Capital Accord (BCBS, 2001). The areas in which they perceive that they face critical resource constraints include technology and data availability. In a small number of less-developed Asian economies lack of well-trained personnel was also seen as an intractable problem. As regards the supervisory authorities, authorities in Japan and more advanced financial markets like Korea, Hong Kong SAR, Singapore and Taiwan reported that when the time comes they would be prepared to take the bull by the horns. Conversely, supervisory authorities in the other Asian

---

[219] The English Common Law system is one of the best examples of this kind of legal arrangement.

[220] For a thorough discussion see Giovanoli (2001).

economies reported serious constraints with respect to staffing, technology and funding.

6.10.1 Credit risk management

In any banking system, counter-party risk is a significant source of credit risk and losses. The BCBS (2000) requires that the board of directors must periodically review and approve the credit risk strategy. Minimum periodicity was required to be once a year. According to the findings of the ABA (2003) survey, in Japan, the boards of directors complied with this requirement. The same applied for the four EMEs of East Asia (namely, Hong Kong SAR, Korea, Singapore and Taiwan) where financial infrastructure was better developed than in the other Asian economies, although their practices in this regard varied considerably and in some countries reviews took place twice in a year. In Brunei Darussalam, Indonesia, Malaysia, the Philippines, Thailand and Vietnam reviews of credit risk strategy were found to take place half-yearly, while in others economies no such review took place. The BCBS (2000) recommended that banks should have well-defined criteria for granting credit, which should include perfect understanding of the counter-party, purpose of credit and mode and sources of repayment. It also stressed that banks must not grant credit on the basis of the reputation of the counter-party. A list of variables was recommended for analysis by the BCBS (2000). All these variables have been included in the credit-granting criteria of the majority of credit-granting banks in Asia. The guidelines are generally adhered to in an earnest manner. However, some banks in the four better-developed EMEs of East Asia did not include some of the variables in the guidelines of the BCBS (2000). They truncated the list of variables to be taken into account before granting credit.

For creating a structured internal credit-rating system and controlling credit risk, BCBS (2000) also recommended the basic principles for the management of credit risk. For the purpose of quantifying the risk involved in exposures to counter-parties, majority of the banks in Brunei Darussalam, Indonesia, Malaysia, the Philippines, Thailand and Vietnam used statistical models as against expert judgment and external ratings. This was truer when they dealt with external borrowers. However, banks in Japan and four EMEs of East Asia where financial infrastructure is relatively better developed than the other Asian economies, banks relied on expert judgment and external ratings. A rule of the thumb in this regard was that in dealing with large corporate borrowers banks relied on expert judgment and external ratings, whereas in dealing with small- and medium-sized borrowers they depended on statistical models.

For internal risk ratings of the counter-parties, BCBS provided clear guidelines. According to the ABA (2003) survey, in the Japanese banks an independent credit unit computed risk ratings of individual counter-parties.

A large number of banks in other Asian economies also complied with the BCBS recommendations, but about a third of the banks in Brunei Darussalam, Indonesia, Malaysia, the Philippines, Thailand and Vietnam still did not conform to this norm.

6.10.2 Market risk management

According to the ABA (2003) survey, in Japan and Brunei Darussalam, Indonesia, Malaysia, the Philippines, Thailand and Vietnam market risk losses for banks came from interest rate and foreign exchange risks. In the four larger EMEs of East Asia interest rate risk was found to be the largest source of loss from market risk, followed by equity position risk and foreign exchange risk. In the Asian economies, except Japan, banks took a basic approach to calculate market risk capital. Banks in four EMEs of East Asia used standardized approach to calculate interest rate, foreign exchange and equity position risk and simplified methodology to calculate options risk. Banks in Southeast Asian economies calculated only interest rate and foreign exchange risk. To this end, they used advanced techniques. The Basel Committee identified several crucial variables that are important and should be covered in reviews of market risk management. In case of banks in the mature economies like Japan, these issues are covered in the internal reviews. In the other Asian economies, banks tend to cover only a third of these critical items in a comprehensive manner.

6.10.3 Operational risk management

The sources of operational risk are (i) execution, delivery and process management, (ii) external fraud, (iii) internal fraud, (iv) clients, products and business services and (vii) business disruption and systemic failures, strictly in this order of priority. While the first, second and third sources of operational risk affect banks universally, the fourth and fifth sources affect banks more in Asian economies, excluding Japan where bankers reported in the ABA (2003) survey that they were not particularly concerned.

The BCBS recommended that the board of directors should be aware of principal aspects of the banks' operational risk and must periodically review banks operational risk management framework. In Japan, this review was done in a rigorous manner but not in the rest of Asia. However, in Hong Kong SAR and Singapore, almost three fourths of the banks managed operational risk in a rigorous manner. More or less the same applied to the Basel Committee recommendation regarding managing of operational risk arising from external market changes and other environmental factors as well as those risks which were associated with new products, activities and systems.

6.11 CONCLUSIONS AND SUMMARY

Financial development in Asia was far from uniform. Financial markets, institutions and systems are highly uneven in their degree of development, quality of performance, financial depth and strength. Therefore, developed and underdeveloped financial markets and institutions coexist in the region. While Hong Kong SAR, Japan, Singapore and Taiwan can be considered to be meeting the international norms in many areas of performance, Korea, Malaysia and Thailand rank average. China, Indonesia and the Philippines are considered to be poor performers from the international standards. Inadequacies and limitations of the financial sector in several Asian economies were considered one of the prime causal factors behind the Asian crisis.

Asian economies are far more dependent on the bank-based financial system than on a market-based, securitized one. The system was characterized as "repressive" in the early stages. Although Japan is a matured industrial economy, its financial structure resembles the other Asian economies instead of the United Kingdom or the United States, where the securities market plays an active role and dominates the financial structure. For bringing about improvements in the financial sector, Asian banking sector needs to be further globalized. Also, development of capital markets for raising securitized finances by the firms was a known natural alternative for strengthening the financial sector. Different sources of finance provide an opportunity to the firms to balance debt and equity.

Bank ownership pattern in Asia reflects a wide variety. Being the dominant part of the financial structure banking industry was appallingly blighted by the Asian crisis. Government ownership of banks increased during the crisis period due to reform and restructuring efforts, albeit the range in this regard is wide. Foreign ownership of banks in Asia is low. The financial system during the post-crisis era is developing into an "intermediate financial structure," which covers the middle ground between a bank-based and a securitized structure. As the banks traditionally dominated the financial structure, and had high reputation and the information advantage in the past, they are ready to play a new role. They can launch into the role of issuers, investors, underwriters, developers, brokers and guarantors in the fledgling corporate bond market during the post-crisis period.

Time had arrived to initiate the required changes in the financial sector. Wide consensuses on a pressing need to diversify it, reduce reliance on bank credit and develop domestic currency bond markets as an alternative source of external finance followed. There are several benefits of active domestic currency bond markets. Asian economies tried to make noteworthy improvements in their bond markets over the post-crisis period, but a great deal more needs to be done. During the post-crisis period, Korea, Malaysia and Thailand took several tangible measures toward improving the corporate bond markets, particularly in the area of strengthening financial market infrastructure and in the establishment of benchmark yield curves. These economies are also opening up their corporate bond markets for the non-residents.

Creation of a regional bond market was another concept that was debated in various regional fora. The second phase of the NMI was launched in May 1999, which also envisioned development of domestic corporate bond markets. This in turn was intended to be the precursor to the development of a regional bond market. The issue of developing an Asian Bond Market was taken up for further deliberation in early 2003 by the APT economies.

The crisis was good for Asia because since then serious efforts were initiated to mitigate these flagrant systemic flaws, which were condoned before. The limitations *inter alia* included unsound risk management practices, lax and inept prudential and supervisory norms and lackadaisical disclosureb practices.

REFERENCES

Aizenmann, J. and N. Marion. 2002, October. *The High Demand for International Reserves in the Far East: What's Going On?* Cambridge, MA: National Bureau of Economic Research. NBER Working Paper No. 9266.

Asia Policy Forum (APF). 2001, October. *Designing New and Balanced Financial Market Structures in Post-Crisis Asia.* Tokyo: Asia Policy Forum. Forum Secretariat. ADB Institute.

The Asian Banker's Association (ABA). 2003. "The regulatory and business environment for risk management practices in the banking sector of APEC economies," was conducted in collaboration with the Pacific Economic Co-operation Council (PECC), and the Chinese Taipei Pacific Economic Co-operation Committee (CTPECC). Circulated at the Second Annual Conference of PECC Finance Forum, held in Hua Hin, Thailand, July 8–9, 2003.

The Asian Development Bank (ADB). 1999. *Compendiums of Sound Practices Guidelines to Facilitate the Development of Domestic Bond market.* Manila: ADB.

The Asian Development Bank. 2004. *Asian Development Outlook 2004.* Hong Kong: Oxford University Press.

The Asian Wall Street Journal (AWSJ). 2003. "Japan proposes regional market for regional bonds." March 3.

Barth, J.R., G. Caprio and R. Levine. 2001, February. *The Regulation and Supervision of Banks around the World: A New Database.* Washington, DC: The World Bank. (mimeo).

Basle Committee on Banking Supervision (BCBS). 2000, September. *Principles for the Management of Credit Risk.* Basle: Bank for International Supervision.

Basle Committee on Banking Supervision (BCBS). 2001, January. *The New Basle Capital Accord: An Explanatory Note.* Basle: Bank for International Supervision.

Basle Committee on Banking Supervision (BCBS). 2002, July. *An Overview of the New Basle Capital Accord.* Basle: Bank for International Supervision.

Das, Dilip K. 2001. "Corporate governance and restructuring: A post-crisis Asian perspective," *The Asia Pacific Journal of Economics and Business.* Vol. 14. No. 2. pp. 98–112.

Das, Dilip K. 2003."Emerging market economies: Inevitability of volatility and contagion," *Journal of Asset Management.* Vol. 4. No. 3. pp. 134–152.

Day, P. and A.H.W. Choi. 2004. "Asia shifts its US dollar risk," *Report on Business, Globe and Mail.* Toronto. p. B10.

de Brouwer, G. 2003. "Financial markets, institutions and integration in East Asia," *Asian Economic Papers.* Vol. 2. No. 1. pp. 96–120.

de Brouwer, G. and J. Corbett. 2003. *A New Financial Market Structure for East Asia.* Asia-Pacific School of Economics and Government. Australian National University. Canberra (unpublished manuscript).

Demirguc-Kunt, A. and R. Levine. 2001. "Bank-based and Market-based financial system: Cross-country comparisons," in A. Demirguc-Kunt and R. Levine (eds) *Financial Structure and Economic Development.* Cambridge, MA: The MIT Press. pp. 81–140.

The Economist. 2004a. "Banking in South-East Asia: Recuperating". May 1, pp. 78–79.

The Economist. 2004b. "Better, not well," May 29. p. 74.

The Economist. 2004c. "Business as usual," February 14. p. 70.

Endo, T. 2001. "Corporate bond market development," in *Bond Market Development in Asia,* Paris: Organization for Economic Co-operation and Development. pp. 237–296.

Executives' Meeting of East Asia-Pacific Central Banks (EMEAP). 2003. *EMEAP Central Banks to Launch Asia Bond Fund.* Available at: http://www.emeap.org:8084. Accessed June 2, 2003.

Freeman, N.J. 2000, July. *A Regional Platform for Trading Southeast Asian Equities: Viable Option or Lofty 'Red Herring'?* Singapore: Institute of Southeast Asian Studies. ISEAS Working Paper No. 3.

Freeman, N.J. and F. Bartels. 2000, August. *Portfolio Investment in Southeast Asia's Stock Markets: A Survey of Institutional Investor's Current Perceptions.* Singapore: Institute of Southeast Asian Studies. ISEAS Working Paper No. 4.

Giovanoli, M. 2001. *A New Architecture for the Global Financial Market: Legal Aspects of International Financial Standard Setting.* Basel, Switzerland: International Monetary Law Association.

Gordon, R.H. and W. Li. 1999. *Government as a Discriminating Monopoly in Financial Maarkets: The Case of China.* Cambridge, MA: National Bureau of Economic Research. NBER Working Paper No. 7110.

Harwood, A. 2000. "Building local bond markets: Some issues and actions," in A. Harwood (ed) *Building Local Bond Markets: An Asian Perspective.* Washington, DC: International Finance Corporation. pp. 3–25.

Herring, R.J. and N. Chatusripitak. 2000, July. *The Case of the Missing Market: The Bond Market and Why it Matters for Financial Development.* Tokyo: The ADB Institute. Working Paper No. 11.

Honohan, P. 2004, February. *Financial Development, Growth and Poverty: How Close Are the Links.* Washington, DC: The World Bank. Policy Research Working Paper No. 3203.

International Monetary Fund (IMF). 2001. *International Capital Markets: Development, Prospects and Key Policy Issues.* Washington, DC: IMF.

International Monetary Fund (IMF). 2003, March. *Global Financial Stability Report.* Washington, DC: IMF.

International Monetary Fund. 2004, April. *Global Financial Stability Report.* Washington, DC: IMF.

International Monetary Fund/World Bank (IMF/WB). 2001, September. *Developing Government Bond Markets: A Hand Book.* Washington, DC: IMF/WB.

Jordan, C. and M. Lubrano. 2002. "How effective are capital markets in exerting governance on corporations?" in *Financial Sector Governance.* Washington, DC: The Brookings Institution Press. pp. 22–40.

Jordan, C. and G. Majnoni. 2002, October. *Financial Regulatory Harmonization and the Globalization of Finance*. Washington, DC: The World Bank. Policy Research Working Paper No. 2919.

Kawai, M. 2002. "Bank and corporate restructuring in crisis-affected East Asia: From systemic collapse to reconstruction," in G. de Brouwer (ed) *Financial Markets and Policies in East Asia,* London: Routledge. pp. 32–66.

Kim, S. and J.H. Park. 2002. "Structural change in the corporate bond market in Korea," in *The Development of Bond Markets in Emerging Economies.* Basel: Bank for International Settlements. Monetary and Economic Department. BIS Paper No. 11. pp. 130–146.

Kobayashi, T. 2001. "Development of international bond markets in the region: New Miyazawa Initiative," in *Bond Market Development in Asia.* Paris: Organization for Economic Co-operation and Development. pp. 173–188.

Krueger, A.O. 2004. *Lessons from the Asian Crisis*. Keynote address at the SEACEN Meeting held in Colombo, Sri Lanka, February 12.

Kuroda, H. 2001. "Future international financial architecture and regional capital market development," in *Bond Market Development in Asia.* Paris: Organization for Economic Co-operation and Development. pp. 73–88.

Levine, R.1997. "Financial development and economic growth: Views and agenda," *Journal of Economic Literature.* Vol. 35. No. 3. pp. 688–726.

Lian, T.S. 2002, June. *The Development of Bond Market in Emerging Market Economies.* Bank for International Settlement. Basel. Switzerland. BIS Paper No. 11.

Mathieson, D.J. and J. Roldos. 2001. "The role of foreign banks in emerging markets," in R.E. Litan, P. Mason and M. Pomerleano (eds) *Open Doors: Foreign Participation in Financial Systems in Developing Countries.* Washington, DC: The Brookings Institution Press. pp. 120–141.

McCauley, R.N. 2003a. "Central bank co-operation in East Asia," paper presented at the *Second Annual Conference of PECC Finance Forum,* held in Hua Hin, Thailand, July 8–9.

McCauley, R.N. 2003b. "Unifying government bond markets in East Asia," *BIS Quarterly Review.* December. pp. 89–103.

McCauley, R.N., J.S. Rudd and P.D Wooldridge. 2002. "Globalizing international banking," *BIS Quarterly Review.* March. pp. 41–51.

Montgomery, H. 2003, January. *The Role of Foreign Banks in Post-Crisis Asia.* Tokyo: The ADB Institute. Research Paper No. 51.

Ohno, K. 1999, February 4. *Capital Account Crisis and Credit Contraction*. Tokyo: The ADB Institute. Working Paper No. 2.

Park, Y.S. 2001. "Development of Asian bond markets," in Y. Hyung and Y. Wang (eds) *Regional Financial Arrangements in East Asia.* Seoul: Korea Institute of International Economic Policy. pp. 53–73.

Powell, A. 2003. *A Capital Accord for Emerging Economies?* Available at: http://econ.worldbank .org/files/13169_wps2808.pdf. Accessed January 28, 2004.

Sakakibara, E. and S. Yamakawa. 2003, "Regional Integration in East Asia: Challenges and Opportunities", June. Part I and Part II. Washington DC. Policy Research Working Paper Nos. 3078 and 3079.

Shirai, S. 2001a, September 4. *Overview of Financial Market Structure in Asia: Cases of the Republic of Korea, Malaysia, Thailand and Indonesia*. Tokyo: ADB Institute. Research Paper No. 25.

Shirai, S. 2001b, September 3. *"Searching for New Regulatory Frameworks for the Intermediate Financial Market Structure in Post Crisis Asia*". Tokyo: ADB Institute. Research Paper No. 24. 3 September.

Shirai, S. 2002, September. *Is the Equity Market Really Developed in China?* Tokyo: ADB Institute. Research Paper No. 41.

Tran, H.Q. and J. Roldos. 2003. "Asian bond markets: The role of securitization and credit guarantees," background paper for the *Second Annual Conference of PECC Finance Forum*, held in Hua Hin, Thailand, July 8–9.

Turner, P. 2002. "Bond markets in emerging market economies," in *The Development of Bond Markets in Emerging Economies* Basel: Bank for International Settlements. Monetary and Economic Department. BIS Paper No. 11. pp. 1–12.

The Wall Street Journal. "Chona plans stock listing for state-owned banks," October 22. p. 16.

Wilson, D. 2000. "Recent developments in Asian financial markets," in G. de Brouwer (ed.) *Financial Markets and Policies in East Asia.* London: Routledge. pp. 17–31.

Wong, M.C.S. and R.Y.K. Ho. 2003. "Road map for building the institutional foundation for regional bond markets in East Asia," paper presented at the *Second Annual Conference of PECC Finance Forum*, held in Hua Hin, Thailand, July 8–9.

World Bank (WB). 2002. *World Development Report 2002. Building Institutions for Markets.* New York: Oxford University Press.

Chapter 7

POST-CRISIS REGIONAL ECONOMIC CO-OPERATION AND THE EMERGING FINANCIAL ARCHITECTURE

7.1 REALISTIC DIMENSION OF THE ASIAN CRISIS

Although some strands of ideas on regional financial and monetary co-operation were broached in the past, a realistic and contemporary proposal was made by Japan in the wake of the Asian currency and financial crisis (1997–98), which was a cataclysmic event for the regional economy.[221] It caused instability in currency values. In many cases the currency depreciations were precipitous. For instance, between June 1997 and August 1998, the Indonesian rupiah depreciated by 82.9 percent vis-à-vis the dollar, the Malaysian ringgit by 40.9 percent, the Philippine peso by 39.3 percent, the Thai baht by 39.7 percent, the Korean won by 33.3 percent, the New Taiwan dollar by 19.6 percent and the Singapore dollar by 18.6 percent. Being on fixed exchange rate, the Hong Kong dollar and the renminbi yuan did not depreciate (Das, 2000a).

---

[221] The Asian economic and financial crisis began in Thailand on July 2, 1997, and its contagion effect spread to several other high-performing Asian economies. Although the crisis mauled the region, the five economies that were most adversely affected were Indonesia, Korea, Malaysia, the Philippines and Thailand. However, there were two exceptions. The People's Republic of China (hereinafter China) and Taiwan were not adversely hit by the crisis. It passed these two economies by. The Asian economic and financial crisis received a great deal of attention from the researchers; consequently voluminous crisis literature emerged. See among others Krugman (1998 and 1999); Das (1999); Radelet and Sachs (1998a); Radelet and Sachs (1998b); Radelet and Sachs (1999); Lindgren et al.(1999); Das (2000a, 2000b); Frankel (2000); Kawai, Newfarmer and Schmukler (2001); Mishkin (2001); Kaminsky and Reinhart (2003).

Global capital flows to Asia fell precipitously from $132.2 billion in 1996 to $12.2 billion in 1997 and further down to minus $44.9 billion in 1998. International credit-rating agencies downgraded the sovereign debt of Republic of Korea (hereinafter Korea), Indonesia and Thailand to "junk" status, seriously impairing their ability to raise the capital needed to work through the region's wrenching downturn. Net financial flows from the Bank for International Settlements (BIS)-reporting countries had turned negative in the third quarter of 1997. Even in 2001, net loans of the BIS-reporting banks to Asia remained negative. This reflected heightened awareness of lending risk and unresolved problems of the Asian financial markets (BIS, 2001).[222] Asian economies had attracted global capital market flows in large volumes since 1990, particularly over the three-year period from 1994 to 1996. Reversal of global capital market flows—particularly short-term capital flows—was the most notable and disturbing feature of the Asian crisis (Das, 2004a, 2004b, 2004c). Monetary instability that spread after the depreciation of the Thai bath was unprecedented and highlighted how financial problems in one economy can have destabilizing ramifications in the region as well as adversely affect the global economy.

The crisis also caused precipitous fall in asset prices, collapse in investment rates and consumer and investor confidence in the region, and destruction of real incomes. It had high economic and social costs for the five crisis-affected economies, for the region as well as for far-reaching implications for the global economy. It caused GDP contraction in the crisis-affected economies and destroyed wealth on a massive scale in Asia and sent absolute poverty soaring. For instance, only in the banking sector "corporate loans equivalent to around half of one year's GDP turned into non-performing loans (NPls)—a destruction of savings on a scale more usually associated with a full-scale war" (Ziegler, 2003). The swiftness of the progression of the contagion surprised all stakeholders within the region as well as outside the region. This included global investors, credit-rating agencies and supranational institutions. The crisis also brought home to public policy community that the regional economy was institutionally ill prepared to live in a globally integrated financial world. The direct outcome of the Asian crisis was a renewed and imperative call for reforms of the financial systems at national, regional and global levels and strengthening of financial infrastructure and institutions, so that the risk of a future crisis can be minimized.

Until the outbreak of the crisis the dynamic Asian economies were widely considered "high performing" and earned fond sobriquet like "miracle economies." In general, they did not suffer from unsound macroeconomic

---

[222] The 2001 *Annual Report* of the BIS shows that in 2001 net exposure of the BIS-reporting banks was rising only for a small group of East European and Latin American economies.

policies and had learned from concepts like the Washington consensus.[223] They were known for their high-saving rates, prudent fiscal policies, low inflation rates, outer-orientation and high real GDP growth. Poor macroeconomic policies were not the causal factor behind the Asian crisis, although Thailand did make some macroeconomic policy errors in 1997.[224] While most crises in the past occurred due to unsustainable current account deficit and poor macroeconomic fundamentals, but *a la* Frankel (2000) Asian crisis was essentially a "capital account crisis." This was a highly unusual characteristic of the Asian crisis (Das 2000a, 2000b).

There was a perception in some quarters that the economic and financial problems were compounded by the long-lasting policy debates over the assisting package, less-than-generous assistance and rigorous conditionality of the international financial institutions (IFIs). IMF's handling of the Asian crisis was considered inapt by most Asian governments as well as many in the academic world. Analysts believed that Asian economies could do better by creating "a zone of financial and monetary stability insulated from these influences" (Eichengreen, 2001). In a rapidly globalizing world economy, it is indeed a difficult, if not unfeasible and arduous, proposition.

The constructive factor in this destructive event was that it gave a dramatic impetus to financial and monetary co-operation-related opinions and endeavors in Asia. Governments and central bankers received a strong impulsion to create a regional mechanism that could forestall any future crises. Several mechanisms and frameworks of regional and bilateral financial and monetary co-operation were debated, devised and implemented. In particular, Japan played a meaningful regional role, one that behooved a regional economic power. It should be recalled that the Japanese economy was going through a bad patch during this period. To manage the Asian crisis, assist the crisis-affected Asian economies and promote financial and monetary co-operation in the region Japanese Government took several initiatives and committed generous financial resources to bilateral and regional support endeavors. Some of these endeavors are profiled below.

---

[223] The term "Washington Consensus" is considered synonymous with "neo-liberalism" and "globalization." John Williamson propounded the concept as a set of neo-liberal policies, which in turn referred to the lowest common denominator of policy advice that was being given by the Washington-based Bretton Woods twins to Latin American countries in 1989. This policy advice essentially entailed fiscal discipline, a redirection of public expenditure priorities toward fields offering both high economic returns and the potential to improve income distribution (such as primary health care, primary education, and infrastructure), tax reforms (to lower marginal rates and broaden the tax base), interest rate liberalization, a competitive exchange rate, trade liberalization, liberalization of inflows of foreign direct investment, privatization, deregulation (to abolish barriers to entry and exit) and secured property rights.

[224] Just before the crisis precipitated, excessive economic expansion did lead to large current account deficits in Thailand.

Indeed, there was a dissenting view, opposing the financial and monetary co-operation in Asia. Contenders of this view proposed that policymakers should instead address the underlying causes behind exchange rate and financial market volatility, which were not difficult to identify. They called for strengthening and deepening of the domestic financial markets. According to them, regional co-operation should take into account the history of bank-dominated financial system in Asia, high corporate leverage and strong business-government ties. Eichengreen (2002) proposed an Asian Financial Institute (AFI), which would (i) have a sharp, albeit limited, focus on technical assistance for strengthening prudential supervision and regulation, (ii) run training programs for bank inspectors, accountants, and securities and exchange commissioners, (iii) provide reserve management, clearing and settlement services as well as central banking services like that of the Bank for International Settlements (BIS), and (iv) provide a forum for regional negotiations on capital and liquidity standards, regulatory process intended to promote financial stability, disclosure norms and corporate governance. However, Asian policy mandarins discarded this proposal.

7.1.1 Manila framework group

The Asian economies were quick to react to the outbreak of the crisis and their self-preservation instinct was reflected in the formation of several plans for managing any future crisis. The Manila Framework Group (MFG) was created in November 1997. This forum was set up by fourteen Asia-Pacific economies (including Australia, Canada, New Zealand and the United States (U.S.) for the purpose of an in-depth dialogue on regional economic surveillance and crisis management.[225] As the Asian economies were unsettled by the crisis, their basic objective in establishing the MFG was to enhance the prospects of financial stability.

Finance Ministers and central bankers from these countries and senior representatives of IFIs like the International Monetary Fund (IMF) and the World Bank met to create a new framework of regional co-operation. Since its inception the MFG has met semi-annually at the level of Deputy Finance Ministers. The IMF and World Bank present the regional economic surveillance reports in the Group meetings. Representatives from the original member countries, IFIs and the BIS have continued to meet but the MFG did not seem to have a great deal of influence. By the early 2000s, the significance of the MFG six-monthly meetings had dwindled and they were reduced to a mere forum for exchange of ideas.

---

[225] The fourteen Asia-Pacific member economies of the MFG are Australia, Brunei Darussalam, Canada, China, Hong Kong SAR, Indonesia, Japan, Korea, Malaysia, New Zealand, the Philippines, Singapore, Thailand and the United States.

7.1.2 ASEAN surveillance process

The next initiative was creation of the ASEAN Surveillance Process (ASP) in October 1998.[226] Its mandate was to coordinate and strengthen the policy-making process in the ASEAN economies and improve macroeconomic and financial surveillance. Peer review of broad regional policy coordination was considered the appropriate instrument for achieving this objective. The overarching objective of the ASP was institutional building, that is, to strengthen the national policymaking apparatuses for the ASEAN economies and regional policy coordination. In the wake of the crisis, many analysts felt that there was an imperious need for the ASP. Some even felt that it was the lack of regional policy coordination that caused the Asian crisis. The peer review and surveillance process was not limited to macroeconomic policies but was to be extended to sectoral and social policies as well. Under the ASP, economies were to exchange information on recent developments in the sub-region, and take note of individual and collective responses to economic and financial events that could have a potentially destabilizing impact. In the latter half of the 1990s, the ASP gradually evolved into the ASEAN-Plus-Three Surveillance Process (APTSP).[227]

To be meaningful and effective, the APTSP and the IMF need to have a close collaborative relationship. Otherwise the two can make inconsistent and incompatible assessments of the sub-regional scenario and come to upshots that are at variance from each other. There is a likely possibility of this, although the APTSP and the IMF both may base their analysis on the same set of information and data. This could undermine the credibility of their policy advice (Eichengreen, 2001). Conversely, a close collaborative relationship may create a good deal of synergy in reading the facts and new developments, analyzing them and coming to effective policy decisions.

7.1.3 New Miyazawa Initiative

A bilateral support mechanism called the New Miyazawa Initiative (NMI) was launched in October 1998 by the Ministry of Finance (MoF), Japan.[228] The objective of the bilateral support was to directly assist the crisis-affected economies and thereby indirectly contribute to the stability of the regional and international financial markets. Under the first phase, the NMI provided

---

[226] The ASP was established during the ASEAN Finance Ministers' Meeting held in Washington DC, in October 1998.

[227] The ASEAN-Plus-Three (APT) group has thirteen members, which included the ten ASEAN members namely, Brunei Darussalam, Cambodia, Indonesia, Lao PDR, Malaysia, Myanmar, the Philippines, Singapore, Thailand, and Vietnam. The three addition members making it the APT are China, Japan and Korea (Republic of).

[228] It was christened after Kiichi Miyazawa, Japan's Minister of Finance, who conceived it.

$30 billion dollar support. It was divided into two halves: The first half was made available to the five crisis-affected economies for medium- to long-term financial assistance as untied loans, so that they are able to recover. The second half was intended to fulfill the short-term financial needs during the implementation of macroeconomic and financial reforms. The Japan Bank of International Co-operation (JBIC) was charged with the implementation of the NMI.[229] This bilateral initiative turned out to be worthwhile and of the $30 billion allocation under the first phase, $21 billion were committed to the five crisis-ridden economies by early 2000 (MOF, 2002). Conscious of the significance of Japan's role in Asia's economic development, *Keidanren*, which is Japan's Federation of Economic Organizations, strongly supported the NMI. It not only acquiesced support for the restructuring measures in the crisis-affected economies but also proposed that Japanese firms should increase their imports from them (*Keidanren*, 2000).

The financial resources under the NMI were made available, as loans not grants, essentially for the purpose of corporate debt restructuring and strengthening the social safety net. In May 1999, Japan's Minister of Finance announced the second phase of bilateral financial support measure under the NMI, under which the MoF—through the JBIC—was to partially guarantee government bonds issued by the crisis-affected economies, totaling up to ¥2 trillion ($17 billion). This support was to be provided outside the framework of the first phase of the NMI (MoF, 1999). The second phase of the NMI also entailed development of domestic currency corporate bond markets, which in turn would be the precursor to the development of a regional bond market (APF, 2001). The two phases of NMI were also intended to enable Japan to utilize its abundant savings for the regional good and promote active use of the Tokyo financial market, in the process enhancing its regional economic and financial significance.

7.1.4 Asian growth and recovery initiative

A joint Japan—U.S. Asian Growth and Recovery Initiative (AGRI) was launched in November 1998.[230] The IFIs were important participants in the AGRI and were also instrumental in its implementation. The AGRI pragmatically emphasized an integrated and comprehensive approach to financial restructuring of problem banks and corporations, supported by adequate financing

[229] The Japan Bank for International Co-operation (JBIC) was created by merging the Export-Import Bank of Japan (JEXIM) and the Overseas Economic Co-operation Fund (OECF).

[230] See the Joint Statement of President Clinton and Prime Minister Obuchi on the Internet at http://www.mof.go.jp/english/if/e1e054.htm.

for bank recapitalization and incentives for creditors and debtors to play a constructive role in debt work-outs. A key element of the strategy to accelerate the pace of bank and corporate restructuring was the Asian Growth and Recovery Program (AGRP), which was financed in part by the World Bank, the Asian Development Bank (ADB) and bilateral support in a variety of forms. The AGRP utilized innovative, cost-effective financing methods to mobilize substantial additional private capital to assist Asian governments to finance bank recapitalization. Support from the AGRP was provided to economies that needed assistance and were implementing an integrated and comprehensive framework for corporate and bank restructuring. This was a precondition of financial support under the AGRP. Japan, the United States, the World Bank and the ADB worked together to establish the program and identify sources of funding. Together they targeted mobilizing $5 billion in bilateral and multilateral support, which in turn was expected to help catalyze significant additional private financing for the five crisis-affected economies. They also worked together to explore ways in which both debtors and creditors could be encouraged to participate constructively in voluntary debt work-outs, which are so essential in resolving financial crises.

While recapitalization of the financial base of banks was considered critical to restore functioning of the financial systems in Asia, companies in the region also faced a more immediate lack of working capital and trade finance necessary to maintain production, employment and exports. To alleviate this problem, the Export-Import Bank of the United States (U.S. ExIm), the Japan Export–Import Bank (JEXIM) and Japan Export Credit and Investment Insurance Agency substantially increased the size of their trade finance programs for the crisis-affected economies.

7.1.5 Asian Monetary Fund

Japan not only took initiative in proposing creation of an Asian Monetary Fund (AMF) in Bangkok, in September 1997, but also proposed to take lead and offered to have a large financial stake in it.[231] The fundamental objective of the proposed AMF framework was to promote financial and monetary co-operation and policy coordination in Asia, so that future crises could not only be averted but if they do materialize, they are managed better than was the last one. The proposed AMF was to be a $100 billion fund. Half of the resources were to be provided by Japan, while the rest were to come from the People's Republic of China (hereinafter China), Hong Kong SAR and Taiwan. The economies

[231] For discussion on the economics and politics of Asian monetary Fund (AMF) see Lin and Rajan (2001) and Rajan (2000).

proposing the AMF believed that rapid disbursement of liquidity from this fund would forestall future speculative attacks on the Asian currencies. The reaction of most of the Asian economies was favorable. They found it a worthwhile and functional concept.

One of the strong motivating factors behind the penchant to create the AMF, as noted above, was the discontentment and disaffection of the Asian governments with the IMF's response to the crisis. It was not the Asian governments alone who felt that the IMF did a sub-par job of handling the Asian crisis, but several academic researchers also concurred with this opinion. By prolonging the dialogues with the governments of crisis-affected countries and delaying the disbursement of liquidity, the IMF worsened the situation in many economies. Therefore, some scholars (see Wade and Venoroso, 1998) strongly supported the creation of AMF. Their plan reasonably tried to exploit Asia's economic strengths, which were manifested by its saving surplus, large foreign exchange reserves and net creditor status in the global economy. As stated in the preceding chapter (Section 6.8), since the crisis, foreign exchange reserves in Asia soared to more than half of the global total (Aizenmann and Marion, 2002; McCauley and Fung, 2003). The foreign exchange reserves of the APT economies were $1,900 billion in early 2004. In the first quarter of 2004, the estimated holdings of Asian central banks were $1 trillion worth of U.S. Treasury bonds (Day and Choi 2004). Numerous policymakers outside Asia concurred with the AMF concept; for instance, Andrew Rose of the U.S. Federal Reserve Bank of San Francisco corroborated the proposal. His AMF concept was to be an exact parallel of the IMF, or an Asian IMF. His validation of the AMF concept was logically based on the fact that currency crises "frequently spread on regional lines of trade linkages, have high regional economic and social costs, and therefore the safety nets devised for them should also be regional" (Rose, 1999).

The European Union (EU), United States and the International Monetary Fund (IMF) were strongly and vocally opposed to the creation of the AMF. It was feared that AMF would duplicate what the IMF does and challenge its global leadership. The IMF also apprehended that AMF would encourage countries to postpone restructuring measures. China, a large and influential economy, was not supportive of the notion of AMF in the early stages. Its complete lack of enthusiasm regarding the AMF was premised on strategic considerations and traditional rivalry between China and Japan in Asia. China's concern was the probability of expansion of Japan's influence over the Asian economies. In addition, many analysts dismissed the premise that a regional institution would have comparative advantage in identifying the Asian problems, comprehending it better than the IMF and prescribing indigenous solutions (Eichengreen, 1999). The AMF proposal was turned down at the Fifth APEC Finance Ministers Meeting in May 1998 in favor of a IMF-World Bank-led multilateral approach, but the concept was far from dead.[232] The Finance Ministers of China, Japan and Korea resuscitated it in 2000.

7.1.6 Other smaller proposals and initiatives

The AMF or other analogous institutional concepts continued to be deliberated upon in different Asian fora and addressed in academic writings, both in Asia and outside Asia. The Institute for International Monetary Affairs (IIMA), an independent think-tank in Tokyo, proposed a regional stability forum, with clear objectives of (i) promoting a regional policy dialogue, (ii) creating a regional framework for emergency financial support and (iii) ensuring that future crises are prevented by active regional economic surveillance (Shinohara, 1999). An identical proposal was made by the Asia Policy Forum, Tokyo, according to which a regional institution should (i) take on the role of the lender of the last resort, (ii) engage in regional economic surveillance and (iii) if the need arises assist in regional financial and corporate restructuring (Yoshitomi and Shirai, 2000).

Academic and policy debates also centered around the theme of a future regional monetary framework. Heiner Flassbeck, the erstwhile Vice Minister of Finance in Germany, saw the need of a steering group of Asian academics and policymakers to devise a regional currency regime. The steering group was to be charged with advising the regional governments on taking logical concrete policy measures for moving toward a unified currency regime, something resembling an Asian Euro (Flassbeck, 1999). Burnie Fraser, the Governor of the Reserve Bank of Australia, proposed a small-scale Bank for International Settlements (BIS) for Asia. This proposal was not made in reaction to the Asian crisis because it was made in 1995. Fraser correctly pointed out that "globalization is elevating the international dimension of monetary co-operation." The Asian BIS was to exchange information on financial and monetary issues and policies. In Fraser's vision regional crisis management was the task of this institution and it was to perform most of the functions that the BIS does for the G-10 industrial economies.

---

[232] The Fifth Asia-Pacific Economic Co-operation (APEC) Finance Ministers Meeting was held in Kananakis, Alberta, Canada, during May 23–24, 1998. It was devoted to the assessment of future prospects for growth and development within the APEC region in light of the Asian crisis and to discuss policies and measures to improve the prospects of post-crisis growth. Refer to the *Joint Ministerial Statement* published by the APEC Secretariat, in May 1998. The deliberations were focused on two broad themes. The first was an assessment of the erstwhile economic situation and policies to restore financial stability and growth, including measures to strengthen social safety nets to help cushion the impact of the crisis on the poor. The second was the development and strengthening of financial markets in the region so as to reduce the likelihood of future financial instability and to facilitate the continued dynamic growth of the region.

This proposal lost steam when the BIS admitted five Asian central banks to its membership and preemptively announced extension of its activities to Asia by establishing (in July 1998) an Asia and Pacific Representative Office in Hong Kong SAR.[233] This was the first overseas office of the BIS. The avowed objectives of the BIS Asian establishment included promoting central bank co-operation in Asia, helping Asia in strengthening its financial sectors, developing the financial infrastructure and restoring financial stability in this region. At the same time, the BIS Representative Office was to improve global understanding of Asia and forge the bonds of global monetary co-operation through its international meetings held in the region.

The BIS attempted to bring in the key elements of the banking reform process of the Basel Committee to the Asia. In 2001, the BIS created the Asian Consultative Council (ACC) with a secretariat in its regional headquarters in Hong Kong SAR. The ACC provides yet another vehicle for communications between the central banks in Asia and the Board of Directors and Management of the BIS. The ACC meets twice a year. Going forward, the Asia and Pacific Representative Office of the BIS has plans to collaborate with the EMEAP (Executives' Meeting of East Asia-Pacific Central Banks) central banks in research on impediments to central bank investment in the domestic currency bond markets (McCauley, 2003). This research would build on the work done by the Bank of Japan[234] and the IMF and the World Bank (IMF/WB, 2001) and other academic researchers. The frenzied manner in which the institution creation activity was undertaken in post-crisis era reflects the determination of the Asian economies to minimize the probability of precipitation of a future crisis and if it does, manage it in an adequate manner.

7.2 LAUNCHING THE CHIANG MAI INITIATIVE

Although policymakers cannot prevent every crisis, they can learn from the past one and minimize the probability of a future one. One of the many lessons of the Asian crisis was the need for a quick disbursing financial facility in periods of financial distress. Holding larger amounts of foreign exchange reserves is the direct and simplistic defense against speculative attacks, but maintaining high reserves has high costs. A pragmatic measure to lighten the cost of holding large reserves is that a group of Asian countries may decide to pool a pre-agreed proportion of their existing reserves to create a credit facility

---

[233] In 1996, the Bank for International Settlements (BIS) admitted (1) the People's Bank of China, (2) the Reserve Bank of India, (3) the Hong Kong Monetary Authority, (4) the Monetary Authority of Singapore and (5) the Bank of Korea. Until this point only the Bank of Japan was the member of the BIS.

[234] Under the Chairmanship of the former Deputy Governor A. Yamaguchi, Bank of Japan.

for the entire group. An individual member country would not have to hold large reserves if it is sure that in periods of financial distress, or a speculative attack, it can count on borrowing from the credit facility created for the entire group (Das, 2001). The current reserve level was quantified above in Section 7.1.5. If only 10 percent of these reserves are pooled for an Asian credit facility, the pool of resources would suffice for a first line of defense against speculative attacks. Looking backwards, in July 1997 if the other Asian economies had succeeded in providing credit to Thailand from such a pool, the spread of contagion to other Asian economies could have been stopped in its tracks and they would have been spared the high costs of economic recession and social dislocation. The basic concept of Chiang Mai Initiative (CMI) was based on this line of thinking.

The Japanese proposal of a framework of financial and monetary co-operation and policy coordination was revisited in Chiang Mai, Thailand, on May 6, 2000, and the Finance Ministers of ASEAN-Plus-Three (APT) countries agreed to create a formal swap arrangement among their central banks. This was named the CMI. The framework was approved at the meeting of the Deputy Finance Ministers of the APT economies on November 7, 2000, in Beijing. Drawings through this arrangement can be utilized for supplementing the drawing from the IMF. They were made subject to IMF conditionality. CMI's first order of business was expansion of the multilateral ASEAN swap arrangement (ASA) from its original five members to all ten. Second, a network of bilateral swap arrangement (BSA) among the thirteen APT economies was created under the CMI. As set out above, the CMI swap framework—which included ASA and BSAs—was intended to provide liquidity support for the APT countries in periods of balance-of-payment difficulties. The expectation was that such liquidity support would prevent national crises from materializing and subsequently turning into a regional contagion.[235] It was also expected that CMI would work toward exchange rate stability in the APT countries.

The CMI was designed as an emergency facility to be a lender of last resort and was to be used infrequently—not unless the member economy is in financial distress or suffers from an acute liquidity crunch—by the 13 participating countries. Like the IMF, the CMI was intended to be proactive. Therefore, there was a need to define the inter-country framework of co-operation among the ATP members, so that an economy can receive the financial and liquidity support of appropriate order when the need arises. It was also needed to be ensured that conditionality should be applied to the group members in a uniform manner. The CMI had to establish a functional relationship with the IMF because conditionality prescribed by the IMF was considered important for restoring

[235] Refer to Das (1999), Das (2000a, 2000b) and Kaminsky and Reinhart (2003) for a detailed discussion on these issues.

stability in the afflicted economy. The probability of the CMI evolving into an AMF remained open.

In comparison to the AMF, liquidity to be provided under the CMI is small. It is sure to fall short when future rescue packages are put together. The liquidity that the global financial markets can provide to an economy in distress is huge as compared to the amount the CMI can provide. Maximum amount that an individual country can draw varies a great deal. There is no gainsaying these facts, but CMI would still be worth it because the rapid disbursement of the first unconditional 10 percent tranche of credit from the ASA and BSAs can send a signal to the market participants and currency speculators. The signals can apprise them that liquidity is not only available to the economy in financial distress but can be further expanded by the APT members. This would in turn change the market perception. Swift IMF assistance could be the next sequential source of liquidity. The lamming-like behavior of the investors would be deterred by the availability of liquidity from more than one source in a short time span. It is reasonable to expect that it would dampen the market volatility. Liquidity demand beyond the 10 percent level—or the remaining 90 percent—will need compliance with the austere IMF conditionality. This linkage makes it clear that the swap arrangements would play a complementary and supplementary role to the IMF. The regional swap facility is secured by IMF conditionality. This is comforting to the financial markets. As the volume of reserves available with the APT economies is substantial, availability of emergency liquidity would make the CMI a helpful and effectual arrangement.

7.2.1 Belated multilateral acceptance

A favorable development for the CMI framework is that the attitude of the multilateral institutions, particularly that of the IMF, has undergone a transformation since 2000. Although acrimoniously critical initially, the IMF is no longer opposed to regional financial and monetary co-operation as long as it took place "not in opposition to the IMF, because the IMF is a global institution. . . " Horst Kohler, the Managing Director of the IMF, made it known that if the CMI operated "in a complementary manner" the IMF would not be averse to the concept. "That is exactly what is happening now and it makes a lot of sense" to have the CMI operating in full swing (Kohler, 2001a). The IMF realized that conceptually the CMI is embedded in the IMF system. The willingness of Asian policymakers to link—subordinate, if you please—the CMI to global financial arrangement helped in mollifying the situation and enhancing its acceptability. Subsequently, the EU and U.S. antagonism with financial co-operation in the form of CMI or AMF was also completely withdrawn (Christie, 2001).

The ASA and BSAs provide short-term liquidity support for balance-of-payment, somewhat like the Emergency Financing Mechanism (EFM) of the

IMF. The EFM facility was intended for periods or circumstances that threaten to give rise to a crisis. The ASA and BSAs are also similar to the Supplemental Reserve Facility (SRF), which was created in 1997 for the purpose of providing short-term support to members experiencing exceptional balance-of-payments difficulty. As the CMI scenario developed in Asia, the IMF grew increasingly convinced and assured that regionalism can support multilateralism. The two need not necessarily work at cross-purposes. Horst Kohler remarked that, "the IMF has increased its support for regional co-operation and integration, as a way to promote strong policies and institutions in neighboring countries and stepping stone towards successful integration into global markets" (Kohler, 2001b). Thus, complementarity was a crucial attribute and the IMF accommodated the ASA and BSAs because they worked in a complementary manner to the IMF by disbursing additional liquidity in an emergency situation.

7.3 MULTILATERAL AND BILATERAL SWAP ARRANGEMENTS

The ASA between the five founding members (Indonesia, Malaysia, the Philippines, Singapore and Thailand) of ASEAN was established fairly long ago, in August 1977, with an objective of alleviating temporary liquidity shortages in the central banks of the member countries. The first step of the CMI was to include the sixth member, namely, Brunei Darussalam in the ASA. Subsequently, details of gradually including Cambodia, Lao PDR, Myanmar and Vietnam without much delay were worked out. Largely based on the suggestion of Bank Indonesia, the terms and conditions of ASA were revised. However, at $200 million the volume of the pooled resources was far from adequate to fend off a crisis of any degree of severity. The magnitude of volatility of capital market that was observed during the Asian crisis was much too large to be handled by the pooled resources under the ASA. As noted in Section 7.1, a sharp reversal of external capital inflows in the crisis-affected economies was observed between 1996 and 1998 (Das, 1999; 2000a, 2000b).

Other than its small size, this multilateral arrangement had several obvious limitations. The first one was that it was created as an equal partnership among the ASA members, which implied that the providing members had equal share in providing the total amount of swap resources, which was not always easy or possible. Second, any swap participant could decline to provide the committed resources and keep out by giving reason to the other ASA members for not providing. Should such a situation arise, the other participants could voluntarily increase their shares. Third, if the total amount offered by the members falls short of the requirement of the borrowing member, the amount of swap would be reduced to the amount available, which could cause considerable difficulties and uncertainty for the borrowing member. Fourth, there was a limit ($80 million) on maximum amount that could be swapped for any member at any one point in time, which was a highly limiting factor (Wang, 2002). The ASA was not only limited in terms of resources but also had its share of weaknesses, which in turn affected its utility for the ASEAN members.

Over the 1979–92 period four ASA members activated the facility, while it was not used during the Asian crisis period.[236] The reason was that liquidity requirement for financing the external balances was large and the ASA was found to be much too small to respond in a meaningful manner. Under the CMI, the new members (Cambodia, Lao PDR, Myanmar and Vietnam) have joined the ASA, but they could not be expected to enlarge its resource base. Of the ten ASEAN members, these countries were the most resource poor and had diminutive foreign exchange reserves of their own. Bank of Indonesia proposed that the equal partnership principle in swaps should not be applied to the four new members and that due to their small resource base they should be made responsible for only 20 percent participation in a swap arrangement. Other ASEAN members found it reasonable and the suggestion was accepted. The size of the ASA facility was raised from to $1 billion in November 2000. The hard currencies available under the ASA were the euro, the dollar and the yen.

Obviously, the ASA was not a comprehensive multilateral swap arrangement, promising a high degree of utility and protection against financial volatility or speculative runs. Under these circumstances, to enhance its utility the ASA had two clear choices. First, expand ASA by including some more Asian economies that have large foreign exchange reserves so that the swap facility could be enlarged to a meaningful amount. The three candidates ready for inclusion in the ASA were China Japan and Korea; all three could contribute meaningful amounts to the multilateral swap arrangement because of their large foreign exchange reserves. Such an enlarged multilateral swap facility would be a region-wide facility. The second possibility was linking ASA to a global liquidity facility, like the IMF.

The BSA, mentioned in Section 7.1, was another feasible regional complementary financial facility. Under the CMI, in 2000 China, Japan and Korea presented the first joint draft of creating a network of BSAs for the region. Japan was the most enthusiastic and active in this regard, while Brunei Darussalam and Singapore seemed the least interested. This proposal was widely regarded as important because it could be used as a prototype for devising a common framework, or a standardized model, for BSAs among the APT economies. On the basis of a pre-agreed framework for BSAs, each participating member

---

[236] These four economies were Indonesia (1979), Malaysia (1980), the Philippines (1981 and 1992) and Thailand (1980).

would negotiate specific conditions of the arrangement bilaterally with the other participating member. One of the BSA-related objectives of the CMI is to design and develop a network that would (i) function as quick disbursing swaps when the need arises, (ii) establish a coordinated process of decision-making for activating the BSAs and (iii) create a monitoring mechanism for the network of BSAs, which would double as an Asian swap secretariat (Park, 2000). The joint draft outline contains a structured framework of the network of BSAs, which includes overall and individual swap sizes, interest rate, collateral, and other related terms and conditions.

A good deal of thought and planning went into this process. The network of BSAs was divided into three groups. First, the network of BSAs was to operate between the three large northeast Asian economies, namely, China, Japan and Korea. The second group of BSAs was to be between the ten ASEAN members. The third network of the BSAs was to be a cross-network between the three northeastern Asian economies on the one hand and the ASEAN members on the other.

One lesson of the Asian crisis was that to keep the currency speculators at bay, pre-emptive measures are indispensable. Equally important are quick access to and activation of the facility and disbursement without delay. To attain this vital objective, as alluded to in Section 7.2, the availability of first 10 percent tranche of the funds under BSAs was made unconditional (Das, 2000a, 2000b). The original plan was to raise the 10-percent limit after the CMI is able to develop its own surveillance unit. For the purpose of institutional backing an Agent Bank was appointed, which was to rotate among the APT members. The Agent Bank receives the ASA fund request, expeditiously assesses it in consultation with other members and disburses the first 10 percent of the request swap amount without delay to fend off the speculators. The central bank from the liquidity-requesting country is allowed to swap its own currency for hard currency for six months (Manupipatpong, 2002). The requesting country can borrow up to twice the amount committed to the ASA facility.[237]

During 2001 and 2002, Japan completed negotiations of BSAs with Korea, Thailand, the Philippines, Malaysia, China and Indonesia, in this chronological order. Other than these, the APT members have negotiated BSA limits among themselves. By the end of 2003, a network of twelve BSAs and Repo (or repurchase) agreements was also put in place. In November 2003, such negotiations were also completed with Singapore. Their combined total size

---

[237] According to Wang and Andersen (2002) each of the following six ASEAN members Brunei Darussalam, Indonesia, Malaysia, the Philippines, Singapore and Thailand committed $150 million to the BSAs, which was in keeping with the principle of equal partnership. However, Vietnam committed only $60 million, Myanmar $20 million, Cambodia $15 million and Lao PDR $5 million.

was $32.5 billion. The repurchase agreement entailed securities, particularly government bonds. In a repurchase agreement the seller agrees to repurchase them at an agreed price and date. Such an agreement allows the borrower use of short-term liquidity.

Under attack from currency speculators, an economy can use the network of BSAs for borrowing the hard currency from another country that is a participant in the BSA network, or use the hard currency to buy its own currency and stabilize its exchange rate. Thus viewed, the BSA entails credit risk for the lending economy. The first borrowing is for 90 days, which can be further extended. There is a renewal limit of seven times (Wang and Andersen, 2002). Interest rate on borrowings is based on London Inter-Bank Offer Rates (LIBOR), plus a spread.[238] As noted earlier, 10 percent of the BSA limit can be automatically disbursed, without any linkage to the IMF program or conditionality. Higher amounts can only be borrowed either in relation to an IMF reform and restructuring program or under a Contingency Credit Line.

The networks of BSAs use dollars. There are two exceptions, namely, China–Japan BSA and China–Korea BSA, which use their domestic currencies. As usual, Cambodia, Lao PDR, Myanmar and Vietnam have been given time for getting ready for accession to this network. This country group is still under the Poverty Reduction and Growth Facility (PRGF) of the IMF and its phasing-in program has not been finalized. As regards the institutional arrangements for the CMI, the informal surveillance system that exists in the central banks of the APT countries is considered adequate for the present to oversee the CMI operations. The only efforts that are currently being made are in the areas of monitoring short-term capital flows and establishing an early warning system for a crisis. If the APT countries decide to multilateralize the BSAs, a reserve pool may be proposed. In that case, a more formal system of surveillance and development of conditionality would be necessary. It would be pragmatic to plan something on the lines of a European Monetary Co-operation Fund that existed in the 1970s, for the APT group.

7.4 FUTURE CHALLENGES FOR THE CHIANG MAI INITIATIVE

Following the Asian crisis, Indonesia, Korea, the Philippines and Thailand received $119 billion from the IMF and the APT group as emergency assistance. The total contribution made by the APT group was $32.5 billion. As a single

---

[238] For the first drawing and first renewal, interest remains 150 basis points, while for subsequent renewals 50 basis points are added. The maximum limit is 300 basis point above the LIBOR.

country contributor, Japan made the largest contributions to the Korean and Thai rescue packages.[239] The European countries and the United States were not involved in the rescue packages, which were prepared in a collaborative manner by the APT economies, Australia and the multilateral institutions (Asami, 2001). As usual, the IMF played the lead role and guided the deliberations on the formation of the packages.

China and Japan favor linking of CMI with the IMF so that its credibility is enhanced, although Malaysia disagrees. They also favor linking BSAs to the IMF conditionality mechanism until CMI is able to develop its own formal regional monitoring and surveillance mechanism. Failure to develop such a framework is being viewed as a serious handicap of the CMI. For functioning in an efficacious manner, CMI would need to develop not only a professional regional surveillance system having credible analytical capabilities but also a well-coordinated decision-making process for rapid activation and disbursement of the swaps. Institutional endeavors were underway in early 2004 to create a regional Surveillance Unit, which would monitor short-term capital flows and have an early warning system. This unit is to monitor (i) liquidity positions and macroeconomic fundamentals, (ii) implementation of common norms agreed among the APT members and (iii) policy reforms and policy harmonization among member economies.

To be sure, the concept of regional financial and monetary co-operation has made some progress. However, at an early stage in its creation, the CMI is also beset with both institutional constraints and political problems. First, due to rapid recovery from the crisis, APT economies are now less interested in financial and monetary co-operation than that in other areas. The political will of the APT governments has considerably sapped. Second, the member economies give an impression that they do not to have an idea of CMI's future direction, and what is its ultimate objective. Whether it is going to remain a regional liquidity support program or would it eventually evolve into an AMF of some genre has not been thought through by them. Although if the multilateral and bilateral swap arrangements are activated collectively along with the surveillance, CMI does give an appearance of a de facto AMF. Third, if the APT economies are collectively ambitious and are aiming at moving in the direction of a future European Monetary System (EMS) and exchange rate mechanism (ERM), they will need to increase both the number and size of the BSAs.[240] Fourth, the

---

239 The individual country rescue packages were as follows: Indonesia received \$42.3 billion (of which \$13 billion came from the APT countries), Korea \$ 58.4 billion (of which \$10 billion came from Japan), the Philippines \$1 billion, and Thailand \$17.2 billion (of which \$9.5 billion came from APT countries).

240 The European Monetary System (EMS) is a system of fixed but adjustable exchange rates between the currencies of many European Union (EU) Member States. It came into effect in

two countries, China and Japan, that are likely to take on the leadership role, have very different perspectives and objectives regarding regional financial and monetary co-operation (Section 7.10).[241]

1979, although agreed a year earlier, and was designed to ensure that currency and exchange rate conditions remain as stable as possible in the EU. The exchange rates of the participating currencies are only allowed to fluctuate upwards or downwards within certain margins, otherwise the participating central banks have to intervene. The EMS system comprises a stable currency zone largely free of serious internal fluctuations in exchange rates. The EMS is made up of three elements: (1) an exchange rate and intervention mechanism, (2) a comprehensive financial assistance system, and (3) the European Currency Unit, the ECU, as a reference value and accounting unit. In the EMS the agreed exchange rates of the participating states are not allowed to fluctuate upwards or downwards beyond a margin of 2.25 per cent. If a currency comes under pressure and its exchange rate approaches the margin limit the participating central banks intervene: they have to buy up the weak currency and sell the stronger one in order to support the exchange rate. This part of the EMS agreements is known as the Exchange Rate and Intervention Mechanism (ERIM). To prevent the central banks running out of funds when they have to make such interventions they grant each other temporary loans (credit mechanism).

The goal of stable exchange rates between the participating states was achieved to a large extent in the 1980s. However, in 1992 the British pound sterling and the Italian lira came under pressure to devalue and they withdrew from the EMS. Subsequently, in order to remove the ever-increasing pressure of speculation from the EMS, the margins were increased in 1993 to 15 per cent in both directions. Otherwise the EMS remained unchanged. By April 1998, 13 of the 15 Member States of the European Union belonged to the EMS exchange rate mechanism, all except Sweden and the United Kingdom.

Twelve of the EU Member States were to join the monetary union on January 1, 1999, or the Euro Zone. New agreements had to be made for the relationship between the new single currency, the euro, and the currencies of those EU Member States that did not participate in the monetary union. The EMS II was devised for this group of countries. The aim was to prevent excessive currency fluctuations between the euro and the other non-Euro Zone currencies. The EU summit in Amsterdam in June 1997 agreed on some basic guidelines for an EMS II. The new entrants to the EU would automatically follow EMS II.

The principal decision on enlargement was made as early as 1993. Back then, at the Copenhagen summit, the EU members agreed that the associated Central and Eastern European Countries (CEEC) should integrate fully into the Union. At the same time, the European Council established political and economic conditions for accession. These "Copenhagen criteria" demand of the accession candidates:

(i) stability of institutions guaranteeing democracy, the rule of law, human rights, and protection of minorities;

(ii) existence of a functioning market economy with the capacity to withstand the competitive pressures in the EU Single Market; and

(iii) adoption of essential EU legislation (*acquis communautaires)* and administrative and judicial structures that ensure its effective implementation.

In addition, the EU set a reform agenda for its own institutions and a legal framework in the "Agenda 2000" put forward by the EU commission in 1997.

[241] See Wang (2003) for a more detailed discussion.

7.5 PROS AND CONS OF INSTITUTIONALIZED REGIONAL CO-OPERATION

As set out above, there were strident dissenting voices against creation of an institution for regional financial and monetary co-operation in Asia in 1997. Concurrently, there were many who equally strongly disagreed with the critics of institutionalized financial and monetary co-operation. They believed that there can be no monopoly in the market for ideas, and that competition in this market is as much valuable as that in markets of goods and services. The supporters of institutionalized co-operation in Asia contended that "competitive pluralism" is certain to provide a novel menu of creative ideas and options to clients. It would put them in the driver's seat for carrying them out, leading to an enhanced regional synergy.

Those who dissented on institutionalized co-operation in Asia posited that Asian economies might not be capable of creating and efficiently managing a regional financial and monetary institution on their own. The European experience was compared to that of Asia. Unlike Europe, institutionalized economic integrationist thinking in Asia was of recent origin. Conversely, since the creation of the European Coal and Steel Community (1951) and signing of the Treaty of Rome (1957) diplomatic and political endeavors for integration in Europe were endemic and indefatigable. They helped in creating a web of interlocking agreements in various areas of economic, social, political and strategic and military affairs. These agreements also encouraged European economies to co-operate in financial and monetary affairs, and made the launch of the euro feasible in 1999.[242] Such a web has not been created in Asia.

The dynamic Asian economies need time to reach the European level of financial and monetary co-operation. For sure, this period would not be as long as half a century as it was for Europe, but it needs to be truncated into a shorter time period (Section 7.9.1). The flip side of this coin is that in the wake of the high-cost Asian crisis, Asian public policymaking community may be on the brink of a policy transformation. They may be ready to put aside their differences and begin to devise a common defense mechanism against any future crises. A silver lining of the crisis cloud was the development of political will for endeavors in this direction. Additionally, Asian countries developed a posse of regional experts having the appropriate analytical skills to monitor macroeconomic and financial developments on the one hand and manage financial co-operation and policy coordination on the other.

As the preceding chapters show, trade policy liberalization in Asia has been progressing for two decades. There is a growing body of empirical

---

[242] The euro was launched on January 1, 1999.

evidence demonstrating that benefits from financial and monetary co-operation strengthen as the level of integration through trade rises (Rose and Engel, 2000). The reverse of this was also found to be correct, that is, joining a financial and monetary union has a multiplier effect on trade (Glick and Rose, 2001; Persson, 2001; Rajan, 2002; Rose, 2000). The principal enabling factors are reduction in transaction cost and currency risks. Other than these, several economic and political economic factors coalesce to produce these results. Rose (2001) also concluded that trade between countries that share a common currency is on an average more than three times of what was predicted by gravity model. Persson (2001) came to the same conclusion but in his computations the increase was less than three times of what was predicted by gravity model.

Soft conditionality and moral hazard have been the long-standing polemical arguments opposing the formation of AMF. It was argued that proliferation of regional endeavors like AMF would exacerbate these two problems because regional institutions might find it difficult to impose politically unpopular policies over the member economies. A lack of policy discipline due to political expediency, or unwillingness to adopt politically unpopular domestic measures, would indeed render a regional financial and monetary institution weak, even ineffective. Even global institutions like the IMF face this problem and a Council of Foreign Relations (CFR) report (1999) advised it to address the moral hazard problem by firmly observing the normal lending limits. There is truth to the contention that Asian economies are not prepared as yet for an intra-regional treaty that has provisions for sanctions for the member economies that do not adjust their domestic macroeconomic and financial policies in accordance with the requirements of the treaty.

The pro-globalizers were also averse to the AMF concept, and found it a retrograde and backward-looking proposal. As they tended to believe in multilateralism, their argument was that in the present era of ongoing globalization, creating AMF would tantamount to backward policy movement. Spread of information and communications technology (ICT) is promoting both financial globalization and virtualization. A regional financial and monetary institution may eventually create impediments in way to financial liberalization and global economic integration. Therefore, the present zeitgeist demands something very different from the new regional institutions. It calls for a new system of global governance, which may *inter alia* include a global central bank and global prudential and regulatory institutions. The pro-globalizers contended that if the markets for financial services are governed globally, they are sure to benefit from scale economies. This would also accommodate the market forces driving the contemporary financial globalization (Das, 2004a). Public goods like services of the lender of the last resort and those of the regulatory institutions can be better provided at the global level. However, Eichengreen (1999) dismissed these contentions as far from today's global financial reality, if not entirely quixotic and impractical. In the area of prudential and regulatory measures, the emerging market economies (EMEs) as well as developing economies have adopted their own codes, norms and standards as a second best.[243] Skepticism has been expressed regarding the ability of global institutions to enforce global norms over the EMEs and developing economies (Park, 2000). Therefore, creation of an Asian financial and monetary institution is not an irrelevant concept. Thus, there has been a strong dichotomy in viewpoints on the issue of institutionalized regional financial and monetary co-operation.

7.6 PREDILECTION FOR A REGIONAL FINANCIAL AND MONETARY INSTITUTION

An honest and accurate answer to the question whether Asia needs a financial and monetary institution would first depend upon the answer to the question whether this genre of regional integration, and creation of a regional institution, would have positive welfare implications for the region. Secondly, it is also essential to answer whether such regional co-operation would impede future multilateral trade and financial liberalization. Knowing whether such regional integration promotes or retards integration of global financial markets as well as integration of the region with the rest of the global economy is important for formulating policy measures in this regard.

As regards the first question, there are benefits of regional monetary co-operation, and trade between countries that share a common currency increases. As for the second question, majority of the experiences of the last decade reveal that regional integration arrangements have not impeded multilateral liberalization and financial globalization. In general, regional endeavors have complemented the global integration endeavors. Over the decade of the 1990s,

---

243 What are the emerging market economies? Other than the rapid endogenous growth endeavors, respect of property rights and respect of human rights are some of the basic prerequisites of becoming an emerging market economy. The national government should offer protection to property and human rights of both, the citizens of the country and the non-residents alike. An indispensable condition for an emerging market economy is its sustained ability to attract global capital inflows. Only an assurance of protection of property rights will attract global investors to a potential emerging market economy. Thus, protection of property rights is a fundamental, non-negotiable, condition, which an economy needs to meet before embarking on its road to becoming an emerging market economy. So far there is little agreement on the country count. In the industrial economies the emerging market economies were thought of as the newly industrialized economies (NIEs) and some middle-income developing countries. The latter group included those countries in which governments and firms are creditworthy enough from the perspective of global investors to successfully borrow from the global capital markets and/or attract institutional portfolio investment. Different international institutions include slightly different sets of countries in this category (Das, 2004b).

when institutionalized regionalism accelerated in Asia, there has been little evidence to show that dynamic Asian economies concurrently withdrew from the global economy and dissociated from the financial globalization process.

Motivation and forces driving the contemporary, or the so-called second wave of regionalism during the late 1980s and the 1990s, are different from those that were behind the first wave of regionalism (of 1950s) and prior to that.[244] The contemporary regional integration initiatives, unlike those in the past, seem to be conducive to global integration. They are not known for strongly supporting dissociation of RIAs from the global economy. In the contemporary period, many developing economies participate in the regional integration initiatives because policy mandarins believe that regionalism would not only help them in liberalizing their economies but also anchor the liberalization measures in the domestic economy. By promoting trade and financial liberalization, regionalism promotes global integration rather than withdrawal from it. Surge in RIA notifications to the GATT–WTO system during the second wave testifies to this fact.[245] Furthermore, in case of dynamic Asian economies that have followed export and FDI-led growth strategies, attempting to thwart the onward march of globalization would not only be counter-productive, but also counter to the mindset of the policymakers. The Asian economies have a great deal to loose by dissociating from the onward march of economic and financial globalization.

Two principal developments during and after the Asian crisis have made Asian economies accelerate their regional integration endeavors in the financial and monetary area. Their disgruntlement with the ill-timed and inadequate response of the supranational financial institutions (set out earlier in this chapter) and slow progress of reforms in the global financial architecture once the recovery took hold. These two developments were the *causae causantes* behind the accelerated interest in forming an Asian financial and monetary institution. However, while a pressing need for reforms was felt during the crisis period, once the Asian economies made a rapid recovery, the interest and political will in the Group-of-Seven (G-7) countries in reforming the global financial architecture receded rapidly. Besides, the Asian economies were impressed with the Japan-led financial assistance package that was put together in September 1997

---

[244] Interested readers are well advised to refer to Das (2004c), which discusses these historical aspects, particularly motivation behind various periods of regionalism in the global economy in great details.

[245] Over 170 regional integration agreements (RIAs) were in force at the end of 2003. The drive toward the conclusion of RIAs, which gathered momentum in the 1990s, has continued unabated. As of October 2003, all 146 WTO members, except Mongolia, were either members of RIAs or actively negotiating one. The period following the Doha Development Agenda, in November 2001, has been one of the most prolific periods in terms of notification of RIAs to the WTO. During these 2 years, 33 RIAs were notified to the WTO (WTO, 2003).

for Thailand. It convinced the Asian governments that in periods of financial distress, they can rely on regional endeavors more than on global ones. The opinion of the Asian governments toward creating a regional financial facility became more favorable than ever before and they began believing that such an institution was indispensable for a rapid recovery from a future crisis.

To be sure, improvements in the global financial architecture were designed following the crisis, but they did not inspire confidence in many, who perceived them as inadequate to promote financial stability in the future periods of crisis in the regional economies. The high cost of the crisis has been highlighted in Section 7.1. Little wonder that they perceived that as long as the structural issues related to the supply side of capital are not effectively addressed and resolved, they would continue to remain vulnerable in future (Park, 2000). Therefore, instead of waiting for the G-7 economies to take initiative in creating the new, viable and effective global financial architecture, they would do well to create a defensive mechanism of their own to safeguard the stability of their economies. Consequently, even after the early rejection of the AMF initiative, regional financial and monetary co-operation received tacit support from the APT economies. Several proposals and initiatives outlined in Section 7.1 and launching of the CMI by the thirteen APT economies are manifestations of the pressing need for regional financial co-operation felt by the APT countries.

There can be no assurance of preventing a future regional crisis. However, creating a regional facility—it matters little whether its name is AMF or not—can be a versatile instrument in minimizing the possibility of future crises in Asia. It could be so structured and managed that it can function without challenging or duplicating the global authority of the IMF (Section 7.2.1). It could provide additional resources and reinforce IMF's endeavors toward managing the financial crisis, if it does precipitate. Second, financial and macroeconomic surveillance in Asia is another area where a future AMF can join hands with the IMF. Third, an AMF can take on the role of the lender of the last resort, or even better, the first lender of the last resort. The IMF can step in at the subsequent stage. Thus, various imaginative and result-oriented collaborative roles between the two institutions can be planned in an imaginative manner.

7.7 AUGMENTING FOREIGN EXCHANGE RESERVES HOLDINGS

It was noted in another context that an immediate concrete measure that was taken early in the post-crisis period by both the crisis-affected Asian economies, and those that were only influenced by it, was a dramatic augmentation in their foreign exchange reserves. These reserves were built up not only in absolute terms but also relative to imports and GDP (Refer to Chapter 6, Section 6.7.2

and Chapter 7, Section 7.1.5). Understanding dawned on the Asian central banks that in a financially globalized world, they were more vulnerable to unfavorable regional and global events, and that this vulnerability was exacerbated by capital account liberalization. There were two more reasons why the new levels of foreign exchange reserves were well above what was considered adequate in the past for smooth operation of import transactions. First was an increased volume of capital account transactions in the Asian economies. Secondly, these economies needed a buffer stock of liquidity for unforeseen speculative attacks to stave off a 1997–98-like crisis. Also, Asian economies ensured that the usable amount of reserves remained high. The reason was that during the crisis a good deal of reserves were locked in various financial products and could not be mobilized to protect the economy from currency speculators.

The elevated levels of reserves vis-à-vis import requirements or GDP appear excessive, have high opportunity cost and represent misallocation of financial resources. To be sure, maintenance of adequate reserves is important for maintenance of investors' confidence and managing pressures of the foreign exchange market. It was *a fortiori* so in the background of the crisis. That being said, holding reserves have a cost; therefore, economies always need to balance the cost with the perceived benefits of high levels of reserves.

7.7.1 Adequacy of foreign exchange reserve holdings

One reason why China, Hong Kong SAR and Taiwan were relatively unaffected by the Asian crisis was their large holdings of foreign exchange reserves. They are a crucial determinant of an economy's ability to avert a crisis, and discourage speculative run. The level of reserve holdings is considered an important determinant of vulnerability to a crisis. Adequate reserves also provide a buffer against the future uncertainties faced by the balance-of-payments (bop). Conversely, depleting holdings of reserves is regarded as an amber signal for the policymakers. For that reason, studies that try to identify variables for predicting a currency and financial crisis consider *ex ante* reserve holdings an important variable (Disystat, 2001).

We saw above that the anxiety response of the Asian central bankers led them to accumulate high levels of reserves in the post-crisis period, which made Asian central banks the biggest and most important investors in the U.S. Treasury bonds. The U.S. economy depended on capital flows from Asia. It helped the United States in financing its high fiscal deficit, while keeping its interest rates low. In turn, the large U.S. deficit kept Asian export growth rate buoyant. However, in early 2004, several central banks were looking for alternative opportunities for these vast reserves that could provide better returns. To this end, Korea, Taiwan and Thailand were making proactive endeavors (Day and Choi, 2004). Another reason for post-crisis accumulation of large reserve holdings was the so-called "fear of floating" among the central banking authorities (Hausmann et al., 2000).

Adequacy of foreign exchange reserve holdings was conventionally assessed against imports because it was believed that only current account can be a source of bop instability. The age-old argument that the level of reserves should be expected to grow with growth in trade originated with Robert Triffin (1947) and the reserves-to-import (R/M) ratio remained a popular measure of adequacy of reserves for a long time. Even the IMF presents reserve adequacy data in this manner in its *World Economic Outlook*. The reserve levels were considered inadequate if they do not cover for four months of imports. However, the popular practice of determining adequacy of reserves exclusively on the basis of imports, or merely computing the R/M ratio, has a weak theoretical foundation (Bird and Rajan, 2002a, 2002b). It's time to expand this narrow view of calibrating adequacy of reserve holdings. This relationship was developed further and the optimal level of reserves was considered an increasing function of uncertainty (measured by average annual imbalances), a decreasing function of the cost of holding reserves and of marginal propensity to import (Heller, 1966).

In relating reserves holdings to the imports or merely to current account transactions, one makes the error of ignoring the fact that the crises of the 1990s and early 2000s, were predominantly the crises of capital account. Therefore, the reserve adequacy benchmark should logically take into account both capital outflows and imports as potential drains on the reserves. A broader view of reserve adequacy needs to see them in the backdrop of the policies that are being followed in this context. That is, while reserve decumulation is one way of addressing the expanding current account deficit, arranging for precautionary credit lines from financial institutions in the global financial markets, treating the IMF as a quasy lender of the last resort and economic adjustment are the other options open for the policymakers (Bird and Rajan, 2002b). This implies that a lower level of reserves may be sufficient when there are other supplementing sources of finance and a probability of policy adjustment. The same level may be inadequate if the alternative sources of finance are absent and there is a reluctance regarding policy adjustment. A partial view based only on the reserves level in isolation is therefore not the right manner of measuring adequacy of the reserve level. In fact, adequacy of reserve holdings should be computed only in the background of "macroeconomic policies, exchange rate regimes, financial sector soundness, and debt management" (Fischer, 2001). Furthermore, in 1995 the IMF created an emergency bailout fund for countries in financial crisis and concurrently moved to increase disclosure requirements of countries borrowing money. In a period of financial distress the IMF can provide additional SDRs because during the post-crisis period, IMF's resources have been beefed up and new lending facilities have been established (Henning, 2002).

After the Asian crisis, short-term indebtedness or short-maturity external capital inflows began to be viewed as a villainous variable. It became a crucial indicator of illiquidity as well as an important crisis predictor. The reversibility of short-maturity capital is exceedingly high. Using data from 33 middle-income developing economies, Dadush et al. (2000) computed the elasticity of short-term debt with respect to external shocks. They inferred that the elasticity of short-term debt with respect to GDP growth was 0.9 when there was a positive shock, and −1.8 when the shock was negative. Because of high reversibility, a negative shock exposes the short-term borrowers to liquidity runs and systemic risk. In view of the high risk, it has been proposed that reserve holdings should also be related to short-maturity debts, as a ratio between the two. Proponents of this view believe that this ratio will have a high utility in determining the adequacy level of reserves and predicting the financial soundness of an economy.

7.8 MONETARY AND CENTRAL BANKING CO-OPERATION

Monetary co-operation is a deceptively wide term covering a large spectrum of policy strands ranging from exchange of information among monetary authorities, a whole range of central banking functions in the management of currency, development of financial infrastructure, supervision of financial institutions, management of foreign exchange reserves, supervisory co-operation leading to standardization of supervisory practices, increasing international or intra-regional co-operation by increasing co-operation in provision of liquidity, to monetary co-operation for creating a monetary union.

Asia had benefited from growth with low inflation due to the monetary discipline imposed by the currency board and prudent fiscal policy, which were the legacy of the colonial era (discussed in the following section). This was the genesis of Asia's future disdain for fiscal profligacy. As Asian economies adopted the outer-oriented policies and developed into successful traders, their stable, dollar-linked, exchange rate became an anchor of high real GDP growth rate. The notion of an EU-like monetary co-operation was alien to them because they essentially traded in dollars with their large trading partners, which included European countries, the United States and the other regional economies.

Co-operation among central banks in Asia has had a changeable geometry. The first endeavor created for such co-operation in 1957 was SEANZA (South East Asia New Zealand Australia). It was the principal central bankers' forum, which had 18 Asia-Pacific economies as members. It provided intensive training to central bankers of the region. Second, established in Kuala Lumpur, Malaysia, in 1966, SEACEN (South East Asian Central Banks) was an identical entity that provided training, organized a range of seminars on central banking and supervision-related subjects and conducted research on period-specific relevant central banking themes (Refer to Chapter 3, Section 3.2.3 also). It had a membership of 11 Asian economies.[246] SEACEN also organizes annual meetings of heads of research and training of the member central banks. The training programs and workshops of SEACEN cover areas like banking supervision, financial market developments, monetary policy and payment systems. Its long-standing ties to bank supervision agencies inside and outside the region have made its courses and workshops well attended by professionals from the regional central banks. In 2000, SEACEN appointed an Expert Group to delve into capital flow, related data accumulation and data-sharing. This Expert Group entered into prolonged dialogue with the IMF on risk management approaches and with the BIS on using international financial statistics for monitoring external debt of varying maturities. The SEACEN has been endeavoring to raise the standard of data collection in the region through its training and research. It has undertaken major research projects on "External Debt: Concept and Monitoring for Crisis Prevention" in 2002 and "Managing and Monitoring the Direct Investment Portfolio Flows" in 2003 (McCauley, 2003).

The Asia Pacific Economic Co-operation (APEC) forum was launched in 1989 (Chapter 4, Section 4.5). The idea of creating a multilateral forum to enhance economic co-operation among Asia and Pacific economies was launched by Australian Prime Minister Bob Hawke. The concept was nurtured jointly by Australia and Japan. APEC had 12 members at the time of launching. Five of them were industrial economies (Australia, Canada, Japan, New Zealand and the United States), six ASEAN members (Indonesia, Malaysia, the Philippines, Singapore, Thailand and Brunei Darussalam) and Korea. Although the founding APEC members discussed trade and investment issues, monetary or central banking co-operation was only a marginal issue.

Breaking away from the past, the APEC members took an important step in 1991 by establishing the EMEAP (Executives' Meeting of East Asia-Pacific Central Banks). The Bank of Japan invited the eleven members of EMEAP for their first meeting to Tokyo.[247] Although initial meetings were devoted to exchange of information but gradually EMEAP evolved into a highly productive forum. The EMEAP began organizing high-level (deputy governors of central banks) meetings and hosted working groups on financial markets, central bank operations and prudentialvadjust supervision. This group of eleven also

---

[246] The 11-member central banks or monetary authorities are those from Indonesia, Korea, Malaysia, Mongolia, Myanmar, Nepal, the Philippines, Singapore, Sri Lanka, Taiwan and Thailand.

[247] The 11 central banks and monetary authorities that participated in EMEAP were those from Australia, China, Hong Kong SAR, Indonesia, Japan, Korea, Malaysia, New Zealand, Philippines, Singapore and Thailand.

included Australia and New Zealand. In 1991, three working groups were established under the EMEAP on (i) financial markets, (ii) banking supervision and (iii) payments systems. In a 2002 review, their operation was adjudged by Gordon de Brouwer (2002) as highly efficient. The strength of EMEAP is that it operates expertly with technical and broad policy issues. The flip side of this coin is that EMEAP has a large distance from the political decision-making process, which in turn results in its complete lack of political clout. It is presently an active forum of central bankers in the region, who participate in EMEAP activities through its six-monthly meeting of deputy governors and annual meeting of governors. Asian monetary co-operation became one of the important points of focus in EMEAP after the Asian crisis.

In January 1995, the Hong Kong Monetary Authority (HKMA) and the central banks of Indonesia, Malaysia and Thailand announced bilateral repurchase agreements of U.S. Treasury Bonds, of which the Asian economies own a massive amount (Section 7.7.1), designed to provide mutual exchange rate support. Singapore, the Philippines and Japan joined this network subsequently. The objective was to enhance the liquidity of the foreign reserves these economies hold. Gradually, all the eleven members of the EMEAP joined in this endeavor. This marked the beginning of monetary co-operation in Asia. In its annual meetings the EMEAP routinely appoints study groups and working groups to address relevant regional monetary issues. Three working groups have been established, on payment systems, financial market development and banking supervision.[248]

The BIS Working Party on Monetary Co-operation has been meeting annually since 1997. It gathers central bankers from Asia, and invites a handful from Europe and North America. A wide range of current regional monetary and central banking issues are discussed under the general guidance of the BIS. Parallel meetings are conducted by the BIS in other regions as well.

7.9 EVOLUTION OF EXCHANGE RATE REGIMES

Currency boards were the colonial legacy of Asian central banks, which provided stability by fixing the exchange rate to an international reserve currency, often the pound or the dollar.[249] During the post-War period, many Asian central

---

248 Executives' Meeting of East Asia-Pacific Central Banks (EMEAP) has a rich website. For more information please access http://www.info.gov.hk/hkma/gdbook/eng/e/emeap.htm.

249 A currency board is an institution that issues notes and coins convertible on demand and at a fixed rate into a foreign currency or other external "reserve" asset. Usually, a currency board does not accept deposits, though in certain cases it may accept those backed 100 percent by external reserves. As reserves, it holds high-quality, interest-bearing securities denominated in the reserve asset. Its reserve ratio is fixed at 100 percent or slightly more of its notes and coins in circulation,

banks evolved from this legacy. Pegged exchange rate regime was found suitable by the Asian economies in the post-war period because it was compatible with the development paradigm pursued by them. They pragmatically pegged their exchange rates at competitive levels, which also provided a nominal anchor to the domestic wages. Stability in wages contributed to profitability in exports and stimulated the early growth of low-wage, labor-intensive exports from Asia. Asian economies testify to the fact that competitive real exchange rate and stable nominal exchange promote investment and GDP growth. Stability in exchange rate was integral to the much-vaunted Asian Miracle.[250] Majority of the Asian economies have gone past this stage of development and old growth paradigm has outlived its profitability.

In the preceding chapter (Section 6.1), I had blamed inflexibility in the exchange rate regime for being one of the foremost policy villains that caused the Asian crisis. It was considered a systemic weakness of the affected economies. The crisis-stricken Asian economies discovered that when fixed exchanges rate fail, currency value misalignment can be large (Das, 1999, 2000a, 2000b). For the financial and monetary *mise-en-scene* of the twenty-first century—which is known for much higher global capital mobility as well as for more open capital accounts in the Asian economies than ever in the past—this exchange rate regime is considered fragile, if not totally inappropriate. While inflexibility in the exchange rate regime can have disastrous consequences, volatility can also leads to the same outcome. Recent research has revealed that volatility in exchange rate has a deleterious impact over both trade and growth rate and that stability in exchange rates, by instruments like a currency union, is good for the long-term performance of the economy.[251] A statistical association of trade with economic growth testifies to this fact. The causation runs through trade rather than macroeconomic influences. That is, if some kind of currency union is formed, exchange rate stability provides a substantial stimulus to trade of the member countries (Frankel and Rose, 2000).

Neither soft- nor hard-pegging the currency comes without its costs. By pegging policymakers lose an important monetary policy instrument, which

as set by law. The currency board makes profits from the difference between the interest on the securities that it holds and the expense of maintaining its note and coin circulation. The currency board has no discretion in monetary policy; market forces alone determine the quantity of notes and coins in circulation.

[250] In this context it needs to be recalled that the yen was also pegged to the dollar between the late 1940s and the early 1970s, which helped turn Japan into a dynamic and highly successful exporting economy (Das, 1992).

[251] For this reason MERCOSUR is seriously debating over the suitability of forming a currency union to achieve the objective of sub-regional exchange rate stability. Its full name is Mercado Comun del Sur, or the common market of the south. Its membership comprises Argentina, Brazil, Paraguay and Uruguay.

has both short- and log-term implications. In the short run, when fiscal policy is substituted for monetary policy, policymakers soon discover that the instrument they are using is a blunt one. In the long run, inflation becomes a built-in feature of the adoption of a hard peg. It is illustrated by Hong Kong SAR, which has had a higher inflation rate than it planned for. Second, cost of adopting a soft peg is speculative attacks at the time of realignment of the rate. Third, there is a high cost associated with the capital controls, which have to be resorted to at the time of financial distress. Whether they mitigate the crisis or not is dubious. A nuanced assessment is that they increase the frequency of currency crises and reduce the incidence of banking crises (Bordo et al., 2001). There is dissenting view, which need not be ignored. Some empirical studies have established that the significance of exchange and their stability has declined over the years. Exchange rate stability contributing to growth was truer in the past than at present. Rapidly growing countries do not subordinate their macroeconomic policies to the demand of maintaining stable exchange rate. Studies that quantified the growth effect of stable exchange rate concluded that this effect was the smallest for the Asian economies (Crosby and Otto, 2001; Moreno, 2001).

We saw in the above section the benefits and costs of exchange rate stability. For a country group or region like Asia that has substantial intra-trade, some degree of currency stability is highly desirable. From the trade and political economic perspective, the rules of the game must be transparent, clearly understood and verifiable by the member countries. Floating—free or managed—does not fit the bill (Reinhart, 2000). A region-wide solution needs to be attempted to resolve the currency volatility problem in periods of financial distress. Resurrecting the peg and thoughtfully pegging the Asian currencies to a basket of currencies that would limit intra-regional fluctuation is one worthy proposition, which has been taken up in Section 7.9.1 below.

7.9.1 Synchronizing exchange rate regimes

Although the EU-like coordination and synchronization of monetary policy and exchange rate regimes was widely considered to be premature in Asia in the past, this issue is increasingly beginning to be mulled over and being assigned a renewed importance. Until the onset of the Asian crisis, co-operation among the Asian economies on monetary, particularly exchange rate issues, was weak, sporadic and unstructured. There was a tradition of some exchange of information among monetary authorities, which was done annually and largely on bilateral basis. There was little policy coordination among the Asian economies. Many of them seemingly accepted in a passive manner the practice of relinquishing their sovereign right over their monetary policy to the central bank of their major trading partner, notably the United States. This was achieved by maintaining a stable exchange rate vis-à-vis the dollar. The Asian crisis changed this complacent situation for ever.

Supporting the early monetary co-operation endeavors, Robert Mundell (2001) argued that Asia is going to need a monetary co-operation that leads to common currency like the euro at some point in not-too-distant future. The Kobe Research Project (KRP), initiated during the third Asia-Europe Finance Ministers' conference in January 2001 is working on this important theme. The KRP was comprehensive, and comprised six technical studies on financial and monetary co-operation in Asia. Experts and institutions from Asia and Europe as well as multilateral institutions are involved in this research project. The first major study was on monetary and financial co-operation in Asia. The Finance Ministers' group also encouraged sharing of information and knowledge on regional economic and monetary co-operation, exchange rate regimes and public debt management. In addition, in March 2001 another study group was set up under the sponsorship of ASEAN for delving into currency and exchange rate mechanism for the ASEAN countries.

Co-operation and synchronization of exchange rate regimes need no longer be relegated to distant future as a long-term strategic priority in Asia. In the post-crisis economic milieu, an economic and monetary union and a euro-like currency need to be short-term policy targets for the Asian economies.[252] Based on openness, trade pattern, and nature of disturbance, Eichengreen and Bayoumi (1999) computed an optimum currency index for the Asian economies. They inferred that this index was not very different from that for the European economies before coming into force of the Maastricht Treaty (1993).[253] With the help of empirical studies, similar conclusions were also reached for the ASEAN economies. Furthermore these studies also contend that some of the conditions for successful economic and monetary integration are endogenous, that is, they fall into place after financial integration has been initiated (Bayoumi and Mauro, 1999; Plummer, 2001).

7.9.2 Post-crisis correction in exchange rate regimes

In the post-crisis era, it was believed that the Asian economic would attempt a region-wide resolution in the area of exchange rate regime, but it was not done. The post-crisis developments in this regard are not encouraging. First,

[252] In an economic and monetary union the member countries integrate their macroeconomic policies and have a common central bank and currency. The European Union (EU) is an example of an economic and monetary union.

[253] On December 1, 1991, agreement was reached in Maastricht on the Treaty on European Union, with a timetable for the Economic and Monetary Union (EMU). The European Single Market was completed on January 1, 1993. On November 1, 1993, the Maastricht Treaty came into force after Danes voted yes at the second try, and the EEC became the European Union (EU).

Table 7.1. Post-Crisis Exchange Rate Regimes in the APT Economies

Country	Regime
1. Brunei Darussalam	Currency-board peg to the Singapore dollar
2. Cambodia	Managed float
3. China	Pegged to the U.S. dollar
4. Indonesia	Float
5. Japan	Float
6. Lao PDR	Managed float
7. Malaysia	Fixed peg to the U.S. dollar
8. Myanmar	Fixed peg to the U.S. dollar
9. The Philippines	Float
10. Korea	Float
11. Singapore	Managed float
12. Thailand	Managed float
13. Vietnam	Managed float

Source: Wang and Andersen (2002).

Williamson (1999) and then Hernandez and Montiel (2001) were critical of inappropriate policy action on this front. As noted in Chapter 2 (Section 2.8) crisis caused Indonesia, Korea and Thailand to move in the direction of greater flexibility in their exchange rate regimes. Malaysia moved in the opposite direction and adopted a fixed exchange rate. The Philippines did not make any changes and retained its pre-crisis independent floating exchange rate regime (Table 7.1).

The bottom line in this regard is that most Asian economies have not made substantial changes in their exchange rate regimes. Currency regimes in the five crisis-affected and other Asian economies are still close to their old sub-optimal strategy by targeting nominal exchange rate stability vis-à-vis the dollar (Calvo and Reinhart, 2000; McKinnon, 2000). It seems that they learned little from the crisis in this important policy area. This mechanism was being followed in an informal and uncoordinated manner. The strategy for exchange rate stability, first, needs to be regionally coordinated and, second, should shift the target of nominal exchange rate stability from the dollar to a basket of three major currencies, namely, the euro, the U.S. dollar and the yen (Williamson 1999). Exchange rate stability of the Asian currencies against this basket has a much greater pay off because it is representative of trade and investment patterns of Asia. The proponents of the basket believe that "pegging to a basket will avoid disruptions to export competitiveness due to Group-of-Three (G-3) exchange rate fluctuations. An agreement on weights will limit intra-regional currency swings" (Eichengreen, 2001).

Although pegging to the basket may not be perfect, the proponents believe that it is better than the available alternatives. Floating exchange rates have proved to be volatile in Asia, which was damaging to the real economy. The alternative of benign neglect of exchange rate is also not feasible for economies with a fragile financial system and high levels of liability. Managing currency boards tends to be extremely difficult at the time of a crisis. Monetary unions are feasible and contribute to exchange rate stability but require a long preparatory phase (GOJ, 2001). A serious shortcoming with pegging to such a basket is that this arrangement comes without any institutional support. It solely relies on separate decisions by individual member countries and their central banks.

Currency stabilization against the euro–dollar–yen basket is sure to contribute to simultaneous stabilization of intra-regional exchange rates compatible with the medium-term policy objectives of stimulating trade, investment and economic growth in Asia. No rigid currency pegs are necessary for this purpose (Kawai and Takagi, 2003). Each Asian economy can choose its currency regime from a menu of currency board, a crawling peg regime or a basket peg with wide margins, and settled down with its own currency regime. Should a crisis strike, the peg can be suspended temporarily. However, once the recovery begins, the economy can return to its original regime. This arrangement appears to be a pragmatic interim option for Asia and could continue until the time when greater political will in the region leads to institutional developments that create an environment appropriate for a robust framework of an EU-like monetary and exchange rate co-operation. This interim currency regime can serve the purpose until that period comes.

7.10 LESSONS FROM THE EU EXPERIENCE

Over the post-war period, European economies experimented with different kind of exchange rate regimes, ranging from the European Payment Union (EPU), which was set up in 1950, to the European Monetary System (EMS), which was agreed upon in 1978 and launched in 1979.[254] The EMS was committed to exchange-rate stability in the member economies. As the EEC and subsequently the EU also grappled with these issues and against all expectations began to successfully implement the Maastricht Treaty[255] in 1993, should it not have some lessons for the Asian economies? Wyplosz (2001) has tried to answer this question. Conviction that exchange rate stability is crucial for economic integration lay behind the creation of the ERM. In keeping with this belief,

[254] Eight of the then nine members immediately became the members of the ERM.

[255] On December 1, 1991, agreement was reached in Maastricht on the Treaty on European Union, with a timetable for the Economic and Monetary Union (EMU). The European Single Market was completed on January 1, 1993. On November 1, 1993 the Maastricht Treaty came into force. A Euro Zone of eleven members came into being. Greece became the 12th member of the Euro Zone in January 2001. The single currency came into being in January 1999, when the Euro was launched.

the member economies acquiesced relinquishing the use of monetary policy for domestic purposes.[256] However, it cannot be overlooked that the European road to successful integration is littered with building of several pragmatic institutions. Two of the most important were the European Commission and the European System of Central Banks (ESCB). The Commission was created with the European Common Market (ECM) and became the repository of each grudging abandonment of national sovereignty by the members. The ECM represented their common interests, which was often at the expense of the national interests, and forced them to "behave in a collectively desirable manner." Likewise, the ESCB or Eurosystem decisions must contribute to the common good of the members and is restrained from working in their national interests. Although these institutions made vital contribution, European integration process has been regarded as slow. Wyplosz (2001) termed it "muddling through, two steps forward and one step backward, with deep and lingering divergences as to what the end objective is." Realistically assessed, any Asian integration process can take a comparable institutional development course, although it can be expected to move faster than the EU integration process. In the post-crisis era, Asia may well be on the brink of an EU-like evolution process.

It is widely agreed that the European Monetary Union (EMU) was made feasible by the presence of a strong currency and a large central economy among the members. Although it took several years, the deutsche mark emerged as the anchor currency within the EMS. In addition, the Bundesbank clearly displayed characteristics of a modern and successful central bank. Its commitment to the price stability objective was unambiguous, and it has a self-determining, stand-alone, monetary policy committee that was called the Dirktorium. China and Japan are the twin candidates for the pivotal role that Germany played in the EU, and so are their currencies. Of the two, Japan is a stronger candidate, but China's economic importance in Asia has been rising for some time. There could be a healthy rivalry or jealous competition between the two for the leadership role.[257]

---

[256] This had to be so because of the Mundellian trilemma. Since the early days of systematic economic analysis, economists have sought to understand how the openness of economies affects their responses to disturbances occurring both at home and abroad. Indeed, the 1999 Nobel Memorial Prize in Economics was presented to Robert A. Mundell in large part for his pioneering studies of the links among economic policy, monetary arrangements and the degrees of international capital and labor mobility. As textbooks reports, the Mundellian trilemma, or "impossible trinity" or "inconsistent trinity" has three policy strands: (i) free capital mobility, (ii) a fixed or stable nominal exchange rate and (iii) an autonomous monetary policy—only two of which can coexist at any point in time.

[257] The two contenders for the leadership position were in different economic and monetary circumstances. In 2004, Chinese and Japanese economies were at two opposite monetary extremes. While China reasonably apprehended inflation, Japan was fighting a strong deflationary trend. Chinese economy grew by 9.1 percent in 2003. But this heartening performance has stoked fears that the Chinese economy is overheating. If it was, it wouldn't have been the first time. China

What is essential is that their leadership—particularly that of Japan—is not perceived as threatening by the other members. Chinese leaders recently called on Japan for a joint leadership in the region, and for proactive collaboration to attain regional strategic goals (Yamazawa, 2004). Other than leadership, regional integration requires confidence-building measures and safety mechanisms. The EU experience demonstrates that they are slow to develop.

The CMI is the partial response to shortcoming of the pegging to the euro–dollar–yen basket. Mutual currency swaps among the member provide a defense against speculative runs. Together with a common basket bands, the CMI can work like the EMS, although there are two essential differences. First, the ERM of the EMS provided for unlimited support of bilateral pegs and, second, it is activated instantly as soon as a member currency demonstrates its need. It works as an effective deterrent to speculators. The message they read into this arrangement is that any isolated attack on one currency is foredoomed because the central bank of the large, central, economy is ready to download large amounts of currency. The Asian situation is different because the CMI arrangement is limited, and the capital market can mobilize much larger resources than the CMI swaps can provide for defense. The basket plus CMI, therefore, would not launch successful interventions in Asia like the EMS can in the EU.

The width of the band is another vital issue. It was expected that the euro–dollar-yen basket with a wide fluctuation band of ±15 percent, as proposed by Williamson (1999), would reduce the risk of speculative attacks. However, a wide band allows large fluctuation of 30 percent and with that the currency stability objective goes out of the window. Such a wide band would encourage higher tariff barriers among the member countries. It is harmful

has suffered from inflationary bouts before. Conversely, in 1994 Japan fell into a deflationary quagmire from which it had difficulty escaping. The GDP deflator, a broad measure of prices, has continued to fall by over 2 percent a year. While the Chinese authorities were acting to head off inflation, the Japanese authorities were actively seeking it. The Bank of Japan was pursuing a policy of "quantitative easing." It could not lower the price of money any further—nominal interest rates were already at zero—so it boosted the quantity of money in the economy instead. Over the 2002–03 period this policy had increased the monetary base by half. In January 2004, the central bank surprised the onlookers by increasing the money supply still further. Its objective was to flood the banking system with reserves of ¥30 trillion to ¥35 trillion ($280 billion to $330 billion), up from its previous target of ¥27 trillion-¥32 trillion. As opposed to this, in China the money supply was increasing, although much to the chagrin of the central bank. To maintain its currency peg, the People's Bank of China had to create enough renminbi yuan to satisfy foreign demand for the currency at the going rate of 8.3 yuan to the dollar. As a result, it was losing its grip on the amount of liquidity in circulation. Broad money was growing by around 20 percent a year. Bank lending is expanding in step. Investment in plant, equipment and other capital assets is growing at rates not seen since the runaway years of 1993–94. Inflation has edged up, from negative territory a year ago to 3.2 percent now (*The Economist,* 2004b).

for intra-regional trade. Furthermore, if it is crawling band to accommodate the Balassa–Samuelson effect, top-to-bottom movement can reach as high as 60 percent. For achieving stable bilateral parities in the region, this outcome is disappointing. Therefore, narrower fluctuation bands are more desirable. From the experience of the EMS one can learn that bilateral parities can be stabilized within narrower bands if they are supported by proper swap arrangements.

In such a backdrop, an economic and monetary union is the ideal arrangement because it not only provides the exchange rate stability but also does not need support by a swap arrangement. A monetary arrangement, however, requires deep economic integration and political commitment from the member countries. In addition, Asia should be ready to build institution comparable to the European Commission. Asian economies need to understand that a battery of agreements that erode national sovereignty and strengthen common regional interests are needed for a monetary union. Wyplosz (2001) pointed out that it would also call for "limits on public debts, the harmonization of banking regulation and supervision, seigniorage sharing rules, and provisions of lender-last-resort operations." To this end, creation of multilateral institutions, like the ESCB, is indispensable, which in turn would raise the prickly political questions of delegation of authority and accountability. Most important of all is the understanding regarding management of the common exchange rate among the regional members. It should, however, be noted that in a monetary union between a diverse group of economies, real exchange rates are unlikely to remain stable for a long time. Asymmetric shocks would always cause short-term variability in it. Besides, different stages and pace of development of the members is sure to lead to long-term variability in the exchange rate (Park and Wang, 2002).

Although Asia need not precisely replicate the European experience because its past and present economic and political circumstances are considerably different from those of Europe, it can take a lesson from the EU, take measured steps, build institutions, plan it own *mutatis mutandis* monetary union and brick-by-brick build it. Fifteen years—between the launching of the EMS and coming in effect of the Maastricht Treaty—were devoted by the European economies to co-operation, coordination and institution building. Asian economies could devote the same length of time for achieving a comparable objective. The CMI is only the beginning.

7.11 MONITORING AND SURVEILLANCE

Both the *Tequila* crisis of 1994–95 and the Asian crisis demonstrated how a contagion is transmitted through various channels to the neighboring economies.[258] A lesson from the Asian crisis and from that of the EU experiences is that the regional economy needs to be vigilantly monitored. In a globalizing financial world, an efficacious surveillance mechanism is *a fortiori* needed. Collaborative endeavors at the regional and global tiers are needed to counter negative spillover of shocks or externalities. Geographical proximity and structural similarities are among the transmission channels of contagion (Das, 2003b). As contagions have a stronger tendency to spread regionally, neighboring economies serve their self-interest in mutual surveillance and in assisting a neighbor when a contagious threat to stability is perceived (Glick and Rose, 1999). The IMF has traditionally provided this global public good.

The three essential elements of regional financial and monetary co-operation are liquidity support in distress situations, monitoring and surveillance and exchange rate stability. An early warning system would help spot the financial vulnerabilities of the region when they arise. As regional integration process progresses, monitoring and surveillance systems would gradually evolve. They can range from a simple system of exchange of information, to consultative fora, to supranational bodies like the EMU. As mutual interdependence increases and turns into integration, integrating member economies lay emphasis on identifying potential common problems and collaborate in resolving them. Peer pressure drives the members to mutually beneficial solutions of common financial and macroeconomic tribulations.

Rule-based penalties may be use for encouraging and enforcing policies that lead to common good. As Asian economies did not have the history of integrationist thinking like Europe, they do not seem to be politically prepared for imposing sanctions and fines against economies that are found to be non-compliant and do not adjust their national policies to reinforce regional good. When formal integration is attempted, this unwillingness and inability to impose politically unpopular decision over the regional economies is likely to create serious moral hazard problems (Wang, 2002). If a regional lender of the last resort comes into being at some point in time during the regional integration process, the moral hazard problem can be addressed by earnestly adhering to the classical Bagehot rule, that is, lending (i) freely to solvent borrowers, (ii) against good collateral, and (iii) at a penalty rate.

As Asia had traditionally followed market-led integration (Chapter 3), regional monitoring and surveillance had no place in it. Asian crisis changed this mindset and an intensive search for a monitoring and surveillance body began. The creation and role of MFG and ASP (or APTSP) has been discussed in this context (Section 7.1). Both of these meet periodically and perform formal

[258] The *Tequila* crisis started in Mexico in December 1994 and had a strong neighborhood effect. The contagion effect transmitted the crisis to several large and small Latin American economies. See Das (2003a) for a discussion on various channels that transmitted the contagion.

and informal monitoring and surveillance of the regional economies. Multilateral institutions—the IMF and the World Bank—collaborate with them in the surveillance process. The Asian Development Bank (ADB) supports the ASP by preparing the *ASEAN Economic Outlook*. With financial support from the Government of Australia, the ADB also created the Regional Economic Monitoring Unit (REMU) in 1999, which provides fairly weak surveillance of the APT economies. The Monitoring of REMU is far from comprehensive and low on analysis. The reason was poor-quality staffing of the REMU.

Acknowledging the inadequacy of monitoring and surveillance in Asia, the APT economies took initiative in this regard and the Finance Ministers from these countries decided to establish a Study Group in their Honolulu meeting on May 9, 2001. Its mandate was to explore ways for enhancing the effectiveness of the review and monitoring process. The APT Study Group report published in November 2001 *inter alia* concluded that the present monitoring is inadequate, has shortcomings and cannot work as an early warning system.[259] The report first stated the obvious weaknesses of the present monitoring and surveillance process, and that little progress has been made in creating an early warning system. Second, it recommended an agenda to be implemented in two stages. The first stage aimed at strengthening the existing process of policy review and policy dialogues. The second stage proposes a new mechanism for this purpose.

As vividly demonstrated by the EU experience, the monitoring and surveillance process is evolutionary in nature. A rising degree of regional integration would indeed call for an intensive and cohesive monitoring and surveillance process. The enthusiasm of the regional economies in creating such a process can only be high if they perceive that the future benefits will be commensurate with endeavors. There is no gainsaying the fact that creating an efficacious monitoring and surveillance mechanism, and running it in a thoroughly professional manner, would have far-reaching implications for Asia. It would make a substantive value-added contribution to the existing mechanisms. Its two principal objectives, namely, early warning system and crisis prevention, cannot be met without concerted endeavors in institution building by the APT economies.

The APT Study Group report made a proposal for an independent monitoring unit in Phase II. This unit will not only be a storehouse of current regional economic and financial data and information but also provide quick professional analyses for the individual and regional economies. Providing warning signals must be a high priority for the proposed unit. The role of the regional unit will expand in keeping with the progress in the future monetary co-operation measures in Asia. For instance, if CMI evolves progressively toward an AMF,

---

[259] The Study Group report was published in November 2001. Its title was *Possible Modalities to Enhance the Effectiveness of Economic Reviews and Policy Dialogue among the ASEAN+3 Countries*.

the role and scope of the proposed surveillance unit will need to be expanded substantially.

Following the May 2001 recommendations of the Finance Ministers of the APT economies, REMU began developing a regional early warning system (EWS) with the help of the IMF and Korea Center for International Finance in 2003. The proposed prototype had four principal components: (i) a set of macroprudential indicators (MPIs), (ii) a non-parametric EWS model, (iii) a parametric EWS model, and (iv) a set of leading economic indicators of business cycle. The MPIs, the first component, focused on the assessment of the health and stability of financial systems in a less formal and qualitative manner. In its endeavors to strengthen the surveillance process, the IMF has made enough progress on the development of MPIs. The other three components make use of statistical techniques and have more specific focuses. The objective of the non-parametric and parametric EWSs is to assess the probability of a currency crisis in a 24-month time horizon. The leading indicators of business cycle are intended to predict the turning points of the business cycle. The latter three components require high-frequency data for computation as well as long-term time series. Therefore, their utility is limited to economies where these are not available, that is, for Indonesia, Korea, Malaysia, the Philippines, Singapore and Thailand.

There are dissenting views regarding creation of EWS. Wang (2004) doubted its utility and contribution in providing a forewarning of an impending crisis. Selecting reliable indicators can be a slippery business because not all crises are alike. While one set of indicators may be useful for a particular crisis, it may not be so for another. Therefore, an EWS may lack credibility and be treated by investors and policymakers as a mere statistics collection exercise. Collecting reliable and current statistics is another possible weakness. The participating economies and supranational institutions in two existing surveillance groups, the MFG and APTSP with mandates for closely monitoring the regional economic and financial signals, had numerous disagreements regarding the focus of their surveillance process. They continued to keep talking at cross-purposes.

Creating a substantial surveillance unit with adequate professional and analytical skills and prowess would not be the end but the beginning. How to get regional members to implement the recommendations of the Finance Ministers of the APT is a thorny issue that peer pressure cannot always resolve. Taking a leaf from the EU experience can yield the desired results. Post-surveillance policy coordination has a two-tier structure in the EU. Accordingly, there are some common recommendations whose implementation is binding for all the EU members, while there are others whose implementation is only based on the discretion of the members. Monetary and exchange rate policies fall in the former category and their implementation is binding over the members for the common good of the EU. As opposed to this, economic policies (like budgetary and structural policies) come in the latter category and are treated as the sovereign right of each member state. However, broad economic policy guidelines are provided by the Board of Economic Policy Guidelines (BEPGs), which was a part of the Maastricht Treaty, and adopted in December 1993. The BEPGs are provided annually for the members. They have gone on becoming progressively specific from year to year. Members are encouraged to adhere to the annual BEPGs. This monitoring, surveillance and implementation process has brought a great deal of consistency to the EU member states. When the APT economies plan to accelerate their monetary integration process, they would do well to *mutatis mutandis* initiate a EU-like structured policy monitoring and implementation process. Monitory integration will not be able to progress without such a structured endeavor. At that point in time, serious capacity building endeavors will be needed at the regional level.

7.12 SUMMARY AND CONCLUSIONS

The Asian currency and financial crisis caused instability in currency values, and in many cases the depreciations were steep. The direction of the global capital flows in Asia reversed and the crisis-affected economies contracted. Two principal developments during and after the Asian crisis have made Asian economies accelerate their regional integration endeavors in the financial and monetary area. They were the disgruntlement of the Asian economies with the untimely and inadequate response of the supranational financial institutions and slow progress of reforms in the global financial architecture once the recovery took hold. These two developments were the *causae causantes* behind the accelerated interest in forming an Asian financial and monetary institution.

In response to the crisis, two top-level consultative groups were set up by the regional governments and the supranational institutions for exchange of information, regional monitoring and collaborative action. They were MFG and ASP, which later became APTSP. Their mandate was to coordinate and strengthen the policymaking process in the region. A bilateral support mechanism called the NMI was launched in October 1998 by the MOF, Japan. The objective of the bilateral support was to directly assist the crisis-affected economies. In May 1999, Japan's Minister of Finance announced the second phase of bilateral financial support measure under the NMI, under which the MOF—through the JBIC—was to partially guarantee government bonds issued by the crisis-affected economies. Also, a joint Japan—U.S. Asian Growth and Recovery Initiative (AGRI) was launched in November 1998.

Japan not only took initiative in proposing creation of an AMF in Bangkok, in September 1997, but also proposed to take lead and offered to have a large financial stake in it. The EU, the United States and the IMF were strongly and vocally opposed to the creation of the AMF. It was feared that AMF would duplicate what the IMF does and challenge its global leadership.

One of the many lessons of the Asian crisis was the need for a quick disbursing financial facility in periods of financial distress. Holding larger amounts of foreign exchange reserves is the direct and simplistic way out of speculative attacks, but maintaining high reserves has high costs. The proposed framework of financial and monetary co-operation and policy coordination was revisited in Chiang Mai, Thailand, in 2000, and the Finance Ministers of the APT countries agreed to create a formal swap arrangement among their central banks. This was named the Chiang Mai Initiative (CMI). Its first order of business was expansion of the multilateral ASEAN swap arrangement (ASA) from its original five members to all ten. Second, a network of bilateral swap arrangement (BSA) among the thirteen APT economies was created under the CMI.

A favorable development for the CMI is that the attitude of the multilateral institutions, particularly that of the IMF, has undergone considerable transformation since 2000. It received belated multilateral and bilateral acceptance. The ASA between the five founding members of ASEAN was set up in August 1977, with an objective of alleviating temporary liquidity shortages in the central banks of the member countries. At $200 million, the original size of the ASA facility was small. It was raised to $1 billion in November 2000. China and Japan favored linking of CMI with the IMF so that its credibility is enhanced, although Malaysia disagrees. They also favor linking BSAs to the IMF conditionality mechanism until CMI is able to develop its own formal regional monitoring and surveillance mechanism.

An immediate concrete measure that was taken early in the post-crisis period by both the crisis-affected Asian economies, and those that were only influenced by it, was dramatic augmentation in their foreign exchange reserves. These reserves were built up not only in absolute terms but also relative to imports and GDP. The elevated levels of reserves vis-à-vis import requirements or GDP appear excessive, have high opportunity cost and represent misallocation of financial resources. To be sure, maintenance of adequate reserves is important for maintenance of investors' confidence and managing pressures of the foreign exchange market.

Monetary co-operation among central banks in Asia has had a changeable geometry. The first endeavor created for such co-operation in 1957 was SEANZA. The APEC members took an important step in 1991 by establishing the EMEAP. The BIS Working Party on Monetary Co-operation has been meeting annually since 1997. It gathers central bankers from Asia, and invites a handful from Europe and North America.

For the contemporary financial and monetary environment, which is known for much higher global capital mobility as well as for more open capital accounts in the Asian economies than in the past, fixed exchange rate regime is considered fragile, if not totally inappropriate. While inflexibility in the exchange rate regime can have disastrous consequences, volatility can also leads to the same outcome. Recent research has revealed that volatility in exchange rate has a deleterious impact over both trade and growth rate and that stability in exchange rates, by instruments like a currency union, is good for the long-term performance of the economy. The post-crisis developments in this regard are not encouraging. Several observers were critical of inappropriate policy action on this front. Many Asian economies have been following their old sub-optimal strategy by targeting nominal exchange rate stability vis-à-vis the dollar. It seems that they learned little from the crisis in this important area.

The proponents of the basket believe that pegging to a basket will avoid disruptions to export competitiveness due to G-3 exchange rate fluctuations. An agreement on weights will limit intra-regional currency swings. Although pegging to the basket may not be perfect, the proponents believe that it is better than the available alternatives. Floating exchange rates have proved to be volatile in Asia, which was damaging to the real economy.

A lesson of the Asian crisis and from that of the EU experiences is that the regional economy needs to be vigilantly monitored. In a globalizing financial world, an efficacious surveillance mechanism is *a fortiori* needed. Collaborative endeavors at the regional and global tiers are needed to counter negative spillover of shocks or externalities. Geographical proximity and structural similarities are among the transmission channels of contagion.

REFERENCES

Aizenmann, J. and N. Marion. 2002, October. *The High Demand for International Reserves in the Far East: What's Going on?* Cambridge, MA: National Bureau of Economic Research. NBER Working Paper No. 9266.

Asami, T. 2001, September. "After the Chiang Mai Initiative," *News Letter*. No. 5. Tokyo: Institute for International Monetary Affairs.

Asia Policy Forum (APF). 2001. *Designing New and Balanced Financial Market Structures in Post-Crisis Asia*. Tokyo: Asia Policy Forum. Forum Secretariat. ADB Institute.

Bank for International Settlements (BIS). 2001. *71st Annual Report*. Basel, Switzerland: BIS.

Bayoumi, T. and P. Mauro. 1999. *The Suitability of ASEAN for a Regional Currency Arrangement*. Washington, DC: The International Monetary Fund. IMF Working Paper No. 99/162.

Bird, G. and R. Rajan. 2002a. "The Evolving Asian Financial architecture," in *Princeton Essays in International Economics*. No. 226. Princeton, NJ: Princeton University. International Economics Section.

Bird, G. and R. Rajan. 2002b. *Too Much of A Good Thing? The Adequacy of International Reserves in the Aftermath of the Crisis*. Discussion Paper No. 0210. Adelaide: Center for International Economic Studies. University of Adelaide.

Bordo. M.D., B.J Eichengreen, D. Klingebiel and M.S. Martinez-Peria. 2001. "Is the crisis problem growing more severe?" *Economic Policy*. Vol. 32. No. 1. pp. 53–82.

Calvo, G. and C. Reinhart. 2000, November. *Fear of Floating*. Cambridge, MA: National Bureau of Economic Research. NBER Working Paper No. 7993.

Council of Foreign Relations (CFR). 1999. *Safeguarding Property in a Global Financial System: The Future International Financial Architecture*. Washington, DC: CFR.

Christie, M. 2001. *Asian Monetary Fund Not a Bad Idea*. Available at: http://dailynew.yahoo.com/h/200108017/pl/economy_asia_usa_dc_1.html. Accessed August 17, 2003.

Crosby, M. and G. Otto. 2001. *Growth and Real Exchange Rate: Evidence from Eleven Countries*. Hong Kong: Hong Kong Institute of Monetary Research. Working Paper No. 8/2001.

Dadush, U., D. Dasgupta and D. Ratha. 2000. "The role of short-term debt in recent crises," *Finance and Development*. Vol. 37. No. 1. pp. 54–57.

Das, Dilip K. 2004a. *The Economic Dimensions of Globalization*. Houndmills, Hampshire, UK: Palgrave Macmillan.

Das, Dilip K. 2004b. *Financial Globalization and the Emerging Market Economies*. London and New York: Routledge.

Das, Dilip K. 2004c. *Regionalism in Global Trade: Turning Kaleidoscope*. Northampton, MA: Edward Elgar.

Das, Dilip K. 2003a. "Managing globalization: Macroeconomic, financial sector and exchange rate volatility," in Dilip K. Das (ed) *An International Finance Reader*. London and New York: Routledge. pp. 27–45.

Das, Dilip K. 2003b "Emerging market economies: Inevitability of volatility and contagion," *Journal of Asset Management*. Vol. 4. No. 3. pp. 22–40.

Das, Dilip K. 2001, January. "Stimulants to capital inflows into emerging markets and the recent role of speculators," *Journal of International Development*. Vo. 22. No. 1. pp. 26–56.

Das, Dilip K. 2000a. "Rejuvenating Asian exports," in Dilip K. Das (ed) *Asian Exports*. Oxford: Oxford University Press. pp. 383–412.

Das, Dilip K. 2000b, December. *Asian Crisis: Distilling Critical Lessons*. Geneva: United Nations Conference on Trade and Development (UNCTAD). Discussion Paper No. 152.

Das, Dilip K. 1999. *Asian Economic and Financial Crises: Causes, Ramifications and Lessons*. San Diego: Graduate School of International Relations and Pacific Studies. University of California. Available at: http://www-igcc.ucsd.edu/igcc2/asiancrisis/asianecon.htm. Accessed July 2004.

Das, Dilip K. 1992. *The Yen Appreciation and the International Economy*. London: The Macmillan Press; New York: New York University Press.

Day, P. and A.H.W. Choi. 2004. "Asia shifts its US dollar risk," *Report on Business, Globe and Mail*, Toronto. p. B10.

Disystat, P. 2001. *Currency Crises and Foreign Reserves: A Simple Model*. Washington, DC: International Monetary Fund. Working Paper No. 01/18.

The Economist, 2004b. "Inflated fears, deflated hopes." 22 January. Available at: http://www.economist.com/agenda/PrinterFriendly.cfm?Story_ID=2366669.

Eichengreen, B. 2002. "Whither monetary and financial co-operation in Asia?" paper presented at the *Second Annual Conference of PECC Finance Forum*, held in Hua Hin, Thailand, July 8–9.

Eichengreen, B. 2001. "Hanging together? On monetary and financial co-operation in Asia," paper presented at the World Bank, conference on *East Asia After the Crisis* in Washington, DC, October 12.

Eichengreen, B. 1999. "Strengthening the international financial architecture: Where do we stand?" paper presented at the East-West Center workshop on *International Monetary and Financial Reforms*, held at the University of Hawai'i, Honolulu, Hawai'i, October 1–2.

Eichengreen, B. and T. Bayoumi. 1999. "Is Asia an optimum currency area? Can it become one?" in S. Collignon, J.P. Ferry and Y.C. Park (eds) *Exchange Rate Policies in Emerging Asian Countries*. London and New York: Routledge. pp. 233–260.

Fischer, S. 2001, April 28. *Opening Remarks*. IMF/World Bank International Reserves, Policy Issues Forum. Washington, DC.

Flassbeck, H. 1999. "Asia urged to launch a joint financial surveillance body," *Kyodo News*. July 14. p. 6.

Frankel, J.A. and A.K. Rose. 2000. "An Estimate of Effects of Currency Unions on Trade and Growth". Cambridge, MA: National Bureau of Economic Research. Working Paper No. 7857.

Glick, R. and A. Rose. 2001, April. *Does a Currency Union Affect Trade? The Time Series Evidence*. (mimeo)

Glick, R. and A. Rose. 1999. "Contagion and trade: Why are currency crises regional?" *Journal of International Money and Finance*. Vol. 18. No. 4. pp. 603–617.

Government of Japan (GOJ). 2001."Exchange rate regime for emerging market economies," background paper prepared by French and Japanese Government officials for the ASEM Finance Minister meeting in Kobe, Japan, January. 16–17. Available at: http://www.mof.go.jp/english/asem/asem03i2.htm. April 5, 2004.

Hausmann, R., U. Panizza and E. Stein. 2000. *Why Do Countries Float the Way They Float?* Washington, DC: Inter-American Development Bank. Working Paper No. 418.

Heller, R. 1966."Optimal international reserves," *Economic Journal*. Vol. 76. No. 2.pp. 296–311.

Henning, R. C. 2002. "The case of regional financial co-operation in East Asia," paper presented at the Pacific Economic Co-operation Council (PECC) conference on *Issues and Prospects for Regional Co-operation for Financial Stability*, Honolulu, Hawai'i, October 11–13.

Hernandez, L. and P. Montiel. 2001. *Post Crisis Exchange Rate Policy in Five Asian Economies: Filling the Hollow Middle?* Washington, DC: International Monetary Fund. IMF Working Paper No. WP/01/170.

International Monetary Fund/World Bank (IMF/WB). 2001, September. *Developing Government Bond Markets: A Hand Book*. Washington, DC: IMF/WB.

Jeffrey, A.F. 2000. "Globalization of the Economy," Cambridge. MA. USA. National Bureau of Economic Research, Inc. NBER Working Papers 7858.

Kaminsky, G. L. and C.M. Reinhart. 2003. "On crisis, contagion and confusion," in Dilip K. Das (ed) *An International Finance Reader*. London and New York: Routledge. pp. 359–360.

Kawai, M. and S. Takagi. 2003, October. *Proposed Strategy for a Regional Exchange Rate Arrangement in East Asia*. Washington, DC: The World Bank. Policy Research Working Paper No. 2503.

Kawai, M., R. Newfarmer and S. Schmukler. 2001, February. *Crisis and Contagion in East Asia: Nine Lessons*. Washington, DC: The World Bank. (mimeo)

Keidanren, 2000. For Asia's Economic Renewal: A proposal by Japan's business community. Available at: http://www.keidanren.or.jp/english/policy/2000/007/proposal.html. Accessed March 13.

Kohler, H. 2001a, June 14. "Focusing the fund on financial stability," *Far Eastern Economic Review*. pp. 48–50.

Kohler, H. 2001b. *A Public-Private Partnership for Financial Stability*. Speech given at the spring meeting of the Institute of International Finance, Hong Kong, May 31.

Krugman, P. 1998, January. *What Happened to Asia?*. Massachusetts Institute of Technology. Unpublished paper.

Krugman, P. 1999. "The return of depression economics," *Foreign Affairs*. Vol. 78. No. 1. pp. 56–74.

Lin, C.L. and R.S. Rajan. 2001. "The economics and politics of monetary regionalism in Asia," *ASEAN Economic Bulletin*. Vol. 18. No. 1. pp. 103–139.

Lindgren, C., T. Balino, C. Enoch, A.M. Gulde, M. Quintyn and L. Teo. 1999. *Financial Sector Crisis and Restructuring: Lessons from Asia*. Washington, DC: International Monetary Fund. Occasional Paper No. 188.

Manupipatpong, W. 2002. "The ASEAN surveillance process and the East Asian monetary fund," *Economic Bulletin.* Vol. 19. No. 1. pp. 111–122.

McCauley, R.N. 2003. "Central bank co-operation in East Asia," paper presented at the *Second Annual Conference of PECC Finance Forum,* held in Hua Hin, Thailand, July 8–9.

McCauley, R.N. and H. Fung. 2003. "Choosing instruments in managing dollar foreign exchange reserves," *BIS Quarterly Review.* March. Vol. 2. pp. 39–46.

McKinnon, R.I. 2000. *After the Crisis, the East Asian Dollar Standard Reconstructed.* Stanford, CA: Stanford University. Available at: http://www-econ.stanford.edu/faculty/workp/swp00013.html. Accessed April 6, 2004.

Ministry of Finance (MOF). Government of Japan. 2002. *Japan's Support for Troubled Asian Neighbors.* Available at: http://www.mof.go.jp/English/qa/my001.htm. Accessed April 6, 2004.

Ministry of Finance (MOF). Government of Japan. 1999. *Japan's Support for Troubled Asian Neighbors Enters New Phase.* Available at: http://www.fpcj.jp/e/shiryo/jb/j9912.html. Accessed May 27.

Mishkin, F.S. 2001, January. *Financial Policies and the Prevention of Financial Crisis in Emerging Market Economies.* Cambridge,. MA: National Bureau of Economic Research. NBER Working Paper No. 8087.

Moreno, R. 2001. "Pegging and macroeconomic performance in East Asia," *ASEAN Economic Bulletin.* Vol. 18. No. 1. pp. 48–68.

Mundell, R. 2001. "Growth and international monetary system," paper presented at an Asian Development Seminar in Manila, February 12.

Park, Y.C. 2002, December. *Regional Financial Arrangements for East Asia: A Different Agenda.* Washington, DC: Latin American/Caribbean and Asia-Pacific Economics and Business Association. Working Paper No. 1.

Park, Y.C. 2000. "Beyond the Chiang Mai Initiative: Rationale and need for decision-making body and extended regional surveillance under the ASEAN+Three framework," paper presented at the meeting of the deputies of APT countries in Prague, the Czech Republic, September 24. (revised version November 2000).

Park, Y.C. and Y. Wang. 2002, September. *Can East Asia Emulate European Economic Integration?* Korea Institute of International Economic Policy. KIIEP Discussion Paper No. 02–09.

Persson, T. 2001. "Currency union and trade: How large is the treatment effect?" paper presented at the Economic Policy Panel meeting at Stockholm, April 5–6.

Plummer, M. 2001. "Monetary union and ASEAN," paper presented at the Australian National University-Kobe University International Conference on Trade and Monetary System in the Asia-Pacific at Kobe, Japan, February 3–4.

Radelet, S. and J. Sachs. 1998a, April. *The Onset of the East Asian Currency Crisis..* Cambridge, MA: National Bureau of Economic Research. NBER Working Paper No. 6680.

Radelet, S. and J. Sachs. 1998b. "The East Asian financial crisis: Diagnosis, remedies, prospects," *Brookings Papers on Economic Activity.* No. 1, pp. 1–74.

Radelet, S. and J. Sachs.1999, March. *What Have We Learned So Far From the Asian Financial Crisis?* Cambridge, MA: Harvard Institute of International Development. CAER Discussion Paper No. 37.

Rajan, R.S. 2002, October. *Examining the Links Between Trade and Monetary Regionalism*". Adelaide, Australia: University of Adelaide. (unpublished paper). Available at: http://www.ips.org.sg/pub/kishen/pa_kishen_Examining%20The%20Links%20Between%20Trade%20And%20Monetary%20Regionalism.pdf. April 10, 2004.

Rajan, R.S. 2000. *Examining the Case for an Asian Monetary Fund.* Adelaide: Center for International Economic Studies. University of Adelaide. Policy Discussion Paper No. 0002.

Reinhart, C.M. 2000. "The mirage of floating exchange rate," *American Economic Review.* Vol. 90. No. 2. pp. 65–70.

Rose, A. 1999. "Is there a case for an Asian Monetary Fund?" *FRBSF Economic Bulletin.* Vol. 30. No.4. pp. 37–62.

Rose, A.K. 2000. "One money, one market: Estimating the effect of common currencies on trade," *Economic Policy.* Vol. 15. No. 1. pp. 7–46.

Rose, A. and C. Engel. 2000. *Currency Unions and International Integration.* Cambridge, MA: National Bureau of Economic Research. NBER Working Paper No. 7872.

Shinohara, H. 1999, August. "On the Asian Monetary Fund," *News Letter.* No. 4. Tokyo: The Institute for International Monetary Affairs.

Triffin, R. 1947. "National central banking and international economy," *Review of Economic Studies.* Vol. 32. No. 1. pp. 122–140.

Wade, R. and F. Venoroso. 1998. "The resources lie within," *The Economist.* November 7. pp. 19–21.

Wang, Y. 2003. "Prospects for financial and monetary co-operation in Asia," paper presented at the international Conference on *Building New Asia: Towards An Asian Economic Community,* organized by the Research and Information System for the Non-Aligned and Other Developing Countries in New Delhi, March 10–11.

Wang, Y. 2002. "Monetary and financial co-operation in East Asia," paper presented at a symposium on *Asian Economic Integration* organized by the United Nations University in Tokyo, April 22–23, 2002.

Wang, Y. 2004. *Prospects for Financial and Monetary Co-operation in East Asia.* Seoul: Korea Institute for International Economic Policy. Discussion Paper No. 02–04.

Wang, S.D. and L. Andersen. 2002. "Regional financial co-operation in East Asia: The Chiang Mai Initiative and beyond," *Bulletin on Asia-Pacific Perspective.* Vol. 8. No. 3. pp. 89–99.

Williamson, J. 1999. "The case for a common basket peg for East Asian currencies," in S. Collignon, J. Pisani-Ferry and Y.C. Park (eds) *Exchange RaTE policies in Emerging Asian Countries.* London: Routledge. pp. 327–344.

World Trade Organization (WTO). 2003. *The Challenging Landscape of RTAs.* Geneva: WTO. Available at: http://www.wto.org/english/tratop_e/region_e/region_e.htm. Accessed April 11, 2004.

Wyplosz, C. 2001. "A monetary union for Asia? Some European lessons," in D.Gruen and J. Simon (eds) *Future Directions of Monetary Policy in East Asia.* Sydney: Reserve Bank of Australia. pp. 124–155.

Yamazawa, I. 2004. *Japan and the East Asian Economies.* Tokyo: IDE-APEC Study Center. Working Paper Series. No. 01.

Yoshitomi, M. and S. Shirai. 2000, October. *Technical Paper for Policy Recommendation on Prevention of Another Capital Account Crisis.* Tokyo: The ADB Institute.

Ziegler, D. 2003. "The weakest link: A survey of Asian finance," *The Economist.* February 8. After p. 52.

BIBLIOGRAPHY

Abu-Lughod, J. 1989. *Before European Hegemony: The World system A.D. 1250–1350.* New York: Oxford University Press.

Ahmed, S. 2004. "Behind the mask: Survey of business in China," *The Economist.* March 20. After p. 60.

Aizenmann, J. and N. Marion. 2002, October. *The High Demand for International Reserves in the Far East: What's Going On?* Cambridge, MA: National Bureau of Economic Research. NBER Working Paper No. 9266.

Akamatsu, K. 1961. "A theory of unbalanced growth in the world economy," *Weltwirtschaftliches Archiv.* Vol. 86. No. 1. pp. 56–68.

Akita, S. 1999. "British informal empire in East Asia, 1880–1939: A Japanese perspective," in R.E. Dumett (ed) *Gentlemanly Capitalism and British Imperialism: The New Debate on the Empire.* New York: Addison Wesley Longman. pp. 141–159.

Anderson, K. 1993. "European integration in the 1990s: Implications for world trade and for Australia," in D.G. Mayes (ed) *External Implications of European Integration.* London: Harvester Wheatsheaf. pp. 120–148.

Anderson, K. and H. Norheim.1993. "History, geography and regional economic integration," in K. Anderson and R. Blackhurst (eds) *Regional Integration and the Global Trading System.* Hertfordshire, UK: Harvester Wheatsheaf. pp. 19–51.

APEC Business Advisory Council (ABSC). 2003, October 21. *The First Decade Since Bogor: A Business Assessment on APEC's Progress.* Bangkok, Thailand.

Ariff, M. 2000. "Trade, investment and interdependence," in S.S. Tay, J. Estanislao, and H. Soesastro (eds) *A New ASEAN in A New Millennium.* Jakarta: Center for Strategic International Studies. pp. 110–133.

Arndt, S.W. 1969. "Customs union and theory of tariffs". *American Economic Review.* Vol. 59. No. 1. pp. 108–118.

Arndt, S.W. and H. Kierzkowski. (eds) 2001. *Fragmentation: New Production Patterns in the World Economy.* Oxford: Oxford University Press.

Arrighi, G., T. Hamashita and M. Selden. 2003. "The rise of East Asia in regional and world historical perspective" in G. Arrighi, T. Hamashita and M. Selden (eds) *The Resurgence of East Asia.* London and New York: Routledge. pp. 1–16.

Asami, T. 2001, September. "After the Chiang Mai Initiative," *News Letter*. No. 5. Tokyo: Institute for International Monetary Affairs.

Asia-Pacific Economic Co-operation (APEC). 1999, September. *Assessing APEC Trade Liberalization and Facilitation.* Singapore: APAC Secretariat. APEC Economic Committee.

Asia-Pacific Economic Co-operation (APEC). 2002, August. *APEC Strengthens Peer review Process for Achieving Open Trade and Investment.* Singapore. Media Release 21.

Asia Policy Forum (APF). 2001, October. *Designing New and Balanced Financial Market Structures in Post-Crisis Asia*. Tokyo: Asia Policy Forum. Forum Secretariat. ADB Institute. (Processed)

The Asian Banker's Association (ABA). 2003. "The regulatory and business environment for risk management practices in the banking sector of APEC economies," conducted in collaboration with the Pacific Economic Cooperation Council (PECC), and the Chinese Taipei Pacific Economic Cooperation Committee (CTPECC). Circulated at the Second Annual Conference of PECC Finance Forum, Hua Hin, Thailand, July 8–9, 2003.

The Asian Development Bank (ADB). 1999. *Compendiums of Sound Practices Guidelines to Facilitate the Development of Domestic Bond market.* Manila.

The Asian Development Bank (ADB). 2000, September. *Asian Development Outlook 2000: Update,* Manila.

The Asian Development Bank (ADB). 2001. *Asian Development Outlook 2003.* Hong Kong: Oxford University Press.

The Asian Development Bank (ADB). 2003. *Asian Development Outlook 2003.* Hong Kong: Oxford University Press.

The Asian Development Bank. 2004. *Asian Development Outlook 2004.* Hong Kong: Oxford University Press.

The Asian Wall Street Journal (AWSJ). 2000. "Free trade in trouble: Kuala Lumpur wrecks a consensus within ASEAN," Hong Kong. October 12. p. 12.

The Asian Wall Street Journal (AWSJ). 2003. "Japan proposes regional market for regional bonds," Hong Kong. March 3.

Association of Southeast Asian Nations (ASEAN). 2000. *Approved AICO Applications*. Jakarta: ASEAN Secretariat. Available at: http://www. aseansec.org/menu.asp?action=4&content=9.

Bairoch, P. 1981. "The main trends in national economic disparities since the industrial revolution," in P. Bairoch and M. Levy-Leboyer (eds) *Disparities in Economic Development Since the Industrial Revolution.* London: The Macmillan Press. pp. 3–17.

Bairoch, P. 1993. *Economics and World History: Myths and Paradoxes.* Chicago: University of Chicago Press.

Balassa, B. 1978. "Exports and economic growth: Further evidence," *Journal of Development Economics.* Vol. 5. No. 1. pp. 181–189.

Balasa, B. and J. Williamson. 1990. *Adjusting to Success: Balance of Payments Policies in the East Asian Economies*. Washington, DC: Institute of International Economics.

Bank for International Settlements (BIS). 2001. *71st Annual Report.* Basel. Switzerland: Bank for International Settlements.

Bardhan, P. 2002. "Disjuncture in the Indian reform process: Some reflections," paper presented at *The Indian Economy Conference,* Cornell University, Ithaca, New York, April 19–20.

Barth, J.R., G. Caprio and R. Levine. 2001, February. *The Regulation and Supervision of Banks around the World: A New Database*. Washington, DC: The World Bank (mimeo).

Basle Committee on Banking Supervision (BCBS). 2000, September. *Principles for the Management of Credit Risk.* Basle: Bank for International Supervision.

Basle Committee on Banking Supervision (BCBS). 2001, January. *The New Basle Capital Accord: An Explanatory Note.* Basle: Bank for International Supervision.

Basle Committee on Banking Supervision (BCBS). 2002, July. *An Overview of the New Basle Capital Accord*. Basle: Bank for International Supervision.

Bayoumi, T. and P. Mauro.1999. *The Suitability of ASEAN for a Regional Currency Arrangement.* Washington, DC: The International Monetary Fund. IMF Working Paper No. 99/162.

Beasley, W.G. 1987. *Japanese Imperialism, 1894–1945.* Oxford: Clarendon Press.

Bennett, M.K. 1954. *The World Food: A Study of the Inter-relations of World Populations, National Diets, and Food Potentials.* New York: Harper.

Bernard, M. and J. Ravenhill. 1995, January. "Beyond production cycles and flying geese: Regionalization, hierarchy, and industrialization of East Asia," *World Politics.* Vol. 47. pp. 171–209.

Bhagwati, J.N. and T.N. Srinivasan.1999. *Outward Orientation and Economic Development: Are Revisionists Right?* Available at: http://www.columbia.edu/~jb38/Krueger.pdf. Accessed September 17.

Bird, G. and R. Rajan. 2002a. *Princeton Essays in International Economics.* No. 226. Princeton: Princeton University. International Economics Section.

Bird, G. and R. Rajan. 2002b. *Too Much of A Good Thing? The Adequacy of International Reserves in the Aftermath of the Crisis.* Discussion Paper No. 0210. Adelaide: University of Adelaide. Center for International Economic Studies.

Birkinshaw, J. 2001. "Strategy and management in MNEs subsidiaries," in A.M. Rugman and T. Brewer (eds) *Oxford Handbook of International Business.* Oxford: Oxford University Press. pp. 134–160.

Bordo. M.D., B.J. Eichengreen, D. Klingebiel and M.S. Martinez-Peria. 2001. "Is the crisis problem growing more severe?" *Economic Policy.* Vol. 32. No. 1. pp. 53–82.

Borrus, M., D. Ernst and S. Haggard (eds). 2000. *International Production Networks in Asia.* London and New York: Routledge.

Bouchon, G. 1999. "Trade in the Indian Ocean at the dawn of the sixteenth century," in S. Chaudhury and M. Morineau (eds) *Merchants, Companies and Trade: Europe and Asia in the Early Modern Era.* Cambridge: Cambridge University Press.

Braga, C., A. Primo, R. Safadi and A. Yeats. 1994, October. *NAFTA's Implications for East Asian Exports.* Washington, DC: World Bank. Policy Research Working Paper No. 1351.

Braudel, F. 1984. *Civilization and Capitalism; 15th to 18th Century.* Vol. III: *The Perspectives of the World.* London: Collins.

Braudel, F. 1992. *Civilization and Capitalism; 15th to 18th Century Vol. III: The Perspectives of the World.* Berkeley: University of California Press.

Bray, F. 1986. *Rice Economics: Technology and Development in Asian Societies.* Oxford: Basil Blackwell.

Calderón, C., S. Loayza and L. Servén. 2004, January. *Greenfield Foreign Direct Investment and Mergers and Acquisitions: Feedback and Macroeconomic Effects.* Washington, DC: The World Bank. Working Paper 3192.

Calvo, G. and C. Reinhart. 2000, November. *Fear of Floating.* Cambridge, MA: National Bureau of Economic Research. NBER Working Paper No. 7993.

Carruthers, R. and J.N. Bajpai. 2002. *Trends in Trade Logistics: An Asian Perspective.* Washington, DC: The World Bank. Transport Sector Unit. Working Paper No. 2.

Carruthers, R., J.N. Bajpai and D. Hummels. 2003. "Trade and logistics: An East Asian perspective," in K. Krumm and H.J. Kharas (eds) *East Asia Integrates: A Trade Policy Agenda for Shared Growth.* Washington, DC The World Bank. pp. 117–139.

Cecchini, P. 1998. *1992, The European Challenge: The Benefits of a Single Market.* London: Aldershot and Hants.

Cernat, L. 2001. *Assessing Regional Trade Agreement: Are South-South RTAs More Trade Diverting?* Geneva: United Nations Conference on Trade and Development. Study Series. No. 16.

Chen, T. and Y.H. Ku. 2000. "Globalization of Taiwan's small firms: The role of Southeast Asia and China," paper presented in a symposium on *Experiences and Challenges of Economic Development in Southeast and East Asia,* Taipei. October.

Chen, S. and M. Ravallion. 2004. *How Have the World's Poorest Fared since the Early 1980s?* Washington, DC: The World Bank. Available at: http://www.worldbank.org/research/

povmonitor/MartinPapers/How_have_the_poorest_fared_since_the_early_1980s.pdf. Accessed April 20.

Cheow, E.T.C. 2002. "Economic and monetary co-operation in Asia: An ASEAN perspective," paper presented at the Euro-Asia Conference organized by the Japan Center of International Finance, Tokyo, May 23–24.

Chia, S.Y. 1997, October 29. *ASEAN: 30 Years of Existence and Challenges Ahead.* Seoul: Korea Institute for International Economic Policy.

Chia, S.Y. 2002. "East Asian regionalism," paper presented at the conference on *East Asian Cooperation: Progress and Future Agenda,* organized by the Institute of Asia-Pacific Studies and Center for APEC and East Asian Cooperation, Beijing, August 22–23.

Christie, M. 2001. *Asian Monetary Fund Not a Bad Idea.* Available at: http://dailynew.yahoo.com/h/200108017/pl/economy_asia_usa_dc_1.html. Accessed August 17.

Clark, C. 1977. *Population Growth and Land Use.* London: The Macmillan Press Ltd.

Cotis, J.P. 2003. "Towards sustainable economic growth in Japan: The new mix of monetary and fiscal policies," presentation made at the Policy Research Institute, Ministry of Finance, Tokyo, June 23.

Council of Foreign Relations (CFR). 1999. *Safeguarding Property in a Global Financial System: The Future International Financial Architecture.* Washington, DC.

Cox, D. and R. Harris. 1992. "North American free trade and its implications for Canada: Results from a CGE model of North American trade," *World Economy.* Vol. 15. No. 1. pp. 31–44.

Crafts, N. and A. Venables. 2001. *Globalization in History: A Geographical Perspective.* London: Center for Economic Policy Research. CEPR Discussion Paper 3079.

Credit Swiss First Boston (CSFB). 2000. *Emerging Market Quarterly: Asia Q1:2001.* Hong Kong. 15 December.

Crosby, M. and G. Otto. 2001. *Growth and Real Exchange Rate: Evidence from Eleven Countries.* Hong Kong: Hong Kong Institute of Monetary Research. Working Paper No. 8/2001.

Dadush, U., D. Dasgupta and D. Ratha. 2000. "The role of short-term debt in recent crises," *Finance and Development.* Vol. 37. No.1. pp. 54–57.

Das, Dilip K. 1991. *Korean Economic Dynamism.* London: The Macmillan Press.

Das, Dilip K. 1992. *The Yen Appreciation and the International Economy.* The London: Macmillan Press; New York: New York University Press.

Das, Dilip K. 1996. *The Asia-Pacific Economy.* London: The Macmillan Press Ltd; New York: St. Martin's Press.

Das, Dilip K. 1996. "Asian exports, not so bad," *The Asian Wall Street Journal.* *<QA>*

Das, Dilip K. 1997 *The Future of Asian Exports.* Singapore and London: Financial Times Business.

Das, Dilip K. 1998. "Changing comparative advantage and changing composition of Asian exports," *The World Economy.* Vol. 21. No. 1. pp. 121–140.

Das, Dilip K. 1999. *Asian Economic and Financial Crises: Causes, Ramifications and Lessons.* San Diego, CA: Graduate School of International Relations and Pacific Studies. University of California. Available at: http://www-igcc.ucsd.edu/igcc2/asiancrisis/asianecon.htm. Accessed June. 1999.

Das, Dilip K. 2000. "Rejuvenating Asian exports," in Dilip K. Das (ed) *Asian Exports.* Oxford: Oxford University Press. pp. 383–412.

Das, Dilip K. 2000. "Asian exports: The present predicament," in Dilip K. Das (ed) *Asian Exports.* Oxford: Oxford University Press. pp. 1–24.

Das, Dilip K. 2000. *Asian Crisis: Distilling Critical Lessons* Geneva: United Nations Conference on Trade and Development (UNCTAD). Discussion Paper No. 152. 33 pp.

Das, Dilip K. 2000. "An action agenda for the next WTO round: A post-Seattle perspective," *The Journal of World Intellectual Property.* Vol. 3. No. 5. pp. 7370–773.

Das, Dilip K. 2001. "Stimulants to capital inflows into emerging markets and the recent role of speculators," *Journal of International Development.* pp. 84–106.

Das, Dilip K. 2001. "Corporate governance and restructuring: A post-crisis Asian perspective," *The Asia Pacific Journal of Economics and Business.* Vol. 14. No. 2. pp. 98–112.

Das, Dilip K. 2001. *The Global Trading System at Crossroads*. London and New York: Routledge.

Das, Dilip K. 2001. "Liberalization efforts in China and accession to the World Trade Organization," *The Journal of World Investment.* Vol. 2. N0. 4. pp. 761–789.

Das, Dilip K. 2001. "Liberalization efforts in China and accession to the World Trade Organization," *The Journal of World Investment.* Vol. 10. No. 6. pp. 44–75.

Das, Dilip K. 2001. *China's Accession to the World Trade Organization: Issues and Implications,* Australian National University. Asia Pacific School of Economics and Management. Canberra. Working Paper No. EA01-1. Available at: http://ncdsnet.anu.edu.au. Accessed July 2001.

Das, Dilip K. 2003. "Managing globalization: macroeconomic, financial sector and exchange rate volatility," in Dilip K. Das (ed) *An International Finance Reader*. London and New York: Routledge. pp. 27–45.

Das, Dilip K. 2003. "Emerging market economies: Inevitability of volatility and contagion," *Journal of Asset Management.* Vol. 4. No. 3. pp. 22–40.

Das, Dilip K. 2003. "Emerging market economies: Inevitability of volatility and contagion," *Journal of Asset Management.* Vol. 4. No. 3. pp. 199–216.

Das, Dilip K. 2003. "Emerging market economies: Inevitability of volatility and contagion," *Journal of Asset Management.* Vol. 4. No. 3. pp. 134–152.

Das, Dilip K. 2004. *Regionalism in Global Trade*. Northampton, MA: Edward Elgar.

Das, Dilip K. 2004. *The Economic Dimensions of Globalization.* Houndmills, Hampshire, UK: Palgrave Macmillan Ltd.

Das, Dilip K. 2004. *Financial Globalization and the Emerging Market Economies.* London and New York: Routledge.

Day, P. and A.H.W. Choi. 2004, "Asia shifts its US dollar risk," *Report on Business, Globe and Mail,* Toronto, Ontario, Canada. p. B10.

Deardorff, A. 2001. "International provision of trade services, trade and fragmentation," *Review of International Economics.* Vol. 9. No. 2. pp. 233–248.

de Brouwer, G. 2003. "Financial markets, institutions and integration in East Asia," *Asian Economic Papers.* Vol. 2. No. 1. pp. 96–120.

de Brouwer, G. and J. Corbett. 2003. *A New Financial Market Structure for East Asia*. Australian National University. Asia-Pacific School of Economics and Government. Canberra (unpublished manuscript).

de Brouwer, G. 2002. "PECC survey of regional arrangements for financial cooperation," paper presented to PECC Finance Forum meeting in Honolulu, Hawai'i, August 12

de Brouwer, G. 2002. "Does a formal common-basket peg in East Asia make economic sense?" in G. de Brouwer (ed.) *Financial Markets and Policies in East Asia.* London and New York: Routledge.

De Gregorio, J. and R.O. Valdes. 2001. "Crisis transmission: Evidence from the debt, Tequila and Asian flu crises," *World Bank Economic Review.* Vol. 15. No. 2. pp. 289–314.

De Melo, J. and A. Panagariya. 1992. *The New Regionalism in Trade Policy*. London: Center for Economic Policy Research.

Demirguc-Kunt, A. and R. Levine. 2001. "Bank-based and market-based financial system: Cross-country comparisons," in A. Demirguc-Kunt and R. Levine (eds) *Financial Structure and Economic Development.* Cambridge, MA: The MIT Press. pp. 81–140.

Denison, C. and P. Chung. 1976. "Economic growth and its sources," in H. Patrick and H. Rosovsky (eds) *Asia's New Giant.* Washington, DC: The Brookings Institution. pp. 94–122.

Department of Foreign Affairs and International Trade (DFAT). 2001. *APEC Progress on Tariffs: Implications for a New Agenda.* Canberra: Commonwealth of Australia.

DeRosa, D.A. 1995. *Regional Trading Arrangements Among Developing Countries: The ASEAN Example.* Research Report 103. Washington, DC: International Food Policy Research Institute.

Disystat, P. 2001. *Currency Crises and Foreign Reserves: A Simple Model.* Washington, DC: International Monetary Fund. Working Paper No. 01/18.

Dollar, D. 1993. "Outward-oriented developing countries really do grow more rapidly: Evidence from 95 LDCs," *Economic Development and Cultural Change.* Vol. 40. No. 3. pp. 523–544.

Drysdale, P. and Y. Huang. 1997. "Technological catch-up and economic growth in East Asia and the Pacific," *Economic Records.* Vol. 73. No. 2. pp. 201–211.

The Economist. 2000. "Asian economies: Happy neighbors," August 26. p. 71.

The Economist. 2001. "Enter the dragon," March 10. pp 21–24.

The Economist. 2003. "Two systems, one grand rivalry," June 21. pp. 21–23.

The Economist. 2003. On a Roll. Available at: http://www.economist.com/agenda/displaystory.cfm?story_id=1872018. Accessed June 27.

The Economist. 2004. "Cheap money, pricey oil," Available at: http://www.economist.com/agenda/displaystory.cfm?story_id=2682614. Accessed May 15.

The Economist, 2004. "Japanese debt: End in sight," February 14. pp. 67–68.

The Economist. 2004. "Still made in Japan," April 10. pp. 57–59.

The Economist. 2004. "Banking in South-East Asia: Recuperating,". May 1, pp. 78–79.

The Economist. 2004. "Better, not well," May 29. p. 74.

The Economist. 2004. "Business as usual," February 14. p. 70.

The Economist, 2004. "Inflated fears, deflated hopes," Available at: http://www.economist.com/agenda/PrinterFriendly.cfm?Story_ID=2366669. Accessed January 22.

The Economist Intelligence Unit (EIU). 2003. *Europe Enlarged: Understanding the Impact.* London: EIU.

The Economic Intelligence Unit (EIU). 2003. *Leaping Dragon, Trailing Tigers? Taiwan Hong Kong and the Challenge of Mainland China.* London: EIU.

The Economic Intelligence Unit (EIU). 2004. *China's Real GDP Forecast.* Available at: http://english.peopledaily.com.cn/200301/25/print20030125_110713.html.

The Economic Intelligence Unit (EIU). 2004, June. *World Investment Prospects.* London: EIU,

The Economist Intelligence Unit ViewsWire (EIU). 2004. *China: Economic Analysis.* London. Available on the Internet at http://www.viewswire.com/index.asp?layout=display_print&doc_id=374521. Accessed May 8.

Eckholm, E. and J. Kahn. 2002. "Asia worries about growth of China's economic power," *The New York Times.* November 24. p. 10.

Edwards, S. 1992. "Trade orientation, distortion and growth in developing countries," *Journal of Development Economics.* Vol. 39. No. 1. pp. 31–57.

Edwards, S. 1993. "Openness, trade liberalization and growth in developing countries," *Journal of Economic Literature.* Vol. 31. No. 3. pp. 1358–1303.

Eichengreen, B. 1999. "Strengthening the international financial architecture: Where do we stand?" paper presented at the East-West Center workshop on *International Monetary and Financial Reforms,* University of Hawai'i, Honolulu, Hawai'i, October 1–2.

Eichengreen, B. 2001. "Hanging together? On monetary and financial cooperation in Asia," paper presented at the World Bank, conference on *East Asia After the Crisis,* Washington, DC., October 12.

Eichengreen, B. 2002. "Whither monetary and financial cooperation in Asia?" paper presented at the *Second Annual Conference of PECC Finance Forum,* Hua Hin, Thailand, July 8–9.

Eichengreen, B. and T. Bayoumi. 1999. "Is Asia an optimum currency area? Can it become one?" in S. Collignon, J.P. Ferry and Y.C. Park (eds) *Exchange Reate Policies in Emerging Asian Countries.* London and New York: Routledge. pp. 233–260.

Elek, A. and H. Soesastro. 2000. "Ecotech At the heart of the APEC: Capacity building in Asia-Pacific," in I. Yamazawa (ed) *Asia-Pacific Economic Co-operation: Challenges and Tasks for the Twenty-First Century.* London and New York: Routledge. pp. 218–254.

Endo, T. 2001. "Corporate bond market development," in *Bond Market Development in Asia.* Paris: Organization for Economic Cooperation and Development. pp. 237–296.

Evans, D. 1998. *Options for Regional Integration in Southern Africa.* Sussex: Institute of Development Studies. IDS Working Paper No. 94.

Executives' Meeting of East Asia-Pacific Central Banks (EMEAP). 2003. *EMEAP Central Banks to Launch Asia Bond Fund.* Available at: http://www.emeap.org:8084. Accessed June 2.

Fagerberg, J. 1996. "Technology and competitiveness," *Oxford Review of Economic Policy.* Vol. 12. No. 3. pp. 39–51.

Feder, G. 1982. "On exports and economic growth," *Journal of Development Economics.* Vol. 12. No. 1. pp. 59–74.

Feldbaek, O. 1999. "Country trade under Danish colours: A study of economics and politics around 1800," in K. R. Haellquist (ed.) *Asian Trade Routes: Continental and Maritime.* London: Curzon Press. pp. 96–133.

Feinberg, R.E. and Z. Ye. 2001. *Assessing APEC's Progress; Trade, Ecotech and Institutions.* Singapore Institute of Southeast Asian Studies.

Ferro, M., D. Rosenblatt and N. Stern, 2002. "Policies for pro-poor growth in India," paper presented at *The Indian Economy Conference* at Cornell University, Ithaca, New York, April 19–20.

Findlay, R. 1996, April. *The Emergence of World Economy: Towards a Historical Perspective.* New York: Columbia University. Economic Discussion Paper No. 9596.

Findlay, R. and K.H. O'Rourke, 2001. "Commodity market integration 1500–2000," paper presented at the NBER Conference on *Globalization in Historic Perspective,* Santa Barbara, CA, May 11–12, 2002.

Fischer, S, 2001, April 28. *Opening Remarks"* IMF/World Bank International Reserves: Policy Issues Forum. Washington, DC.

Flassbeck, H. 1999. "Asia urged to launch a joint financial surveillance body," *Kyodo News.* July 14. p. 6.

Flynn, D.O. and A. Giraldez. 1995. "Born with silver spoon: The origin of world trade in 1571," *Journal of World History.* Vol. 6. No. 2. pp. 201–221.

Frank, A.G. 1998. *ReOrient: Global Economy in the Asian Age.* Berkeley: University of California Press.

Frankel, J.A. 1997. *Regional Trading Blocs in the World Economic System.* Washington, DC: Institute for International Economics.

Frankel, J.A. 2000. "The Asian financial crisis in perspective," in P.A. Petri (ed) *Regional Co-operation and Asian Recovery.* Singapore: Institute of Southeast Asian Studies. pp. 20–35.

Frankel, J.A. and A.K. Rose. 2000. *An Estimate of Effects of Currency Unions on Trade and Growth.* Cambridge, MA: National Bureau of Economic Research. Working paper No. 7857.

Freeman, N.J. 2000, July. *A Regional Platform for Trading Southeast Asian Equities: Viable Option or Lofty 'Red Herring'?* Singapore: Institute of Southeast Asian Studies. ISEAS Working Paper No. 3.

Freeman, N.J. and F. Bartels. 2000, August. *Portfolio Investment in Southeast Asia's Stock Markets: A Survey of Institutional Investor's Current Perceptions*. Singapore: Institute of Southeast Asian Studies. ISEAS Working Paper No. 4.

Fujita, N., P. Krugman and A.J. Venables. 1999. *The Spatial Economy: Cities, Regions, and International Trade.* Cambridge, MA: The MIT Press.

Fukasaku, K. and F. Kimura. 2002. "Globalization and intra-firm trade: Further evidence," in P.J. Lloyd and H.H. Lee (eds) *Frontiers of Research in Intra-Industry Trade.* Basingstoke: Palgrave Macmillan. pp. 130–162.

Fukase, E. and W. Martin. 2001. *Free Trade Area Membership As A Stepping Stone to Development: The Case of ASEAN.* Washington, DC: The World Bank. Policy Research Working Paper No. 421.

Fukuda, S. and H. Toya.1995. "The conditional Convergence in East Asian countries: The role of exports for economic growth," in T. Ito and A. O. Krueger (eds.) *Growth Theories in Light of the East Asian Experience.* Chicago: University of Chicago Press, 1995. pp. 178–200.

Gaastra, F.S. 1999. "Competition or collaboration? Relationship between the Dutch East India Company and Indian merchants around 1680," in S. Chaudhury and M. Morineau (eds) *Merchants, Companies and Trade: Europe and Asia in the Early Modern Era.* Cambridge: Cambridge University Press.

Gilbert, J., R. Scollay and B. Bora. 2001. *Assessing Regional Trading Arrangements in the Asia-Pacific*. Geneva: United Nations Conference on Trade and Development. Policy Series. No. 15.

Giovanoli, M. 2001. *A New Architecture for the Global Financial Market: Legal Aspects of International Financial Standard Setting*. Basel, Switzerland: International Monetary Law Association.

Glick, R. and A. Rose. 1999. "Contagion and trade: Why are currency crises regional?" *Journal of International Money and Finance.* Vol. 18. No. 4. pp. 603–617.

Glick, R. and A. Rose. 2001, April. *Does a Currency Union Affect Trade? The Time Series Evidence*. (mimeo)

Gordon, R.H. and W. Li. 1999. *Government as a Discriminating Monopoly in Financial Markets: The Case of China*. Cambridge, MA: National Bureau of Economic Research. NBER Working Paper No. 7110.

Goto, J. and M. Kawai. 2001. "Macroeconomic interdependence in East Asia," paper presented at the *International Conference in on Economic Interdependence: Shaping Asia-Pacific in the 21st Century*, jointly organized by the Institute for International Monetary Affairs, the IMF and the World Bank, in Tokyo, March 22–23.

Government of Japan (GOJ). 2001. "Exchange rate regime for emerging market economies," background paper prepared by French and Japanese Government officials for the ASEM Finance Minister meeting in Kobe, Japan, January 16–17. Available at: http://www.mof.go.jp/english/asem/asem03i2.htm.

Grossman, G. and E. Helpman. 1991. *Innovation and Growth in the Global Economy.* Cambridge, MA: The MIT Press.

Gundlach, E., U. Hiemenz, R. Langhammer, P. Langhammer and P. Nunnenkamp, 1993. "Regional integration in Europe and its impact on developing countries," in K. Ohno (ed.) *Regional Integration and Its Impact on Developing Countries.* Tokyo: Institute of Developing Economies. pp. 134–158.

Hallward-Driemeier, M., G. Iarossi and K.L. Sokoloff. 2002, October. *Export and Manufacturing Productivity in East Asia: A Comparative analysis with Firm Level Data*". Cambridge, MA: National Bureau of Economic Research. NBER Working Paper No. W8894.

Hansen, G. 2001. *Should Countries Promote Foreign Direct Investment?* Geneva: United Nations Conference on Trade and Development. G-24. Discussion Paper Series No. 9.

Harris, R. and D. Cox. 1986. "Quantitative assessment of the economic impact on Canada of sectoral free trade with the United States," *Canadian Journal of Economics*. Vol. 19. No. 2. pp. 377–394.

Harwood, A. 2000. "Building local bond markets: Some issues and actions" in A. Harwood (ed) *Building Local Bond Markets: An Asian Perspective.* Washington, DC: International Finance Corporation. pp. 3–25.

Hausmann, R., U. Panizza and E. Stein. 2000. *Why Do Countries Float the Way They Float?* Washington, DC: Inter-American Development Bank. Working Paper No. 418.

Hayami, A. 1992. "The industrious revolution," *Look Japan.* Vol. 38. pp. 8–10.

Hayami, Y. 1997. *Development Economics: From the Poverty to the Wealth of Nations.* Oxford: Oxford University Press.

Heller, R. 1966. "Optimal international reserves," *Economic Journal.* Vol. 76. No. 2. pp. 296–311.

Henning, R. C. 2002. "The case of regional financial co-operation in East Asia," paper presented at the Pacific Economic Co-operation Council (PECC) conference on *Issues and Prospects for Regional Co-operation for Financial Stability,* Honolulu, Hawai'i, October 11–13.

Hernandez, L. and P. Montiel. 2001. *Post Crisis Exchange Rate Policy in Five Asian Economies: Filling the Hollow Middle?* Washington, DC: International Monetary Fund. IMF Working Paper No. WP/01/170.

Herring, R.J. and N. Chatusripitak. 2000. *The Case of the Missing Market: The Bond Market and Why it Matters for Financial Development.* Tokyo: The ADB Institute. Working Paper No. 11.

Hew, D. 2003, June 16. *Towards an ASEAN Economic Community by 2020: Vision or Reality? Viewpoints.* Singapore: Institute for Southeast Asian Studies.

Heydon, K. 2002. "RIA market access and regulatory provisions," paper presented at the conference on *The Changing Architecture of the Global Trading System,* organized by the World Trade Organization, Geneva, April 23.

Hilpert, H.G. 2003. "Japan: Is the crisis over?" *CESifo Forum.* Vol. 4. No. 4. pp. 49–61.

Hoekman, B.M., M. Schiff and L.A. Winters. 1998. *Regionalism and Development: Main Message From Recent World Bank Research.* Washington, DC: The World Bank. (mimeo)

Honohan, P. 2004, February. *Financial Development, Growth and Poverty: How Close Are the Links*". Washington, DC: The World Bank. Policy Research Working Paper No. 3203.

Huang, J. and S. Rozelle. 2002. "The nature of distortions to agricultural in China and implications of WTO accession," paper presented at the Seminar on *The WTO Accession, Policy Reforms and Poverty Reduction in China*, organized by the World Bank and held in Beijing, June 28–29.

Hufbauer, G. and J. Schott. 1994. "Regionalism in North America," in K. Ohno (ed) *Regional Integration and Its Impact on Developing Countries.* Tokyo: Institute of Developing Economies.

Hummels, D., J. Ishii and K.M. Yi. 2001. "The nature and growth of vertical specialization in World Trade," *Journal of International Economics.* Vol. 54. No. 1. pp. 75–96.

Humphrey, J. and H. Schmitz. 2001. "Governance in global value chain," *IDS Bulletin,* Vol. 32. No. 3. pp. 112–138.

Hutchison, M. 1997. *The Political Economy of Japanese Economic Policy.* Cambridge, MA: The MIT Press.

Ianchovichina, E. 2003. *Economic Impact of China's Accession to the WTO*. Washington, DC: The World Bank.

Ianchovichina, E. and W. Martin. 2001. "Trade liberalization in China's accession to the World Trade Organization," *Journal of Economic Integration*. Vol. 15. No. 4. pp. 421–445.

Ianchovichina, E., S. Suthiwart-Narueput and M. Zhao. 2003. "Regional impact of China's WTO accession," in K. Krumm and H. J. Kharas (eds) *East Asia Integrates: A Trade Policy Agenda for Shared Growth*. Washington, DC: The World Bank. pp. 57–79.

Ianchovichina, E. and T. Walmsley. 2002. *Regional Impact of China's Accession*. Washington, DC: The World Bank.

Iida, Y. 1997. "Fleeing the West, making Asia home: Transposition of the otherness in Japanese Pan-Asianism," *Alternatives*. Vol. 22. No. 3. pp. 409–432.

Ikeda, S. 1996. "The history of the capitalist world system vs. the history of East-Southeast Asia," *Review*. Vol. 19. No. 1. Winter. pp. 49–78.

Ikenberry, J. G. 2000. "The political economy of Asia-Pacific regionalism," *East Asian Economic Perspective*. March. pp. 35–61.

International Monetary Fund (IMF) 2001. *International Capital Markets: Development, Prospects and Key Policy Issues*. Washington, DC: IMF.

International Monetary Fund (IMF). 2002. *India: Selected Issues and Statistical Appendix*. Washington, DC: IMF. IMF Country Report No. 02/193.

International Monetary Fund (IMF). 2003. *Global Financial Stability Report*. Washingon, DC: IMF.

International Monetary Fund (IMF). 2003. *World Economic Outlook*. Washington, DC: IMF.

International Monetary Fund (IMF). 2004. *World Economic Outlook*. Washington, DC: IMF.

International Monetary Fund (IMF). 2004. *Global Financial Stability Report*. Washington, DC: IMF.

International Monetary Fund/World Bank (IMF/WB). 2001. *Developing Government Bond Markets: A Hand Book*. Washington, DC: IMF/WB.

International Trade Center (ITC). 2000. *Offshore Back-Office Operations: Supplying Support Services to Global Markets*. Geneva: ITC.

Ito, T. 2000. "Principal causes of Asian export deceleration," in Dilip K. Das (ed) *Asian Exports*. Oxford: Oxford University Press. pp. 75–114.

Japan Bank of International Co-operation (JBIC). 2002. "JBIC FY 2001 Survey: The outlook of Japanese foreign direct investment," *Journal of the Research Institute of Development and Finance*. No. 9. January. pp. 4–38.

Japan External Trade Organization (JETRO). 2001, October. *Japanese Investment in China*. Tokyo: JETRO.

Jordan, C. and M. Lubrano. 2002. "How effective are capital markets in exerting governance on corporations?" in *Financial Sector Governance*. Washington, DC: The Brookings Institution Press. pp. 22–40.

Jordan, C. and G. Majnoni. 2002, October. *Financial Regulatory Harmonization and the Globalization of Finance*. Washington, DC: The World Bank. Policy Research Working Paper No. 2919.

Kaminsky, G. L. and C.M. Reinhart. 2003. "On crisis, contagion and confusion," in Dilip K. Das (ed) *An International Finance Reader*. London and New York: Routledge. pp. 359–360.

Kawai, M. 2002. "Bank and corporate restructuring in crisis-affected East Asia: From systemic collapse to reconstruction," in G. de Brouwer (ed) *Financial Markets and Policies in East Asia*. London: Routledge. pp. 32–66.

Kawai, M., R. Newfarmer and S. Schmukler. 2001. *Crisis and Contagion in East Asia: Nine Lessons*. Washington, DC: The World Bank. (mimeo).

Kawai, M. and S. Takagi. 2003, October. *Proposed Strategy for a Regional Exchange Rate Arrangement in East Asia.* Washington, DC: The World Bank. Policy Research Working Paper No. 2503.

Kawai, M. and S. Urata. 2002. "Trade and foreign direct investment in East Asia," paper presented at the international conference on *Linkages in East Asia: Implications for Currency Regime and Policy Dialogue,* held in Seoul, September 12–13.

Keidanren. 2000. *Urgent Call for Active Promotion of Free Trade Agreements.* Tokyo. Available at: http://asia.neww.yahoo.com. Keidanren. or.jp.english/policy/2000/003/proposal.html.

Keidanren. 2000. For Asia's Economic Renewal: A Proposal by Japan's Business Community. Available at: http://www.keidanren.or.jp/english/policy/2000/007/proposal.html. Accessed March 13.

Kim, J. I. and L. Lau. 1994. "The sources of economic growth of the East Asian newly industrialized economies," *Journal of Japanese and International Economics.* Vol. 8. No. 3. pp. 235–271.

Kim, S. and J.H. Park. 2002. Structural change in the corporate bond market in Korea," in *The Development of Bond Markets in Emerging Economies.* Basel: Bank for International Settlements. Monetary and Economic Department. BIS Paper No. 11. pp. 130–146.

Kobayashi, T. 2001. "Development of international bond markets in the region: New Miyazawa initiative," in *Bond Market Development in Asia.* Paris: Organization for Economic Cooperation and Development. pp. 173–188.

Kohler, H. 2001a. "Focusing the fund on financial stability," *Far Eastern Economic Review.* June. pp. 48–50.

Kohler, H. 2001b. *A Public–Private Partnership for Financial Stability.* Speech given at the spring meeting of the Institute of International Finance, Hong Kong, May 31.

Kormendi, R.C. and P.G. Meguire. 1985. "Macroeconomic determinants of growth: Cross-country evidence," *Journal of Monetary Economics.* Vol. 16. No. 1. pp. 141–163.

Kose, M. A. and R. Riezman. 1999, October. *Understanding the Welfare Implications of Preferential Trade Agreements.* Coventry: The Center for the Study of Globalization and Regionalization. University of Warwick. CSGR Working Paper No. 45/99.

Krause, L.B. 1997. *Korea's Economic Role in East Asia.* Stanford: Stanford University. Asia-Pacific Research Center.

Kreinen, M. 1982. "Effect of EC enlargement on trade in manufactures," *Kyklos.* Heft 108. No. 3. pp. 110–138.

Kreinen, M. 1998. "Multinationalism, regionalism and their implications for Asia," paper presented at the Conference on *Global Interdependence and Asia-Pacific Cooperation*, Hong Kong, June 8–10.

Kremer, M. 1993, August. "The O-ring theory of economic development," *Quarterly Journal of Economics.* Vol. 106. No. 3. pp. 551–575.

Krueger, A.O. 1980. "Trade policy as an input to development," *American Economic Review.* Vol. 70. No. 4. pp. 288–292. (Papers and Proceedings).

Krueger, A.O. 1995. "East Asian experience and endogenous growth theory," in T. Ito and A.O. Krueger (eds) *Growth Theories in the Light of East Asian Experience.* Chicago: University of Chicago Press.

Krueger, A.O. 1997. *Trade Policy and Economic Development: How We Learn?* Cambridge, MA: National Bureau of Economic Research. NBER Working Paper No. W5895.

Krueger, A.O. 2000. "Factors affecting export growth and performance and the Asian case," in Dilip K. Das (ed) *Asian Exports.* Oxford: Oxford University Press. pp. 25–74.

Krueger, A.O. 2004. *Lessons From the Asian Crisis.* Keynote address at the SEACEN Meeting held in Colombo, Sri Lanka, February 12.

Krugman, P. 1996. *Pop-Internationalism.* Cambridge, MA: The MIT Press.
Krugman, P. 1998. *What Happened to Asia?* Massachusetts Institute of Technology. Massachusetts. Unpublished paper.
Krugman, P. 1999. "The return of depression economics," *Foreign Affairs.* Vol. 78. No. 1. pp. 56–74.
Krumm, K. and H.J. Kharas. 2003. *East Asia Integrates: A Trade Policy Agenda for Shared Growth.* Washington, DC: The World Bank.
Kuroda, H. 2001. Future international financial architecture and regional capital market development," in *Bond Market Development in Asia.* Paris: Organization for Economic Cooperation and Development. pp. 73–88.
Kwan, C.H. 2002, August. *The Rise of China and Asia's Flying Geese Pattern of Economic Development.* Tokyo: Nomura Research Institute. NRI Papers No. 52.
Laffont, J.J. and Y. Quin. 1999. "The dynamics of reform and development in China: A political economy perspective," *European Economic Review.* Vol. 24. No. 4. pp. 1105–1114.
Laird, S. 1997, September. "Mercosur: Objectives and achievements," paper presented at the Third annual World Bank Conference on *Development in Latin America and the Caribbean,* Montevideo.
Langois, J.D. 1981. *China Under Mongol Rule.* Princeton, NJ: Princeton University Press.
Lardy, N. R. 2002. *Integrating China into the Global Economy,* Washington, DC: Brookings Institution Press.
Lau, L.J., Y. Qian and G. Ronald. 2000. "Reforms without losers: An interpretation of China's dual-track approach," *Journal of Political Economy.* Vol. 108. No.1. pp. 120–143.
Lee H. and D. Roland-Holst. 1998. "Prelude to the Pacific century: Overview of the region," in H. Lee and D. Roland-Holst. (eds) *Economic Development and Cooperation in the Pacific Basin.* Cambridge: Cambridge University Press. pp. 3–36.
Levine, R. 1997. "Financial development and economic growth: Views and agenda," *Journal of Economic Literature.* Vol. 35. No. 3. pp. 688–726.
Levine, R. and D. Renelt. 1992. "A sensitivity analysis of cross-country growth regression," *American Economic Review.* Vol. 82. pp. 942–963.
Lewis, J.D. and S. Robinson. 1996. *Partners or Predators? The Impact of Regional Trade Liberalization on Indonesia.* Washington, DC: The World Bank. Policy Research Working Paper No. 1626.
Lian, T.S. 2002. *The Development of Bond Market in Emerging Market Economies.* BIS Paper No. 11.
Liang, C.Y. 2002. *The Total Factor Productivity Growth in Taiwan 1960–1993*, Taipei, Taiwan: The Institute of Economics. Academia Sinica. Discussion Paper 2002–04.
Limao, N. and A. Venables. 2001. "Infrastructure, geographical disadvantage, transport cost and trade," *The World Bank Economic Review.* Vol. 15. No. 2. pp. 451–471.
Lin, C.L. and R.S. Rajan. 2001. "The economics and politics of monetary regionalism in Asia," *ASEAN Economic Bulletin.* Vol. 18. No. 1. pp. 103–139.
Lindgren, C., T. Balino, C. Enoch, A.M. Gulde, M. Quintyn and L. Teo. 1999. *Financial Sector Crisis and Restructuring: Lessons from Asia.* Washington, DC: International Monetary Fund. Occasional Paper No. 188.
Lipsey, R. 1960. "The theory of customs unions: A general survey," *Economic Journal.* Vol. 10. No. 2. pp. 498–513.
Lo, C. 2004. *China's Economic Reform Myth.* Hong Kong SAR. (unpublished manuscript)
Maddison, A. 1995. *Monitoring the World Economy.* Paris: Development Center. The Organization for Economic Cooperation and Development.
Maddison, A. 1998. *Chinese Economic Performance in the Long Run.* Paris: Development Center. The Organization for Economic Cooperation and Development.

Maddison, A. 2001. *The World Economy: A Millennial Perspective.* Paris: OECD Development Center.

Manupipatpong, W. 2002. "The ASEAN surveillance process and the East Asian monetary fund," *Economic Bulletin.* Vol. 19. No. 1. pp. 111–122.

Marshall, R. 1993. *Storm From the East: From Genghis Khan to Kublai Khan.* Los Angeles: University of California Press.

Mathews, J. A. 2001. *Dragon Multinationals: A New Model of Global Growth.* New York: Oxford University Press.

Mathieson, D.J. and J. Roldos. 2001. "The role of foreign banks in emerging markets," in R.E. Litan, P. Mason and M. Pomerleano (eds) *Open Doors: Foreign Participation in Financial Systems in Developing Countries.* Washington, DC: The Brookings Institution Press. pp. 120–141.

Mattoo, A. and S. Wunsch. 2004, March. *Preempting Protectionism in Services: The WTO and Outsourcing.* Washington, DC: The World Bank. Policy Research Working Paper No. 3237.

Meade, J.E. 1955. *The Theory of Customs Union.* Amsterdam. North Holland.

McCauley, R.N. 2003. "Central bank cooperation in East Asia," paper presented at the *Second Annual Conference of PECC Finance Forum,* held in Hua Hin, Thailand, July 8–9.

McCauley, R.N. 2003. "Unifying government bond markets in East Asia," *BIS Quarterly Review.* December. pp. 89–103.

McCauley, R.N. and Fung. 2003. "Choosing instruments in managing dollar foreign exchange reserves," *BIS Quarterly Review.* March. pp. 39–46.

McCauley, R.N., J.S. Rudd and P.D. Wooldridge. 2002. "Globalizing international banking," *BIS Quarterly Review.* March. pp. 41–51.<QA>

McCleery, R.1993. "Modeling NAFTA: Macroeconomic effects." in K. Ohno (ed.) *Regional Integration and Its Impact on Developing Countries.* Tokyo: Institute of Developing Economies. pp. 42–60.

McCombie, J.S.L. and A.P. Thirlwall. 1994. *Economic Growth and Balance of Payments Constraints.* New York: St. Martin's Press.

McKinnon, R.I. 2000. *After the Crisis, the East Asian Dollar Standard Reconstructed.* Stanford: Stanford University. Available at: http://www-econ.stanford.edu/faculty/workp/swp00013.html.

Michaely, M. 1998. "Partners to a preferential trade agreement: Implications of varying size," *Journal of International Economics.* Vol. 46. No. 1. pp. 73–85.

Midelfart-Knarvik, K.-H. and H.G. Overman. 2002 "Delocation and European integration: Is structural spending justified?" *Economic Policy.* Vol. 35. No. 2, pp. 321–359.

Midelfart-Knarvik, K.-H., H.G. Overman, S. Redding and A.J. Venables 1999. *The Location of Industry in Europe.* London: Center for Economic Policy Research.

Ministry of Finance (MOF). Government of Japan. 1999. *Japan's Support for Troubled Asian Neighbors Enters New Phase.* Available at: http://www.fpcj.jp/e/shiryo/jb/j9912.html. Accessed May 27.

Ministry of Finance (MOF). Government of Japan. 2002. *Japan's Support for Troubled Asian Neighbors.* Available at: http://www.mof.go.jp/English/qa/my001.htm.

Ministry of Foreign Trade and Economic Co-operation (MOFTEC). 2001. *Foreign Trade Statistics,* Beijing: MOFTEC.

Ministry of International Trade and Industry (MITI). 2001. *White Paper on International Trade 2001: External Economic Policy Challenges in the 21st Century.* Tokyo: MITI.

Mishkin, F.S. 2001, January. *Financial Policies and the Prevention of Financial Crisis in Emerging Market Economies* Cambridge, MA: National Bureau of Economic Research. NBER Working Paper No. 8087.

Montgomery, H. 2003, January. *The Role of Foreign Banks in Post-Crisis Asia.* Tokyo: The ADB Institute. Research Paper No. 51.

Moreno, R. 2001. "Pegging and macroeconomic performance in East Asia." *ASEAN Economic Bulletin*. Vol. 18. No. 1. pp. 48–68.

Mortimore, M. 2000. "Corporate strategies for FDI in the context of New Economic model," *World Development.* Vol. 28. No. 9. pp. 1611–1626.

Mote, F.W. 1999. *Imperial China: 900–1800.* Boston, MA: Harvard University Press.

Mundell, R. 2001. "Growth and international monetary system," paper presented at an Asian Development Seminar in Manila, February 12.

Myerson, R.B. 1999. "Nash equilibrium and the history of economic theory," *The Journal of Economic Literature.* Vol. 36. No. 3. pp. 1067–1082.

Nagarajan, N. 1998. "On the evidence for trade diversion in MERCOSUR," *Integration and Trade.* Vol. 2. No. 6. pp. 3–30.

Needham, J. 1954. *Science and Civilization in China,* Vol. I. Cambridge: Cambridge University Press.

Ng, F. and A. Yeats. 2003, June. *Major Trade Trends in Asia.* Washington DC: The World Bank. World Bank Policy Research Working Paper 3084.

Noland, M. 1994. "Asia and the NAFTA," in Y. S. Kim and K. S. Oh (eds.) *The US–Korea Economic Partnership*. Vermont: Ashgate Publishers. pp. 134–148.

Nomura Research Institute (NRI). 2002. *Medium Term Outlook for the Japanese Economy.* Tokyo: NRI. Research Paper No. 2002–27.

Ohno, K. 1999, February. *Capital Account Crisis and Credit Contraction*. Tokyo: The ADB Institute. Working Paper No. 2.

Okfen, N. 2003, June. *Towards An East Asian Community? What ASEM and APEC Can Tell Us.* University of Warwick. Center for the Study of Globalization and Regionalization. CSGR Working Paper No. 117/03.

Organization for Economic Co-operation and Development (OECD). 2002. *Foreign Direct Investment for Development: Maximizing Benefits, Minimizing Costs. OECD Policy Brief.* Paris: OECD.

Organization for Economic Co-operation and Development (OECD). 2003. *Attracting International Investment for Development.* Paris: OECD.

Organization for Economic Co-operation and Development (OECD). 2003. *Investment Policy Review of China—Progress and Reform Challenges.* Paris: OECD.

Page, S. 2000. *Regionalism Among Developing Countries.* London: The Macmillan Press.

Panagaria, A. 2004, March. *India in the 1980s and the 1990s: A Triumph of the Reforms*. Washington, DC: IMF. IMF Working Paper No. Wp/04/43.

Park, Y.C. 2000. "Beyond the Chiang Mai initiative: Rationale and need for decision-making body and extended regional surveillance under the ASEAN+Three framework," paper presented at the meeting of the deputies of APT countries in Prague, the Czech Republic, September 24. (revised version November 2000).

Park, Y.S. 2001. "Development of Asian bond markets," in Y. Hyung and Y. Wang (eds) *Regional Financial Arrangements in East Asia.* Seoul, Korea: Institute of International Economic Policy. pp, 53–73.

Park, Y.C. 2002, December. *Regional Financial Arrangements for East Asia: A Different Agenda*. Washington, DC: Latin American/Caribbean and Asia-Pacific Economics and Business Association. Working Paper No. 1.

Park, Y.C. and Y. Wang. 2002, September. *Can East Asia Emulate European Economic Integration?* Seoul: Korea Institute of International Economic Policy. KIIEP Discussion Paper No. 02–09.

Persson, T. 2001."Currency union and trade: How large is the treatment effect?" paper presented at the Economic Policy Panel meeting at Stockholm, April 5–6.

Petri, P.A. 1993. "The East Asian trading bloc: An analytical history," In *Regionalism and Rivalry: Japan and the United States in Pacific Asia.* Chicago: University of Chicago Press. pp. 21–52.<QA> editor name

Petri, P.A. 1994. "The East Asian trading bloc: An analytical history," in R. Garnaut and P. Drysdale (eds.) *Asia Pacific Regionalism : Readings in International Economic Relations.* Sidney: Harper Educational Publishers. pp. 107–124.

Petri, P.A. 1997. "Measuring and comparing progress in APEC," *ASEAN Economic Bulletin.* Vol. 14. No. 1.*<QA>*

Phillips, E.D. 1969 *The Mongols.* New York: Frederick A. Praeger Publishers.

Pinto, B. and F. Zahir. 2004. *India: Why Fiscal Adjustment Now?* Washington, DC: The World Bank. Policy Research Working Paper 3230.

Plummer, M. 2001. "Monetary union and ASEAN," paper presented at the Australian National University-Kobe University International Conference on Trade and Monetary System in the Asia-Pacific at Kobe, Japan, February 3–4.

Polaski, S. 2004. *Job Anxiety is Real—and It is Globa*". (Policy Brief). Washington, DC: Carnegie Endowment.

Pomeranz, K. and S. Topik. 1999. *The World that Trade Created: Society, Culture, and the World Economy.* New York: M.E. Sharpe.

Powell, A. 2003. *A Capital Accord for Emerging Economies?* Available at: http://econ.worldbank.org/files/13169_wps2808.pdf. Accessed March.

Prasad, E. and T. Rambaugh. 2003. "Beyond the Great Wall," *Finance and Development.* December 2003. pp. 46–51.

Radelet, S. and J. Sachs. 1998, April. *The Onset of the East Asian Currency Crisis.*. Cambridge, MA: National Bureau of Economic Research. NBER Working Paper No. 6680.

Radelet, S. and J. Sachs. 1998. "The East Asian financial crisis: Diagnosis, remedies, prospects." *Brookings Papers on Economic Activity.* No. 1. pp. 1–74.

Radelet, S. and J. Sachs. 1999. *What Have We Learned So Far From the Asian Financial Crisis?* Cambridge, MA: Harvard Institute of International Development. CAER Discussion Paper No. 37.

Rajan, R.S. 2000. *Examining the Case for an Asian Monetary Fund.* Adelaide, Australia: University of Adelaide. Center for International Economic Studies. Policy Discussion Paper No. 0002.

Rajan, R.S. 2002. *Examining the Links Between Trade and Monetary Regionalism.* Adelaide, Australia: University of Adelaide. (unpublished paper). Available at: http://www.ips.org.sg/pub/kishen/pa_kishen_Examining%20The%20Links%20Between%20Trade%20And%20Monetary%20Regionalism.pdf.

Rajan, R.S. 2003. *Emergence of China as an Economic Power: What Does it Imply for Southeast Asia?* Adelaide: School of Economics. University of Adelaide. Available at: http://www.economics.adelaide.edu.au/staff/rrajan/unpub/PRCASEAN-1.pdf. Accessed June 30.

Rajan, R.S. and R. Sen. 2002, April. *The Japan-Singapore "New-Age" Partnership Agreement: Background, Motivation and Implications*. Singapore: Institute of Policy Studies. IPS Working Paper No. 13.

Ravenhill, J. 2003, June. *The Move to Preferential Trade in the Western Pacific Rim.* Honolulu, Hawai'i: East-West Center. Asia-Pacific Issues No. 69.

Reid, A. 1993. *Southeast Asia and the Age of Commerce 1450–1680*, Vol. 2. New Haven, CT: Yale University Press.

Reinhart, C.M. 2000. The mirage of floating exchange rate," *American Economic Review*. Vol. 90. No. 2. pp. 65–70.

Reyes, A.R. 2004. "ASEAN: A single market and production base," *The Jakarta Times*. June 14. p.10.

Riezman, R. 1999, October. *Can Bilateral Trade Agreements Help induce Free Trade?* Coventry: The Center for the Study of Globalization and Regionalization. University of Warwick. CSGR Working Paper No. 44/99.

Roach, S. 2004. *Global Economy: When China Sneezes*. New York: Morgan Stanley Global Economic Forum. Available at: http://www.morganstanley.com/GEFdata/digests/20040503-mon.html#anchor0. Accessed May 3.

Rodrik, D. and A. Subramanian. 2004. *From Hindu Growth to Productivity Surge*. Cambridge, MA: National Bureau of Economic Research. NBER Working Paper No. w10376.

Ronald-Holst, D. 2002, October. *An Overview of PRC's Emergence and East Asian Trade Patterns to 2020*. Tokyo: ADB Institute. Research Paper Series. No. 44.

Rose, A. 1999. "Is there a case for an Asian monetary fund?" *FRBSF Economic Bulletin*. Vol. 30. No. 4. pp. 37–62.

Rose, A. K. 2000. "One money, one market: Estimating the effect of common currencies on trade," *Economic Policy*. Vol. 15. No. 1. pp. 7–46.

Rose, A. and C. Engel. 2000. "Currency unions and international integration. Cambridge, MA: National Bureau of Economic Research. NBER Working Paper No. 7872.

Rossabi, M. 1983. *Khubilai Khan: His Life and Times*. Los Angeles: University of California Press.

Rozman, G. 1991. *The East Asian Region: Confucian Heritage and Its Modern Adaptation*. Princeton, NJ: Princeton University Press.

Rutherford, T.F. and J. Martinez. 2000. "Welfare effects of regional trade integration of central American and Caribbean nations with NAFTA and MERCOSUR," *The World Economy*. June. pp. 799–825.

Sachs, J. and A. Warner. 1995. "Economic reforms and the process of global integration," *Brookings Papers on Economic Activity*. No. 1. pp. 1–118.

Safadi, R. and A. Yeats. 1993. "The North American ree Trade Agreement: Its effect on South Asia," *Journal of Asian Economics*. Vol. 5. No. 2. pp. 197–216.

Sager, M.A. 1997. "Regional trade agreements: Their role and the economic impact on trade flows," *The World Economy*. Vol. 20. No. 1. January. pp. 239–273.

Sakakibara, E. and S. Yamakawa. 2003. *Regional Integration in East Asia: Challenges and Opportunities*", Part I and Part II. Washington, DC: Policy Research Working Paper Nos. 3078 and 3079.

Samuelson, R.A. 2004. "Keeping US jobs at home," *The Washington Post*. April 28. p. A21.

Sanderson, S.K. 1995. *Social Transformation: A General Theory of Historical Development*. Oxford: Blackwell.

Scoffield, H. 2004. "Outsourcing a major boon to Canada," *Globe and Mail, Report on Business*. April 2. p. B4.

Schiff, M. 1999, August. *Will the Real "Natural Trading Partner" Please Stand Up?* Washington, DC: World Bank. Policy Research Working Paper No. 2161.

Schiff, M. and L.A. Winters. 2003. *Regional Integration and Development*. New York: Oxford University Press.

Schill, M. 1996, October. *Small is Beautiful* Washington, DC: World Bank. Working Paper No. 1668.

Sender, H. 2001. "China steps up chip production," *The Asian Wall Street Journal*. January 10, p. N1–N2.

Shin, K. and Y. Wang. 2003. "Trade integration and business cycle: Synchronization in East Asia," *Asian Economic Papers.* Vol. 2. No. 3. pp. 1–29.

Shinohara, H. 1999, August. *On the Asian Monetary Fund.* News Letter. No. 4. Tokyo: The Institute for International Monetary Affairs.

Shirai, S. 2001, September 3. *Searching for New Regulatory Frameworks for the Intermediate Financial Market Structure in Post Crisis Asia.* Tokyo: ADB Institute. Research Paper No. 24.

Shirai, S. 2001. *Overview of Financial Market Structure in Asia: Cases of the Republic of Korea, Malaysia, Thailand and Indonesia.* Tokyo: ADB Institute. Research Paper No. 25.

Shirai, S. 2002, September. *Is the Equity Market Really Developed in China?* Tokyo: ADB Institute. Research Paper No. 41.

Smith, M. and A.J. Venables. 1988. "Completing the internal market in European community: Some industry simulations," *European Economic Review.* Vol. 32. No. 8. pp. 1501–1525.

Soesastro, H. and C.E. Morrison. 2001. "Rethinking the ASEAN formula," in *East Asia and the International System,* A Report to The Trilateral Commission. New York. Paris. Tokyo. pp. 57–75.

Srinivasan, T.N. 2001. *India's Fiscal Deficits: Is There a Crisis Ahead?* Palo Alto, CA: Stanford University. Center for Research on Economic Development and Policy Reform. Working Paper No. 92.

Stern, N. and J. Stigllitz. 1997, April. *A Framework for a Development Strategy in a Market Economy: Objectives, Scope, Institutions and Instruments.* London: European Bank for Reconstruction and Development. Working Paper No. 20.

Sugihara, K. 1985 "Ajiakan-Boeki no Keisei to Kozo 1880–1913" [Patterns and Development of intra-Asia Trade], *Shakai Keizai Shigaku* [The Socio-Economic History]. Vol. 51. No. 1. pp. 123–146.

Sugihara, K. 1990. "Japan as an engine of the Asian international economy, 1980–1936," *Japan Forum.* Vol. 2. No. 1. April. pp. 127–145.

Sugihara, K. 2003. "The East Asian path of economic development: A long-term perspective," in G. Arrighi, T. Hamashita and M. Selden (eds) *The Resurgence of East Asia.* London and New York: Routledge. pp. 78–123.

Tan, G. 2000. *ASEAN Economic Development and Co-operation.* Singapore: Times Academic Press.

Tarling, N. 1992. *The Cambridge History of Southeast Asia,* Vol. I. Cambridge: Cambridge University Press.

Tay, S.S. 2000. "Institutions and processes: Dilemmas and possibilities," in S.S. Tay, J. Estanislao and H. Soesastro (eds) *A New ASEAN in a New Millennium.* Jakarta: Center for Strategic International Studies. pp. 3–24.

Tongzon, J.L. 1998. *The Economies of Southeast Asia: Growth and Development of ASEAN Economies.* Cheltenham, UK: Edgar Elgar.

Tran, H.Q. and J. Roldos. 2003. "Asian bond markets: The role of securitization and credit guarantees," background paper for the *Second Annual Conference of PECC Finance Forum,* held in Hua Hin, Thailand, July 8–9.

Trewin, R. and M. Azis. 2000. *Updated Impediments Report: Measuring Tariff-related Impediments.* Trade Policy Forum. Pacific Economic Cooperation Council.

Triffin, R. 1947. "National central banking and international economy," *Review of Economic Studies.* Vol. 32. No. 1. pp. 122–140.

Turner, P. 2002. "Bond markets in emerging market economies," in *The Development of Bond Markets in Emerging Economies.* Basel: Bank for International Settlements. Monetary and Economic Department. BIS Paper No. 11. pp. 1–12.

Turner, A.G. and S.S. Golub. 1997. *Towards a System of Multilateral Unit Labor Cost-Based Competitiveness Indicators for Advanced, Developing, and Transition Countries.* Washington, DC: IMF. IMF Working Paper WP/97/151.

United Nations Conference on Trade and Development (UNCTAD). 1993. *World Investment Report: Transnational Corporations and Integrated Production.* Geneva and New York: UNCTAD.

UNCTAD. 1996a. *Investment, Trade and International Policy Arrangements.* Geneva and New York: UNCTAD.

UNCTAD. 1996b. *World Investment Repor.*, Geneva and New York: UNCTAD.

UNCTAD. 1999. *World Investment Report.* Geneva and New York: UNCTAD.

UNCTAD. 2001. *World Investment Report: Promoting Linkages.* Geneva and New York: UNCTAD.

UNCTAD. 2002. *World Investment Report: Transnational Corporations and Export Competitiveness.* Geneva and New York UNCTAD.

UNCTAD. 2003a. *World Investment Report.* Geneva and New York: UNCTAD.

UNCTAD. 2003b. *China: An Emerging FDI Outward Investor: A Research Note.* Geneva and New York: UNCTAD Available at: http://r0.unctad.org/en/subsites/dite/fdistats_files/pdfs/China_Researchnote.pdf. Accessed December 4.

United States Trade Representative (USTR). 2002. *NAFTA at Eight: A Foundation for Economic Growth.* Available at: http://www.ustr.gov/naftareport/nafta8_brochure_eng.pdf.

Urata, S. 2001. Emergence of FDI-trade nexus and economic growth in East Asia," J.E. Stiglitz (ed.) *Rethinking the East Asian Miracle.* New York: Oxford University Press. pp. 409–459.

Urata, S. 2004. *Regional Economic Integration, Economic Growth and Infrastructure in East Asia.* Tokyo: Wased University. Available at: http://www.countryanalyticwork.net/CAW/Cawdoclib.nsf/0/AEC725C4F7D9241E85256E440058A724/$file/Manila+Wrkshop_SESSION+3_Urata.pdf.

Venables, A.J. 2002. *Winners and Losers From Regional Integration Agreement*". Available at: http://econ.lse.ac.uk/staff/ajv/research_material.html#regint.

Venables, A.J. in press. "Regional integration agreements: A force for convergence or divergence?" *The Economic Journal.*()

Venables, A.J. and L.A. Winters. 2003, February, 26. *Economic Integration in the Americas: European Perspectives.* London: London School of Economics. (unpublished manuscript)

Viner, J. 1950. *The Customs Union Issue.* New York: Carnegie Endowment for International Peace.

Wade, R. and F. Venoroso. 1998. "The resources lie within," *The Economist.* November 7. pp. 19–21.

Wain, B. 2002. "Outgoing chief says lack of integration puts off foreign investors," *The Asian Wall Street Journal.* November 5. p. A3.

The Wall Street Journal. 2003 "China plans stock listing for state-owned banks," New York. 22 October. p. 16.

Wallerstein, I. 1989. *The Modern World System,* Vol. 3. New York: Academic Press.

Wang, Y. 2002. "Monetary and financial cooperation in East Asia," paper presented at a symposium on *Asian Economic Integration,* United Nations University, Tokyo, April 22–23, 2002.

Wang, Z. 2002. "WTO accession, greater China free trade area and economic relations across the Taiwan strait," paper presented at the *Fifth Conference on Global Economic Analysis,* Taipei, Taiwan June 5–6.

Wang, Y. 2003. "Prospects for financial and monetary cooperation in Asia," paper presented at the International Conference on *Building New Asia: Towards An Asian Economic Community,* Research and Information System for the Non-Aligned and Other Developing Countries, New Delhi, March 10–11.

Wang, Y. 2004. *Prospects for Financial and Monetary Cooperation in East Asia*. Seoul, Korea: Institute for International Economic Policy. Discussion Paper No. 02–04.

Wang, S.D. and L. Andersen. 2002. "Regional financial co-operation in East Asia: The Chiang Mai initiative and beyond," *Bulletin on Asia-Pacific Perspective.* Vol. 8. No. 3. pp. 89–99.

Wei, S.J. and W. Yi. 2001, March. *Globalization and Inequality: Evidence from China.* Cambridge. MA: National Bureau of Economic Research. NBER Working Paper No. 8611.

Williamson, J. 1999. "The case for a common basket peg for East Asian currencies," in S. Collignon, J. Pisani-Ferry and Y.C. Park (eds) *Exchange Rate policies in Emerging Asian Countries.* London: Routledge. pp. 327–344.

Wilson, D. 2000. "Recent developments in Asian financial markets," in G. de Brouwer (ed.) *Financial Markets and Policies in East Asia.* London: Routledge. pp. 17–31.

Wilson, J., C. Mann, Y.P. Woo, N. Assani and I. Choi. 2002. "Trade facilitation: A development perspective in the Asia Pacific region," paper prepared for the APEC conference. Washington, DC: The World Bank.

Winters, L.A. 1999. "Regionalism for developing countries: Assessing costs and benefits," in J. Burki, G. Perry and S. Calvo (eds) *Trade: Towards Open Regionalism.* Washington, DC: The World Bank. pp. 141–185.

Wolf, M. and E. Luce. 2003. "India's slowing growth: Why a hobbled economy cannot meet the country's needs?" *The Financial Times.* April 4. p. 11.

Wong, J. and L. Ding. 2003. *China's Economy Into The New Century: Structural Issues And Problems*. Singapore: East Asian Institute. National University of Singapore.

Wong, M.C.S. and R.Y.K. Ho. 2003. "Road map for building the institutional foundation for regional bond markets in East Asia," paper presented at the *Second Annual Conference of PECC Finance Forum*, 0ua Hin, Thailand, July 8–9.

World Bank (WB). 2002. *World Development Report 2002. Building Institutions for Markets.* New York: Oxford University Press.

The World Bank (WB). 2003. *Global Economic Prospects 2004.* Washington, DC The World Bank.

The World Bank (WB). 2004. *Global Development Finance 2004.* Washington, DC: The World Bank.

WEF. 2002. *Global Competitiveness Report 2001–2002.* New York and Oxford: Oxford University Press.

World Economic Forum (WEF). 2004. *Global Competitiveness Report 2003–2004.* New York and Oxford: Oxford University Press.

WTO. 1995. *Regional and the World Trading Systems.* Geneva: WTO. March.

WTO. 1995. *Regional and the World Trading Systems*. Geneva: WTO. March.

WTO. 1996. *Annual Report 1996.* Geneva: WTO.

WTO. 1999. *Annual Report 1999.* Geneva: WTO.

WTO. 2001. *Market Access: Unfinished Business. Post Uruguay Round Inventories and Issues*. Geneva: Economic research and Analysis Division, WTO.

WTO. 2002. "Regional trade integration under transformation," background paper prepared by the Trade Policy Review Division of the WTO for the conference on *The Changing Architecture of the Global Trading System,* World Trade Organization, Geneva, April 26.

WTO. 2003, November 14. *A Changing Landscape of RTAs*. Geneva: WTO.

WTO. 2003. *Annual Report 2003*. Geneva: WTO.

WTO. 2003. *The Challenging Landscape of RTAs*. Geneva: WTO. Available at: http://www.wto.org/english/tratop_e/region_e/region_e.htm. Accessed November 14

World Trade Organization (WTO). 2004, April 5. *World Trade 2003, Prospects For 2004*. Press Release. No. Press/373.

Wyplosz, C. 2001. "A monetary union for Asia? Some European lessons," in D. Gruen and J. Simon (eds) *Future Directions of Monetary Policy in East Asia.* Sydney: Reserve Bank of Australia. pp. 124–155.

Yamazawa, I. 2004. *Japan and the East Asian Economies.* Tokyo: IDE-APEC Study Center. Working Paper Series. No. 01.

Yamazawa, I., A. Hirata and K. Yokota. 1991. "Evolving patterns of comparative advantage in the Pacific economies," in M.A. Ariff (ed) *The Pacific Economy: Growth and External Stability.* Sydney, Australia: Allen and Unwin. pp. 213–232.

Yamazawa, I. and S. Urata. 2000. "Trade and investment liberalization and facilitation," in I. Yamazawa (ed) *Asia Pacific Economic Co-operation: Challenges and Tasks for the Twenty-First Century.* London and New York: Routledge. pp. 57–97.

Yoshitomi, M. and S. Shirai. 2000, October. *Technical Paper for Policy Recommendation on Prevention of Another Capital Account Crisis.* Tokyo: The ADB Institute.

Young, A. 1991. "Learning by doing and the dynamic effects of international trade," *Quarterly Journal of Economics.* Vol. 106. No. 2. pp. 369–405.

Young, A. 1994. "Lessons from the East Asian NICs: A contrarian view," *European Economic Review.* Vol. 38. No. 5. pp. 946–973.

Young, A. 1995. "The tyranny of numbers: Confronting the statistical relationship of the East Asian growth experience," *Quarterly Journal of Economics.* Vol. 110. No. 3. pp. 641–680.

Yusuf, S. 2003. *Innovation is Key to Asia's Growth.* New York: Oxford University Press.

Yusuf, S. and S. Evenett. 2003. *Can East Asia Compete? Innovation for Global Markets.* New York: Oxford University Press.

Zhan, X.J. and S. Ge. 2002. "Multilateral framework for investment and its implications for China," *Journal of World Economy and Policy.* Vol. 4. No. 2. pp. 12–21.

Zhang, W.W. 2000. *Transforming China: Economic Reforms and Its Political Implications.* Basingstoke, Hampshire, UK: Macmillan Press.

Ziegler, D. 2003. "The weakest link: A survey of Asian finance," *The Economist.* February 8. After p. 52.

INDEX

Afro-Eurasia, 2
Akamatsu's hypothesis, 88
APEC International assessment Network, 138
the ASEAN way, 118
ASEAN Surveillance Process, 245
A-shares, 230
Asian Bankers' Association, 209, 211
Asian Bond Fund, 224–225
Asian Bond Market Initiative, 220
Asian crisis, 64–65, 67, 68–71, 93, 168, 205, 209, 214, 241–242, 243, 256, 277
Asian Financial Institute, 244
Asian "miracle", 21–23
Asian Monetary Fund, 247
Asset Management Companies, 213

backward linkage, 106
Bangkok Declaration, 117
bilateral investment treaties, 108–110, 152
bilateral swap arrangement, 251
Bogor Declaration, 133
  goals, 134
B-shares, 230
business-process services, 186–87

capital account crisis, 243
chaebol, 176, 206
Chiang Mai Initiative, 129, 250–252, 257
competition, 188–189
competitiveness, 165–172,
  financial crisis, 168–169
  high-technology, 171–72
  policy structure, 165–167
  quantifying, 166
contingency credit line, 256
credit rating agencies, 242
credit risk, 234–236
cronyism, 67
cumulative causation, 105
CUSFTA, 91–92

Doha Development Agenda, 134
Dow Jones composite, 228
dynamic Asia, 27–33

East Asia Economic Grouping, 127–128
economic evolution, 3–25
  heritage, 1–25
  sub-groups, 27–33
Ecotech, 136–137
EFTA, 93
emerging-market economies, 150–151, 154–155, 211, 212, 261
equity markets, 227–230,
exports and growth, 158–160
  deceleration, 159
exchange rate regimes, 270–273
export-oriented, 148

financial markets, 201–210
financial repression, 205
foreign direct investment, 172–182
  in China, 173–174, 178
  prospects, 175–176
  regional flows, 174–175
forward linkage, 106

global capital flows, 150–153, 242
Greenfield investment, 152
Group-of-Three, 109

heterogeneity, 27–33, 35
High Level Task Force, 127
historical perspective, 1–25
hollowing out, 188
hot money, 216

Individual Action Plans, 133–135, 138
Industrial revolution, 20–21
industrious revolution, 10–11
ISI strategy, 77–78
integrated production networks, 182–187
  competition, 183–84
  expanding opportunities, 184–85
  splitting the value chain, 184
intermediate financial structure, 214
investment-grade rating, 226

kaizen, 130
keidanren, 140
Kennedy Round, 105
Khubilai Khan, 4–6, 16

liquidity trap, 39
laissez faire stance, 63

Manila, 8
Manila Declaration, 137
Manila Framework Group, 244–245
market-driven regionalization, 80–82
mergers and acquisitions, 152
MFN liberalization, 102
Ming Dynasty, 6–7, 16–17
"miracle" economies, 21–23, 242–243
Mundellian trilemma, 247

Nash non-co-operative equilibrium, 93
National People's Congress, 48
Natural trading partners, 115
neo- mercantalism, 31
"new age" trade liberalization, 139
New Miyazawa Initiative, 245–246
non-institutional groups, 232
non-performing loans, 212–214, 229
  in China, 213
North American Free Trade Area, 91, 109, 119–120, 165
NYSE composite, 228

open-door policy, 44, 80, 164
open regionalism, 132–133
outer-orientation, 147–150
  adoption, 148
outward-orientation of growth, 78–79, 170–171
Organization of Petroleum Exporting Countries, 66
Osaka Action Plan, 133, 136

Plaza Accord, 82
post-crisis restructuring, 68–71, 226–228

quality of financial infrastructure, 203–205

regional diversity, 27–28
  bond market, 223–225
  groupings, 33–36
Regional Integration Agreements, 89–93, 101
  proliferation, 101–105
  sectoral specialization, 107–108
  tariff barriers, 103
repo market, 222
repressive financial markets, 236
regionalism, 116–117, 186
regionalization, 94–95, 116–117
  of production, 88–89

S&P 500, 228
Settle Ministerial Meeting, 134
second millennium, 4–8
Silicon Valley, 105
Single European Market, 114–115
Single Market Program, 119
soft institutionalism, 124–125, 138
spatial cluster, 106
Special Economic Zones, 178–180
structure of financial markets, 201–203
sudden reversal, 216
sun-set industries, 88
Supplemental Reserve Facility, 253
swadeshi, 53, 59

Tequila crisis, 207–208, 276–277
Trade
  Creation, 92–93
  entrepot, 17–18
  intra-regional, 13–15, 31–32, 79–80, 83–84

Japan and Asia, 15–16
past trend, 12–18
performance, 155–156
structural transformation, 156–158
triangle, 160–162
transnational corporations, 153–154
Treaty of Rome, 259

unity in diversity, 27–28
Uruguay Round, 120

virtuous circle, 89

Washington consensus, 243

Yuan Dynasty, 5